D1784697

Rights, Gender and Family Law

There has been a widespread resurgence of rights talk in social and legal discourses pertaining to the regulation of family life, as well as an increase in the use of rights in family law cases, in the UK, the US, Canada and Australia. *Rights, Gender and Family Law* addresses the implications of these developments – and, in particular, the impact of rights-based approaches upon the idea of welfare and its practical application. There are now many areas of family law in which rights- and welfare-based approaches have been forced together. But while, to many, they are premised upon different ethics – respectively, of justice and of care – for others, they can nevertheless be reconciled. In this respect, a central concern is the 'gender-blind' character of rights-based approaches, and the ontological and practical consequences of their employment in the gendered context of the family. *Rights, Gender and Family Law* explores the tensions between rights-based and welfare-based approaches: explaining their differences and connections; considering whether, if at all, they are reconcilable; and addressing the extent to which they can advantage or disadvantage the interests of women, children and men. It may be that rights-based discourses will dominate family law, at least in the way that social policy and legislation respond to calls of equality of rights between mothers and fathers. This collection, however, argues that rights cannot be given centre stage without thinking through the ramifications for gendered power relations, and the welfare of children. It will be of interest to researchers and scholars working in the fields of family law, gender studies and social welfare.

Julie Wallbank is Senior Lecturer in Law at the University of Leeds.

Shazia Choudhry is Senior Lecturer in Law at Queen Mary, University of London.

Jonathan Herring is a Fellow at Exeter College, Oxford University.

Rights, Gender and Family Law

Edited by
Julie Wallbank, Shazia Choudhry
and Jonathan Herring

Routledge
Taylor & Francis Group
LONDON AND NEW YORK

First published 2010
by Routledge
2 Park Square, Milton Park, Abingdon, Oxon, OX14 4RN

Simultaneously published in the USA and Canada
by Routledge
270 Madison Ave, New York NY 10016

A GlassHouse book
Routledge is an imprint of the Taylor & Francis Group, an informa business

Transferred to Digital Printing 2010

Typeset in Times New Roman by
Taylor & Francis Books

British Library Cataloguing in Publication Data
A catalogue record for this book is available from the British Library
Library of Congress Cataloguing in Publication Data
Rights, gender, and family law / edited by Julie Wallbank, Shazia Choudhry and
Jonathan Herring.
　　p. cm.
　ISBN 978-0-415-48267-7
　1. Domestic relations–English-speaking countries. I. Wallbank, Julie A. II.
Choudhry, Shazia. III. Herring, Jonathan.
　K670.R545 2010
　346.01'5–dc22
　　　　　　　　　　　　　　　　2009013226

ISBN10: 0-415-48267-4 (hbk)
ISBN10: 0-415-58958-4 (pbk)
ISBN10: 0-203-86947-8 (ebk)

ISBN13: 978-0-415-48267-7 (hbk)
ISBN13: 978-0-415-58958-1 (pbk)
ISBN13: 978-0-203-86947-5 (ebk)

Contents

The contributors

Jo Bridgeman, University of Sussex

Shazia Choudhry, Queen Mary, University of London

Richard Collier, Newcastle University

Alison Diduck, UCL, London

Brid Featherstone, University of Bradford

Lisa Glennon, Queen's University, Belfast

Jonathan Herring, Exeter College, Oxford University

Caroline Jones, University of Southampton

Felicity Kaganas, Brunel University

Christine Piper, Brunel University

Helen Rhoades, University of Melbourne

Julie Wallbank, University of Leeds

Chapter 1

Welfare, rights, care and gender in family law

Shazia Choudhry, Jonathan Herring and
Julie Wallbank

INTRODUCTION

This book is concerned with critically examining the various approaches which have been adopted in family law, understood herein as an institution, a set of practices but also as an academic and theoretical endeavour. The aim of this chapter is to assess some of the broad themes which will run through this book. We will focus on approaches to family law based on welfare, rights and an ethic of care and evaluate the various merits and demerits of each approach. Throughout our analysis we place gender centrally and draw upon the rich body of feminist contributions to the study of family law. What we are concerned with here is the shifting social and legal constructions of gendered power relations and with how the various case studies examined in this book offer important insights into the discursive constitution of masculinity and femininity in relation to the main themes covered, i.e. rights, responsibilities, welfare and care.[1]

This collection of essays therefore adopts a case-study approach to the use and usefulness of rights in family law. The effects of rights and the associated gendered discourses upon the power relations between parents and between children is a central focus of the book. The contextual analysis adopted herein is particularly useful for understanding how rights can have important ontological and practical consequences for the balance of power between women as mothers and men as fathers and for children's welfare. As such, the book offers some critical reflections on the increasing significance of the relationships between rights, responsibility and welfare in family law and social policy.

The case-study approach to gender is important precisely because it allows for an in-depth understanding of the workings of gendered power in small-scale studies. We are therefore concerned with the interplay between socially and legally

---

[1] The case study approach to gender and power in law and social policy undoubtedly owes a debt to the work of M. Foucault, e.g. *Discipline and Punish* (A. Sheridan trans.) Harmondsworth: Peregrine, 1977; *History of Sexuality* Vol. 1 (R. Hurley trans.) London: Penguin, 1981 and to the critical or socio-legal studies communities.

constructed gender identities and the interrelationship between the production of gender sameness/difference and the construction and relative power effects on gender of the adoption of and weight given to the values of rights, responsibilities, welfare and care in the elected contexts. In addition, other cultural categories of analysis have been drawn upon, including class, ethnicity, sexuality, age, disability. Fortunately, we have available to us a wide range of theoretical commentary on the various approaches to family law. Not all this work emanates from within feminism but it offers critical and important insights into the various approaches, both in a theoretical and practical sense. It is not the aim of the chapter to come down on the side of one approach over another. Rather, our chapter seeks to offer some justification for the book's subject matter by flagging up the importance of keeping a critical eye on the potential and actual gendered impacts of the adoption of each of the approaches. Before looking at these theoretical approaches, the basic legal principles will briefly be introduced.

An introduction to key legal principles

The welfare principle

The Children Act 1989 opens in s. 1 with one of the central principles of English family law:[2]

> When a court determines any question with respect to—
>
> (a) the upbringing of a child; or
> (b) the administration of a child's property or the application of any income arising from it the child's welfare shall be the court's paramount consideration.

When a judge is considering what is in the welfare of the child s 1(3) provides a checklist of factors to consider. There has been considerable debate over the meaning of the word 'paramount' in s 1(1). The accepted interpretation is that it means that the welfare of child is the sole consideration.[3] The interests of adults and other children are only relevant in so far as they may impact on the welfare of the child.[4]

---

[2] A detailed analysis of the welfare principle and its interpretation can be found in J. Herring, *Family Law*, Harlow: Pearson, 3rd edn 2008; Ch 9.

[3] UN Convention on the Rights of Children, in Art 3, states that the child's welfare should be the primary consideration. This appears to place slightly less weight on children's interests than s 1 of the Children Act 1989.

[4] Lord Hobhouse in *Dawson* v *Wearmouth* [1999] 1 FLR 1167. Although see J. Herring, 'The welfare principle and the rights of parents', in A. Bainham *et al. What is a Parent?* Oxford: Hart, 1999 for an argument that despite this the courts have in fact found means of giving weight to parents and other children.

The Human Rights Act 1998

The implementation of the 1998 Human Rights Act has added a new layer of analysis to family law cases. It is designed to ensure the protection of individuals' rights under the European Convention on Human Rights (ECHR) in two main ways. First, s 3 requires judges to interpret domestic legislation in a way which complies 'so far as is possible' with the ECHR. If the court is unable to interpret a statute in line with the Convention rights, then it must apply the statute as it stands and issue a declaration of incompatibility in order that Parliament can consider whether the legislation needs amending.[5]

Second, s 6 requires public authorities to act in a way which is compatible with the Convention rights. Failure to do so gives a cause of action under s 7 of the Human Rights Act 1998 which provides a wide range of remedies.

Family law cases often involve a clash between competing rights of the children and adults. The European Court on Human Rights (ECtHR) and English and Welsh courts are still developing the jurisprudence on how to deal with such clashes but some clarification is emerging. As Shazia Choudhry and Helen Fenwick point out, one way in which the welfare principle could be interpreted compatibly with Convention rights is to interpret 'paramount' to mean 'primary'.[6] In other words, the interests of the child will be the most important consideration for the court but will not inevitably determine the outcome, particularly where there are weighty countervailing interests.[7] On this interpretation, the welfare principle can be read compatibly with the approach of the ECHR which requires a balancing exercise between all of the rights involved, but with particular importance given to the rights and interests of the child.[8]

The nature of this balancing exercise in cases where rights of individuals conflict has produced some complex jurisprudence. A popular view is that the courts must undertake a 'parallel analysis'[9] of the rights involved. The starting point is to look at the interests of each individual and consider

[5] See *Bellinger* v *Bellinger* [2003] UKHL 21 for an example of a case where a declaration of incompatibility was issued.

[6] S. Choudhry and H. Fenwick, 'Taking the rights of parents and children seriously: Confronting the welfare principle under the Human Rights Act' (2005) 25 *Oxford Journal of Legal Studies* 480.

[7] For another way of reconciling the welfare principle and the HRA see J. Herring, 'The Human Rights Act and the welfare principle in family law – conflicting or complementary?' [1999] *Child and Family Law Quarterly* 223.

[8] There is a debate as to whether it is the interests of the child or her rights that should be given particular weight in the ultimate balancing exercise and, indeed, whether the child's interests and rights can be separated in any meaningful way, see J. Fortin, 'Accommodating Children's Rights in a Post Human Rights Act Era' (2006) 69 *Modern Law Review* 299.

[9] H. Rodgers and H. Tomlinson, 'Privacy and expression: Convention rights and interim injunctions' [2003] *European Human Rights Law Review* 37.

whether they engage a right under the ECHR. The point being that not every interest an individual has is necessarily protected by a right under the ECHR. If the interest does engage a right, then the court will need to consider whether an infringement of that right is justified. So, a parent may have a right under Art 8(1) to have contact with a child, but under Art 8(2) it may be permissible to interfere with that right if necessary in the interests of the child. It would be necessary to consider the right of each party involved (each parent and the child) and consider in each case whether the rights and interests of others are sufficiently strong to justify an interference with that right. This process will provide the solution, if there is only one person's right which cannot be justifiably interfered with.[10]

However, the above process may produce a clash between two rights for neither of which can justifiably be infringed. The ECtHR, to date, has offered little guidance on how to resolve such a stalemate. We will mention a couple of options.

One is to privilege the rights of children. According to the ECtHR when considering the competing rights of adults and children the rights of children should be regarded as being of crucial importance.[11] Although the ECtHR has referred to the child's interests as being paramount, it has only done so very rarely[12] and usually describes children's interests as being of crucial importance.[13] Shazia Choudhry and Helen Fenwick[14] have suggested that, in accordance with the ECtHR's approach, once the competing rights of all concerned have been considered, the rights of children should be 'privileged' even if that means going against the interests of either of the adult parties. However, Jane Fortin[15] complains that this is too vague and believes that it needs to be explained how the interests of children are privileged. However, in Choudhry and Fenwick's article the authors do, in fact, go into some detail as to how in a contact dispute their analysis would apply and have suggested that in a case of clashing rights the court should look at the values underpinning the right. For example, in the case of Art 8, which is the most common right used in family cases, the underlying value may be that of

[10] For a detailed application of the 'parallel analysis' to such a dispute see S. Choudhry and H. Fenwick, 'Taking the rights of parents and children seriously: Confronting the welfare principle under the Human Rights Act' (2005) 25 *Oxford Journal of Legal Studies* 453.

[11] See, e.g. *Yousef* v *The Netherlands* [2000] 2 FLR; *Sahin* v *Germany* [2003] 2 FCR 619; *Hasse* v *Germany* [2004] 2 FCR 1.

[12] *Yousef* v *The Netherlands* [2000] 2 FLR; *Kearns* v *France* (App No 35991/04) [2008] ECHR {35991/04}, para 79.

[13] See, e.g. *Haase* v *Germany* (App No 11057/02) [2004] 2 FLR 39, para [93].

[14] S. Choudhry and H. Fenwick, 'Taking the rights of parents and children seriously: Confronting the welfare principle under the Human Rights Act' (2005) 25 *Oxford Journal of Legal Studies* 453.

[15] J. Fortin, 'Accommodating children's rights in a post Human Rights Act era' (2006) 69 *Modern Law Review* 299.

autonomy: the right to pursue your vision of the 'good life'.[16] A judge could consider the extent to which the proposed order would constitute a blight on each of the party's opportunities to live the good life and make the order which causes the least blight.

As will be clear from this discussion, the exact relationship between the welfare principle and the Human Rights Act is still being worked out. Under the welfare principle it is only the interests of children which count.[17] The welfare principle is capable of restricting any parental right in order to maximise the welfare of the child, no matter how small increase in welfare.[18] While under a human rights analysis a balancing between the different rights of the parties is required. Despite these differences, the English courts have denied that there is any difference between an approach based on the welfare principle and one based on rights. For example, in *Payne* v *Payne*[19] Lord Justice Thorpe considered that:

> [the HRA] requires no re-evaluation of the judge's primary task to evaluate and uphold the welfare of the child as the paramount consideration, despite its inevitable conflict with adult rights.[20]

Lord Justice Thorpe went on to deny any conflict between the welfare principle and an approach based on the ECHR. That view has received little, if any, support from academics.[21] There are two key differences between the welfare principle and the ECHR approach. First, the ECtHR has clearly stated that in cases involving conflicting interests it is engaged in an exercise balancing the rights of the parties. The welfare principle does not involve a balancing exercise as parental interests are only relevant if they affect the welfare of the child. There is no balancing because all that matters is the welfare of the child. Second, the ECHR approach implies that the interests of the child will not always override those of the parent.

The welfare-based approach to family law has been well entrenched since the Children Act 1989 and this may explain the reluctance to accept that it

---

[16] This seeks to develop dicta of Lord Steyn in *Re S (A Child) (Identification: Restrictions on Publication)* [2005] 1 AC 593 para 17 which refers to the need to consider the values underlying the right when considering cases of clashing rights.

[17] Although if the interest of an adult affects the welfare of the child it can thereby become relevant.

[18] A point emphasised in J. Eekelaar, 'Beyond the Welfare Principle' [2002] *Child and Family Law Quarterly* 237.

[19] *Payne* v *Payne* (2001) EWCA Civ 166, [2001] 1 FLR 1052, paras 35–37 (Thorpe LJ) and para 82 (Butler Sloss LJ).

[20] Ibid, para 57.

[21] E.g. S. Harris-Short, 'Family law and the Human Rights Act 1998: judicial restraint or revolution' [2005] CFLQ 329, 355; S. Choudhry and H. Fenwick, 'Taking the rights of parents and children seriously: Confronting the welfare principle under the Human Rights Act' (2005) 25 *Oxford Journal of Legal Studies* 453.

may be challenged under an HRA analysis.[22] As well as the practical issues of how the tests should be used in particular cases, questions have been raised about the theoretical relationship between the two approaches, which can be said to contain two different sets of ethics.[23] There are now many areas of family law in which the two strands of rights and utility have been forced together and the chapters of Julie Wallbank and Jo Bridgeman, for example, examine the ways in which the courts have reconciled the two approaches. Although there has been a good deal of debate about the link between rights and welfare, as illustrated by the above discussion, there has been rather less discussion in respect of the relationship and the category of gender which this book seeks to rectify.[24]

Welfarism

Welfarism is at the heart of s 1 of the Children Act 1989. At its simplest it involves a desire to protect children and promote their best interests. It is motivated by a concern that all too often children's interests are overlooked and children end up being used by adults or regarded as their property. Elevating the interests of the child to the paramount position ensures that the most vulnerable parties to a family dispute are given the highest possible level of protection.

Arguments seeking to justify the welfare principle

There are several justifications for the welfare principle which we outline below.[25] It sends an important symbolic message emphasising the value, importance and vulnerability of children. It also recognises, that without a particular focus on them, children's interests are easily lost from the picture. In family disputes children are the ones with the least social, emotional and financial capital to deal with the aftermath of a family breakdown. It is

---

[22] See S. Choudhry and H. Fenwick, 'Taking the rights of parents and children seriously: Confronting the welfare principle under the Human Rights Act' (2005) 25 *Oxford Journal of Legal Studies* 456 and S. Harris-Short, 'Family law and the Human Rights Act 1998: Judicial restraint or revolution' [2005] CFLQ 329, 329.

[23] S. Parker, 'Rights and utility in Anglo-Australian family law' (1992) 55 *Modern Law Review* 311. For a discussion of whether or not it is significant to make a distinction between children's rights and welfare see A. Bainham, 'Can we protect children and protect their rights?' (2002) 32 *Family Law* 279 and J. Herring, *Family Law*, Harlow: Pearson, 3rd edn 2008, pp 405–6.

[24] A recent exception being an essay by Carol Smart in respect of her discussion about 'rights talk' and 'welfare talk' ('The ethics of justice strikes back: changing narratives of fatherhood', in A. Diduck and K. O'Donovan, *Feminist Perspectives on Family Law*, Routledge: London, 2006.

[25] The following paragraphs draw from J. Herring, 'Farewell welfare?' (2005) 27 *Journal of Social Welfare and Family Law* 159.

therefore appropriate that their interests are at the forefront of a court's concern. This message has significance not only for legal language, but also the wider social discourse. It encourages parents to focus on their children rather than their own rights and interests. It has support worldwide and is central to international conventions promoting children's rights and interests.[26]

The welfare principle is particularly important in respect of legal disputes when children's voices are rarely heard in courts.[27] It centralises the importance of looking at the dispute from the perspective of the child.[28] It also is sufficiently broad to enable courts to fashion the best response for the particular child in question, rather relying on abstract rights or generalisations about what is good for families or children.

Criticisms of welfarism: indeterminacy

Probably the most common criticism of welfarism is that its application is unpredictable.[29] It can be difficult enough to predict what factors the courts will weigh up, let alone predict what the result will be. The welfare principle requires the court to predict the possible outcomes for a child. That is extremely difficult; not least because the courts and professionals are required to assess parents at a time of life when they are in emotional turmoil. Even if the outcomes were known and calculable, there might still be much uncertainty over which outcomes a court would think was in the best interests of the child.

In the face of complaints of indeterminacy, some supporters of the welfare principle argue that court decisions are far more predictable than is often assumed. In many cases it would not be difficult to predict the result. This is because the welfare principle operates against a background of widely accepted norms.[30] Solicitors are very familiar with informing clients that the courts will never make the order they seek. For example, it is widely assumed that contact is in the child's interests and this acts as a widely accepted norm. Courts reach decisions by drawing upon this norm and also upon the acceptance that children's outcomes are improved by it. Therefore, it will only be in exceptional cases, such as extreme domestic violence or child abuse that courts will not make an order. Despite this, it is a commonly heard complaint that the welfare principle means that the outcome of the case depends on the personality or mood of the judge, rather than any legal principle.

---

[26] E.g. the United National Convention on the Rights of the Child.

[27] A. L. James, A. James and S. McNamee 'Constructing Children's Welfare in Family Proceedings' [2003] 33 *Family Law* 889.

[28] Ibid, however, James *et al.* point out that the legal system should also rely on other means to ensure the child's voice is heard.

[29] E.g. R. Mnookin, 'Child-custody adjudication: judicial functions in the face of indeterminacy' (1975) 39 *Law and Contemporary Problems* 259.

[30] C. Schneider, 'Discretions, rules and law', in K. Hawkins (ed) *The Uses of Discretion*, Oxford: Oxford University Press, 1993.

Criticisms of welfarism: feminism and gender

Feminist critics of welfarism have been alert to the potential for welfare discourses to have gendered dimensions and application in the family law context. In respect of contact disputes, for example, the application of the welfare principle has meant that children and fathers' interests potentially become one. This is due to the great emphasis placed on the alleged benefits to children of being in contact with their fathers (see further Julie Wallbank's chapter). This causes problems for mothers who have strong concerns about it. Where mothers object to contact, the strength of the assumption that contact benefits children's welfare is so strong that only in the most exceptional cases will courts refuse to order it. Further, because women are more usually the resident parent, the sometimes onerous burden of maintaining contact more frequently falls upon them.[31] Therefore, although the law's formal approach to child welfare is gender neutral, there will be cases where the responsibility for ensuring child welfare lodges squarely with women.

As this discussion shows, there is a danger that the welfare discourse, with its focus on the child in isolation from those caring for him, disguises the burdens that can be placed on mothers. Notably, welfare is now increasingly drawn upon by fathers' rights activists as a framing mechanism in order to stake their claims to either shared residence or contact.[32] As Smart maintains:

> parents are obliged to frame their disputes in terms of which parent has the welfare of the child most closely at heart. It is therefore little more than a rhetorical device; yet if it is absent, then parents are seen as making illegitimate claims.[33]

Looking at the Canadian context Susan Boyd has noted how fathers' rights activists have aligned their claims with the welfare of children 'in order to ensure their [children's] psychological well-being'.[34] Although child welfare is central to family law and difficult to resist in a theoretical and practical

---

[31] H. Reece, 'UK women's groups' child contact campaign: 'So long as it is safe' (2006) 18 *Child and Family Law Quarterly* 538.

[32] See further C. Smart, 'The Ethic of Justice Strikes Back: Changing narratives of Fatherhood' in A. Diduck and K. O'Donovan, *Feminist Perspectives on Family Law* Routledge-Cavendish: London, 2006, pp 132–3.

[33] Ibid, p 133.

[34] S. Boyd, '"Robbed of their Families"? Fathers' Rights Discourses in Canadian Parenting Law Reform Processes', in R. Collier and S. Sheldon (eds) *Fathers' Rights Activism and Law Reform in Comparative Perspective*, Oxford: Hart, 2006, p 29. See also S. Gilmore, 'Contact/shared residence and child well-being: Research evidence and its implications for legal decision-making' (2006) 20 *International Journal of Law, Policy and the Family* 344 for a demonstration of the lack of empirical evidence for the claims often made surrounding the benefits of contact.

sense, feminists concerned with the gendered implications of both the rhetorical and practical force of welfare-based frameworks need to continue to be vigilant about the gender discriminatory implications.

These concerns are bolstered by looking back to the past and the way that the welfare principle has led to various forms of discrimination – as a means of reinforcing patriarchal power over women and children;[35] as working in a way that is prejudicial to gay and lesbian parents;[36] and as working against the interests of minority cultures.[37] Although developments in family law have to a great extent eliminated many forms of discrimination, it is imperative that sexuality and gender are kept to the forefront of the analysis of the application of the welfare principle to ensure that discrimination is kept at bay.

Criticisms of welfarism: child welfare knowledge

A further criticism of welfarism is that the courts' understanding of what is in the best interests of the child is sometimes lacking. There are cases where a court has boldly declared what was in the child's best interests but which are now regarded as clearly wrong and discriminatory. For example, cases stating that children were harmed when raised by same-sex parents because they were not part of a 'normal family' are now read with shock, anger or shame.[38] Over time, well-accepted psychological or social theories fall into disrepute. For example, in the 1970s a predominantly held view was that contact with non-resident parents may not benefit children.[39] Despite the development of an extensive knowledge base in respect of child welfare and contact there remains little agreement about the issue and the research findings are far from conclusive.[40]

Criticisms of welfarism: children's rights

Another major challenge to welfarism is that it fails adequately to take account of children's rights. Welfarism is paternalistic and leaves children as

---

[35] E.g. S. Maidment, *Child Custody and Divorce*, London: Croom Helm, 1984.
[36] E.g. H. Reece, 'The paramountcy principle: Consensus or construct?' (1996) 49 *Current Legal Problems* 267.
[37] S. Toope, 'Riding the fences: Courts, charter rights and family law' (1991) 9 *Canadian Journal of Family Law* 55.
[38] E.g. H. Reece, 'The paramountcy principle: Consensus or construct?' (1996) 49 *Current Legal Problems* 267.
[39] J. Goldstein, A. Freud and A. Solnit, *Beyond the Best Interests of the Child*, New York: Free Press, 1973.
[40] See, e.g. the disputes over the benefits of contact, usefully summarised in S. Gilmore, 'Contact/shared residence and child well-being: Research evidence and its implications for legal decision-making' (2006) 20 *International Journal of Law Policy and the Family* 344, p 347.

little more than objects of adult concerns, to be simultaneously controlled and protected. Early child liberationists argued for children having exactly the same rights as adults. In recent times, those who support children's rights have made more moderate claims. Much has been written on children's rights, and the issues are discussed in several chapters of this book, but here we will focus on whether an advocate of children's rights must necessarily reject the welfare principle in order to protect children's legal rights.

One important point worth making is that most leading exponents of children's rights include a powerful element of paternalism or welfarism within their accounts of rights. For example, John Eekelaar, Michael Freeman and Jane Fortin have all argued that children's rights are not to be used in ways that seriously harm children.[41] It is also important to note that the framework employed by the ECHR and the HRA does not preclude the consideration of welfare issues in relation to claims made under the qualified articles.[42] This means that in many cases a welfare and rights approach will produce the same result. For example, in cases concerning child protection, the same legal response is likely, regardless of whether resolved by a rights or welfare approach. The kinds of cases which divide those taking a rights or a welfare approach are cases where the welfare calculation is finely balanced, and those involving children's autonomy.[43] So, in cases where the welfare calculation is finely balanced, the right of an adult may prevail, with there being insufficient justification in the name of the child's welfare for its infringement. By contrast a welfare-based approach would never allow an adult's interests to trump a child's. Similarly a rights-based approach may allow a child to make a decision which causes the child a small amount of harm, while a welfare-based approach might not. However, the extent of the differences between the approaches depends, in part, on how one interprets welfare and rights.

A children's rights proponent can readily accept that children's choices should be restricted in order to promote their welfare. Indeed, it would be quite possible for a children's rights advocate to be less willing than a child welfarist to allow children to make their own decisions. For example, where

---

[41] For a full discussion see, e.g. M. Freeman, *The Rights and Wrongs of Children*, London: Frances Pinter, 1983; J. Eekelaar 'The interests of the child and the child's wishes: The role of dynamic self-determinism' (1992) 8 *International Journal of Law, Policy and the Family* 42; J. Fortin, 'Accommodating children's rights in a post Human Rights Act era' (2006) 69 *Modern Law Review* 299.

[42] This is because the ECHR is not a purely deontological instrument by virtue of the inherently consequentialist qualifications that are present in Arts 8–11. See S. Choudhry and H. Fenwick, 'Taking the rights of parents and children seriously: Confronting the welfare principle under the Human Rights Act' (2005) 25 *Oxford Journal of Legal Studies* 453.

[43] J. Eekelaar, 'The interests of the child and the child's wishes: The role of dynamic self-determinism' (1992) 8 *International Journal of Law, Policy and the Family* 42.

a children's rights advocate emphasises children's rights to protection from harm, the right to a safe environment or the right to discipline and/or where a child welfarist placed much weight on the benefit to children of developing their own personalities through making their own decisions and learning from their mistakes. Jane Fortin has written: 'the claim that a rights-based approach must necessarily be devoid of any element of any paternalism or "welfare" misconstrues the concept of rights'.[44] On the other hand, any claim that a welfare approach would necessarily be devoid of any element of rights would be equally false.

Criticisms of welfarism: the interests of others

As outlined above, the welfare principle has been interpreted by the courts to mean that the child's welfare is the sole consideration. The court will therefore pursue the course which best promotes the interests of the child, regardless of the impact on the interests of others. However, in practice courts have found ways of protecting parents' interests while adhering to the welfare principle.[45] As Jonathan Herring has argued there is no difficulty in interpreting the welfare principle in a way which takes account of the rights or interests of others and is based on a notion of relationship-based welfare which rests on the idea that children are raised in relationships and that child welfare is promoted by ensuring that the child is raised in healthy relationships. Under such an approach, cases can be resolved by recognising and acting in the child's interests while heeding parental interests and the integrity of the family as a whole.[46] Relationship-based welfare provides a means of holding onto the welfare principle while respecting the rights and interests of caregivers.

One criticism of this approach is that there is a need to adopt a 'more detached view' of children's interests in order that they are centralised and not sidelined by those of others.[47] However, to see children's interests outside their relationship with their carers could be said to be artificial and as excluding much of what is of value to a child. Similarly, to view the interests of the carer without accounting for the interests of the child is to exclude many important issues. Relationship-based welfare allows for a clear focus on the child's past, ongoing and future relationships, though there is some

---

[44] J. Fortin, 'Children's rights: Are the court now taking them more seriously' (2005) 15 *Kings College Law Journal* 253, 259.

[45] J. Herring, 'The welfare principle and the rights of parents', in A. Bainham *et al.*, *What is a Parent?*, Oxford: Hart, 1999.

[46] J. Herring, 'The Human Rights Act and the welfare principle in family law – conflicting or complementary?' (1999) 11 *Child and Family Law Quarterly* 223.

[47] J. Eekelaar 'Beyond the Welfare Principle' (2002) 14 *Child and Family Law Quarterly* 237.

force in John Eekelaar's complaint that the model fails to provide clear guidance as to how to balance the interests of the parties involved.[48]

Rights-based approaches

The Human Rights Act 1998 (HRA) has prompted a resurgence of rights in social and legal discourses pertaining to the regulation of family life. Family members now commonly bring cases based upon their rights which are protected under the European Convention of Human Rights (ECHR). The Act has had a great impact upon the way that family case law is argued and decided and legislation is structured,[49] although there is also evidence that there is a certain amount of misapplication and misunderstanding of it by the judiciary which has its own dangers.[50] Nevertheless, the incorporation of a rights-based framework necessitates a debate around how rights impact upon mothers, fathers and children, particularly when they conflict in some way. Although, family law tends to use the gender-neutral term 'parent' when referring to the rights of the adults involved in disputes, experiences of family life, conflict and the resolution of disputes is often highly gendered. As emphasised earlier, under a human rights approach it is necessary to consider the rights of each party involved in the case. The complex analysis that may be required where rights clash was discussed earlier. Moreover, the incorporation of the ECHR through the HRA has meant that rights-based discourse is frequently centralised in debates on family law and social policy without any clear articulation of the need to consider what significance rights-based approaches have upon the idea of welfare and its practical application.[51] It may be the case, therefore, that rights-based discourses could come to dominate family law at the very least in respect of the way that social policy and legislation respond to calls of equality of rights between mothers and fathers and in respect of the ways those families who are identified as potentially problematic are managed.

The benefits of a rights-based approach

The benefits of rights have been highly contested, particularly by feminist commentators. In this section we outline those aspects of rights which have been heralded as relevant to transformative projects in family law. Elizabeth Kingdom has stated that the potential to exploit the political power of the

---

[48] J. Eekelaar 'Children beyond cultures' (2004) 18 *International Journal of Law, Policy and Family* 178.

[49] See further J. Herring (2007) *Family Law* (3rd edn), Harlow: Pearson Education, pp 30–1.

[50] S. Choudhry and H. Fenwick, 'Taking the rights of parents and children seriously: Confronting the welfare principle under the Human Rights Act' (2005) 25 *Oxford Journal of Legal Studies* 453.

rights-oriented framework cannot be ignored or discarded as irrelevant.[52] Her argument rests on the idea that rights discourse is so entrenched in the 'legal–political context' 'that for any intervention to be successful it ... must be cast in those terms'.[53] The firm entrenchment in the legal context of rights–values is demonstrated by Alison Diduck's chapter in this book where she argues that rights discourse has been shown to have been appropriated by the judiciary even in disputes where the parties have not claimed Convention rights. Alison's eloquent chapter considers the ways in which the HRA 'its "culture" or "values"' have influenced judicial reasoning in the House of Lords in claims for property division or financial provision when intimate partners separate.

Focusing particularly on the judicially created objective of fairness, Alison demonstrates how the courts have implied widely accepted values about family life which include 'public, democratic values such as equality and non-discrimination between separating partners'.[54] She concludes that rather than relying upon welfare and dependence, financial awards are rather constructed, evaluated and articulated through the language of entitlement. Therefore, even when 'equality and non-discrimination have not been claimed as *rights* between separating partners, the House of Lords has adopted them as *values* to give meaning to fairness between those partners'.[55] Having made such pithy observations she goes on to heed caution at the use of 'liberal, individualistic norms formulated for public, political living'.[56] Her chapter flags up the importance of keeping a critical eye on these new developments in family law and it is within the ambit of this book to engage in that critical enterprise.

As Vanessa Munro has recently argued:

> The ability of rights analysis to politicise contentious issues and to provide protection to the individual against state intervention has been illustrated repeatedly in liberal legal theory and can barely be disputed.[57]

Associated with this is the fact that law is a powerful mechanism for enforcing rights. It is therefore questionable whether women would be wise to ignore it.[58]

---

[51] See further F. Kaganas, and S. Day Sclater, 'Contact disputes: Narrative constructions of "good parents"' (2004) 12 *Feminist Legal Studies* 1.

[52] See further E. Kingdom, *What's Wrong with Rights? Problems for Feminist Politics of Law*, Edinburgh: Edinburgh University Press, 1991.

[53] E. Kingdom, 'Body Politics and Rights', in J. Bridgeman and S. Millns (eds), *Law and Body Politics: Regulating the Female Body*, Dartmouth: Aldershot, 1995.

[54] See p 201.

[55] Ibid.

[56] See p 218.

[57] V. Munro (2007) *Law and Politics at the Perimeter: Re-Evaluating Key Debates in Feminist Theory*, Oxford: Hart, 2007, p 74.

[58] Ibid.

Rights-based claims have been extremely important in improving women's lives, for example, in first-wave feminist claims for the right to vote, to participate in public life, equal pay and sex discrimination. Rights influence wider social changes and social acceptance for example of lesbian, gay, bisexual and transgender (LGBT) issues, race discrimination and gender discrimination. In putting forward rights-based claims minority groups seek to establish their interests and 'impose duties on others'. In addition, rights which are the product of international and regional instruments can also impose positive obligations upon individual states to ensure that the individual rights of their citizens are adequately protected and promoted. Shazia Choudhry discusses how such obligations could carry a great deal of potential for the further protection of the victims of domestic violence by implementing certain arrest and prosecution policies. However, there is a need to ensure that states consider the impact of their policies along gender lines when formulating policies that are designed to fulfil the state's positive duties towards its citizens. The chapters of Christine Piper and Felicity Kaganas demonstrate these dangers with respect to government policy on youth justice and child protection. Against the criticism that rights-based claims are individualistic which we discuss below, the argument is that: 'those claiming rights implicitly invest themselves in a larger community, even in the act of seeking to change it'.[59] Therefore, rights-based claims establish a place for traditionally marginalised groups in the wider community and help to shape the socio-political climate.

Carol Smart has noted the appeal of rights in respect of forwarding claims of those who believe themselves to be in need of protection through a perceived diminution of their rights. She has argued that rights are constructed as offering:

> the protection of the weak against the strong, or the individual against the state ... There is little doubt that a reduction in rights is equated with a loss of power or protection.[60]

Feminists remain concerned about the continuing restrictions on women's autonomy in respect of reproductive rights in the context of abortion and continue to challenge the restrictions of the Abortion Act 1967 whereby an abortion is only permissible if two doctors agree to it.[61] In the post-separation context fathers have sought to re-establish rights which they perceive to have lost in respect of their children. They have, in the past, extensively drawn on rights-based discourse in order to assert their claims for fair child

---

[59] M. Minow, *Making All the Difference: Inclusion, Exclusion and American Law*, Ithaca Cornell University Press, 1990 p 294.
[60] C. Smart, *Feminism and the Power of Law*, London: Routledge, 1989 p 144.
[61] See letter to the editor *The Times* 17 October 2008.

support and contact law.[62] That rights-based strategies oversimplify complex power relationships has been seen as both a positive and negative feature of them.

Below, we outline some of the compelling critiques of rights but also flag up a way of reconceptualising rights in order to make them more relevant to strategies of law reform. As Munro has argued we need to acknowledge the creative aspects of rights while at the same time holding a critical position on them:

> What feminist theorists and activists really need to avoid is not so much the use of rights but rather the assertion of any blanket position on their utility.[63]

This book project pays heed to this call and seeks to explore the socio-political significance and usefulness of rights in the family law context on a case-study basis.

Criticisms of rights: rights and individualistic autonomy

A powerful critique of rights is that they are based on an image of individuals living isolated lives, protected by their rights of privacy and autonomy. Rights, it is said, place no weight on relationships and imagine a society full of independent self-interested individuals unaffected by gender roles, ethnicity and social status. Many of the chapters in this collection seek to both reveal and explore how gender impacts upon both the formulation of rights-based claims and how gender as a category is sometimes elided as a result of equality of rights claims. In other words, some of the contributors seek to (en)gender rights discourse, which by its very nature, attempts to evacuate it as a relevant category of analysis. Examples of the gendering of rights are immediately apparent in the area of contact which is discussed in this edition by Richard Collier and Julie Wallbank. Richard maintains there may be 'more going on "under the radar" with fathers' rights groups than the high-profile protests of recent years and the collective "staking out" of rights and equality claims would indicate'.[64]

He draws attention to the relationship between fathers' emotionality and their rational thought and actions in respect of their constructed masculinity, their situation in social policy, family law practices and their relationships with

---

[62] See further J. Wallbank, 'The campaign for change of the Child Support Act 1991: reconstituting the "absent" father' (1997) 6 *Social and Legal Studies* 191 and J. Wallbank, *Challenging Motherhood(s)* Longman: London, 2001. See also R. Collier, 'The campaign against the Child Support Act, "errant fatherhood" and "family men"' [1994] *Family Law* 384.

[63] V. Munro (2007) *Law and Politics at the Perimeter: Re-Evaluating Key Debates in Feminist Theory*, Oxford: Hart, 2007.

[64] See p 136.

their children. Richard posits convincing arguments for a recognition of and response to the emotional aspects of fathers' needs in developing social policy. Julie demonstrates in her chapter how a wide range of discourses have given support to the idea, particularly in relation to the law of contact, that there should be no rights without responsibilities. These discourses have in turn, she argues, constructed an aspirational view of fatherhood where fathers' claims to be increasingly involved in the practical and emotional aspects of child-care are not borne out by the research evidence, which continues to illustrate that familial responsibilities remain highly gendered. Rather than relying on a utopian vision of gender-neutral patterns of care and responsibilities courts, she argues that courts should take into account the gendered investments made by parents before any breakdown in their relationship, as such invest-ments may well impact upon the way that they come to address the issue of contact at the end of it.

The chapter by Felicity Kaganas exemplifies the importance of ensuring that the false image of the isolated individual, free of gender and responsibilities is not allowed to dominate. Felicity notes that while the HRA may protect parents from unwarranted intervention into their family life in the child protection context, she pithily argues that the development of universal and targeted strate-gies in order to bypass the courts and compulsory intervention means that parents, mainly mothers, 'are faced with even more potential sources of pres-sure or reasons for coercion; if they do not accept the advice and attend the parenting classes as instructed, for example, they face the risk of being adjudged irresponsible'[65] due to the social reality of their caring responsibilities.

Additionally, Brid Featherstone illustrates how feminist commentators 'have noted, the term parent when mobilised by policy makers and attached to initiatives or legislation is problematic. It obscures material inequalities in caretaking and the difficulties this poses for mothers'.[66] She also seeks to show how fathers' organisations have also begun to challenge how the term 'parent' obscures the needs of fathers. The Fatherhood Institute has sought to challenge employment policies and the practices of child welfare services. Though the impetus to challenge employment practices emerges from a concern with gender equity, she argues that fathers' concerns are often framed around the idea that men are 'missing out'. What is missing from the debate, according to Brid, is a lack of acknowledgement of the difficulties women often face. Thus, these chapters seek to challenge and refute the values commonly associated with rights as individualistic autonomy.

As Mary Ann Glendon shows, rights can create 'hyperindividualism' and 'exceptional solitariness'.[67] It can also lead to an analysis which bears little

[65] See p 68.
[66] See p 40.
[67] M. A. Glendon, *Rights Talk: The Impoverishment of Political Discourse*, New York: Free Press, 1991, p 15.

connection with real life. By emphasising individual rights, rather than lived-in relationships, in effect 'rights talk' means that 'real experiences' are converted into 'empty abstractions'.[68] As Smart puts it: 'the rights approach takes and translates personal and private matters into legal language. This is evident in Lisa Glennon's chapter which looks at the use of equality discourse in the legal regulation of adult relationships. She argues that recent government policy has sought to achieve equality between relationships, regardless of the sexual orientation of the parties. Most obviously this has been done through the Civil Partnership Act 2004. But it has also involved judicial use of the HRA to ensure that statutes were interpreted in a way which did not discriminate between same-sex and opposite-sex relationships.[69]

Lisa argues that the Civil Partnership Act led to increasing political pressure to consider the position of cohabitants. Indeed she sees reform of the law on cohabitation and civil partnership as having common ideological underpinnings, with an emphasis on autonomy and a move away from seeing marriage as an ideal. She is, however, critical of the proposed reforms of the law on cohabitation. To her it is caregiving which provides the strongest reason for justifying financial orders on relationships breakdown. The Law Commission proposals, which she characterises as 'marriage minus', protect cohabiting caregivers to a lesser extent than married ones. She powerfully argues that 'familial caregiving is not considered as a valued activity in its own right, but is conceptualised through the lens of the relationship form in which it takes place.' As her chapter shows, the notion of fairness, especially when it is combined with references to autonomy, can obscure the realities of relational life. Legal constructions of equal status and views that persons have a completely free choice to enter or not enter them, is no guarantee of substantive fairness. Lisa's chapter shows how the law reformulates private issues into legal ones which may have little or no relevance to the lives of ordinary people.[70] It is neither possible nor desirable to consider one person's interests in isolation from those with whom they are in a relationship.[71]

A related aspect is that the focus on rights may downplay or even ignore the importance of responsibilities.[72] Rights fail to place value on issues such as commitment and obligation.[73] Sir John Laws has argued that a

---

[68] M. Tushnet, 'A critique of rights' (1984) *Texas Law Review* 1363, 1364.

[69] *Fitzpatrick v Sterling Housing Association* [2000] 2 FLR 271.

[70] C. Smart, 'Children and the transformation of family law', in J. Dewar and S. Parker, *Family Law Processes, Practices, Pressures*, Oxford: Hart, 2003, pp 238–9.

[71] J. Nedelsky, 'The practical possibilities of feminist theory' (1993) 87 *Northwestern University Law Review* 1286, 1295–6.

[72] M. Regan, *The Pursuit of Intimacy*, New York: New York University Press, 1995; K. Bartlett, 'Re-expressing parenthood' (1988) 98 *Yale Law Journal* 293, 295; M. Glendon, *Rights Talk: The Impoverishment of Political Discourse*, New York: Free Press, 1991.

[73] M. Regan, *The Pursuit of Intimacy*, especially Ch 2.

rights-based society which fails to place appropriate weight on duty and self-sacrifice is at an 'immature stage of development'.[74] Many, particularly feminist, academics sympathetic to these cogent critiques of rights have turned to support an ethic of care approach which is discussed below.[75] Others have sought to reconceptualise rights in a more relational way. Most prominent among these is the concept of relational autonomy, which Jonathan Herring develops in his chapter. Arguing against the growing use of autonomy in family law, Jonathan mounts a powerful case for abandoning 'individualistic conceptions of autonomy'. He argues that such a use of autonomy is antithetical to how families actually live their lives – that family life is, by its very nature, a fundamentally relational activity. He further argues that individualistic autonomy also works against the interests of women who are very often primarily responsible for children and other dependants.

Criticisms of rights: misuse of rights

Whatever the merits of rights in theory, feminists have shown that in practice, they can work to the disadvantage of women and children.[76] The history of rights is replete with examples of cases where the rights of women are subsumed within the rights of men and the rights of children within the rights of adults.[77] Rights are of particular use to those with the power to assert and claim them. Where gendered and inter-generational power relations are unequal the enforcement of rights operates unequally. The rights of weaker people (e.g. children) can be used to pursue the agenda of stronger people (e.g. adults).[78] It is not difficult to find in the English and Welsh case law examples of parents' rights which have been presented as children's rights; or cases where human rights have been considered but the rights of children and women are ignored and are not used to protect women and children who may be vulnerable.[79] Caroline Jones in her chapter on claims to rights to genetic identity, explores the hidden meanings behind such claims

---

[74] J. Laws, 'The limitation of human rights' [1998] PL 254, 255.
[75] E. C. Gilligan, 'Moral orientation and moral development', in E. Kittay and D. Meyers (eds), *Women and Moral Theory*, London: Rowman & Littlefield, 1987; S. Sevenhuijsen, *Citizenship and the Ethics of Care*, London: Routledge, 1998; V. Held, *The Ethics of Care*, Oxford: Oxford University Press, 2006.
[76] M. Guggenheim, *What's Wrong with Children's Rights?* Cambridge, MA: Harvard University Press, 2005, Ch 1.
[77] J. Fortin, 'Accommodating children's rights in a post Human Rights Act era' (2006) 69 *Modern Law Review* 299.
[78] E.g. C. Gilligan, 'Moral orientation and moral development', in E. Kittay and D. Meyers (eds), *Women and Moral Theory*, Ottowa: Rowman & Littlefield, 1987; S. Sevenhuijsen *Citizenship and the Ethics of Care*, London: Routledge, 1998; V. Held, *The Ethics of Care*, Oxford: Oxford University Press, 2006.
[79] C. Ungerson 'Thinking about the production and consumption of long-term care in Britain: does gender still matter?' (2000) 29 *Journal of Social Policy* 623.

and the inconsistent ways in which the law protects the alleged right to know one's genetic identity.

Criticisms of rights: failure to use rights

Christine Piper, for example, discusses an area where, although rights discourse has been given a high level of prominence via the incorporation of a number of rights-based international instruments, there is little evidence of any real consideration in policy terms of the impact this may have along gender lines. By focusing on the apparent invisibility of gender in the rights discourse around girls and boys who behave badly she argues for a greater attention to difference in administering punishment and rehabilitation – not just between adults and children but also between boys and girls, young men and young women – and for a greater attention to potential discrimination in decision making.

There are also some areas of law where rights discourse has, rather surprisingly, not been given a high enough level of prominence, even where it may result in providing greater protection for women in particularly vulnerable situations. Shazia Choudhry demonstrates, in her chapter, the relative failure to harness the full potential of the HRA and the ECHR for the benefit of the victims of domestic violence. By focusing on mandatory prosecution and arrest policies as a means to comply with the duties created by both the HRA and ECHR towards such victims, she provides an analysis of their gender implications and how, ultimately they may offer a further opportunity to reduce the patriarchal nature of the state.

Although all the above concerns are justified, it is arguable that they can be met within a human rights framework. After all, the key right in many family law cases is the right to respect for family life: a right which emphasises the importance of relationships. In addition, a central principle of the ECHR and HRA framework is that of proportionality, which should ensure that the right to family life can only be interfered with after a careful balancing exercise has taken place in respect of any other relevant rights. Any resultant interference with a person's right to family life must not therefore be any more than is absolutely necessary to achieve the aim.

The ethic of care

Both the welfare and rights-based approach have been criticised for taking an over-individualistic approach. Those sympathetic to this complaint have turned to an ethic of care to find an analysis which is more sympathetic to the importance of relationships. An ethic of care, perhaps unsurprisingly, has attracted attention from feminist commentators.[80] Caring is a gendered

---

[80] C. Gilligan *In a Different Voice: Psychological Theory and Women's Development*, Cambridge, MA: Harvard University Press, 1984, p 73.

activity. It is traditionally regarded as 'women's work' and as such it has not been given the respect or recognition that higher valued 'economically productive' activities have. By describing care work as 'voluntary' and 'informal' it is marginalised. The lack of respect owed to caring has played a significant role in the unequal economic and social position of women.[81]

The ethic of care promotes a vision of mutually interdependent relationships as the norm around which legal and ethical responses should be built. Carol Gilligan explains:

> The ideal of care is thus an activity of relationships, of seeing and responding to need, taking care of the world by sustaining the web of connection so that no one is left alone.[82]

Care is an inevitable part of life.[83] The balance between caring and being cared for may shift but caring is the very essence of life.[84] It is part of being human. Without it, society would soon collapse.[85] The law must regard relationships as key to its thinking and not ignore them. Care ethicists would argue that not only is care an inevitable part of life, but that it is a good part of life, providing 'meaning' 'security and emotional sustenance'.[86] Caring, then, is a 'major life activity' that benefits the person receiving the care, but also and importantly, the person giving the care and society, more widely.[87] From a feminist perspective there is the danger that the ethic of care merely reinforces women's responsibility for unpaid care work. However, care ethics seek to ensure that value is attached to care so that those who undertake 'love labour'[88] are not disadvantaged. The aim is to attach importance and value to care and to get men and women to partake equally in it.[89]

---

[81] M. Fineman, *The Autonomy Myth: A Theory of Dependency*, New York: The New Press, 2004, p xvii.

[82] C. Gilligan, *In a Different Voice: Psychological Theory and Women's Development*, Cambridge, MA: Harvard University Press, 1984, at 62.

[83] M. Daly 'Care as a good for social policy' [2002] 31 *Journal of Social Policy* 251.

[84] R. West, 'The right to care', in E. Kittay and E. Feder (eds), *The Subject of Care: Feminist Perspectives on Dependency*, Lanham: Rowman & Littlefield, 2002, p 89.

[85] A. Hubbard 'The myth of independence and the major life activity of caring' [2004] 8 *Journal of Gender, Race and Justice* 327.

[86] K. Silbaugh 'Turning labor into love: Housework and the law' (1996) 91 *Northwestern University Law Review* 1.

[87] J. Williams, 'From difference to dominance to domesticity: Care as work, gender as tradition' (2001) 76 *Chicago-Kent Law Review* 1441. There would also need to be changes in the employment market to ensure that employed work was a realistic and attractive option for women: T. Knijn and C. Ungerson 'Introduction: Care work and gender in welfare regimes' 9 (1997) 32 *Social Politics* 323.

[88] G. Clement *Care, Autonomy and Justice: Feminism and the Ethic of Care*, New York: Westview, 1996, p 11.

[89] V. Held, *The Ethics of Care*, Oxford: Oxford University Press, 2006, p 1.

The attraction of an ethic-of-care approach is that it seeks to move away from an atomistic picture of individuals, with rights that compete against each other, to a model that emphasises the responsibilities of people towards each other in mutually supporting relations.[90] So rather than being rights focused it is concerned with relational obligations.[91] In contrast to the ethic of justice approach discussed above 'an ethic of care sees the interest of carers and cared-for as importantly intertwined rather than as simply competing'.[92] Held makes clear though that while: 'There can be care without justice', 'There can be no justice without care ... for without care no child would survive and there would be no persons to respect.'[93]

There is another important aspect of this issue. The emphasis on inter-dependence and mutuality means that the division between carer and cared for dissolves. Michael Fine and Caroline Glendinning argue that care is not something that one takes and the other receives but is 'best understood as the product or outcome of the relationship between two or more people'.[94] In the context of domestic violence for example, to say, as the law does, that a father can be violent towards his child's mother, but be committed to the child, is to separate individuals inappropriately.[95] The relationship between carer and cared for is marked by interdependency.[96] As Diane Gibson has argued, our society is increasingly made up of overlapping networks of dependency.[97] These themes are picked up particularly in Jo Bridgeman's chapter where she considers the law's treatment of children with exceptional needs and their parents.

Criticisms of an ethic of care

The ethic of care rose to prominence with the writing of Carol Gilligan[98] who distinguished between a 'male' approach to ethical issues, which focused

---

[90] Ibid, p 15.
[91] Ibid, p 15.
[92] M. Fine and C. Glendinning 'Dependence, independence or inter-dependence? Revisiting the concepts of care and dependency' (2005) 25 *Ageing and Society* 601 p 619.
[93] *Re JS* [2002] 3 FCR 433.
[94] T. Shakespeare, *Help* Birmingham: Venture, 2000 and T. Shakespeare 'The social relations of care', in G. Lewis, S. Gewirtz and J. Clarke (eds), *Rethinking Social Policy*, London: Sage, 2001.
[95] D. Gibson, *Aged Care: Old Policies, New Solutions*, Melbourne: Cambridge University Press, 2005.
[96] C. Gilligan *In a Different Voice: Psychological Theory and Women's Development*, Cambridge, MA: Harvard University Press, 1982, pp 1–4, 24–63.
[97] O. Hankivsky, *Social Policy and the Ethic of Care*, Vancouver and Toronto: UBC Press, 2004, p 2.
[98] Repeats of the experiments used by Carol Gilligan in European countries have not found the differing responses to ethical issues tied to sex in the way she did: A. Vikan, C. Camino and A. Biaggio 'Note on a cross-cultural test of Gilligan's ethic of care' (2005) 34 *Journal of Moral Education* 107.

on concepts of justice; and a 'female' approach to ethical issues, which focused on concepts of care. The 'second generation'[99] of care ethicists has tended to downplay the argument that the ethic of care is a female way of thought.[100] They have focused instead on advocating that value be attributed to care and on emphasising that women and men can perform caring roles.

Another concern is that an ethic-of-care approach elevates the importance of relationships over concepts of justice and fairness, the danger being that in doing so abusive relationships become protected, despite the harm done to those in them. However, as Held's work has shown the sharp divide between justice and care is not normally relied upon nowadays. An ethic of care does not seek to promote unjust relationships, but rather just ones. Arguments that an ethic of care perpetuates assumptions that women are naturally drawn to caring roles,[101] or that it overlooks the potential for abuse within relationships, are usually based on a rather old-fashioned (mis)understanding of what the ethic of care is about.

One of the most powerful criticisms of an ethic of care is that care relationships, despite their cosy-sounding image, are in fact about power. John Eekelaar writes:

> to exercise care is also to exercise power. True, it is to be hoped that it is a beneficent exercise of power, but it is power nonetheless. The key element, overlooked in some communitarian accounts, is the role of force or coercion. There are many examples where the role of caregiver, even if applied with good intentions, has adverse consequences.[102]

As mentioned earlier it is a mistake to assume that the caregiver exercises power over the person cared for. Caring relations often involve a complex interplay of dependencies and vulnerabilities.[103] As Michael Fine and Caroline Glendinning argue:

> Recent studies of care suggest that qualities of reciprocal dependence underlie much of what is termed 'care'. Rather than being a

---

[99] E. Jackson, *Medical Law*, Oxford: Oxford University Press, 2006, p 22.

[100] J. Eekelaar, *Family Law and Personal Life*, Oxford: Oxford University Press, 2007, pp 178–79. See also R. Wood, 'Care of disabled people', in G. Dalley (ed) *Disability and Social Policy*, Policy Studies Institute, 1991.

[101] C. Chorn and J. Harms Cannon, '"They're still in control enough to be in control": Paradox of power in dementia caregiving' (2008) 22 *Journal of Aging Studies* 45.

[102] M. Fine and C. Glendinning, 'Dependence, independence or inter-dependence? Revisiting the concepts of care and dependency' (2005) 25 *Ageing and Society* 601, p 619.

[103] J. Herring, 'Where are the carers in healthcare law and ethics?' (2007) 27 *Legal Studies* 51; J. Herring, 'Caregivers in medical law and ethics' (2008) 25 *Journal of Contemporary Health Law and Policy* 1.

unidirectional activity in which an active care-giver does something to a passive and dependent recipient, these accounts suggest that care is best understood as the product or outcome of the relationship between two or more people.[104]

Eekelaar is right to be concerned about the power that can undoubtedly be exerted in a caring relationship. However, that is not an automatic consequence of caring and it reminds us how important it is to emphasise the elements of justice and responsibility within an ethic of care.

Putting an ethic of care into practice

Under an ethic of care the practice of caring would be hugely valued within society and social structures and attitudes established to encourage and enable caring. This would require adequate remuneration of carers: not the payment of benefits of the kind paid to those 'unable to work', but payment acknowledging the key role they play.[105] Work would need to be done to ensure that the burden of caring did not fall on the few, often women, but was shared across the community. Fully participatory and responsible care practices would therefore come to represent the norm.[106] Many of the contributors to this edition have drawn on the work of Martha Fineman and her impact on discussions of family law is considerable. Her writing stresses the importance of ensuring that caring work is attributed with the value it deserves and there is much support for this in the academic community in England and Wales as the chapters of Bridgeman, Herring and Wallbank particularly demonstrate.

When assessing the rights of any individual, they would have to be considered in a situational context. Rather than looking at rights in isolation each person's needs and rights would have to be considered in the context of their relationships. This highlights the problems with the welfare principle as traditionally understood. Seeking to promote the welfare of the child without consideration of the web of relationships within which the child lives is impossible and undesirable. No parent could possibly undertake the task of caring if every decision which has to be made was solely on the basis of what is in the interests of the child. The relationship of caring does, and should, involve give and take. It would not be in the interests of a cared-for person to be in a relationship which was utterly oppressive to their carer. What is in

---

[104] See further M. Fineman, *The Autonomy Myth: A Theory of Dependency*, New York: The New Press, 2004 for a discussion of what such a model would look like.

[105] J. Herring, 'Where are the carers in healthcare law and ethics?' (2007) 27 *Legal Studies* 51; J. Herring, 'Caregivers in medical law and ethics' (2008) 25 *Journal of Contemporary Health Law and Policy* 1.

[106] See further M. Fineman, *The Autonomy Myth: A Theory of Dependency*, New York: The New Press, 2004 for a discussion of what such a model would look like.

their interests is to be in a relationship with their carer which promotes the interests and well-being of both of them. However laudable the ethic of care is in theory, and we suggest that it has many advantages over the more individualistic approaches, it too has problems which have been to an extent highlighted above. Some of the issues with it are related to how it might be applied in a legal context. Feminist projects on family law would still need to keep a watchful eye on individual contexts in which it might arise.

CONCLUSION

This chapter has examined the broad themes of care, rights and an ethic of care. In respect of welfarism generally and the welfare principle in particular we have outlined how it has been used in order to centralise the importance of child well-being in respect of the resolution of familial disputes and also in respect of emanating the message of the need for the state to protect children's interests in the context of public family law and the treatment of children in the wider legal arena. However, we have also reflected on some of the cogent criticisms that have been made, such as its indeterminate nature and the way that child welfare may, in some significant contexts where there is a clash between the interests of the parents, be used as a means of aligning the child's welfare with the interests of fathers to the effect of marginalising the interests of the main carers, usually mothers. We argue that welfare discourses also need to be capable of accounting for and responding to the needs of those connected to the child.

Additionally, it has been suggested that child welfare knowledge is in constant development and understandings of what is in a child's best interests shift over time. Critical commentaries on the development of this increasingly visible bank of knowledge needs to be scrutinised in order to ensure that gender and other forms of discrimination are resisted, while at the same time it is ensured that child welfare is attended to. However, children's rights advocates have also flagged up the paternalism of the welfarist approach, although we tend to agree with those commentators who argue that to imagine the welfare approach and the rights-based approach to be in stark contrast and in opposition are quite simply mistaken and that in many instances, whichever approach is used is likely to produce the same result. In respect of the practical applications of the welfare principle as opposed to the rights approach, we have shown that there are important differences in the way that outcomes are achieved as the emphases in the two approaches are distinct.

We have outlined the benefits of rights-based approaches as outlined by various feminist commentators while noting the potential problems of them. One of the most potent critiques is that rights are over-individualistic and conjure up a world of independent self-interested individuals unaffected by gender roles, ethnicity and social status and their connections with others.

Responding to this we have argued for a reconceptualisation of rights based on the concept of relational autonomy which seeks to centralise the importance of relationships while noting the feminist concern that women should not be expected to sacrifice personal autonomy for the sake of others, such as in the context of domestic violence.

Those who have criticised both welfare and rights for their individualism have developed an ethic-of-care approach which promotes a model of mutually interdependent relationships as the norm around which legal and ethical responses should be built. However, writers have noted how care as a practice is a highly gendered activity and that a danger with the ethic of care is that women's responsibility for unpaid care work may merely be reinforced. That said, care ethics has developed in such a way that value is attributed to care so that those who undertake it are valued and rewarded. It is hoped that once care values become embedded in a society women and men will participate equally in it. In order to put an ethic of care into practice there would need to be a radical reordering of societal and political institutions to ensure that those who do caring work are adequately rewarded. Currently, it is women that undertake the bulk of caring work and it is important that the ethic of care and the sets of expectations that accompany it, such as in responsibility discourses and practices, do not work against women in a way that men as fathers quite simply do not experience. This book then seeks to herald caution in prospective and actual developments where rights are given centre stage without thinking through the ramifications for gendered power relations and the welfare of children.

Chapter 2

Gender, rights, responsibilities and social policy

Brid Featherstone

Introduction

This chapter outlines the background to thinking about rights in social policy.[1] It explores the apparent intensification of concern with responsibilities over the last decades and, in this context, highlights how New Labour, in particular, developed some of their key social policies in relation to parents and their responsibilities. The chapter discusses the gendered implications of such policies and the perspectives of some of those seeking to rethink rights and responsibilities and their relationship.

Background

The academic discipline of social policy has championed the classic socio-logical formulation espoused by Marshall who identified three kinds of citizenship rights: civil or legal rights, political or democratic rights and social or welfare rights.[2] The capitalist welfare state gave expression to the latter and, during what has been called the golden age of the welfare state, there was a broad, if fragile, consensus between those who stressed collective responsibility for human welfare and those who stressed mutual obligation and social protectionism. This resulted in a commitment to welfare provision, which had an emphasis on distributing resources, providing directly for needs and pooling resources to protect against various risks.[3]

As Dean notes, 'the crowning achievement of the twentieth century – brought to fruition following the end of the Second World War – has been the consolidation of more or less systematic forms of social policy across the capitalist world, providing certain rights to social security, health care, education, housing, social protection and, for example, legal aid for the

---

[1] H. Dean, (2004) 'Human rights and welfare rights: contextualising dependency and responsibility' in H. Dean (ed) *The Ethics of Welfare*, Bristol: Policy Press, 7–29.

[2] H. Dean, 'Social policy and human rights: Re-thinking the engagement', (2008) 7 *Social Policy and Society*, 1.

[3] Ibid.

poor'.[4] He further notes that the form and substance of welfare rights has always been contested with different welfare regimes exhibiting different notions of rights. For example, some such as the more 'liberal' English speaking countries have operated with a notion of welfare rights as a form of safety net, whereas corporatist continental European welfare states have tended to see such rights as compensatory rights for their workers. Social democratic welfare states, by contrast, have been inclined to regard welfare more in terms of universal rights for all citizens.

The consensus outlined by Dean has now broken down and the last decades have seen many countries redesigning their social policies.[5] A key point in the context of this chapter is that, while conditionality was always a feature of welfare provision in most countries, it has become more clearly entrenched and tied to notions of responsibility. The relationship between rights and responsibilities is deeply contested[6] and the last decades have seen a range of differing debates and developments. Neo-conservatives have questioned the rights of social citizenship because they were considered to undermine the responsibilities of citizens to provide for themselves through paid work and neo-liberals have questioned them because they were considered to undermine the ethical freedoms and civic duties of the individual property-owning subject.[7]

As has been well documented the Third Way was a political development articulated initially in the USA by Clinton and then by Blair[8] which had, as central, the notion 'no rights without responsibilities'.[9] In order to locate this mantra and understand its impact upon a range of policies, this chapter now turns to explore some of the policies in relation to parents and their responsibilities that have been developed under New Labour.

From welfare to investment

A range of writers have documented how New Labour has sought to construct a social investment state.[10] Others have located this within an exploration of policies across the EU.[11] The notion of the social investment

[4] Ibid, p 1.
[5] J. Jenson, 'Writing women out, folding gender in: The European Union "Modernises" Social Policy' (2008) 15 *Social Politics*, 131–54.
[6] H. Dean, Social policy and human rights: Re-thinking the engagement p 6.
[7] ibid, p 6.
[8] As Dean notes, its influence has spread to a range of countries.
[9] A. Giddens, *The Third Way: The renewal of social democracy*, Cambridge: Polity, 1998, p 65.
[10] See, e.g. B. Featherstone, *Family Life and Family Support: A Feminist Analysis*, Basingstoke, Palgrave/Macmillan, 2004; R. Lister, 'Children (but not women) first: New Labour, child welfare and gender' (2006) 26 *Critical Social Policy* 315–35.
[11] Jenson 'Writing Women out, Folding Gender in'.

state can be understood as both an ideal and an analytical tool.[12] Basically, it is argued the old welfare state sought to protect people from the vagaries and insecurities of the market, whereas a social investment state seeks to facilitate the integration of people into the market. Jenson and Saint-Martin[13] compare what they call the citizenship regime of the old post-war welfare state and its social rights with social investment regimes. Post-war social rights accrued to the model citizen who was the waged – usually the male – worker. Full employment policies responded to his primary interest as did the politics of workplace representation and a range of social rights to protect against risks. The other social rights were to meet the needs of non-participants in the workforce who, apart from women and children, were expected to be few in number.

Jenson[14] identifies three features of the 'new' paradigm: constant learning; a future orientation; we all benefit from good social investments or success-ful individuals enrich our common future.

Briefly, security depends on learning for employability.[15] In modern industrial societies income security depended upon the earnings of a salaried or independent worker. But in recent decades, that pattern has changed. Rising rates of female employment have impacted upon the role of the male breadwinner and the restructuring of wages has decreased the capacity of the family to live on a single wage. These changes have generated new ways of thinking about income security. It is considered that individuals' security depends less on protection from threats to male breadwinning and more on the capacity to confront and adapt successfully to challenges over the life course or coming from unstable markets. The key challenges are defined as those at life transition points, such as entry into school, the school–work transition, breakdown of a couple relationship, as well as labour market conditions, such as unemployment or sickness.[16]

Reliance on acquired human capital rather than specific skills or training is proposed as a response to the changes associated with deindustrialisation, the growth of the service sector and the emergence of a knowledge-based economy. Spending on early years increasingly becomes emphasised – 'good behaviours follow from a "strong start"'.[17]

Moreover, it is argued that we all benefit from good investments and that investment now is less costly than solving problems later. In addition,

---

[12] Lister, 'Children (but not women) first: New Labour, child welfare and gender', p. 316.
[13] J. Jenson and D. Saint-Martin, *Changing Citizenship Regimes: Social Policy Strategies in the Investment State*, Université de Montréal, 2001.
[14] Jenson 'Writing Women out, Folding Gender in'.
[15] Ibid, pp 133–34.
[16] Ibid, pp 133–34.
[17] Ibid, p 135.

certainly in the EU, attention to demographic considerations obliges efforts to respond to social risks, such as decreased fertility rates. 'Never in history has there been economic growth without population growth – if appropriate mechanisms existed to allow couples to have the number of children they want, the fertility rate could rise overall.'[18] The future of European society is linked to the capacity to address new social risks such as there may be too few adults of working age to provide care and support for the elderly.

Such social risks are considered in terms of the methods needed to reconcile work and family responsibilities. Certainly in the UK there has been considerable development in this area.[19] Lewis and Campbell examine such developments and assess how far they promote gender equality which they define 'in terms of the possibility of making a "real" or "genuine" choice for men and women to "work and care"'.[20] They note that part of the construction of UK as a 'liberal welfare regime' was linked to the extent to which care of dependants was treated as a private family issue and the UK long occupied a place towards the bottom of EU league tables on most aspects of family policy including care leaves and care services for children. However, under New Labour, the position has changed with an explicit family policy being developed along a number of dimensions. New forms of leave have been introduced and existing ones extended. There has been an investment in childcare and a new statutory right to request a flexible working pattern.

The next section considers the gendered implications of the policies that have been developed in relation to reconciling work and family before locating these within a discussion of the gendered implications of wider policies directed at parents.

Work, parental responsibilities and gender equity

> The wage as the best form of welfare, employment as a means of social inclusion, and a flexible labour market as the best means of promoting economic growth and increasing employment have been core New Labour ideas.[21]

The responsibility to work is at the heart of New Labour's approach and, in particular, central to the goal of abolishing child poverty. For example, the consultation paper on welfare reform published in 2008 outlines the aim of an 80 per cent employment rate and the enshrining of the responsibility to work

---

[18] European Commission quoted in Jenson, ibid, p 137.
[19] J. Lewis, and M. Campbell, 'UK work/family balance policies and gender equality, 1997–2005' (2007) 14(1) *Social Politics*, 4–30.
[20] ibid, p 4.
[21] ibid, p 9.

at the heart of the approach.[22] 'For those who are capable of working, there will be no right to a life on benefits.'[23] The entrenching of conditionality is explicitly articulated within this document in the context of a commitment to ensuring that it is 'personal, appropriate and fair for every individual'.[24]

Securing gender equality has not been an explicit priority in the policies which have been developed under the rubric of work–family balance policies.[25] Two overlapping agendas have been evident – the promotion of flexibility and fairness was most prominent before 2000 and since 2000, flexibility and choice have been stressed. Choices are treated in all the relevant policy documents as gender neutral, although there is evidence that the erosion of the male breadwinner model has been understood.[26] Policies have addressed the issues of enabling women's choices to balance work and care and, to a much lesser extent, men's, but they have ignored the extent to which expanding women's choices depends on changing men's behaviour in the home. However, as Lewis and Campbell acknowledge, this neglect is relatively commonplace outside a small number of Nordic countries.

In the case of men paid work is assumed to take precedence over unpaid work, and the initiatives that have been directed at them have been considered disappointing by those seeking genuine possibilities to exercise choice. However, as we shall see in a subsequent discussion, a recent analysis of fatherhood and paid work opens up interesting issues in terms of what should be aimed for.[27] Lewis and Campbell argue that there is considerable evidence from cross-national research on what parental leave should look like if fathers are to take it. It must be an individual entitlement, paid at a high rate of compensation, and be flexible, making possible shorter and longer blocks of leave either full or part-time. New Labour, by contrast, has instituted a low flat rate of compensation for its two weeks paternity leave. Additional paternity leave is not an individual right (it is a transfer from the mother's leave), and is not well compensated and flexible. Indeed, the government's own regulatory impact assessment makes it clear that it does not expect many fathers to take up this leave.

Furthermore, it would appear long male working hours is not considered a problem by the government. By contrast with other countries in the EU, the UK is distinguished by the extent to which men work 48 plus hours

---

[22] DWP (2008) *No One Written Off: Reforming Welfare to Reward Responsibility*, London, The Stationery Office.

[23] Ibid, p 12.

[24] Ibid, p 12.

[25] Lewis and Campbell discuss the different terminology that has been used on occasion by the government. They suggest that the kinds of policies that have been adopted mean they should be called work–family balance policies rather than, for example, work–life balance which implies the balancing of a wider set of considerations.

[26] Lewis and Campbell 'UK Work/Family Balance Policies and Gender Equality'.

[27] See E. Dermott, *Intimate Fatherhood*, London: Routledge, 2008.

weekly. The opt-out from the limitation placed on working hours by the EU's 1993 Directive was ended in a vote cast by the European Parliament in 2008.[28] Indeed, it is clear that exhortation has been preferred rather than legislative change in this area. Featherstone[29] suggests that this tendency to favour exhortation, rather than entrench legislative rights, extends across a range of policy initiatives directed at men as fathers.

In relation to women the clear preference that paid work be undertaken by lone mothers, dependent on welfare benefits, has gradually been underpinned by compulsion. Much of the financial aid in work–family balance policies has been channelled into childcare with the explicit aim of encouraging women, especially lone mothers, to enter paid work. However, the picture is more complex than in relation to men. For example, budget speeches have repeatedly stressed the value of tax credits to two-parent families in which mothers stayed at home.

In terms of supporting women to fulfil their responsibilities in relation to paid work, the government has opted for arrangements that do little to improve gender equality in terms of the division of unpaid care. The UK now has the longest maternity leave entitlement of any EU member state, whereas the research suggests that short leaves are better for gender equality. However, as Lewis and Campbell note, there is considerable evidence that working mothers wanted and welcomed longer maternity leaves and there has been some suggestion of unease about employing the mothers of very young children. In addition, research on the benefits of one-to-one care in the first year has been influential with the government.[30] It is recognised that policies that promote the future welfare of mothers and their children are not easy to design. Galtry and Callister have concluded that the best compromise may be a six-month leave for the mother followed by a six-month leave for the father.[31] These leaves would have to be adequate financially however. In the current policy context mothers may have to or feel they need to sacrifice gender equality for child welfare consideration.

Economic deprivation may be alleviated, but not dealt with adequately, by the emphasis upon paid work. Currently, for example, over half of those classified as poor are in employment.[32] The 'new economy' is characterised by job insecurity and employment practices, such as flexible working, homeworking and teleworking.

---

[28] Indeed, the government has been attempting to produce their response to this matter since that time.

[29] B. Featherstone, *Contemporary Fathering: Theory, Policy and Practice*, Bristol: Policy Press, 2009.

[30] Lewis and Campbell, 'Work/Family Balance Policies and Gender Equality'.

[31] J. Galtry and P. Callister 'Assessing the optimal length of parental leave for child and parental well-being: how can research inform policy?' (2005) 6 *Journal of Family Issues* 219–46.

[32] P. Toynbee and D. Walker, *Unjust Rewards*, London: Granta, 2008.

'The growth of flexible capitalism has been regarded by some as making a contribution to the resolution of the tensions between employment and family "work". The non-flexible career bureaucrat was enabled to work in full-time, long term employment because he could rely upon the unpaid work of a full-time homemaker.'[33] However, flexible employment, which is concentrated among women, is not usually associated with individual success in the labour market, and flexible workers often tend to be in lower-level positions. Crompton argues that facilitating flexibility is convenient for employers and such policies are relatively cheap. The UK business world has facilitated 'extreme flexibility' and, alongside the USA,[34] has the highest incidence of evening and night-time work among employed parents.

Crompton's finding that it is problematic to combine employment success and caring is not new. The tensions are, she argues, greatest for two groups who have 'responded positively' to the competitive changes of reflexive modernity, and seek advancement within increasingly individualised career structures: aspirant managerial and professional women and men in routine and manual occupations who want to move up the career ladder. While much of the contemporary discussion of the problems of combining career success and family responsibilities has focused on individuals in high-flying managerial and professional occupations, her qualitative data suggests that even a move out of a lower rung of the occupational ladder will be associated with increased pressures on domestic life. Full-time employment and longer working hours are required to move off the first rung of the job ladder. This means that, as mothers and carers, most women are simply not able to compete on equal terms with most men. Thus despite formal gender equality policies in respect of employment, men still predominate in higher-level jobs.

A recent campaign by the Fawcett Society[35] points out that mothers are at greater risk of poverty in the UK than in any other Western European country. In the UK it is often the event of having a child itself which puts women at risk of moving into poverty. One factor is that, despite it being illegal, 30,000 women every year lose their jobs as a result of becoming pregnant. Many more face disadvantage and reduced opportunities. After having a child, many mothers become trapped in part-time, low-paid and low-status work. The gap in pay between men and women is the largest in Europe and it more than trebles when women reach their thirties, as a result of the financial penalties associated with motherhood. As already outlined,

---

[33] R. Crompton (2006) *Employment and the Family: The Reconfiguration of Work and Family Life in Contemporary Societies*, Cambridge: Cambridge University Press, p 7.

[34] Crompton's study was of Britain, USA, France, Portugal, Finland and Norway.

[35] The Fawcett Society is a charity campaigning to close the inequality gap between men and women. The campaign alluded to here is 'Mum's the Word' and details are available at www.fawcettsociety.org.uk.

women often have to give up more responsible and better-paid jobs because the work is not flexible enough to be combined with caring for a child. Despite attempts by New Labour through the tax credit system to 'make work pay', recent research found that only 50 per cent of lone mothers felt they were better off financially after a move into work. Two-thirds of vulnerable and low-paid workers are women and while jobs, such as homeworking, can allow the combining of work and childcare, they offer little in the way of rights and good pay.

Feminist debates

As has been well documented, there is a substantial body of literature from a range of disciplines which argues for an ethic of care to infuse social policies. This requires a political commitment to value care and to reshape institutions to reflect that changed value.[36] The ethic of care, undoubtedly, speaks to the concerns of those who see New Labour's pursuit of independence through paid work as ill-conceived and undesirable. However, feminists such as Lister, while sympathetic to the arguments for valorising care work, caution against dismissing the importance of a long-standing feminist emphasis upon the importance of paid work for women arguing that: 'True interdependence between individual men and women will not be possible so long as the economic and power relationships underpinning their interdependence are so unequal.'[37] She suggests that an overreaction to the valorisation of paid work loses sight of the social, economic and psychological value of paid work for many women. What is crucial is to interrogate the conditions under which women and men work and parent. She adapts Fraser's notion of the universal caregiver model, as outlined below, and argues this should underpin policies in relation to work and care.

Fraser[38] has identified two approaches for reforming the welfare state in gender egalitarian directions – the 'universal breadwinner' and 'caregiver parity' approaches. 'The former would allow and encourage women to act as men do in the economy, as breadwinners, earning a family supporting wage, and ceding carework to others – not the unpaid housewife of the "traditional" household, but the paid service workers of the state, thus commodifying everyone while also commodifying care.'[39] By contrast, the 'caregiver parity' model does not neglect care, or women's work as caregivers, but

[36] J. Tronto, (1993) *Moral Boundaries*, New York: Routledge.
[37] R. Lister (2003) *Citizenship: Feminist Perspectives*, 2nd edn, p 115.
[38] N. Fraser (1994) 'After the family wage: Gender equity and the welfare state', 22 *Political Theory* 591–618, see also A. Orloff, (2007) 'Should feminists aim for gender symmetry? Why a dual-earner/dual-carer society is not every feminist's utopia' accessed 18 August 20008, http://www.ssc.wisc.edu/~mscaglio/2006documents/Orloff_2007_Gender_Symmetry.pdf.
[39] Orloff, ibid, p 8.

instead tries to compensate them for the disadvantages this work creates. Thus women and men continue to be different, but women are protected from the consequences.

Fraser outlines the problems with both approaches and has advanced an influential synthesis of them – the 'universal caregiver' model in which men are made the focus of efforts to change rather than women. Therefore, the problem is considered to be that most men are unlike most women (caregivers who are also women). As Orloff notes, this is an important analytic innovation, decentring the masculine and valorising care while not leaving it solely to women. Fraser does note that a precondition for this kind of gender equity would be to end gender as we know it which, as Orloff notes, is a revolutionary demand indeed. But a more reformist version is to attempt to make men more like women by finding ways to encourage their participation in care with policies, such as individual leave entitlements.

However, Orloff argues that such a position does not adequately engage with the deep investments people have in gender and the ways in which subjectivity and knowledge are grounded in gender categories. She argues that taking account of these investments matters insofar as it points to men's investments in preserving the power that current social arrangements give them, but also women's concerns to preserve their power in the domain of the private, caregiving realm: identities are formed in relation to whether men and women see themselves as caregivers or not.

Recent research with fathers in the UK would suggest that the model of fatherhood, which is favoured, is based upon establishing a strong emotional relationship between father and child and not a gender equality model of parenthood. There is, therefore, little appetite from fathers themselves for an extension of policies to advance gender equality.[40] Dermott argues that her research does not support suggestions that some men wish to reduce their working hours when they become parents, even if they are not able to do so. Rather her research supports previous survey material indicating that satisfaction with work–life balance only reduces significantly when fathers work extremely long hours. Fathers do make an adjustment when a new child arrives but this reduction is not maintained through the child's years of dependency.

Overall, Dermott suggests that the relationship between paid work and employment is very different for mothers and fathers in the UK. She argues that fathers do not have shorter working hours than non-fathers and, moreover, that they do not find this problematic. There is no evidence that fathers, as a whole or as a significant sub-group, are adopting a 'female model' by taking on part-time and reduced hours. She notes that while this does not necessarily undermine arguments for the existence of a different discourse

---

[40] E. Dermott, *Intimate Fatherhood.*

around fathering behaviour (emphasising the emotional and nurturing elements) it does clarify that this is not translated into alterations to working hours.

Unlike mothers and non-mothers, the part-time–full-time distinction does not apply to fathers and non-fathers. Fathers' behaviour will need to be thought about in ways which do not assume female models. According to Dermott, fatherhood has changed, but it has not become motherhood and does not provide the backdoor route to gender equality.

Dermott seems to be suggesting that present policies accord with men's preferences, whereas others such as Lewis and Campbell see current policies as part of the problem and wish to challenge men's preferences in the interests of fostering gender equity,

There have been challenges by feminists to current policies also 'in the name of the mother'. For example, Hollway, from a psycho-social perspective, contests the contemporary widespread substitution of the term parent for mother as it signifies a huge ideological and political shift to the 'principle that fathers should be involved in parenting beyond their traditional breadwinner roles, even to being the primary caretakers of infants and young children … it claims, in its gender neutrality, that the sex (and gender) of the carer is unimportant, even irrelevant'.[41]

A key point made by Hollway is that mothers and fathers *cannot* fill identical positions in early childcare. The early experience of the mother as holding the baby in her body is crucial and, therefore, the father represents separateness in a way the mother never will. 'Perhaps, we can conclude that, while fathers can perform the maternal and paternal functions (and mothers both these functions too), in the internal world of the child, these will never be entirely interchangeable as long as the infant is born out of the mother's body.'[42]

Hollway concludes that if boys are to grow up with the capacity to care as fathers, much depends on whether they succeeded as boys themselves in retaining their positive identifications with maternal capacities to care for them, while at the same time coming to terms with being boys.

An interesting sociological exploration by the Canadian writer Doucet[43] with men who self-defined as primary caregivers suggests that most fathers believed that fathers and mothers have a different connection to their children and that the one held by the mother is stronger, vaster and more profound. Fathering was a mother-led dance. Moreover, fathers found the negotiation of a range of spaces such as schoolyards and childcare nurseries could be quite problematic and most spoke of having felt a mother's

[41] W. Hollway, *The Capacity to Care: Gender and Ethical Subjectivity*, London: Routledge, 2006.
[42] Ibid, p 90.
[43] A. Doucet, *Do Men Mother?*, Toronto: University of Toronto Press, 2006.

watchful eye on them at times. Yet there was also evidence of significant movement and flow which disrupted this picture. Moreover, primary care-giver fathers clearly articulated a 'care' voice, although they were very clear that they were not mothering. Doucet's research is very valuable, reminding us that gendered investments are, indeed, deep but may also be fluid and changing in differing contexts. Moreover, gender is not all there is. Social class featured for some. One father, a doctor, articulated a sense that his occupation allowed him the ability to navigate women-only spaces in ways which he suspected might not be available to a plumber. A gay bookshop owner who adopted a child spoke of the way in which 'being known' in the community seemed to break down barriers.

The next section turns to consider the emergence of legislative and policy developments seeking to emphasise parents' responsibilities on a range of levels other than paid work, many of which have impacted upon those who are poor and more likely to be subject to state scrutiny.

Widening the emphasis on parents and their responsibilities

Fox Harding[44] noted that from 1979 onwards the Conservative government had developed an interest in family responsibility and was particularly con-cerned about the relationship with state responsibility and the financial implications of who took responsibility for what. She noted the emergence of key pieces of legislation using the term 'parental responsibility': the Children Act 1989, the Criminal Justice Act 1991 and the Child Support Act 1991. The different types were not always consistent but it was argued that the then Conservative government was using the concept in a unified way. 'The concept meshes with a wider strategy for broader family responsibility, more private dependency, and fewer state-dependent families.'[45]

The Children Act was extremely wide-ranging and, according to Fox Harding, its vastness allowed some sections to become law without enough questioning. These were the definition of parents as having responsibilities rather than rights in ss 2 and 3 and the principle of minimum intervention as set out in s 1(5) which states that a court may not make any order regarding a child unless satisfied that this is a better outcome for the child than no order. She suggests that these sections illustrate the government's aim of leaving more responsibility to parents and less to the state.

The Criminal Justice Act made parents more accountable for their chil-dren's behaviour. The main provisions of the Child Support Act related to how maintenance from a non-resident parent usually, but not invariably, the

---

[44] See L. Fox Harding, 'Parental responsibility: the reassertion of private patriarchy?' in E. Silva, (ed) *Good Enough Mothering? Feminist Perspectives on Lone Mother-hood*, London: Routledge, 1996.
[45] Ibid, p.136.

father, whether ever married to the child's mother or not, should be calculated and enforced.

Looking at parental responsibility in the three acts the following, not always consistent, threads were identified: responsibility emphasising an emotional and psychological commitment; financial responsibility for children; blame for a failure of parental responsibility which contributes to criminality.[46]

When New Labour came to power in 1997, it reinforced the emphasis on parental responsibilities. Moreover, the social investment emphasis on the importance of social policy facilitating good outcomes for children contributed to a discourse which increasingly constructed parents as central to ensuring such outcomes were achieved.

The legislative infrastructure inherited from the Conservatives was built upon. Child support policies have been subject to at least two major reform attempts as they have proved deeply problematic in practice. Current proposals seem to be emphasising private arrangements with tougher enforcement powers in certain situations. The emphasis on getting mothers, especially those on benefits, to enter paid work seems to suggest the state has, to some extent, given up on trying to get some fathers to exercise their responsibilities, although the recent decision to make joint birth registration mandatory suggests this is by no means clear-cut.[47]

Parents' responsibilities in relation to their children's delinquency and criminality have been expanded. As Parton has documented, throughout the 1990s, as New Labour was developing its political identity, the case was made by a number of diverse constituencies for developing new policies on crime and delinquency reduction and this was to become an important area of policy.[48] Eschewing a conservative view that the collapse of a particular model of family was responsible for a range of social ills and the left view that parents and children were victims of economic and social changes, a growing consensus emerged. 'It was recognised that turning the clock back to the 1950s was neither a serious nor a desirable option and that policies to "strengthen families" and "help parents" needed development. Family change should be managed not anathematised, with a firm policy emphasis on supporting parents, not stigmatising them.'[49] In a changing world parents and parenting behaviours were seen as important mediators between the stresses of adult life and children's development. Parton documents the family-based factors which were increasingly considered by influential researchers to be linked to an increased risk of offending:

[46] See S. Edwards and A. Halpern, 'Parental responsibility: an instrument of social policy' (1992) 92 *Family Law*, 113–18 and Fox Harding ibid.

[47] Featherstone, *Contemporary Fathering*.

[48] N. Parton, *Safeguarding Childhood: Early intervention and surveillance in a late modern society*, Basingstoke: Palgrave Macmillan, 2006.

[49] Ibid, p 78.

Neglect – where parents spend little time interacting with and supervising children;

Conflict – where parents exert inconsistent or inappropriate discipline and where one party rejects the other;

Deviancy – where parents are themselves involved in offending and/or condone lawbreaking;

Disruption – where neglect and conflict arise from marital discord and the break-up of the marriage with the subsequent absence of one parent, usually the father.[50]

Anti-Social Behaviour Orders for Children aged 10 or older were introduced in the Crime and Disorder Act 1998. This Act also introduced parenting orders. These court orders could require parents to attend for counselling or guidance sessions, and to exercise control over the child's behaviour, ensuring, for example, that their child went to school every day. Local authorities gained the powers to apply local curfew schemes where police could return children home if they broke the curfew notices.

Within the Respect Agenda[51] a range of developments has ensued also expanding the responsibilities of parents in unprecedented ways. It is interesting in this regard to note Eekelaar's comments on responsibility.[52] By the 1980s, both public child protection law and private family law placed the interests of children (at least as perceived by courts and welfare agencies) above those of adult family members. The Children Act 1989, at the behest of the Law Commission, felt it necessary to attempt to banish the concept of a parent's 'rights' with respect to children, saying that parents had only responsibilities towards them. Eekelaar explores the faultlines which have emerged in relation to the rights–responsibility axis. For example, the responsibility of parents in relation to divorce now includes an expectation that the agent should demonstrate an appreciation of the effects of their actions, or inactions, on other people by modifying their behaviour accordingly even if this means modifying claims to one's entitlements'.[53] So while we can say that a responsible person follows their legal obligations, responsibility does not stop there. A fuller conception of responsibility exists which is well established and well developed in people's behaviour. Responsible people will exercise restraint within their legal rights, but they will also act beyond their legal duties. For example, a child who keeps in regular contact with her parents when she leaves home has no legal duty to do this but will usually be seen as acting more responsibly than one who does not. Responsible parents will try to ensure that their children behave considerately

---

[50] Ibid, p 79.

[51] See P. Squires, 'New Labour and the politics of anti-social behaviour' (2006) 26 *Critical Social Policy* 144.

[52] J. Eekelaar, *Family Law and Personal Life*, Oxford: Oxford University Press, 2006.

[53] Ibid, p 128.

towards others. None of these, hitherto, have been legal obligations. However, it is now interesting that the government is trying to embrace this through the provisions in relation to anti-social behaviour within the law. As Eekelaar notes, the legislation in relation to anti-social behaviour clearly covers behaviour which, hitherto, escaped any form of legal action (but would probably have been thought to be irresponsible). The apparent failure of parents to have prevented such behaviour might previously have been considered irresponsible: but it would have fallen outside the scope of official intervention. Eekelaar argues that there is no difficulty in principle with a policy which seeks to bring about such changes in behaviour. But the difference between encouraging and enforcing is pivotal as one loses the fuller sense of responsibility referred to above. The behaviour is now a legal duty.

Henricson and Bainham[54] have considered whether attributing blame to parents for children's behaviour can be considered compatible with human rights considerations. They also point out such an attribution underestimates children's independence and overestimates the ability of parents to control the behaviour of their children as they grow older. Indeed, in an evaluation of a parenting programme with fathers who were compelled by the courts to attend because of their sons' offending, fathers made this very point.[55]

A number of writers have highlighted the gendered implications of policies which emphasise parents' responsibilities towards their children.[56] For example, the research evidence suggests that it has been mothers, not 'parents' who have been made the subject of parenting orders because of their sons' behaviour.[57] Indeed there is some agreement that such orders should be more accurately named 'mothering' orders.

The imposition of the order is determined not by legal concerns about who has parental responsibility, but by who accompanies the child to court and this is usually related to residency. Holt[58] notes that the mothers in her research were more likely to attend court because they were either unemployed or working part-time or flexible hours. She also notes the evidence from the research on parenting orders that economic difficulties were a key concern for mothers. This links with themes from the research identified in a previous section and suggests the importance of attending to the feminisation of poverty in many families.

---

[54] C. Henricson and A. Bainham, *The Child and Family Policy Divide: Tensions, Convergence and Rights*, York: Joseph Rowntree Foundation, 2005.

[55] B. Featherstone, *Contemporary Fathering*.

[56] B. Featherstone, *Family Life and Family Support*.

[57] D. Ghate and M. Ramalla, *Positive Parenting: The National Evaluation of the Youth Justice Board's Parenting Programme*, London: Policy Research Bureau, 2002.

[58] A. Holt (2007) Parenting Orders, Youth Justice Policy and the discursive shaping of subjectivity, paper presented at Monitoring Parents: childrearing in the age of 'intensive parenting', University of Kent, 21–22 May.

Moreover, Lister has noted that it is women-headed households who fail to control the behaviour of male children or boyfriends who are most likely to be the subject of complaints under anti-social order legislation and subject to sanctions, such as eviction from their homes.[59]

As many feminist commentators have noted, the term parent, when mobilised by policy makers and attached to initiatives or legislation, is problematic. It obscures material inequalities in caretaking and the difficulties this poses for mothers. Fathers' organisations have, in recent years, also begun to challenge the term suggesting that it obscures the needs of fathers. The Fatherhood Institute has sought to challenge employment policies and the practices of child welfare services. While the challenging of employment practices emerges from a concern with gender equity, concerns about services are often posed in terms of men 'missing out' and are not adequately accompanied by any acknowledgement of the difficulties women often face in their dealings with services

The Fatherhood Institute invests in the government-promoted discourse of the importance of facilitating good outcomes for children. Fathers are construed as central to such a project. In the process, mothers and their wishes, needs or desires can become invisible. A more robust engagement with the difficulties posed by men who do not cooperate with women financially or in terms of caretaking is missing with the dominant message being that services are obstructing men's involvement with their children.[60] As has been well documented, although it is beyond the scope of this chapter to explore further, other fathers' organisations employ a fused language of rights, equality and care to make claims in relation to their children in the private law arena, but appear to have little to say about gendered inequities in broader arenas.[61]

Returning to rights or not?

The ethic of care has attracted substantial support and speaks to the concerns of those who see New Labour's pursuit of independence through paid work as an unattractive vision. The increased emphasis upon responsibilities by New Labour (and its link with conditionality) does appear, however, to have reinforced the continuing importance of a language of rights and the often associated concept of justice. For example, Lister argues for the importance of rights to citizenship, both generally and with respect to subordinated groups and the potential for a language of social justice to reconcile the political claims of radical pluralism and universalism. She argues for an approach to citizenship that embraces both ethics of care and justice. In

---

[59] Lister, 'Children (but not women) first'.
[60] B. Featherstone, *Contemporary Fathering*.
[61] See R. Collier and S. Sheldon, *Fathers' Rights Activism and Law Reform in Comparative Perspective*, Oxford and Portland: Hart Publishing 2006; see also chapters by Collier and Wallbank in this volume.

so doing she recognises that she is by no means alone with writers from within both the care and the justice paradigm increasingly embracing such a position.

As Dean[62] notes, mid-twentieth century 'social liberalism had been willing to concede rights to welfare as a means to equality of status and opportunity. The "advanced liberalism" of the new millennium is rather more insistent that rights should not precede the responsibilities of the citizen.' He further notes that the language of welfare rights was once capable of accommodating either a contractarian or a solidaristic interpretation of human dependency. He defines a contractarian as being averse to dependency, celebrating independence and seeking to enable people to engage with one another as freely contracting parties. By contrast, the solidaristic approach acknowledges dependency, celebrates human interdependence and seeks to enable people to engage with one another in mutually protective solidarity. By and large, it is the contractarian approach that has achieved ascendancy.

Dean argues that the language of human rights has displaced that of welfare rights in the global poverty context. He recognises that human rights can represent a discursive resource upon which social policy can draw in the current climate, but the challenge is how to re-establish concretely claims to welfare rights within public debate. He suggests that Nancy Fraser's notion of a 'politics of needs interpretation' may be of help here. Fraser argued that through such a politics specific human needs may be translated into claims and asserted as rights.[63] This would be in a context which combined struggles over the redistribution of resources with identity-based struggles for recognition. 'It is through the language of welfare rights and the processes by which they are negotiated that people may lay claim to the satisfaction of their own needs, while also recognising the claims of distant strangers'.[64]

As already argued, many feminists increasingly call for a synthesis of the ethics of care and justice recognising the importance of a language of rights in a political context where responsibilities are stressed so strongly and a language of care in a context where independence through paid work is stressed so strongly. However, there remain ongoing discussions between feminists, as outlined above, particularly about what should be campaigned for in order to balance paid work and care responsibilities.

Conclusion

This chapter has explored the development of social policies concerned with investing in children and reinforcing their parents' responsibilities towards

---

[62] H. Dean, *Social Policy and Human Rights*.

[63] N. Fraser (1994) 'After the family wage: gender equity and the welfare state', 22 *Political Theory* 591–618.

[64] H. Dean, *Social Policy and Human Rights*, p 9.

those children. It highlights the continued importance of exploring gendered inequalities in relation to such responsibilities. It draws on the work of feminists who suggest the need for a synthesis of an ethics of care and an ethics of justice in order to develop the possibilities for men and women to care and earn, although it suggests that areas of debate remain.

Acknowledgements

I would like to thank Ruth Lister and the contributors to this book, especially Julie Wallbank, for their help with this chapter. I would also like to thank Ann Orloff for permission to cite her paper which was most helpful.

Chapter 3

Child protection, gender and rights

Felicity Kaganas*

INTRODUCTION

The need to strike a balance between protecting children and respecting family privacy has long been a concern of the liberal state. The question it faces is how the way that families raise children can be made into a matter of public concern and how child rearing can be monitored 'without destroying the ideal of the family as a counterweight to state power, a domain of voluntary, self regulating action'.[1]

Coercive intervention in the family is regarded as a last resort and the Children Act 1989 was drafted to reflect this. In particular, the notion of partnership, which is implicit in the legislation and which is explicitly promoted in government documents, demands that local authorities make every effort to work with parents on a cooperative, voluntary basis. The Human Rights Act 1998 and the jurisprudence that has developed around the European Convention on Human Rights (ECHR) place further restrictions on agents of the state. These are consistent with the partnership principle and with the notion of family participation in decision making. In addition, in so far as it safeguards family privacy and parents' rights, the Human Rights Act reinforces the idea that compulsory intervention in the family is to be reserved for cases where there is no alternative.

Yet while family privacy is protected by law and while it appears to be accorded considerable respect within family policy, there is a potentially contradictory, or at least divergent, strand of family policy that is gaining increasing prominence in government programmes. This aspect of family policy could lead to greater intrusion in the family. It is aimed at breaching the ramparts of the private family to inculcate in parents 'better' attitudes to their children and to promote 'better' childcare practices. Of course, in a

---

* My thanks for their comments goes to Christine Piper, Alison Diduck and all the other participants in the conference on Rights, Gender and Family Law held in Oxford on 26th September 2008.
[1] R. Dingwall, J. Eekelaar and T. Murray, *The Protection of Children: State Intervention and Family Life*, Oxford: Blackwell, 1983, pp 214–15.

society that assumes that children can and should be protected,[2] it is well established that family privacy must yield to the demands of child protection. But it seems that it is now also considered acceptable to seek to intervene in families other than those posing an immediate risk to children. It seems that whereas previously family policy was concerned primarily with ensuring that parents did no harm to their children, the state is now demanding more: parents are expected to do good. Concerns about child abuse and about youth offending are driving initiatives aimed not only at saving children from bad families but at making most families into 'good' families. And where parents are considered deficient in some way, there is now a preoccupation with effecting change. Problem, potential problem or marginalised families must be moulded into better families in order to transform them into suitable environments for raising children.

The aim of government and of policy makers is to create responsible parents who will raise responsible children. Parents who acknowledge and seek to address their parenting deficits may be offered help but those who do not will be subject to compulsion. This is not new. Donzelot[3] tells us that in the nineteenth century 'moralization' and 'normalization' were used as strategies to facilitate penetration into and moralisation of the family in the face of a strong tradition of family privacy. What is new about the current policy is the scope of its reach; the new re-moralisation[4] project is embedded in an ambitious project to improve parenting throughout the nation by means of universal and targeted services.

This chapter will examine the extent to which the law, and in particular the Human Rights Act, does in fact constrain intervention in the family. It will argue that, in practice, the statute does little to fortify parental rights. In addition this chapter will explore the risks for families of the new extra-legal initiatives. These initiatives expose parents to monitoring and to intervention by welfare professionals in circumstances where there are few safeguards in place and with no real counterweight to the power of those professionals. More specifically new measures have the potential to make more families, or, to be more accurate, more mothers, visible and susceptible to varying levels of surveillance and coercion to transform them into 'good' mothers.

The Human Rights Act 1998

The government and policy makers are at pains to re-emphasise that children should be raised within their families. So, for example, the new Guidance and Regulations under the Children Act 1989 reaffirm that '[t]he Act is

---

[2] H. Ferguson, *Protecting Children in Time. Child Abuse, Child Protection and the Consequences of Modernity*, Basingstoke: Palgrave Macmillan, 2004, p 3.

[3] J. Donzelot and R. Hurley (tr), *The Policing of Families*, London: Hutchinson, 1980.

[4] S. Day Sclater and C. Piper, 'Remoralising the family? – Family policy, family law and youth justice' (2000) 12 *Child and Family Law Quarterly* 135.

based on the belief that children are generally best looked after within the family with their parents playing a full part in their lives and with least recourse to legal proceedings'.[5]

In contrast, Art 3 of the ECHR has had the effect of requiring local authorities to split up families under certain circumstances. It provides redress in cases where there has been a failure to protect children from abuse. Of course, local authorities have a duty under the Children Act 1989 to investigate cases of suspected abuse and the power to intervene in abusive families. Art 3 goes even further. It imposes a duty on the state to ensure that people, especially 'children and other vulnerable persons' are not subjected to torture or inhuman or degrading treatment.[6] The state therefore must take steps to prevent children being assaulted or neglected[7] and this duty extends to the need to take 'reasonable steps to prevent ill-treatment of which the authorities had or ought to have had knowledge', even where that ill-treatment is meted out by a private individual.[8]

However, the HRA also has the potential, in theory, to buttress parents' claims to privacy and to strengthen their position in disputes with local authorities and other agencies. Before the statute was enacted, it was thought that it might prove 'helpful to those wishing to challenge the ways that courts and local authorities deal with ... care proceedings'.[9] It was also argued, and continues to be argued, that the balancing exercise required by Art 8[10] necessitates a re-evaluation or reinterpretation of the paramountcy principle.[11] Nevertheless, the courts have taken a different view and the effect of the HRA in cases where the welfare principle applies has not been very significant.

Art 8 has been applied by the ECtHR in cases where there has been over-zealous intervention to remove a child who was not at risk.[12] In particular,

[5] DCSF, *The Children Act 1989 Guidance and Regulations, Volume 1, Court Orders,* London: TSO, 2008, para 1.8.

[6] See *E v UK* [2002] 3 FCR 700, para 88.

[7] *Z v United Kingdom* (2002) 34 EHRR 3.

[8] *E v UK* (above n 6) para 88; *A v UK* (1999) 27 EHRR 611. In addition, where abuse is detected the state has an obligation to punish the offender (*A v UK* (above)). See also M. Hayes, 'Criminal trials where a child is the victim: extra protection for children or a missed opportunity?' (2005) 17 CFLQ, 307 p 311; S. Choudhry and J. Herring, 'Righting domestic violence' (2006) 20 IJLPF 95.

[9] J. Wadham and H. Mountfield, *Blackstone's Guide to the Human Rights Act,* 1999, p 97.

[10] In terms of Art 8(2) ECHR, local authorities are not permitted to interfere with the right to private and family life of parents and children unless that interference is justified by, for instance, 'the protection of health or morals, or for the protection of the rights and freedoms of others'.

[11] See, e.g. J. Herring 'The Human Rights Act and the welfare principle in family law – conflicting or complementary?' (1999) 11 CFLQ 223. See also F. Kaganas and C. Piper 'Grandparents and contact: rights v welfare revisited' (2001) 15 IJLP&F 250 for a critical analysis of the arguments put forward.

[12] See, e.g. *K and T v Finland (app 25702/94)* (2001) 36 EHRR 255 [2001] 2 FLR 707. The state has positive obligations also under Art 8: *MC v Bulgaria* (2005) 40 EHRR 20, para 150.

Art 8(2) has been applied in some cases so that intervention in the family has been held to be unjustified because it was not necessary and proportional.[13] These have tended to be cases, however, where there is no evidence of ill-treatment or neglect;[14] where the state agencies have failed to consider alternatives to removing the children or have failed to provide support for the family;[15] where a newly born infant is removed;[16] where emergency measures are taken despite the absence of immediate risk,[17] especially if the parents have not been consulted or involved in the decision making;[18] and where contact between children and their families has been denied.[19]

The domestic courts have taken a similar approach. One important change has been that Art 8 of the ECHR has led the English courts to circumscribe the situations in which children's services authorities are permitted to take emergency action. Most notably, Art 8 led Munby J in *X Council* v *B*[20] to devise guidelines placing stringent limitations on the use of Emergency Protection Orders (EPOs). He expressed doubt as to whether some provisions in the Children Act 1989 dealing with EPOs, such as the restriction of parents' right to appeal, are human rights compatible. Nevertheless he did accept that the removal of children in terms of EPOs is in principle compatible with the Convention. He stressed, however, that an EPO is a 'drastic' measure;[21] courts must have 'scrupulous regard for the Convention rights of both the child and the parents'.[22] Intervention in the family is only justified where it is necessary and proportionate to the legitimate aim of protecting the welfare and interests of the child. Courts must therefore confine the use of emergency orders to situations where 'no other less radical form of order will achieve the essential end of promoting the welfare of the child'.[23]

When it comes to applications for care orders, the courts require 'extraordinarily compelling' justification for the removal of an infant from its mother at or shortly after birth.[24] In addition, Art 8 requires public

---

[13] I am obliged to Shazia Choudhry for pointing out that the ECtHR has shown itself more willing than domestic courts to invoke this provision.

[14] *Kutzner* v *Germany* [2003] 1 FCR 249.

[15] *Kutzner* v *Germany*, above n 14; *Haase* v *Germany* [2004] 2 FLR 39.

[16] *Haase* v *Germany*, above n 15.

[17] See, e.g. *P, C and S* v *United Kingdom* [2002] 3 FCR 1. There it was held that emergency measures to remove a newly born infant contravened Art 8 because the risk to the child while in the hospital could be contained by supervising the mother. The risk was not imminent and it was not life-threatening.

[18] *Haase* v *Germany*, above n 15.

[19] *Moser* v *Austria* [2007] 1 FLR 702, para 66. See also *HK* v *Finland* [2007] 1 FLR 633.

[20] [2004] EWHC 2015 (Fam); [2007] 1 FCR 512, para 57.

[21] *X Council* v *B (Emergency Protection Orders)*, above n 20, para 34.

[22] Ibid, paras 41–42.

[23] Ibid.

[24] *Re M (Care Proceedings: Judicial Review)* [2003] EWHC 850 (Admin), [2004] 1 FCR 302, para 44.

authorities to consider alternatives before embarking on child protection proceedings in respect of any child.[25] Removal of a child ought to be considered a temporary measure and the aim should be to reunite the family where possible.[26] Restrictions on contact warrant strict scrutiny.[27]

It is perhaps in relation to the procedures adopted by local authorities and courts that the influence of Art 8, and also Art 6, is most apparent. There must be a 'transparent and transparently fair procedure at all stages of the process', both in and out of court.[28] Art 8 guarantees fairness at all stages of decision making in the child protection process[29] and parents must be involved in that process, 'seen as a whole, to a degree sufficient to provide them with the requisite protection of their interests'.[30] The demands of fairness require that ex parte proceedings be justified;[31] that documents be fully disclosed;[32] and that parents know the evidence against them and be allowed to present their own evidence.[33]

So, both the ECtHR and the domestic courts have shown themselves willing to criticise procedural defects, precipitate action by state agencies[34] and also restrictions on contact between family members after removal of a child.[35] However the courts appear more reluctant to question the merits of a decision to place a child in state care. The ECtHR said, in *K and T v Finland*, that the importance of protecting children means that a wide

---

[25] See, e.g. *Haase v Germany*, above n 15, para 95, cited in *X Council v B (Emergency Protection Orders)* above n 20 para 45.

[26] *Down Lisburn Health and Social Services Trust v H* [2006] UKHL 36 [2007] 1 FLR 121, para 33. But the case law should not be interpreted to prioritise reunion over the protection and welfare of the child or over the provisions of Art 8(2) and the need to strike a fair balance (*Re R (Care: Disclosure: Nature of Proceedings)* [2002] 1 FLR 755, 770).

[27] *Haase v Germany*, above n 15, cited in *X Council v B (Emergency Protection Orders)*, above n 20, para 45.

[28] *Re L (Care: Assessment: Fair Trial)* [2002] EWHC 1379 (Fam) [2002] 2 FLR 730, para 151.

[29] Ibid, para 88.

[30] *W v United Kingdom* (1988) 10 EHRR 29, paras 63–64: *Re G (Care: Challenge to Local Authority's Decision)* [2003] EWHC 551 (fam); [2003] 2 FLR 42, para 31. *Re L*, above n 28, para 98. Parents must be involved in decision making even after the care order is made and the local authority is implementing it (*Re G*, above, para 36).

[31] *X Council v B*, above n 20, para 57.

[32] *Re G*, above n 30, para 33.

[33] *Re L*, above n 28, paras 102–5.

[34] See further on the ECHR cases, J. Masson with D. McGovern, K. Pick and M. Winn Oakley, *Protecting Powers. Emergency Intervention for Children's Protection*, Chichester: NSPCC, Wiley, 2007, p 48ff.

[35] See, e.g. *K and T v Finland*, above n 12. See also *Gorgulu v Germany* [2004] 1 FCR 410. In *Olsson v Sweden (no 2) (app no 25702/94)* [1992] ECHR 13441/87, the court upheld a prohibition on removing children from their foster parents, pointing out that the lack of contact was the fault of the biological parents.

margin of appreciation is accorded to the state when it comes to decisions to take children into care.[36] And it appears that domestic courts are vehement in refusing to allow rights to override welfare; courts almost always place the exigencies of child protection before the rights of the parents.

The Human Rights Act – the limits for parents

In general, the approach of the courts appears to have been to assume that there is no conflict between Art 8 and the paramountcy principle or, for that matter, between the Children Act 1989 and the Human Rights Act 1998. They have, on numerous occasions, asserted that, in relation to child protection, the Children Act 1989 was framed in the light of the HRA and that the balancing exercise between the need to intervene to protect a child and to avoid intervening in private family life is implicit in the earlier statute.[37] 'Domestic law has long been applying the concepts inherent in Art 8(2) in all but name';[38] no change in approach is needed:

> The social workers have to conduct a balancing exercise both in domestic law and under the European Convention.[39]

> The obligations imposed on local authorities are the same whether pre or post the implementation of the Human Rights Act 1998, because the expectations in relation to the protection of children are the same. The Children Act 1989 anticipated the introduction into English law of the European Convention.[40]

Decisions of the ECtHR are cited in support of the contention that the Convention prioritises children's welfare. In *Yousef* v *The Netherlands*[41] it was held that the child's rights are paramount and must prevail over the parents' Art 8 interests. In *Johansen* v *Norway*, the ECtHR said that consideration of the child's best interests is of 'crucial importance'.[42] The court, it explained, will attach 'particular importance to the best interests of the

---

[36] *K and T v Finland*, above n 12, para 155.
[37] *Re S (Sexual Abuse Allegations: Local Authority Response)* [2001] EWHC Admin 334, [2001] 2 FLR 776, para 54.
[38] *Re S (Sexual Abuse Allegations: Local Authority Response)*, above n 37, para 54. See also *Re S (Adoption Order or Special Guardianship Order)* [2007] EWCA Civ 54, [2007] 1 FLR 819, para 49.
[39] *Re S (Sexual Abuse Allegations: Local Authority Response)*, above n 37, para 53.
[40] *Re S (Sexual Abuse Allegations: Local Authority Response)*, above n 37, para 60. See also *Re KD (A Minor) (Ward: Termination of Access)* [1988] AC 806; *Re L and H (Residential Assessment)* [2007] EWCA Civ 213, [2007] 1 FLR 1370, para 82.
[41] (2003) 36 EHRR 20 [2003] 1 FLR 210, para 73.
[42] (1997) 23 EHRR 33, para 64.

child, which, depending on their nature and seriousness, may override those of the parent'.[43]

There are arguments for interpreting both cases restrictively. *Yousef* has been described as an 'isolated and weak decision'.[44] Baroness Hale has also sought to lessen the potential impact of the case, saying that, although in terms of *Yousef* the child's interests prevail, the court is expected to examine the 'relevance and sufficiency' of the reasons for intervention and consider whether the intervention is 'necessary and proportionate'.[45] Herring and Taylor[46] in turn have pointed out that *Johansen* implies that the interests of the child will not always override those of the parents; the decision will depend on the 'nature and seriousness' of the interests concerned. And according to Harris-Short,[47] in some cases only weighty welfare considerations will render interference with the parents' Art 8 rights proportionate. Yet, as Freeman says, the paramountcy principle has 'enormous symbolic importance' and, in the context of litigation over children, 'it is not difficult to construct a right that their welfare should assume overriding importance'.[48]

The preponderance of the reported case law indicates that the courts are currently not prepared to allow parental rights to stand in the way of child protection. Also, the available empirical evidence bears out the observation that courts put safety first. It appears that orders are not difficult to obtain. According to the professionals surveyed by Masson and her colleagues,[49] the threshold for an EPO presents few problems for local authorities. Indeed, the researchers found that it was almost unknown for magistrates to refuse an order.[50] Even in cases where emergency proceedings are considered inappropriate, families are not necessarily shielded from compulsory intervention.

---

[43] Ibid, para 78.

[44] S. Harris-Short, 'Family law and the Human Rights Act 1998: judicial restraint or revolution?' (2005) 17 CFLQ, 329 p 357.

[45] *Down Lisburn Health and Social Services Trust* v *H*, above n 26, para 134. See also *In re B (Children) (Care Proceedings: Standard of Proof) (CAFCASS Intervening)* [2008] UKHL 35 [2008] 3 WLR 1, para 78.

[46] J. Herring and R. Taylor, 'Relocating relocation' (2006) 18 CFLQ 517, p 528.

[47] S. Harris-Short, 'Family law', p 356.

[48] M. Freeman, 'Feminism and child law' in J. Bridgeman and D. Monk (eds), *Feminist Perspectives on Child Law*, London: Cavendish Publishing, 2000, p 31. See further, Kaganas and Piper, 'Grandparents and contact'.

[49] J. Masson 'Research – emergency intervention to protect children: using and avoiding legal controls' (2005) 17 CFLQ 75. This research, conducted between 2001 and 2004, preceded *X Council* v *B*, above n 20, but presumably the courts should have been mindful of the ECHR at that time.

[50] Masson *et al.*, *Protecting Powers*, report that approximately 90 per cent of applications are granted and, in their study, no application was refused. A small number of applications were withdrawn following agreements (p 177). The authors speculate that this may be because local authorities bring only strong cases and also perhaps because of legal advice to parents not to oppose orders (pp 175, 180–82).

Courts are not precluded from protecting children in other ways, namely care or interim care orders.[51] And it appears that care orders are not often refused either.[52] Domestic courts have followed the lead of the ECtHR and the latter has been slow to criticise orders. As one judge has noted, '[t]he European Court of Human Rights has only rarely held that the initial taking of a child into care violates Art 8, although it has done so in the case of newborn babies'.[53] So courts in this jurisdiction have found little difficulty in adopting an approach that does not allow the issue of rights to get in the way of what they consider most important: the welfare[54] and protection of children. For instance, in *Re M-J (Adoption Order or Special Guardianship Order)*, the Court of Appeal indicated that, while it might be appropriate to consider the proportionality of whatever order is sought to the child's needs, and to consider whether a less interventionist order would suffice, 'insofar as any such consideration is allowed to derogate from the welfare principle, it is plainly unacceptable'.[55]

Even in relation to procedure, where the HRA seems to have had its greatest impact,[56] there needs to be a substantial departure from good practice before it can be said that the parents' human rights have been infringed.[57] A failure to comply with good practice does not necessarily entail a breach of either Art 6 or Art 8; there will be an infringement only if the departure is 'sufficiently substantial to infect the fairness of the proceedings'.[58] According to Freeman, the courts are reluctant to find there has been interference with parents' procedural rights.[59] They are hostile to any attempt to obstruct child protection by relying on technicalities and in one

[51] *Re X (Emergency Protection Orders)* [2006] EWHC 510 (fam); [2006] 2 FLR 701, para 101. An EPO should not normally be sought in non-urgent cases of sexual abuse, emotional abuse or fabricated illness.

[52] Masson *et al.*, *Protecting Powers*, report that in the 'overwhelming' majority of cases, an emergency order is followed by a change of carer or a long-term protective order (p 207). See also DfES and DCA, *Review of the Child Care Proceedings System in England and Wales*, 2006, para 4. 7; J. Masson, J. Pearce and K. Bader with O. Joyner, J. Marsden and D. Westlake, *Care Profiling Study, Ministry of Justice Research Series 4/08*, 2008, para 55.

[53] *Down Lisburn Health and Social Services Trust v H*, above n 26, para 33.

[54] *Re R (Care: Disclosure: Nature of Proceedings)*, above, n 26, pp 770–71; *Re V (Care: Pre-Birth Actions)* [2004] EWCA Civ 1575, [2005] 1 FLR 627, para 33.

[55] [2007] EWCA Civ 56, [2007] 1 FLR 691, para 19.

[56] In *Re L and H (Residential Assessment)*, for example, Wall LJ confined his discussion of the European Convention to questions of procedure and fairness, while applying only the Children Act in relation to the grounds for an order (above n 40, para 85). See Masson *et al.*, *Protecting Powers*, pp 158, 178 for examples of the impact of the HRA.

[57] *Re J (A Child) (Care Proceedings: Fair Trial)* [2006] EWCA civ 545 [2006] 2 FCR 107 para 19; *Re L*, above n 28, para 122.

[58] *Re J (A Child) (Care Proceedings: Fair Trial)*, above n 57, para 26. Failure to give a parent access to legal representation in a complex case with potentially serious consequences may infringe Art 6. See *P, C and S v United Kingdom*, above n 17.

[59] M Freeman, *Understanding Family Law*, London: Thomson Sweet & Maxwell, 2007, p 278.

case it was stressed that courts should be careful to 'weed out barren arguments' under the HRA which do not relate to the identification of the s 31 threshold or the welfare disposition of the case.[60] In *Re J*, although Wilson LJ said that infringements of parents' human rights should be exposed in court, he went on to state that judicial guidelines[61] relating to procedural fairness,

> must not be used as a bandwagon, to be drawn across the tracks of the case and to de-rail the proceedings from their prompt travel towards the necessary conclusions referable to, and in the interests of the child. ... [W]e will support those who deal robustly with suggestions of such minor non-compliance ... as could never sensibly be translated into an infringement of human rights.[62]

It is not easy, then, to establish a breach of Art 6 or Art 8 by reason of some procedural defect. It is probably even more difficult to establish a breach arising from the substantive decision to take a child into care. Even if it is correct to emphasise the need for proportionality, this does not change the court's priorities. As Masson *et al.* observe:

> The introduction of human rights law has brought further scrutiny to child protection practices but has not resulted in a clear basis for balancing the rights of children to physical safety and of parents to respect for family life, interpreted in this context as involvement in all decisions about their children and the limitation of intervention to cases where it is essential. Human rights judges, recognising the vulnerability of children, especially babies, the huge responsibility child protection laws place on social workers and the wide variety of circumstances where protection may be required, have found it difficult to identify either minimum procedural standards or substantive tests which can distinguish legitimate and illegitimate intervention.[63]

This is not surprising. Human rights jurisprudence cannot be expected to point to the 'right' answers when it comes to asking whether a child should be removed from his or her parents. Human rights law in this field is a vessel that has to be filled by family policy; the two cannot be considered separately.[64] Focusing on non-intervention (and privacy) obscures the 'ethical and political choices we make'.[65] Indeed the notion of family privacy cannot be divorced from those choices.

---

[60] *Re V (Care: Pre-Birth Actions)*, above n 54, para 33.
[61] Set out in *Re L*, above n 28.
[62] *Re J (A Child) (Care Proceedings: Fair Trial)*, above n 57, para 30. See also *Re V (Care: Pre-Birth Actions)*, above n 54, paras 24, 29.
[63] Masson *et al.*, *Protecting Powers*, p 54.
[64] See F. Olsen, 'The myth of state intervention in the family' (1985) 18 *Journal of Law Reform* 835, 842.
[65] Ibid, 861.

Moreover, it is not surprising that the legislation has not made decisions easier or more clear-cut. Human rights norms and rules cannot tell us whether a child is at risk and, if so, what should be done; they cannot produce certainty in an area of law where decisions often hinge on prediction and opinion. The Art 8 balancing exercise is self-evidently an exercise involving discretion and the information available to inform this exercise is derived from risk assessment and expert evidence formulated in the context of a body of knowledge that is characterised by shifting perceptions of harm, by uncertainty and by change.

Once the professional assessment is that a child is at risk, the impetus is towards obtaining a court order. Both social workers and police fear that they will be exposed to criticism unless they are seen to be doing all they can to protect children.[66] This anxiety means that social workers tend to favour removing children from what they consider to be unacceptably risky situations.[67] And it is not surprising that magistrates appear loath to refuse applications for orders unless satisfied that the child will be made safe by means of other arrangements.[68] While there is research suggesting that orders are sought only in circumstances where the need for one is 'self evident',[69] it appears that magistrates generally do not want the responsibility of leaving a child in a situation deemed by the welfare professionals to be unsafe.[70] Magistrates assume there is 'no smoke without a fire'[71] and, unless there is evidence to contradict the testimony of the social worker and the experts before it, a court would not be in a position to gainsay the assessment of risk presented to it.[72]

It is true that human rights law may put parents in a better position than they would otherwise be because it gives them the opportunity to present evidence challenging that of the authorities. Yet as long as there is sufficient evidence to convince a court that the s 31 threshold is satisfied, it is difficult to imagine a successful challenge to an application for a care order on the basis of proportionality except in very unusual circumstances. It is unlikely that the courts will be prepared to expose children even to moderate levels of risk in the name of parental rights.[73]

---

[66] Masson *et al.*, *Protecting Powers*, p 203.
[67] Ibid.
[68] Masson *et al.*, *Protecting Powers*, p 203.
[69] J. Hunt, A Macleod and C Thomas, *The Last Resort. Child Protection, the Courts and the 1989 Children Act*, London: TSO, 1999, p 111.
[70] See Masson *et al.*, *Protecting Powers*, p 182.
[71] Local authority lawyer quoted by Masson *et al*, *Care Profiling*, p 179.
[72] In the event of differing expert opinions, a court will tend to use rules of thumb, unconnected with the substance of the opinions, to decide between them. For example, a court might prefer the opinion of an experienced professional over a less experienced one, or an expert whose views conform with the professional orthodoxy rather than someone adjudged a maverick by peers (M. King and F. Kaganas, 'The risks and dangers of experts in court' (1998) *Current Legal Issues*, 221, 233).
[73] But see *P, C and S v United Kingdom*, above n 17, paras 132–33. The courts' attitude to risk in cases dealing with contact disputes is somewhat different; there is evidence that courts frequently prioritise fathers' rights even in cases where there is some risk to the children.

Avoiding the courts

The HRA, then, provides little comfort for parents faced with compulsory intervention through the courts. Nevertheless, it appears that even those relatively easily surmounted procedural obstacles that the ECtHR creates for local authorities have led them to seek ways of circumventing the need to go to court at all. For example, there is evidence that, rather than seek an EPO, a local authority is now more likely than previously to invoke police protection.[74]

More importantly, and whether this is to avoid the strictures imposed as a result of the HRA or not, local authorities are using agreements rather than seek emergency orders.[75] Also, it appears that accommodation is used, at least by some local authorities, as an alternative to applying for court orders.[76] Moreover, the practice of relying on 'voluntary' arrangements may become all the more prevalent in the wake of the Public Law Outline, which imposes significantly heavier burdens on local authorities in the preparation of applications.[77] Similar concerns have also been voiced in relation to the new public law family fee structure.[78] Moreover, there is a move to increase the use of Family Group Conferences and alternative dispute resolution (ADR) as well as to promote consideration of informal care arrangements by family or friends.[79] These changes have given rise to suggestions that fewer cases will go before the courts, to the detriment of children at risk.

However what is being suggested here is that while there might be a drop in the number of applications to court,[80] this does not necessarily mean that

---

[74] Masson, 'Research – emergency intervention'; Masson *et al.*, *Protecting Powers*, pp 105, 160.

[75] Masson, 'Research – emergency intervention'.

[76] J. Brophy, *Research Review: Care Proceedings under the Children Act 1989*, London: DCA, 2006, p 53. See also Masson, 'Research – emergency intervention'.

[77] See Ministry of Justice, The Public Law Outline. Guide to Case Management in Public Law Proceedings, 2008.

[78] See, e.g. for reference to some of these concerns, B. Prentice (2008) 'Outcome of consultation on public law family fees' accessed 18 April 2008, www.justice.gov.uk/news/announcement210408b.htm.

[79] See P. Welbourne 'Safeguarding children on the edge of care: policy for keeping children safe after the *Review of the Child Care Proceedings System, Care Matters* and the Carter Review of Legal Aid' (2008) 20 CFLQ 335.

[80] Although Welbourne, 'Safeguarding children', suggests there may be more emergency applications because there will be fewer planned interventions. In addition, at the time of writing, the effects of the Baby P case have yet to be documented. However, it appears that applications for care orders are proliferating.

families are not going to be regulated. What it might mean is that families will be subject to forms of regulation that take even less account of their rights and give them even less chance of making their side of the story heard or of resisting the assessments of the professionals. It is true that the safeguards offered by the HRA are triggered at all decision-making stages of the child protection process,[81] but since they relate primarily to information, consultation and presence at meetings, they do not necessarily provide a bulwark against pressure to reach agreement.

Partnership/agreements – the limits for parents

Employing extra-legal measures to deal with risky families is not new. The partnership principle has always been crucial to child protection under the Children Act 1989. Yet even in the early days of the legislation, concerns were voiced that partnership would leave considerable scope for coercion.[82] Recent studies have borne out these predictions. Many parents report that they agreed to accommodation or other arrangements under pressure, with court action being threatened as an alternative.[83] As Brophy says, research shows that the sanction of removing children 'galvanised even the most vulnerable mothers and some fathers into taking seriously the concerns of welfare and health agencies'.[84] The threat of court proceedings can have the effect of prompting parents to co-operate and to comply with the professionals' requirements. However, this does not mean that they do so willingly or on the basis of shared understandings about the child's needs.[85] Brophy notes that parents report feeling confused and powerless within the social services system. The way they experience accommodation is 'some distance from the ideal notion of partnership between officials and parents'.[86]

Indeed, the partnership between social workers and parents is generally weighted in favour of the professionals. The balance of power between parents and professionals is not equal[87] and professionals are in a position to dictate what is expected of families. In all cases it is the professionals who ultimately determine what has to change and they impose the terms of any

---

[81] *Re L*, above n 28, para 88.
[82] See, e.g. F. Kaganas. 'Partnership under the Children Act 1989 – an overview' in F. Kaganas, M. King and C. Piper (eds), *Legislating for Harmony*, London: Jessica Kingsley Publishers, 1995.
[83] See Brophy, *Research*, pp 53–54; Hunt *et al.*, *The Last Resort*, 'Research – emergency intervention', p115; Masson, *Research*, pp 82–3.
[84] Brophy, *Research*, p 23.
[85] See Masson *et al.*, *Protecting Powers*, p 148.
[86] Brophy, *Research*, p 54.
[87] See Kaganas, 'Partnership'; Department of Health, *The Challenge of Partnership in Child Protection: Practice Guide*, London: HMSO, 1995, para 2.13.

agreement reached.[88] This presents risks for parents. Masson, for example, comments that '[p]ressure to agree, uncertainty about what has been agreed, for how long and why, and the lack of both independent advice and external scrutiny may lead to practice that is oppressive to families'.[89] The pressure exerted, coupled with parents' lack of understanding, means that they may agree to arrangements they cannot maintain. Failure to abide by the terms of the agreement can be used to demonstrate parents' unfitness or refusal to co-operate. Partnership failure can be used to demonstrate that voluntary measures are ineffective; non-compliance can be presented, without other proof of increased risk, as evidence in support of an application for a court order.[90] It is assumed that '[p]utting your children first means co-operating ... Allowances are not made for clients' lack of pragmatism and inability to read the professionals' etiquette'.[91]

Clearly then, partnership and co-operative working can involve monitoring and regulation of the family. And that regulation is unimpeded by the kind of scrutiny that court proceedings would entail. The arrangements are not open to challenge by, for example, lawyers or a children's guardian.[92] And any challenge on the part of the parents carries the risk of court proceedings in which they could be branded as unco-operative and unreasonable.

For almost two decades, then, the state has operated a system designed to facilitate child protection by voluntary means backed up as a last resort by legal proceedings. However, the state has recently espoused more ambitious goals. It has moved from the relatively narrow objective of protecting children at risk to a much broader objective of helping all parents to become better parents. This help, in the form of universal services, is offered on an entirely voluntary basis. Yet the new policy, initially conceived of to improve outcomes for children and to combat social exclusion although strengthening the family and improving children's health and development, appears to make intervention in the family more likely and to extend the reach of the professionals. The national strategy appears to facilitate monitoring and

---

[88] See, e.g. HM Government, *Working Together to Safeguard Children. A guide to inter-agency working to safeguard and promote the welfare of children*, London: TSO, 2006, para 5.120. Families are expected to understand the concerns of the local authority and address those concerns (DfES and DCA, *Review* para 1.9). See also J. Scourfield, *Gender and Child Protection*, Palgrave Macmillan: Basingstoke, 2003, pp 53–54.

[89] Masson, 'Research – emergency intervention', p 78.

[90] M. King, 'Partnership in politics and law; a new deal for parents' in F. Kaganas, M. King and C. Piper (eds), *Legislating for Harmony*, London: Jessica Kingsley Publishers, 1995 pp 149–50; Masson *et al.*, *Protecting Powers*, p 143. See also Brophy, *Research*, above n 76, p 14.

[91] J. Scourfield 'Constructing women in child protection work' (2001) 6 *Child and Family Social Work* 77 p 82.

[92] Masson, 'Research – emergency intervention', p 80. See also Masson *et al.*, *Protecting Powers*, above n 34, p 148.

regulation and, when the universal services offered do not have the desired effect, targeted services can be deployed. These 'voluntary' measures are, in turn, backed up by the threat of compulsory intervention, leaving open the potential for coercion.

Universal services

Policy documents announcing the new measures are careful to reiterate the importance of family privacy and autonomy. But they also emphasise the responsibility that families have to raise good citizens. And they set out the government's intention to endeavour to see to it that they receive the appropriate direction to do this.

The Children's Plan published by the Department for Children, Schools and Families stipulates as one of its five underpinning principles that 'government does not bring up children – parents do'.[93] 'Families are the bedrock of society', it goes on, 'and the place for nurturing happy, capable and resilient children'.[94] In order to produce such children, parents want (and need) information and support, it says.[95] Advice and support will, presumably, help them to be 'good' parents: 'The aim of all parenting support services is to enable parents to exercise their parental responsibilities effectively for their children in a way which safeguards and promotes their welfare'.[96] To ensure that parents are given what is considered to be the correct advice and help, the professionals working with them will be trained to impart the necessary knowledge and skills. The government-funded National Academy for Parenting Practitioners (NAPP) is intended to 'enable the delivery of quality parenting support in … Children's Centres and in schools'.[97] It is expected to provide training for professionals such as social workers and clinical psychologists and also to act as a national source of advice.[98]

A number of initiatives have also been developed to support parents directly.[99] The government has established Sure Start Children's Centres, extended schools, integrated youth services and also more specialist

---

[93] DCSF, *The Children's Plan. Building Brighter Futures.* Cm 7280, London: HMSO, 2007, Executive Summary, para 4.

[94] Ibid, para 6.

[95] Ibid.

[96] DfES, *Care Matters: Time for Change*, Cm 7137, London: HMSO, 2007, para 2.14.

[97] J. Barlow, S. Kirkpatrick, D. Wood, M. Ball and S. Stewart-Brown, *National Evaluation Report, July 2007: Family and Parenting Support in Sure Start Local Programmes. Sure Start Report 023.* Research Report NESS/2007/FR/023, London: HMSO, 2007, 53.

[98] DfES, *Care Matters*, above n 96, para 2.15.

[99] See, for a description of some of these initiatives, HM Government, *Reaching Out: an Action Plan on Social Exclusion*, 2006, para 5.11, Box 4.1; Box 5.3.

services.[100] Services and support in the early years are intended to be universal.[101]

Sure Start programmes are expected to provide support for all families and they offer 'health services, good quality play and early learning services, outreach and home visiting services and services for families with special needs'.[102] Support for parenting can take the form of enabling parents to 'enhance their parenting'[103]and improve their parenting practices. Services of this nature include 'formal and informal interventions to increase parenting skills, improve parent/child relationships, parenting insight, attitudes and behaviours, confidence in parenting and so on'. Other services are 'aimed to reduce the stresses associated with parenting'.[104] These include informal activities giving access to social contact and support. The National Evaluation Report records that most services offered as part of the programmes evaluated were of the former type,[105] involving parenting programmes, early learning programmes, perinatal programmes and home visiting programmes.[106]

Sure Start is offered on a voluntary basis; coercion is seen as undesirable. Recruitment of parents relies primarily on their own wish to become better at the business of parenting. With the proliferation of expertise and information on how to be a good parent, there is perhaps an increasingly prevalent view among parents themselves that they need help and advice, that parenting cannot be something left to 'common sense' or instinct. As Rose put it in another context, the parental search for advice is impelled by 'the activation of individual guilt [and] personal anxiety'.[107] The new services now available may appear to offer ways of bridging the gaps between 'expectation and realisation',[108] and offer the promise of assuaging anxieties about how to be a 'good' parent.

Parents who come into contact with professionals such as health visitors and midwives might be encouraged to attend Sure Start but there is no compulsion.[109] Even where families 'need more intensive help'[110] it is

---

[100] DfES, *Care Matters*, paras 1.9, 2.14.
[101] HM Government, *Reaching Out*, para 4.11. See also Barlow *et al.*, *National Evaluation Report*, p 38; J. Tunstill and D. Allnock, *National Evaluation Report, July 2007. Understanding the Contribution of Sure Start Local Programmes to the Task of Safeguarding Children's Welfare, Report 026*. Research Report NESS/2007/FR/026, London: HMSO, 2007, p 12.
[102] Barlow *et al.*, *National Evaluation Report*, Executive Summary, p i.
[103] Ibid. See also Ch 3.
[104] Ibid, p i.
[105] Ibid, p ii.
[106] Ibid, Ch 3.
[107] N. Rose, 'Beyond the public/private division: law, power and the family' (1987) 14 JLS, 61, 73.
[108] Ibid.
[109] Barlow *et al.*, *National Evaluation Report*, pp v, 38–9.
[110] DCSF, *The Children's Plan*, Executive Summary, para 7.

expected that parents will simply receive the 'encouragement' they need to come forward.[111]

However, encouragement is not always enough. Attendance at Sure Start is low, with the government noting that those with the 'greatest need or at greatest risk' are sometimes the least likely to receive services.[112] These families are 'typically harder to reach and harder to engage'; they may not know that help is available or they might reject it.[113] The aim, therefore, is to find those families and to draw them in. In order to achieve this, all families must be made more visible and transparent. Home visiting and outreach[114] enable professionals to penetrate the home and identify those who are deemed to be in need of help.

Once a family in difficulty is identified, and if parents do not present themselves willingly to take advantage of whatever services are offered, they must, it seems, be persuaded to do so.[115] Where families are judged to be risky, the plan is that there should be early and intensive intervention.[116] This intervention is targeted and it undoubtedly entails putting pressure on parents to comply with what is required of them by the child welfare professionals.

Early intervention

The targets of early intervention are primarily the parents of children who are on the verge of being taken into care and children who are offending or exhibiting antisocial behaviour. If there are concerns about a family, those providing services must not give up in the face of 'an unanswered door, letter or call' but must redouble their efforts to engage that family.[117] The family is expected to accept help and if they do not, they are deemed irresponsible:

> [T]he flip-side to this support is that, as far as possible, individuals need to share and take responsibility themselves, and particularly where their actions have an impact on those around them. For example, the parent of an at-risk child should be given support, but it is also incumbent on them to take this support. This approach is illustrated by intensive family support projects – a highly personalised approach, but one that

---

[111] Ibid, Executive Summary, para 1.13.
[112] HM Government, *Reaching Out*, para 4.11. See also Barlow *et al.*, *National Evaluation Report*, p 31.
[113] HM Government, *Reaching Out*, para 4.12.
[114] The government has stated that outreach services will be used to bring parents to Sure Start Children's Centres (See DCSF, *The Children's Plan*, para 1.2).
[115] See Barlow *et al.*, *National Evaluation Report*, p 24.
[116] See, DfES, *Care matters*, para 2.16.
[117] HM Government, *Reaching Out*, para 3.22. See also para 1.29.

requires a clear sense of personal responsibility on the part of the adults involved, with clear consequences if those responsibilities are not met.[118]

Irresponsibility may be met with coercive legal measures when all other means of control have been exhausted. However, even where the children's services authority is contemplating recourse to the court, it should first seek to reach an agreement with the family. Persuasion and partnership are still important. Section 17 of the Children Act 1989 is interpreted as placing an obligation on local authorities to explore the possibility of voluntary arrangements before making an application under section 31, provided that to do so would not jeopardise the child's safety and welfare.[119] Section 1(5) of the Children Act also ensures that court orders should not be seen as routine. Moreover it is clearly government policy that court proceedings should be a last resort.[120] So the professionals seek to avoid court proceedings by means of monitoring, persuasion and sometimes threats. And when cases do reach court, an order becomes almost inevitable.

The very fact that there is a preference for dealing with cases outside the legal process presents parents with risks and these have not gone unremarked. It was suggested that parents should have access to advice and advocacy[121] and the Review of Child Care Proceedings accordingly recommended 'more consistent local use of early advice, advocacy and support initiatives such as Family Group Conferences'.[122] The Guidance and Regulations now stipulate that where a local authority decides to apply for a care or supervision order, it must immediately notify the parents and others with parental responsibility for the child.[123] The parents, on receipt of this Letter Before Proceedings, are entitled to non-means-tested publicly funded legal advice which covers 'liaison and negotiations with the local authority with the aim of avoiding proceedings or limiting the issues'.[124]

Helping and empowering parents?

Parents, then, are offered assistance and support on a voluntary basis to enable them to raise their children responsibly. Even potentially irresponsible

---

[118] Ibid, para 3.66.
[119] DCSF, *Children Act Guidance*, para 3.7. See also DfES and DCA, *Review*, para 1.9.
[120] See also DfES and DCA, *Review*, para 1.9; HM Government, *Reaching Out*, para 1.13. The effects of the Baby P case are yet to be seen at the time of writing.
[121] Hunt *et al.*, *The Last Resort*, p 164.
[122] DfES and DCA, *Review*, para 5.10. See also HM Government, *Working Together*, para 10.5.
[123] DCSF, *Children Act Guidance*, above n 5 para 3.3. See also Ministry of Justice, Public Law Outline, pp 22, 39; DfES and DCA, *Review*, above n 52, para 5.11.
[124] DCSF, *Children Act Guidance*, para 3.26.

parents are offered the possibility of a co-operative partnership with the professionals. Their interests are to be represented by advisers and some space for autonomous decision-making is to be afforded by the use of FGCs.[125] Perhaps most importantly, their rights are potentially of more weight as a result of the enactment of the HRA. Yet, it seems, while these measures may have some impact on child protection practice and they may force professionals and local authorities to be prepared to justify their actions, the relative position of parents in conflict with the authorities over child protection has not been significantly strengthened. Whether the case is being dealt with in or out of court, parental rights and demands generally do not and cannot determine outcomes.

In particular, it is open to doubt whether the provision of advice and the use of FGCs will significantly empower parents. Nor is this what the government intends. The Review makes it clear that the purpose of advice and of FGCs is to 'help vulnerable families to understand local authority concerns and to be encouraged to address these as early as possible and before proceedings are issued'.[126] The discussion with parents and others with parental responsibility after the issue of a Letter Before Proceedings is meant to focus on what steps, if any, can be taken to avoid proceedings. More specifically, consideration should be given to ways of 'improving parental engagement with the local authority' and to 'further explaining the local authority's position and concerns'.[127] At these discussions, the parents are to be given a new plan indicating what will be done by them and by the local authority to safeguard the child and 'what action will be taken by the Local Authority to safeguard the child if this is not followed'.[128] The intention, then, is to get parents to see things from the professionals' point of view and to persuade them to change their behaviour accordingly.

Moreover, this is an aim which parents' advisers often help to achieve. By the time a Letter Before Proceedings is issued, it is unlikely that an application to court can be averted and the role of the adviser may well be confined to advocating on ancillary matters such as contact. This may mean that parents will be enabled to negotiate better terms than they would on their own. However research reveals that advisers tend to seek to persuade parents to co-operate.[129]

---

[125] However the professionals decide on the parameters of the Family Group Conference (FGC). They decide what issues are open for negotiation and those which are non-negotiable, for example. See HM Government *Working Together*, above n 88, para 10.3. See further A. Diduck and F. Kaganas, *Family Law, Gender and the State*, Oxford: Hart Publishing, 2006, p 365.

[126] DfES and DCA, *Review*, above n 52, para 5.10.

[127] DCSF, *Children Act Guidance*, above n 5, para 3.27.

[128] Ibid, Foreword.

[129] See also Masson *et al.*, *Protecting Powers*, above n 34, pp 147, 169. Once court proceedings are imminent, advisers tend to advise their clients not to oppose the order but do assist them in negotiations over matters such as contact (Mavis Maclean – oral communication July 2008).

Lindley *et al.*[130] found that advocates supported parents at meetings and assisted them, but they also managed parents' behaviour and, by doing so, added to the pressure on parents to accede to the demands being made of them:

> Much of the advocate's function is to support, encourage, advise and even cajole the parents to co-operate with social services' specifications of what they need to change in their own behaviour in order to overcome the child protection concerns.[131]

Monitoring families

The aim of changing behaviour lies at the heart of the new services. Universal and targeted services are to a large extent designed to help parents to learn to parent in ways that are considered acceptable within the parameters of child welfare knowledge. And those parents who do not meet the requisite standards must be identified and must be dealt with. The family support project might therefore be seen as having not only a helping but also a regulatory function. Moreover, the networks and organisations established to implement the government policy of assisting and advising parents also facilitate surveillance of families. Home visiting and outreach are intended to be used to identify, target and monitor families considered to be in need of assistance. The government has referred to the need to equip 'front-line practitioners' such as health visitors and community midwives with predictive tools designed to facilitate better identification of children at risk and also to facilitate early intervention.[132]

Intervention might, of course, simply take the form of encouraging parents to access services such as those offered by Sure Start. And when families are identified as being in difficulties, the early intervention agenda is meant to reduce 'the risk that individuals or families will experience problems later in life', and to prevent existing problems from escalating.[133] But these services are not divorced from the child protection process.[134] There is evidence

---

[130] B. Lindley, M. Richards and P. Freeman, 'Research: advice and advocacy for parents in child protection cases – what is happening in current practice?',(2001) 13 *CFLQ* 167, p 182–83.

[131] B. Lindley, M. Richards and P. Freeman, 'Advice and advocacy for parents in child protection cases – an exploration of conceptual and policy issues, ethical dilemmas and future directions' (2001) 13 *CFLQ* 311, p 323.

[132] HM Government, *Reaching Out*, above n 99, para 1.14. See also para 4.13. The government favours 'intensive health-led home visiting' during pregnancy and the first two years of the child's life (para 1.18).

[133] Ibid, Box 2.2.

[134] See e.g. K. Clarke, 'Childhood, parenting and early intervention: a critical examination of the Sure Start National Programme' (2006) 26 *Critical Social Policy* 699, p 711.

that more families in Sure Start areas are becoming enmeshed in the system. For instance, a report evaluating Sure Start Local Programme areas records that there has been an increase in the rate of s 47 enquiries in these areas.[135] The rate of registrations on the Child Protection Register has also gone up.[136]

Of course, this means in many cases that children are being protected from harm; Sure Start areas, for example, have seen a reduction in the number of children hospitalised for severe injury.[137] However there are concerns about the effects of the safeguarding agenda. It may be that the concept is clouding public understanding about the possible consequences of contact with child welfare professionals. Sure Start staff liaise with Children's Services[138] and, although it is normal practice to warn parents of the risk of child protection concerns being reported,[139] some parents might not be aware of the actions that might be taken by the professionals they are dealing with.[140] And these parents may find themselves, instead of being offered help, the subject of a formal investigation. Engagement with child welfare workers and exposure to the professional gaze carry risks for parents.[141]

Some parents consider this risk worth taking. Ferguson describes the positive outcomes that some parents experience; they take the opportunity offered by professional intervention to review their lives, seek protection and make new life plans.[142] So advice, both about personal matters and on how to improve parenting, may not be experienced as oppressive.[143] As for those who do experience help negatively as unjustified interference, there may be strong evidence in many cases that they are endangering their children and intervention in some form is warranted. But there will also be cases, particularly where neglect is in issue, where the assessment of the family is based not only on objective, 'scientific' grounds but also on a class-based and moral judgement.[144]

---

[135] J. Barnes, H. Cheng, B. Howden, M. Frost, G. Harper, D. Sapna and J. Finn, *Changes in the Characteristics of SSLP Areas Between 2000/2001 to 2003/04*. Research report NESS/2006/FR/016, Nottingham: DfES Publications, 2006, p 6.

[136] Ibid, pp 6–7.

[137] Barnes *et al.*, *Changes in Characteristics*, above n 135, p 8, attribute this to improved inter-agency working, better monitoring and education of parents about safety.

[138] Tunstill and Allnock, *National Evaluation Report*, above n 101, pp 25, 34, 37, 127.

[139] Ibid, p 37; L. Niven and M. Ball, *National Evaluation Report: Sure Start Local Programmes and Domestic Abuse, Report 025*. Research Report NESS/2007/FR/025, London: HMSO, 2007, para 7.7.

[140] Tunstill and Allnock, *National Evaluation Report*, above n 101, p 115.

[141] Ferguson, *Protecting Children*, above n 2, pp 147–8.

[142] Ibid, pp 150–51.

[143] I am indebted to Brid Featherstone for pointing out that Sure Start practices vary from area to area and that the services offered in some Sure Start areas are considered beneficial, non-coercive and non-stigmatising by many parents.

[144] Ferguson, *Protecting Children*, above n 2, pp 180, 182.

Moreover assessment and monitoring do not always lead to help.[145] It appears that many families, often because of limited local authority resources, are left to their own devices, as long as they are functioning at the most basic level:[146]

> Access to family support for many families is severely restricted. Families in considerable stress on the threshold of family breakdown and serious harm are not getting the sustained support they need. Some services operate inappropriately high thresholds in responding to child protection concerns and taking action to protect children and young people. As a result, some families do not receive support when they need it

> Parents with long standing or complex problems may need longer term help, but too often are given short term irregular support at times of crisis, which may be withdrawn as soon as they feel able to cope.[147]

Most families who become involved in care proceedings have been 'struggling along the bottom rung of acceptable parenting for some time'.[148] They are left unaided until problems become so acute that voluntary measures no longer can suffice. Proceedings are usually precipitated by a particular event, a decline in parenting or by the parents' failure to abide by the terms of their agreement with social services.[149] When events like this occur, the focus of social services is on the risk to the children, rather than on the needs of the family as a whole.[150] Children's services sets the child protection process in

---

[145] Ferguson reports that professionals may fail to engage with some families where those families are seen as repellent or threatening (*Protecting Children*, above n 2, p 186).

[146] See Commission for Social Care Inspection, Children's Services. CSCI, Findings 2004–2007, CSCI, 2007, p 1. See also Commission for Social Care Inspection, *Supporting Parents, Safeguarding Children. Meeting the needs of parents with children on the child protection register*, CSCI, 2006 paras 1.1, 4.29, 6.7, 8.1; Masson *et al.*, *Care Profiling*, above n 52, p 29; Hunt *et al.*, *The Last Resort*, above n 69, p 133. Brophy's review of the relevant research suggests that parents tend to under-report the extent of the assistance they receive. However they do testify to unmet needs (*Research Review*, above n 76, pp 51–52). See also Ferguson, *Protecting Children*, above n 2, p 166. Broadhurst *et al.* are concerned that Sure Start may not be leading to the provision of support but that surveillance may instead emerge as the priority (K. Broadhurst, C. Mason and C. Grover, 'Sure Start and the "re-authorization" of Section 47 Child Protection Practices' (2007) 27 *Critical Social Policy* 443, p 448).

[147] Commission for Social Care Inspection, *Children's Services. CSCI Findings 2004–2007*, CSCI, 2007, pp 9–10.

[148] Brophy, *Research Review*, above n 76, p 7.

[149] Ibid. See also DfES and DCA, *Review*, above n 52, para 4.11.

[150] See Commission for Social Care Inspection, *Supporting Parents*, above n 146, para 4.22.

motion and begins to gather evidence of what went wrong.[151] The professionals put all their efforts into getting the parents to understand their concerns, to co-operate with them and to change:

> When asked for their views about the care needs of parents, a number of respondents – but particularly those working in children's services – interpreted the question in an unexpected way. They interpreted it in terms of the needs that result from having to help parents to understand the child protection system and manage the stresses associated with it.

> The biggest challenge is to get them to understand and acknowledge our concerns. That is the first step. If they don't do that we can't get them to change their attitudes and behaviour within the time-scale of the child.[152]

Broadhurst et al. argue that there is too much emphasis on parental deficiency and not enough on the poverty and social exclusion faced by the mostly lone female-headed households targeted.[153] The focus has come to be on 'causes of poor outcomes' with the spotlight on the behaviour of parents and, more specifically, of mothers.[154]

Monitoring mothers

While government publications (and much of the relevant research) refer to 'families' and 'parents',[155] it is really all about mothers; it is primarily mothers who are and who will continue to be the focus of the remoralisation project.

In the majority of cases, it is mothers who are the primary caretakers of their children, whether they are lone mothers or in relationships with fathers or with other men.[156] Fathers' involvement is largely mediated by mothers and their contribution is usually a passive one in the sense of 'being there'.[157] This reality is reflected in social work practice in the sense that child welfare professionals expect to deal mainly with mothers.[158] But they also appear to

---

[151] Ibid, para 6.27.
[152] Ibid, para 6.5.
[153] Broadhurst et al., 'Sure Start', above, n 146, pp 452–53.
[154] Clarke, 'Childhood', above n 134, p 710.
[155] The use of this term in this chapter was intentional to avoid pre-empting the argument that follows.
[156] See, e.g. J. Lewis and E. Welsh, 'Fathering practices in twenty-six intact families and the implications for child contact' (2005) 1 International Journal of Law in Context 81 pp 94–5; Masson et al., Care Profiling, above n 52, p 16.
[157] Lewis and Welsh, Fathering, above n 156, pp 94–5.
[158] See, e.g. Ferguson, Protecting Children, above n 2, pp 154–5.

assume that it is mothers and not fathers who *should* bear the responsibility of child rearing and child protection.

Government policy, in contrast, is increasingly focused on fatherhood. The goal is avowedly to increase the involvement of fathers in the care and upbringing of their children. Government guidance stresses the importance of fathers to children and makes it clear that those working with children and parents are expected to nurture the relationships between fathers and their children. For example the Sure Start guidance states that all Sure Start Children's Centre services should help to support fathers in their role as a parent and to promote the role of fathering.[159]

Yet whether government initiatives will mean that, in future, social workers will look upon fathers as being responsible for child care and child protection is open to doubt. It seems that, in practice, little is expected in the way of paternal involvement. There is still an emphasis on the goals of getting fathers to find work or undertake training to enable them to support their families financially.[160] Child care appears to be regarded, to some extent, as a leisure activity. Fathers are thought to need services where they can meet other fathers and engage in activities related to 'traditional male interests'.[161] In this vein, Sure Start centres offer fathers the opportunity to spend time with their children working on allotments, attending sports facilities, and participating in music or photography sessions.[162]

What is more, it appears that few fathers exceed professional expectations. For instance, the degree to which fathers are involved in Sure Start is very limited. Most of those parents attending are women and, when fathers do get involved, they tend to prefer 'outdoor, active, Funday-type activities' rather than 'indoor sessions with children or ... sessions related to parenting skills'.[163] Impediments to paternal involvement include the restricted hours when Sure Start services are available as well as the female environment of Sure Start. However, fathers also seem to be deterred by traditional attitudes to gender roles.[164]

In any event, Sure Start is an initiative aimed primarily at mothers.[165] This is apparent in the emphasis on home visiting and outreach. It is even more apparent in the importance attached to visiting shortly after the birth of a child[166] because of concerns about post-natal depression as well as health,

---

[159] DfES, *Sure Start Children's Centres. Practice Guidance. Every Child Matters. Change for Children*, Nottingham: DfES Publications, 2006, p 81.
[160] Ibid, p 82.
[161] DfES, *Every Parent Matters*, Nottingham: DfES Publications, 2007, para 3.29.
[162] Ibid.
[163] N. Lloyd, M. O'Brien and C. Lewis, *Fathers in Sure Start. National Evaluation of Sure Start*, Report 04, London: NESS, 2003, p iii. See also pp 20–21.
[164] Ibid, pp 42–3.
[165] Clarke, 'Childhood', above n 134, p 716.
[166] See DfES, *Sure Start*, above n 159, pp 3, 9, 10.

hygiene and safety. These preoccupations all suggest that it is mothers who are intended to be the targets of help, advice and education.[167] The 'health-led parenting support demonstration projects' which are meant to provide support from pre-birth until the age of 2[168] are undoubtedly aimed at women, as is the nurse–family partnership.[169]

Clearly, the risks inherent in being assessed and monitored, and the responsibility of behaving in a way that withstands scrutiny, do not rest on both parents equally. Nor do the burdens of co-operating with the professionals[170] and maintaining a partnership relationship. The risk assessments carried out by social workers 'promote the rapid scrutiny and classification of parents, largely mothers, through a filter of cultural, class and gender assumptions'.[171] Failure to measure up can 'easily be construed as ... pathological'[172] and can result in removal of the children.[173]

According to Krane and Davies, it is thought that mothers should be able to cope, despite extremely trying circumstances.[174] Women are seen to be responsible for protecting children, even if family difficulties are caused by socio-economic conditions or by other people.[175] Social workers do not engage with men even in cases where it is the father who is identified as the abuser.[176] They tend to ignore fathers and conceive of men as a threat, as irrelevant, as useless or as absent.[177] Fathers are regarded as irresponsible when absent and as making demands on mothers or as possibly violent when present. But it is not their conduct that the professionals seek to change; mothers are the 'focus of intervention'.[178] As Scourfield observes, it has always been assumed that children's services are delivered by women working with women.[179] It is mothers who have to conform to the dominant

---

[167] See Clarke, 'Childhood', above n 134, pp 172–3.

[168] See HM Government, *Reaching Out*, above n 99, para 1.18.

[169] Ibid, Box 4.1.

[170] See Scourfield, 'Constructing women', above n 91, p 82; L. Davies and J. Krane, 'Collaborate with caution: protecting children, helping mothers' (2006) 26 *Critical Social Policy* 412 p 415.

[171] J. Krane and L. Davies, 'Mothering and Child Protection Practice: Rethinking Risk Assessment' (2000) 5 *Child and Family Social Work* 35, 42.

[172] Clarke, 'Childhood', above n 134 p 701.

[173] See Scourfield, 'Constructing women', above n 91, p 78.

[174] Krane and Davies, 'Mothering', above n 171, p 42.

[175] Scourfield, 'Constructing women', above n 91, p 85; B. Daniel and J. Taylor, *Engaging with Fathers. Practice Issues for Health and Social Care*, London: Jessica Kingsley Publishers, 2001 p 23.

[176] Daniel and Taylor, *Engaging with Fathers*, above n 175, pp 21, 23–4.

[177] See J. Scourfield, 'The challenge of engaging fathers in the child protection process' (2006) 26 *Critical Social Policy* 440 p 443; Daniel and Taylor, *Engaging with Fathers*, above n 175, pp 21–24.

[178] Daniel and Taylor, *Engaging with Fathers*, above n 175, p 21.

[179] Scourfield, 'The Challenge', above, n 177, p 441.

norms of 'good' parenting or, more specifically, 'good' motherhood. It is mothers, not fathers, who are expected to make the changes considered necessary by the professionals.[180]

In cases of physical and emotional neglect, it is mothers who are 'overwhelmingly identified as perpetrators';[181] they, and not fathers, are the ones who are charged with caring and nurturing. In child sexual abuse cases the focus is on the mother's failure to protect.[182] Women who are the victims of domestic violence are also deemed to be failing to protect their children.[183] And intervention may not lead to help for the woman. Instead she may be threatened with the removal of her children if she does not get rid of the violent partner.[184] On the other hand, if a mother refuses to allow contact between her child and the non-resident father on the basis of allegations that he is violent or abusive, but cannot prove those allegations, she runs the risk of finding herself branded as an abuser.[185] At the very least she may be regarded as deviating from the professionals' image of the 'good' post-separation mother and may face pressure to conform.

Programmes, such as Sure Start, while intended to help mothers, and which indeed may help many, have the potential to enable professionals to assess and find wanting[186] an increased number of mothers. At the same time as offering services, they have the potential to extend the reach of the professionals, and to broaden the scope of the advice or instructions with which mothers are expected to comply. Moreover, according to Clarke,

---

[180]   Ibid, p 444. See also Scourfield, 'Constructing women', above n 91, pp 83– 85.

[181]   Daniel and Taylor, *Engaging with Fathers*, above n. 175, p 24. See also Scourfield, 'Constructing women', above, n. 91 p 79. Herring points out that s 5 of the Domestic Violence, Crime and Victims Act 2004 has been most commonly deployed to prosecute mothers (often victims of domestic violence) who are accused of 'standing by' while their male partners killed a child. It is mothers in these cases, rather than the men, who are vilified in the media and on the Internet (J. Herring 'Familial homicides, failure to protect and domestic violence: who's the victim?' [2007] *Crim. L.R.* 923).

[182]   Daniel and Taylor, *Engaging with Fathers*, above n. 175, p 24.

[183]   See Scourfield, 'Constructing women', above n 91 pp 83–5; Scourfield, 'The challenge', above n 177, p 442.

[184]   See Scourfield, 'Constructing women', above n 91, pp 84–5; Scourfield, 'The challenge', above n 177, p 442; Davies and Krane, 'Collaborate', above n 170, pp 416, 418–19. See generally S. Holt, 'Child protection social work and men's abuse of women: an Irish study' (2003) 8 *Child and Family Social Work* 53.

[185]   See, e.g. *Re M (Intractable Contact Dispute: Interim Care Order)* [2003] EWHC 1024 (Fam) [2003] 2 FLR 636; *V v V (Contact: Implacable Hostility)* [2004] EWHC 1215 (Fam) [2004] 2 FLR 851.

[186]   Krane and Davies are sceptical as to the accuracy of risk assessment tools in identifying risk or abuse. They argue that the use of ostensibly scientific methods obscures the 'moral and political judgments made in child protection cases' ('Mothering', above n 171, p 42).

professionals 'promote a middle class conception of motherhood and the role of mothers'.[187] This, say Broadhurst et al.,[188] means there is increased surveillance and regulation of poor women, without addressing the causes of their disadvantage.

CONCLUSION

The HRA might appear, at first sight, to promise protection for the rights of parents who are in conflict with local authority children's services. This protection, however, is mainly procedural and takes the form of restricting the use of emergency measures and of imposing a requirement to inform and consult; the substantive outcome of the case is unlikely to be affected. The HRA affords parents a better opportunity to be involved in decision making and to put their case before the courts. But the impact of the legislation is limited in the context of child protection and it is even counter-productive for some parents in that local authorities sometimes seek to avoid its requirements.

That the HRA and other measures may be having the effect of deterring applications to court does not mean that families are immune from regulation. If the professionals take the view that the family can be managed without a court order, informal support and 'voluntary' agreements are used to educate them and to change their behaviour.

We are, arguably, witnessing, as an adjunct to and sometimes as a substitute for coercive measures, an increasing reliance on parents' aspirations to be 'good' parents. Most parents who become involved in services such as Sure Start undoubtedly do so willingly; they are not forced or duped into taking advantage of what is offered.[189] Yet we are also, arguably, witnessing the creation of new mechanisms for identifying 'bad' parents, especially 'bad' mothers. Universal and targeted services have the potential to render 'problem' families more visible and, once identified, these families face the risk of unwanted intervention to regulate their conduct.

While intervention can save children and can help parents, it can also be coercive and oppressive. The introduction of advice and education for parents may mean that parents are faced with even more potential sources of pressure or reasons for coercion; if they do not accept the advice and attend the parenting classes as instructed, for example, they face the risk of being adjudged irresponsible. And since it is overwhelmingly mothers who are, and who are expected to be, responsible for children's safety and well-being, it is

---

[187] Clarke, 'Childhood', above, n 134, p 701.
[188] Broadhurst et al., 'Sure Start', n 146, p 454.
[189] See Rose, 'Beyond the public/private', above n 107, p 73.

they who must co-operate and conform to the professionals' norms of good mothering. It is mothers who are examined, it is mothers who might be found wanting and it is mothers who must change so as to fit the mould of the 'good' mother. Engaging in the new programme for supporting families carries risks for mothers and the offer of support has, paradoxically, the potential to burden them.

Chapter 4

Rights and responsibility: Girls and boys who behave badly

Christine Piper

Introduction

The development of youth justice policy has been – at least over the last fifty years – at the mercy of political vicissitudes and anxieties. In the last ten years in particular, policy has suffered from being required to respond to a conflicting mix of political imperatives, ranging from a perceived need to be seen as accepting '*No More Excuses*'[1] in relation to offending by children and young people, to the economic necessity of 'selling' preventative early intervention programmes as a good investment[2] and diversion from expensive custody as effective alternatives,[3] through pressure to employ measures designed to reduce the fear of crime and respond to nuisance behaviour in local communities. The current political importance of law and order policies in the context of the declining legitimacy of the criminal justice system has, however, meant that perceptions of community safety and public confidence in the youth justice system have often been higher priorities than either the rights or the welfare of children and young people who publicly behave badly.

So, in the context of an apparently punitive public, the 'talk' on juvenile crime and antisocial behaviour has been 'tough' and New Labour's 'Third Way' ideology has emphasised that the individual must be held responsible for his or her offending even though socio-economic factors are acknowledged as causes of crime. The result has been that, despite a social inclusion policy agenda, the focus on the responsibility of children and young people who misbehave and commit offences in England, Wales and Northern Ireland now means that children as young as 10 can be held

---

[1] Home Office, *No More Excuses: A New Approach to Tackling Youth Crime in England and Wales.* Cm 3809, London: The Stationery Office, 1997.

[2] See, e.g. Audit Commission, *Youth Justice 2004*, London: Audit Commission, 2004; C. Piper, *Investing in Children: Policy, Law and Practice in Context*, Cullompton: Willan Publishing, 2008.

[3] See, e.g. Audit Commission, *Misspent Youth, Young People and Crime.* London: Audit Commission, 1996; Home Office, *Youth Justice: The Next Steps*, London: Home Office, 2003.

legally as well as morally responsible.[4] Section 34 of the Crime and Disorder Act 1998 marked a reversal of the historical trend to reduce the age of criminal responsibility when it removed the presumption that children between 10 and 14 are *doli incapax* (incapable of being held criminally liable).

Children and young people above the age of 10 can, therefore, be punished for committing a wide range and variety of 'adult' offences and so need, and can call on, the protection of those human rights which have been used to improve the conditions and procedures for all offenders. However, for over a century, and particularly since the establishment of a juvenile court in the UK in 1908, separate and different treatment has been advocated for children simply because they are not adults and because adult offenders can 'contaminate' them. Children and young people facing the legislated consequences of criminal or antisocial behaviour have consequently become the focus for extra rights, different processes and different conditions, and rights have been used to challenge an inappropriate focus on responsibility, inappropriate state responses and inappropriate treatment.

Article 40 of the United Nations Convention on the Rights of the Child (UNCRC) focuses on the need to 'promote the establishment of laws, procedures, authorities and institutions specifically applicable to children alleged as, accused of, or recognized as having infringed the penal law' with dispositions and alternatives to institutional care which will 'ensure that children are dealt with in a manner appropriate to their well-being'. In challenging practices which are not appropriate, several rights in the European Convention on Human Rights (ECHR) have been useful: Articles 3 ('No-one shall be subjected to torture or inhuman or degrading treatment or punishment'), 5 (which deals with the right to liberty and security of a person and the procedural rights to safeguard those arrested or detained by the state), 6 (which provides further rights for those charged with a criminal offence), and 8 (the right to respect for private and family life). This chapter will focus on the use of these rights and then go on to assess the utility of the UNCRC and other relevant conventions. It will then focus on the apparent invisibility of gender in the rights discourse around girls and boys who behave badly and argue for a greater attention to difference in administering punishment and rehabilitation – not just between adults and children but also between boys and girls, young men and young women – and for a greater attention to potential discrimination in decision making.

The ECHR: young 'prisoners' and the Children Act 1989

Since the implementation of the HRA 1998 there have been several high profile cases which have been hailed quite rightly as victories for children as

---

[4] The Republic of Ireland raised its minimum age from 7 to 12 in 2006. The minimum age for Scotland is 8 but young offenders are dealt with in the welfare-based Children's Hearings system.

well as for a rights-based approach to improving the lives of children. As regards young offenders the most significant ones have, arguably, related to prisoners, those young people held in various forms of penal detention, and the most important case – in terms of publicity and impact on policy and practice – was that brought by the Howard League for Penal Reform in 2002 as part of a deliberate strategy to use courts to secure improvements for children in, and leaving, prison.

This case sought to test the applicability of certain provisions of the Children Act 1989 to those in young offender institutions (YOIs)[5] but it is also significant because Munby J, giving the judgment, explicitly drew on the principles of the UNCRC when assessing whether the obligations imposed on local authorities by ss 17 (to children in need) and 47 (to children at risk of significant harm) applied to children in prison service establishments. Using the principles contained within Arts 3 and 37[6] of the UNCRC and also Art 24[7] of the Charter of Fundamental Rights to the European Union 2000 (the European Charter) he interpreted Arts 3 and 8 of the ECHR as imposing *positive* duties on the Prison Service 'to take reasonable and appropriate measures designed to ensure that':

> i) children in YOIs are treated ... with humanity, with respect for their inherent dignity and personal integrity as human beings, and not in such a way as to humiliate or debase them;
> ii) children in YOIs are not subjected to torture or to inhuman or degrading treatment or punishment by fellow inmates or to other behaviour by fellow inmates which impacts adversely and disproportionately on their physical or psychological integrity.[8]

He then acknowledged that the Prison Service needed to balance the interests of the child with those of the 'community as a whole' but stated that, while doing so, they must have regard to the principle that the best interests of the child are at all times a 'primary consideration',[9] and that,

---

[5] *The Queen (On the Application of the Howard League for Penal Reform) v Secretary of State for the Home Department* [2002] EWHC 2497 (Admin) [2003] 1 FLR 484.

[6] Article 3: 'in all actions concerning children, whether undertaken by public or private social welfare institutions, courts of law, administrative authorities or legislative bodies, the best interests of the child shall be a primary consideration'; Article 37: prohibits 'cruel, inhuman or degrading treatment or punishment' and provides principles in relation to loss of liberty.

[7] Article 24 provides three general statements in relation to the rights of the child including the statement that 'the child's best interests must be a primary consideration'.

[8] *The Queen (On the Application of the Howard League for Penal Reform) v Secretary of State for the Home Department* [2002] para 66.

[9] Ibid, para 67.

consequently, 'human rights law imposes on the Prison Service enforceable obligations':

> i) to have regard to the 'welfare' principle encapsulated in the UN Convention and the European Charter; and
> ii) to take effective steps to protect children in YOIs from any ill-treatment, whether at the hands of Prison Service staff *or of other inmates*, of the type which engages either article 3 or article 8 of the European Convention.[10]

The second arm of this is important given that the current rates of assault in YOIs and juvenile establishments are the highest rates of any prisons in England and Wales.[11]

The result of this case was extensive new guidance, issued to all local authorities and governors of prisons and young offender institutions, which quoted Munby J and made clear a range of duties to implement the judgment.[12] Where a child had been receiving services under Part III of the Children Act 1989 before entering custody then the youth offending team (YOT) worker responsible for the child's sentence and discharge planning must request information about the child from the local authority children's services; further, the local authority will need to make a judgement as to whether any other child will be 'in need' on release or whether any child with special needs requires those needs to be met while in custody. In relation to s 47 duties the local authority must investigate any reports that a child is suffering significant harm while in custody or that a child was being abused prior to custody and might be abused again on release. The local authority must also now take a role in investigating deaths in custody.

The Prison Service also revised Prison Service Order (PSO) 4950, which deals with the regime for juveniles,[13] to incorporate a range of child protection measures, noting that Munby J's judgment 'confirmed that the Prison Service has a legal obligation to safeguard the well-being of children in its care by virtue of Section 6(1) of the Human Rights Act and Article 8 of the European Convention on Human Rights'.[14] The Order therefore included specific guidance in relation to the investigation of children at risk of harm:

[10] Ibid, para 68, italics in the original.
[11] Prison Reform Trust, *Bromley Briefings: Prison Factfile*, London: PRT, 2007, p 20.
[12] DfES, *Safeguarding and promoting the welfare of children and young people in custody*, Local Authority Circular LAC 2004(26), London: DfES, 2004, para 3.
[13] PSO 4950 deals with children serving a detention and training order; guidance in relation to the special characteristics of the s 92 population of young offenders in detention can be found in HM Prison Service, *Detention Under Section 92 of the Powers of Criminal Courts (Sentencing) Act 2000: Young People Serving Longer Sentences for Serious Offences*, PSO 4960, London: HM Prison Service, 2001.
[14] HM Prison Service, *Regimes for Juveniles*, PSO 4950, London: HM Prison Service, 2004, para 2.1.

for example, '*Area Managers must make every effort to ensure that all establishments holding children have their needs represented on the local Area Child Protection Committee (ACPC)*' [Italics in original to indicate that the duties are mandatory].[15] The case also led to a Youth Justice Board (YJB) decision to place a social worker in each YOI although only 10 of the posts had been filled by the beginning of 2008. From 2009–10 local authorities must fund this post.[16]

There have also been two further cases which, whilst not argued in relation to rights in the ECHR and UNCRC, have dealt with issues related to the application of the Children Act 1989. In *R (K)* v *Manchester City Council*[17] the Howard League challenged the practice of assessment by a YOT worker, as opposed to a local authority social worker, as to whether a child in custody would be 'in need' on release.[18] The context to this case is that there are different assessment tools and different training approaches for social workers in the local authority children's social services and the workers in the YOT.[19] The Howard League's concern, shared with many, is that assessment by members of a YOT using the YJB 'Asset' assessment tool and without the statutory authority to determine a child as being 'in need' of services and support, leaves a young prisoner at a disadvantage[20] unless they have previously been 'looked after'.[21] Further, he or she has argued to the House of Commons Children, Schools and Families Committee that current pressure on resources and 'failings in the intended culture of cooperation' has resulted in 'children getting less than the enhanced service that was originally envisaged'.[22]

[15] Ibid para 2.2.
[16] Howard League, *Children in custody, children in need*, submission on looked after children to the House of Commons Children, Schools and Families Committee, London: Howard League, 2008, para 2.9; see also NACRO, 'Children in custody: local authority duties, responsibilities and powers', *Youth Crime Briefing*, NACRO, March 2008.
[17] *The Queen (on application of K)* v *Manchester City Council* [2006] EWHC 3164 (Admin). This was another case bought by the Howard League.
[18] This was a successful application for judicial review which focused on the reasonableness or otherwise of the local authority's conduct in relation to an assessment under s 17 of the Children Act 1989. But see, re developing judicial review principles, T.M. Poole, 'Between the devil and the deep blue sea: administrative law in an age of rights' (July 30, 2008). *LSE Law, Society and Economy Working Paper* No. 9/2008.
[19] See C. Piper, 'Assessing Assessment' (2004) 34 *Family Law*, 736–40.
[20] Howard League, *Children in custody, children in need*.
[21] The Howard League argues that 'for those children entering custody who do not have looked after status, custody is effectively an alarm bell ringing that should trigger an assessment of the child's vulnerabilities, which the local authority can then act on' (ibid, para 2.5). A 'looked after child' is one accommodated by the local authority, either voluntarily under ss 17 or 20 of the Children Act 1989, or under a care order.
[22] Ibid, para 2.6. The Howard League believes that a partnership approach 'will not work if no one takes the lead or takes responsibility where appropriate'.

In *R(K)* v *Manchester City Council* Mr Justice Lloyd Jones decided that the YOT was not the 'agency best suited to meeting the needs of K' and stated that the defendant authority is required itself to carry out an assessment. It is not entitled to delegate that function'.[23] The judgment also made clear that YOTs can, and should, refer children to children's services, whether under s 47 as a child at risk or under s 17 as a child in need. In *R (on the application of M)* v *Hammersmith and Fulham LBC*,[24] although the appeal was dismissed on a legal technicality, Baroness Hale laid down procedures in relation to homeless 16–17 year-olds – often involved with the youth justice system – and again mandated a detailed assessment of the needs of the young person. She made clear that the local authority should have referred the child to children's social services – with Children Act duties – and not the housing authority.

Rights in detention

The problem is that most of the gains made by the above cases are more important for young people when they leave detention than when they are experiencing it. Further, until there is a social worker post in each YOI it is difficult to see how the Children Act 1989 duties can kick in fully. Therefore there is a need for specific rights regarding treatment in custody, particularly because of the problems arising from the need appropriately to discipline or restrain those young people who are behaving particularly badly. One disciplinary measure is segregation and the case of *R (on the application of BP)* v *Secretary of State for the Home Department*[25] queried whether its use with minors was lawful. This case concerned a 17-year-old (18 at the time of the hearing) who claimed that his treatment at Warren Hill YOI had been in breach not only of the Young Offender Institution Rules (2000) but also of Arts 3 and 8 of the ECHR. He had been in what amounted to solitary confinement in the segregation unit of a YOI for over 23 hours a day during two periods of 5 and 4 days in relation to two disciplinary offences – that of having an unauthorised article in his possession (a 'dead' mobile phone) and failing to turn up at a roll check.

The court decided that the rules of the institution had been breached and that, given the documented medical history of the offender, in particular his self-harming and suicide attempts, insufficient account had been taken of the young man's vulnerability. Moses J referred to Munby J's endorsement in the 2002 case of the principle that the child's best interests are the primary consideration and he accepted that 'solitary confinement of a child (in other words someone under 18) could amount to a breach of Article 3 in circumstances where it would not in relation to an adult'. However, he concluded as follows:

[23] [2006] EWHC 3164 (Admin), para 45.
[24] [2008] UKHL 14.
[25] [2003] EWHC 1963 Admin.

But the facts of this case, and particularly the facilities afforded to this claimant within his cell – the number of visits; the length of time which he was kept there, and its purpose preclude – any finding or anything approaching a finding of a breach of Article 3.[26]

The case points up the difficulties of using rights in practice because of the need for evidence and for evidence of considerable 'extra' deprivation. Further, this case did not forbid the use of segregation but stated that a breach of Art 8 requires evidence of significant adverse effects. Moses J, noting that Art 8.1 'turns on the extent to which this young claimant's physical and psychological integrity were in fact violated', concluded that there was insufficient evidence of adverse effects of segregation in this case which, therefore, leaves open the use of these Articles in relation to segregation of vulnerable young offenders and clearly alerts the Prison Service to this fact,[27] but that is all.[28]

It is not only segregation which is a cause of concern: concerns about other methods of restraint in YOIs and secure training centres (STCs) have been highlighted by two deaths in custody following the use of restraint techniques.[29] The YJB issued a draft Code of Practice 'for managing the behaviour of the troubled and troublesome young people' in secure accommodation in 2005 and a final version the following year[30] but problems continue. Some commentators argue that what currently occurs[31] is 'tantamount to institutional child abuse'[32] and the Chief Inspector of Prisons, Anne Owers, recently recommended the closure of Oakhill STC, a privately run centre, because of the 'staggering levels of use of force by staff'.[33] The

---

[26] Ibid, para 27.

[27] Ibid, see para 34.

[28] Indeed, in the context of the very good report on Warren Hill YOI by HM Inspector Prisons, the young claimant was in effect reprimanded by Moses, J: 'That makes it all the more disappointing that the claimant should have persisted in allegations of a very serious charge under Article 3 of the European Convention on Human Rights. That seems a poor reward for the hard work demonstrated by the independent inspector in relation to staff at that particular institution': ibid, para 33.

[29] Adam Rickwood, aged 14, and Gareth Myatt, aged 15.

[30] YJB, *Managing Children and Young People's Behaviour in the Secure Estate: A code of practice.* London: Youth Justice Board, 2006.

[31] This has been documented by the report of the inquiry into restraint chaired by Lord Carlile of Berriew, QC: see Howard League for Penal Reform, *An independent inquiry into the use of physical restraint, solitary confinement and forcible strip searching of children in prisons, secure training centres and local authority secure children's homes,* London; Howard League, January 2006.

[32] B. Goldson, 'Damage, harm and death in child prisons in England and Wales: questions of abuse and accountability' (2006) 45 *Howard Journal,* 449–67.

[33] See HM Inspectorate of Prisons, *Report on an announced inspection of the management, care and control of young people at Oakhill secure training centre.* London, HM Inspectorate, 2008; see also, S. Easton and C. Piper, *Sentencing and Punishment, The Quest for Justice,* 2nd edn, Oxford: Oxford University Press, 2008, pp 440–41.

government's review of the use of restraint in juvenile secure settings has not yet reported.

Criticism has also focused on the rules under which YOIs and STCs operate and a report by the Parliamentary Joint Committee on Human Rights in March 2008 on the use of physical restraint, notably the use of painful 'distraction techniques' was very critical of the government.[34] The report stated that restraint was used on more than 3,000 occasions in STCs in 2006 meaning that, on average, restraint is used on ten occasions per child, per year,[35] and asked for the immediate suspension of the use of distraction techniques, arguing that restraint was not compatible with the UK's human rights obligations.[36] Further, *R (on the application of C)*,[37] found that the government had breached the duty to consult on its amendments to the Secure Training Rules 1998 which extended the possibilities for using restraint techniques and in July 2008, the Court of Appeal, reviewing this decision, with C supported by the Children's Commissioner and the Equality and Human Rights Commission, ruled that the government's breaches of duty were sufficient to quash the Amendment Rules. The Court also found that the Rules breached Art 3 and 8 of the ECHR.[38]

There is another rather different issue which has been subject to judicial scrutiny in relation to the ECHR. This is the minimum period (formerly referred to as the 'tariff' period) to be served before the young offender on an indeterminate sentence, notably the sentence for murder of detention at Her Majesty's pleasure under s 90 of the Powers of Criminal Courts (Sentencing) Act 2000, can be considered by the Parole Board for release on licence. This became a high-profile issue after the conviction of Thompson and Venables for the murder of James Bulger when they were 11 years old. They challenged – ultimately in the European Court of Human Rights before the implementation of the HRA 1998 – the raising by the Home Secretary of their minimum period. That court decided that the Home Secretary's power to set the minimum period was contrary to Arts 5(4)[39] and 6(1)[40] on the grounds that such decisions should be made and reviewed by a judicial body and set the minimum period for Venables and Thompson at eight years.[41]

---

[34] Joint Committee on Human Rights *The Use of Restraint in Secure Training Centres*, Eleventh Report, HL 65/HC 378 (2008); see 'Conclusions and recommendations'.

[35] Ibid, para 32.

[36] Ibid, paras 6 and 7 and 13–15.

[37] *R (on the application of C)* v *the Secretary of State for Justice* [2008] EWHC 171 (Admin).

[38] *R(C)* v *The Secretary of State for Justice* [2008] EWCA Civ 882.

[39] 'Everyone who is deprived of his liberty by arrest or detention shall be entitled to take proceedings by which the lawfulness of his detention shall be decided speedily by a court and his release ordered if the detention is not lawful.'

[40] 'In the determination of his civil rights and obligations or of any criminal charge against him, everyone is entitled to a fair and public hearing … '

[41] *V and T* v *United Kingdom* (1999) 30 EHRR 121.

The sentencing court must now set the minimum period[42] and children are now allowed adult assistance in making a subsequent application to the Parole Board and have a right to an oral hearing in that context.[43] However, Parliament has since legislated guidelines for the courts: s 269 and Sched 21 of the Criminal Justice Act (CJA) 2003 require the court to have regard to a 'starting point' of 12 years in setting the minimum period for an offender who was aged under 18 years when he committed the offence. This is higher than the period set by the court for Venables and Thompson and indicates the vulnerability of rights-based jurisprudence to populist punitiveness.

The ability of individuals to use ECHR rights in the courts does not, however, address the issue of the very high rate of imprisonment in the UK which has a 'long and inglorious'[44] history of incarcerating children. The UN Conventions stress that detention should be used very sparingly for minors: Art 37 of the UNCRC states that detention should be 'a measure of last resort' and the UN Committee on the Rights of the Child (the Committee) has criticised the UK on this account. The number of 15–17-year-olds in prison increased 86 per cent 1995–2006[45] and, at the end of 2007, there were 2,742 boys and girls in prison (minors on remand or sentenced) in England and Wales, double the number in 1993.[46] Further, legislation has over the last 15 years introduced earlier ages at which detention is available to the courts and longer periods for which detention can be imposed, greater numbers have been detained, and conditions in young offender institutions have been deemed unacceptable.[47] Consequently, both the Children's Rights Alliance for England (CRAE) and the UK's four Children's Commissioners published reports to the UN Committee in June 2008 which were highly critical of the UK's breaches of the UNCRC and, in particular, the increasing criminalisation of children and the high rates of detention.[48]

---

[42] In *R (Smith)* v *Home Secretary* [2005] UKHL 51 the House of Lords ruled that detainees whose minimum periods were reset by the Lord Chief Justice following the *V* v *UK* judgment at the European Court are entitled to have periodic reviews of their progress. *R* v *Secretary of State for the Home Department ex parte Dudson* [2005] UKHL 52, however, the House of Lords decided that oral hearings need not be held in all circumstances, although in *Easterbrook* v *UK* [2003] 37 EHRR 40 the ECtHR had decided that the lack of an oral hearing when setting the tariff was in breach of Art 6. The court in *Dudson* argued this did not always apply.

[43] See NACRO, *Youth Crime Section Update*, March, London: NACRO, 2008, pp 2–3.

[44] Howard League, *Children in Prison: Provision and Practice at Lancaster Farms*, London: Howard League, 2001.

[45] Prison Reform Trust, *Bromley Briefings*, p 21.

[46] See www.Howardleague.org.uk: figures are for December 2007.

[47] Committee on the Rights of the Child, 2002, paras 59–62.

[48] UK Children's Commissioners' Report to UN Committee on the Rights of the Child, accessible at www.11million.org.uk/resource/31f7xsa2gjgfc3l9t808qfsi.pdf; CRAE, *Analysis of Children's Rights in England 2008*, Joint Report to the UN Committee by England's children's charities, London: Children's Rights Alliance for England, 2008.

Further, the ECHR is limited in its scope and, notably, it has not led to a successful challenge to the age of criminal responsibility in England, Wales and Northern Ireland. This is now one of the lowest ages in Europe but the European Court of Human Rights, in the case of *T* v *UK*[49] held that this minimum age did not of itself breach Art 3. In 2007 a case[50] questioned whether the doctrine of *doli incapax* might have survived the abolition of the presumption relating to 10–13-year-olds but a subsequent case has removed this doubt.[51] The age of 10 appears to be fixed and non-negotiable for the foreseeable future.

Diversion decisions and processes

Another focus of concern has been the rights of children at the other end of the youth justice process when they come to the attention of the police and about whom a crucial decision to divert or prosecute must be made. Of particular concern has been the amount of discretion available to the police and the Crown Prosecution Service (CPS) and the increasing intrusiveness of a range of interventions which might mean that the rights of children may not be given sufficient weight in the judicial exercise of balancing competing rights and interests. The result may be net-widening rather than diversion. Rights have therefore also been seen as a tool to challenge public responses and practices in this area.

The Crime and Disorder Act (CDA) 1998, ss 65–66, introduced for the first time a statutory scheme of police-controlled diversion. By the Act a pre-court system of reprimands and warnings replaced cautions[52] but, unlike cautions they do not require the consent of the minor. The *Durham* (2005)[53] case focused on the rights issues raised by this omission. The case concerned a young person who had not been told that a final warning for indecent assault involved a registration requirement as a sex offender but the House of Lords concluded that reprimands and warning do not constitute punishment[54] and that informed consent is not required of children and young people in connection with the use of these provisions. Counsel for R drew the court's attention to concerns expressed by the Parliamentary Joint

---

49 *V and T* v *United Kingdom* (1999) 30 EHRR 121.
50 *Crown and Prosecution Service* v *P* [2007] EWHC (Admin) 946.
51 *R* v *T* [2008] EWCA Crim 815; see NACRO, *Youth Crime Section Update*, June 2008, London: NACRO, p 3.
52 However, the statutory provisions have many similarities to the procedures established by a series of Circulars: see C. Piper, 'Who are these youths? Language in the service of policy' (2001) 1 *Youth Justice* 30–39.
53 *R (on the application of R)* v *Durham Constabulary and Another* [2005] UKHL 21, [2005] 2 All ER 369.
54 'A process which can only culminate in measures of a preventative, curative, rehabilitative or welfare-promoting kind will not ordinarily be the determination of a criminal charge' ibid, per Lord Bingham of Cornhill para 14.

Committee on Human Rights[55] at the registration requirements imposed on young offenders reprimanded or warned for sex offences, and also to Art 40(2) of the UNCRC[56] but Lord Bingham in response drew attention to Art 40(3)'s encouragement of non-judicial measures to deal with children who offend.[57] Baroness Hale, however, raised much wider issues about the relevance of international conventions to the reasoning of the court:

> The Beijing Rules are not binding on Member States, but the same principle [the welfare of the child] is reflected in the *United Nations Convention on the Rights of the Child* 1989 (UNCRC), which has been ratified by all but two of the Member States of the United Nations. This is not only binding in international law; it is reflected in the interpretation and application by the European Court of Human Rights of the rights guaranteed by the European Convention: see, for example, *V v United Kingdom* (1999) 30 EHRR 131; to that extent at least, therefore, it must be taken into account in the interpretation and application of those rights in our national law.[58]

Baroness Hale also noted that the focus on prevention and diversion to be found in Art 40 of the UNCRC is reinforced by the *United Nations Guidelines for the Prevention of Juvenile Delinquency (The Riyadh Guidelines)* 1990.[59] She argued that the lack of a requirement for consent 'appears inconsistent with rule 11 of the *Beijing Rules*',[60] and so she concluded, 'I have grave doubts about whether the statutory scheme is consistent with the child's rights under the international instruments dealing with children's rights'.[61] She also noted that reprimands and warning, though preventative, can have punitive consequences.[62] Lord Steyn shared her 'misgivings'[63] but all members of the court held the procedure to be lawful under the 'less extensive' rights[64] contained in the ECHR.

---

[55] 'Scrutiny of Bills: Further Progress Report', *Twelfth Report of Session 2002–03*, HL Paper 119, HC 765, paras 2.26–2.37.

[56] Particularly that '(b) Every child alleged as or accused of having infringed the penal law has at least the following guarantees: (iii) To have the matter determined without delay by a competent, independent and impartial authority or judicial body in a fair hearing according to law … '; see para 18 of *R (on the application of R)* v *Durham Constabulary and Another* [2005].

[57] Ibid.

[58] Ibid, para 26.

[59] Ibid, para 28.

[60] Ibid, para 39.

[61] Ibid, para 42.

[62] Ibid, para 45.

[63] Ibid, para 22.

[64] Ibid, per Baroness Hale para 44.

While, therefore, 'unnecessary prosecution represents an erosion of the rights of the child',[65] the current system of diversion, as Baroness Hale noted, has several features which are contrary to the spirit of these rights: reprimands and warnings – and failure to complete any rehabilitation programme attached to a warning – are citable in court in the same way as are previous convictions and they also restrict the options available to a court on a subsequent appearance.[66] Further, they are seen as disproportionate, they lack flexibility and they are not available for young people who have already been convicted.[67] It is possible to argue, as do Koffman and Dingwall,[68] that juveniles are in fact being diverted, not from punishment, but to a different form of punishment and that such diversion can 'have the undesirable effect of stigmatising young offenders and ensuring that their rights and freedoms are circumvented'.[69]

The powers of the police are increased when ss 48–50 and Sched 9 of the Criminal Justice and Immigration Act 2008 are implemented. These provisions provide a new pre-court disposal, the youth conditional caution (YCC), which is available for 10–17-year-olds[70] who have previously been given a reprimand and/or warning. Those existing two options can be bypassed but they will not be available after a YCC has been given. Its objectives are stated as one or more of the following: to facilitate the rehabilitation of the offender, to ensure that he makes reparation for the offence, and to punish.[71] The YCC gives the police extensive powers to add a fine and attendance at specified activities up to a total of 20 hours[72] but will also not be available after a conviction while the adult conditional caution is. This might be seen as contrary to the stress on diversion in rights conventions.

Another type of police controlled outcome is that of penalty notices – either penalty notices for disorder (PNDs) or fixed penalty notices (FPNs) – which can be given by constables or, in some circumstances, community support officers.[73] PNDs are financial penalties for low-level offences which have been available for use with 16–17-year-olds since 2004 (although the Anti-Social Behaviour Act (ASBA) 2003 allows the imposition of PNDs on children aged 10 and above and their use for 10–15-year-olds has been

---

[65] NACRO, 'Out of Court: Making the most of diversion for young people', *Youth Crime Briefing*, London: NACRO, 2005, p 3.

[66] Crime and Disorder Act 1998 ss 66(5) and 66(4) respectively.

[67] See NACRO *Youth Crime Update* March 2008, p 4.

[68] L. Koffman and G. Dingwall, 'The diversion of young offenders: a proportionate response?' (2007) *Web Journal of Current Legal Issues* 2.

[69] Ibid.

[70] Piloted first on 16–17-year-olds.

[71] The Police and Justice Act 2006 s 17 added the third objective to the other two aims given in s 22(3) of the Criminal Justice Act 2003 which introduced conditional cautions for adults although that third more punitive aim is not yet in force.

[72] New s 66A in the Crime and Disorder Act 1998.

[73] Anti-Social Behaviour Act 2003 s 89.

piloted in seven areas since 2005). By 2006 19,598 such notices were issued.[74] A youth court magistrate has argued that the PNDs are used 'to punish a crime without proper consideration as to the underlying causes' and often without the involvement of the YOT.[75] The latest UK report to the UNCRC Committee defends PNDs as diversion[76] but failure to pay the fine is resulting in attendance at the magistrates' court.[77]

Civil orders for 'offenders'

The last decade has seen an expansion of the youth justice system into new areas of work such that the boundaries of the system have 'become increasingly blurred with a variety of options open to the police, and other agencies, to deal with behaviour which might not otherwise have led to a substantive response'.[78] Consequently, there is now another set of options for boys and girls who behave badly and these options have been far more contentious than those relating to reprimands and warnings. The CDA 1998, ss 1(1)(a) and 12(3)(c) introduced in England and Wales anti-social behaviour orders (ASBOs)[79] and child safety orders with a common criterion that the child or adult has acted 'in a manner that caused or was likely to cause harassment, alarm or distress' to one or more persons outside the family. Section 85 of ASBA 2003[80] widened the scope of ASBOs and the Police Reform Act 2002 (and the Criminal Procedure (Scotland) Act 1995) empowered the criminal courts to impose an order – sometimes referred to as a CRASBO – on a conviction.[81]

---

[74] For detailed information see: NACRO, 'Fixed Penalty Notices for Disorderly Behaviour and Fixed Penalty Notices for Children and Young People', *Youth Crime Briefing*, June, NACRO: London, 2007; NACRO, 'Some Facts about Children and Young People who Offend – 2006' *Youth Crime Briefing*, March, London: NACRO, 2008.

[75] J. Fassenfelt, 'Penalty notices for disaster?' *YJ* March/April, London: Youth Justice Board (2008) p.10.

[76] UK Government, *The Consolidated 3rd and 4th Periodic Report to UN Committee on the Rights of the Child*, 2007, para 112, p.172.

[77] Fassenfelt, 'Penalty notices for disaster?'.

[78] NACRO, 'Some facts about children and young people who offend – 2006' *Youth Crime Briefing*, NACRO: London, 2008, p 6. See, also, A. Millie, 'Anti-Social Behaviour, Behavioural Expectations and an Urban Aesthetic' *British Journal of Criminology*, 48(3), 2008, 379–94.

[79] The Anti-social Behaviour (Scotland) Act 2004 made ASBOs available in Scotland for 12–15-year-olds.

[80] This Act incorporated the proposals in Home Office, *Respect and Responsibility*, Cm 5778, London: The Stationery Office, 2003.

[81] As first implemented in England and Wales ASBOs could be awarded only by magistrates in their civil jurisdiction (and in Scotland by Sheriff's Courts): see, for detailed information about ASBOs, NACRO, 'Further developments in measures related to anti-social behaviour' *Youth Crime Briefing* March, London: NACRO, 2007.

ASBOs raise several issues. MacDonald and Telford argue that, in relation to civil applications 'on both sides of the border, the choice of forum for applications against young people displays a failure to make adequate concessions for their youthfulness'.[82] They further argue that the statutory minimum of two years for an ASBO in England and Wales (but not in Scotland) makes them disproportionate in length and in the range and type of negative conditions that can be attached.[83] Even the Youth Justice Board (YJB) is concerned about the impact on young people of the restrictions on liberty:

> Geographical 'exclusions' and 'non-association' with anti-social peers were regarded on all sides as the most problematic prohibitions in terms of compliance. Young people and their parents/carers reported that being prohibited from associating with friends in familiar local territories resulted in a serious – and in some cases counter-productive – restriction of normal daily activities. The qualitative data confirmed that the majority of breach cases centred on failure to comply with these types of prohibition.[84]

Another significant issue is that of the publicity given to children and young people in connection with these orders. The Home Office 'Respect' website states that 'It is important to remember that everyone has rights under the European Convention of Human Rights (ECHR), including those individuals who behave in an anti-social manner. There must be a balance between their rights and those of the victims of the anti-social behaviour' and the web page provides justifications for interference with the rights in Arts 6, 8, 10 and 11 of the ECHR as well as Art 40 of the UNCRC.[85] However, Government guidance on 'Publicising Anti-social Behaviour Orders' includes the, to my mind, indefensible argument that a similar impact of actions by those under and over 18 justifies a similar 'punishment':

---

[82] S. McDonald and M. Telford 'The use of ASBOs against young people in England and Wales: lessons from Scotland' (2007) 27 *Legal Studies*, 604–29, p 615. See, also, N. Cobb, 'Governance through Publicity: Anti-social Behaviour Orders, Young People, and the Problematization of the Right to Anonymity' (2007) 34 *Journal of Law and Society*, 342–73.

[83] McDonald and Telford, ibid, p 618; see also S. Mackenzie 'Second-chance Punitivism and the Contractual Governance of Crime and Incivility: new Labour, Old Hobbes' (2008) 35 *Journal of Law and Society* 214–39 for a critique of forms of regulation which amount to 'second chance punitivism' in that they legitimate criminal sanctions for non-compliance in circumstances which would not otherwise be legitimate.

[84] YJB, *Anti-social Behaviour Orders* (Summary). London, Youth Justice Board, 2006, p 8.

[85] www.respect.gov.uk/members/article.aspx?id=7838, accessed 10 July 2008.

The age of the person against whom the ASBO was obtained should be a consideration when deciding whether or how to inform people about the order.

Factual information should be obtained about whether an individual is particularly vulnerable. This should be done as early as possible so as to avoid delays in informing the public once an order has been obtained.

The fact that someone is under the age of 18 does not mean that their anti-social behaviour is any less distressing or frightening than that of an adult.

An ASBO made against a juvenile (a person under 18) is made in open court and is not usually subject to reporting restrictions. The information is in the public domain and newspapers are entitled to publish details.[86]

The case of *Stanley* v *Metropolitan Police* (2004)[87] considered under Art 8(1) of the ECHR the practice of naming and shaming children and young people given ASBOs and exonerated these from censure on the ground of overriding community interests. The continuing use of such publicity has been criticised by the EU Commissioner on Human Rights.[88]

Some victories – but not for children's rights?

The above selective review reveals gains through the use of ECHR rights in the courts, sometimes buttressed by reference to the UNCRC. But there have also been 'failures' and, further, cases which apparently give rights to children in the youth justice system are not always based on rights reasoning. For example, the ASBA 2003 provided the police with further powers to disperse groups in 'designated areas' and with the power to return home any such people under 16 years of age (ss 30–36). This power was challenged in *Re (W)* v *Commissioner of Police of the Metropolis and Another*[89] which established that s 30(6) of ASBA did not give the police the power to use reasonable force to return a child home. However, as Hollingsworth notes, Brooke LJ's judgment did not mention Convention

---

[86] *Publicising Anti-social behaviour orders*, Home Office Guidance March 2005. However, s 141 of the Serious Organised Crime and Police Act 2005 amends the Crime and Disorder Act 1998 to remove the automatic reporting restrictions on breach proceedings involving juveniles.

[87] *R v Stanley (and others)* v *Metropolitan Police Commissioner* [2004] EWHC 222 (Admin).

[88] A. Gil-Robles, *Report by the Commissioner for Human Rights on his Visit to the UK*, Strasbourg: Council of Europe, 2005, p 37; see also J. Donoghue, 'The judiciary as a primary definer of Anti-Social Behaviour Orders' *Howard Journal*, Vol 46(4), 2007, 417–30, pp 420–21; MacDonald and Telford, 'The use of ASBOs against young people in England and Wales' pp 620–23.

[89] [2005] EWHC 1586 (Admin).

rights at all[90] so that the case does not establish any entitlements under the ECHR.[91] Similarly, *S* v *Miller*[92] established that the procedure of Scottish Children's Hearings was not compliant with Art 6 of the ECHR in denying the child a right to legal representation. However, the judgment was conveyed as encouraging more family participation. Such cases do not refer to and so do not significantly enhance the status of a child as a rights-bearing person.

The government also undermines rights while seemingly upholding the child's best interests. In the UK's Consolidated 3rd and 4th Periodic Report to the UN Committee on the Rights of the Child the government defends its decision not to raise the minimum age of criminal responsibility[93] by reference to both justice and welfare. The Report argues that the rebuttable doctrine of *doli incapax* for children aged 10–14 'led to difficulties such as delaying cases or even making it impossible for the prosecution to proceed' and that 'The UK Government, in relation to England and Wales, believes that children of this age generally can differentiate between bad behaviour and serious wrongdoing, and that it is not in the interests of justice, victims or the children themselves to prevent offending from being challenged through formal criminal justice processes'.[94] Further, it explained, 'The Government is concerned about 10- and 11-year-olds becoming drawn into offending behaviour and believes that commencing criminal responsibility from the age of 10 helps children develop a sense of personal responsibility for their behaviour'.[95]

It appears, then, that the UNCRC is essentially international law whose impact on policy and legislation depends on the political pressure on signatory states generated by the negative publicity resulting from non-compliance. Its influence in relation to judicial reasoning and professional practice depends on the extent to which the judiciary and others use UNCRC principles to influence practice guidance and add authority. Mumby J and Baroness Hale have, for example, referred extensively to UNCRC rights in their judgments while policy documents currently make reference to the importance of such rights, and all parts of the UK now have Children's Commissioners, albeit with different roles and responsibilities.[96]

---

[90] Hollingsworth, K. (2006) '*R(W)* v *Commissioner of Police for the Metropolis and Another* – Interpreting child curfews: a question of rights?' (2006) 18 *Child and Family Law Quarterly*, 253–68, p 265.

[91] Ibid, p 268.

[92] 2001 SLT 531.

[93] See, for criticisms made by the UN Committee, CRC/C/15/Add.188 para 61.

[94] UK Government, *The Consolidated 3rd and 4th Periodic Report to UN Committee on the Rights of the Child*, paras 54 and 55 p 160.

[95] Ibid, para 55.

[96] See J. Williams, 'Effective government structures for children? The UK's four Children's Commissioners' (2005) 17 *Child and Family Law Quarterly*, 37–53.

However, the UN Committee on the Rights of the Child has, as we have already seen in relation to the age of criminal responsibility, been very critical in its reports in 1995 and 2002 of aspects of the UK's treatment of children who offend.[97] Further, recent 'clarification' of Arts 37 and 40 of the UNCRC in the General Comment on rights in juvenile justice issued in 2007[98] prompts concern relative to UK compliance particularly in regard to the priority given to the welfare of the child.[99] The welfare test ('have regard to') in s 44 of the 1933 Children and Young Person's Act (CYPA) is weak and the Criminal Justice and Immigration Act (CJIA) 2008 s 9(3) makes clear that the court must also have regard to the principal aim of the youth justice system – to prevent offending[100] – and the purposes of sentencing.[101]

There has been insufficient space in this chapter to focus on the serious rights issues raised by suicides and self-harm in young offender institutions (YOIs) and secure training centre (STCs) which have led critics to argue that the UK is in breach of Art 24 of the UNCRC for failure to provide adequate facilities for, in particular, the mentally ill, drug abusing or otherwise vulnerable young offender.[102] Article 24 includes the right to enjoy 'the highest attainable standard of health' and enjoins States Parties to provide appropriate facilities to treat illness and promote the health of children and young people. It is here, however, that concern has increasingly been gender based, with a focus on the particular vulnerabilities of girls and young women. Research done for the YJB by Douglas and Plugge with a sample of young women aged 17 years old found, for example, that before imprisonment, 81 per cent smoked and 61 per cent drank more than the recommended limit while nearly all had taken drugs, over one-third had harmed themselves in the previous month, and nearly half suffered from depression. In terms of overall physical and mental health the young women scored even lower than women

---

[97] See Concluding Observations of the Committee on the Rights of the Child – UK (2002), CRC/C/15/Add.188; Concluding Observations of the Committee on the Rights of the Child – UK (1995), CRC/C/15/Add.34. These are available on the treaty-bodies database of the United Nations at www.unhchr.ch/tbs/doc.nsf.

[98] Committee on the Rights of the Child, General Comment No. 10 (2007), 'Children's rights in juvenile justice', CRC/C/GC/10, available at: www.ohchr.org/english/bodies/crc/docs/CRC.C.GC.10.pdf.

[99] Rule 5 of the Beijing Rules is also relevant: 'The juvenile justice system shall emphasise the well-being of the juvenile and shall ensure that any reaction to juvenile offenders shall always be in proportion to the circumstances of both the offenders and the offence'.

[100] Section 37(1) of the Crime and Disorder Act 1998.

[101] Listed in s 9(3) of the CJIA. This fudged position is, however, a considerable improvement on an earlier cl 9 of the Bill which stated that 'The court must have regard primarily to the principal aim of the youth justice system, that is, to prevent offending by children and other persons aged under 18'.

[102] See, e.g. N. Douglas and E. Plugge, 'The health of young women in custody: emerging concerns and a case for advocacy' Childright, 2007, CR 238, pp 4–17.

from social class five (those in the general population with the poorest health) and adult women.[103]

Gender

Until this point, this chapter has not discussed gender issues. The Convention Articles which have been referenced are couched in gender-neutral terms and the cases discussed have not raised gender issues. This is not surprising as a focus on rights has encouraged the search for equality of treatment – a lack of discrimination on any ground – above a minimum acceptable level set by rights conventions. Consequently, issues of differential impact of policies and practice have had less priority. Youth justice audits have tended to take account of differential impact only to the extent which they legally have to. So the Audit Commission report on youth justice in 2004 mentioned differences in terms of race – which is a mandatory requirement under s 95 of the Criminal Justice Act 1991 – but not gender, so 'males' are referred to but only in the context of 'black',[104] and gender is not an issue anywhere in the report. Likewise, the 2005 *Youth Matters* Consultation Paper mentioned gender only in reference to the need for career advisers to challenge gender stereotypes:[105] the words 'girl', 'boy', 'young women' and 'young men' do not feature in the report. In the relevant prison service order for juveniles, 'young women' are only dealt with separately in relation to initial health screening procedures, the provision of a booklet for young mothers and the clothing to be supplied after a full search; 'young men' are not referred to separately:

> Every young person must be screened on the day of arrival to ensure their safety and to identify all immediate health care needs, as supported in the YJB's KEEP document on 'Assessment, Planning Interventions and Supervision' ... For young women, the screening must ensure that any sanitary needs, child care needs or pregnancy issues are identified, and child care options are discussed, e.g. applying for a place on a mother and baby unit.[106]

Further, despite the fact that more girls than boys have suffered domestic violence or sexual abuse before entering prison[107] – with clear implications

---

[103] Ibid, p 16.
[104] Audit Commission, *Youth Justice*, London: Home Office, 2004, p 81.
[105] DfES, *Youth Matters*, Cm 6629, London: The Stationery Office, 2005, para 169.
[106] PSO 4950, para 5.5.
[107] See, e.g. S. Creighton, *Prevalence and Incidence of Child Abuse: International Comparisons*, London: NSPCC, 2004, Table 1. This survey of child sexual abuse data revealed higher figures for women and girls in all the jurisdictions included.

for strip searching and the gender of prison staff – the relevant passage in PSO 4950 does not mention young women separately.

> For young people, particularly those new to custody, a full search is an undignified and stressful experience. *Whilst recognising that it is an essential and very important part of the reception procedure, officers must conduct the search with consideration and courtesy. The searching procedure to be followed must be explained to the young person prior to the search taking place.* This is particularly important with this age group because of their youth and the likelihood of them having experienced physical or sexual abuse. [italics in original][108]

There is simply elsewhere the reference, noted above, to the provision of suitable clothing for girls and young women after the search.

There is however one particular relevant Convention which focuses on women – the United Nations Convention on the Elimination of All Forms of Discrimination Against Women (CEDAW).[109] As with the UNCRC, states must provide periodical reports[110] and the 5th Periodic Report of the United Kingdom of Great Britain and Northern Ireland of June 2003 dealt with girls who offend in relation to Art 2. The report acknowledged the difference–equality debate:[111]

> Moreover, research to identify the factors leading to young women and girls offending (*What works*) is being conducted. Specifically, the aim is to identify the characteristics and needs of girls and young women, in order to tailor programmes that will meet those needs, and reduce the numbers entering or re-entering the Criminal Justice System. An important development during the reporting period, is the Women's Estate Policy Unit, set up to develop gender-responsive regimes and policy. The Government recognises that consideration needs to be given to the differential impact that sentences can have on women and men.[112]

---

108 PSO 4950, para 5.17.
109 See www2.ohchr.org/english/bodies/cedaw/index.htm and, for the website giving information up to December 2007, www.un.org/womenwatch/daw/cedaw/.
110 In addition an optional protocol effective since 2000 mandates the committee to receive and investigate claims of violations from individuals and groups.
111 'States Parties condemn discrimination against women in all its forms, agree to pursue by all appropriate means and without delay a policy of eliminating discrimination against women.' This statement is followed by a list of seven specific ways in which the Parties undertake to eliminate discrimination.
112 Para 79; see also paras 82, 83, 86 and Annex 1 (community programmes). For the 6th Periodic Report (2007) see: http://daccessdds.un.org/doc/UNDOC/GEN/N07/398/67/PDF/N0739867.pdf?OpenElement pp 48–49 for an update on developments.

This statement reflects and responds to long-standing pressures on the government to treat women differently within the criminal justice system, notably within prison. The pressure has been in response to evidence that women have been 'invisible' in policy making and in the operation of the penal system. Until very recently girls have also been invisible in the youth justice system although, in relation to detention, the last few years have seen major research reports which have focused on the different needs of girls and young women. At the pre-prison level girls are still largely invisible. Campaigners argue that the current provisions and processes are not gender neutral and are in reality based on a male standard, stemming from the much larger numbers of boys and young men in the penal system. Consequently, the equal application of that standard may be unjust to females and hide their specific needs.

There are therefore two sets of issues: whether the decision-making system operates to discriminate against female youths and whether the ways in which preventative programmes and detention are organised and delivered disadvantage them.

Gender issues in decision making

A considerable amount of research was done in the 1980s about sentencing women and the treatment of girls in relation to police cautioning but detailed data is not currently available to be able to assess whether the factors identified in the 1980s are still valid[113] and whether law and rights are being applied differentially at the sentencing stage. There is, however, an emerging consensus that current diversionary strategies have differentially affected the rates of reprimands, warnings and prosecutions for boys and girls in that the recent decrease in the use of informal responses by the police and the CPS – possibly because of police targets to increase sanction detections – has had a greater impact on the prosecution rate of girls and young women than on boys and young men.[114] NACRO argues that this is probably the most significant factor in the rise of the prosecution and conviction rates for young female offenders.[115] Further, there is a suggestion that the 'net widening' which has occurred has had a greater impact on girls and young women, with girls in an ethnic minority being the most vulnerable to the new final warning scheme.[116]

---

[113] See C. Piper, 'Feminist perspectives on youth justice', in A. Diduck and K. O'Donovan, *Feminist Perspectives on Family Law*, London: Routledge-Cavendish, 2006, p 175.

[114] See NACRO, *Some facts about children and young people who offend – 2006*, Youth Crime Briefing, London: NACRO, March 2008, pp 3–4, 6.

[115] Ibid, p 6.

[116] D. Fox, M. Dhami, and G. Mantle, G. 'Restorative final warnings: policy and practice' (2006) 45 *Howard Journal* 129–40, p 137.

The nature of assessment is also a contentious issue in relation to gender. Assessment is the gatekeeper for access to resources, entry into the penal system and the choice of penal or rehabilitative responses. Player argues that for women, 'risk-based classifications are particularly problematic in the criminal justice context': the accuracy of the actuarial method is reduced for women and girls because risk tools have been developed by reference to male profiles.[117] They may, therefore, not be sufficiently 'sensitive' to pick up the needs of girls and young women. It has also been suggested that restorative final warnings differentially impact on girls and boys: 'restorative justice interventions are seen as having a welfare orientation, emphasising particular "feminine" traits such as mothering, nurturing, and relationship building'.[118]

While the greater number of males in the prison population is the reason why the apparently neutral assessments, procedures and conditions are inherently male orientated, it does not follow that boys and young men are always treated appropriately. One might argue that there is discrimination against the boys and young men who make up the vast majority of those given ASBOs as such orders are seen as a suitable response to typically male bad behaviour. The vulnerability of boys and young men may also be underestimated by those dealing with detainees, whilst those detainees may feel it 'unmanly' to express their anxieties.

Punishment issues

There is also inherent discrimination in relation to allocation to detention sites. PSO 4960 notes that 'Girls below the age of 18 and boys below the age of 15 will, as a general rule, continue to be placed outside the Prison Service Estate, either in local authority secure units or secure training' centres. Consequently, there are currently approximately 2,600 young men aged 15–17 years and 70 young women aged 17 being held in YOIs run by the Prison Service. However, generally girls and women are held further away from home because there are fewer establishments for them,[119] and reports have provided evidence of discriminatory treatment of girls in custodial establishments. *Girls in Prison*[120] and *Advice, Understanding and Underwear*,[121] provide

---

[117] E. Player 'Remanding women in custody: concerns for human rights' (2007) 70 *Modern Law Review* 402.

[118] Fox, Dhami and Mantle 'Restorative final warnings' p.136.

[119] Cookham Wood, until recently providing only female accommodation, has been redeveloped to take only boys and young men since early 2008.

[120] Office for Standards in Education, *Girls in Prison: The Education and Training of Under-18s Serving Detention and Training Orders*, London: Her Majesty's Inspectorate of Prisons, 2004.

[121] Howard League for Penal Reform, *Advice, Understanding and Underwear: Working with Girls in Prison*, London: Howard League, 2004.

numerous examples of inappropriate practice and suggest that there are insufficient numbers of staff trained to deal with the specific problems of vulnerable (young) females.[122]

There are also concerns about the treatment of girls and young women in relation to punishment in the community.[123] The OFSTED report on girls in prison suggested problems in relation to the 'training' half of a detention and training order (DTO) – that part served in the community – in relation to girls:

- The community aspect of the DTO was fraught with risk for the majority of young women; it did not provide them with sufficient structure or support to cope with personal problems or help them to progress to further education, training or employment;
- The availability of suitable programmes and support structures for young women on licence was inconsistent from one Youth Offending Team area to another.[124]

There has been some suggestion from previous criminal statistics that girls may receive more regulatory, and fewer practical, penalties but the latest quarterly figures do not provide a gender breakdown by type of community penalty imposed on juveniles and so this must remain speculative.[125] Research on women and community penalties suggests that their needs – both welfare and criminogenic – are not being properly addressed within male dominated service provision[126] and it is very likely this conclusion is also valid for girls.

What is clear is that over the last decade girls – whether they have offended or behaved anti-socially – have been drawn into a system in which the 'child as youth' is the dominant concept'.[127] What is also clear is how rarely CEDAW is referred to in the policies, cases and commentaries on youth justice and anti-social behaviour. Rights and gender appear to be uneasy bedfellows in regard to young offenders. However, since April 2007 the government has had a statutory duty to take positive action to eliminate gender discrimination and promote equality under the Equality Act and this may be the trigger which is needed. Certainly, the Corston Report on the treatment

---

[122] See, also, Easton and Piper, *Sentencing and Punishment, The Quest for Justice*, 2nd edn, pp 441–42.

[123] The Tokyo Rules 1990, adopted by the General Assembly in 1990, provide the UN Standard Minimum Rules for Non-Custodial Measures in criminal justice but there is nothing specifically in relation to juveniles; see: www.unhchr.ch/html/menu3/b/h_comp46.htm.

[124] Office for Standards in Education, *Girls in Prison*, part of the summary on the 'Main findings' of the report given on pp 8–9.

[125] *Sentencing Statistics Quarterly Brief*, England and Wales, October – December 2007 (Crown Court and magistrates' courts), London: Ministry of Justice/NOMS, 2008.

[126] L. Gelsthorpe, G. Sharpe and J. Roberts, *Provision for Women Offenders in the Community*. London, Fawcett Society, 2007.

[127] See Piper, 'Feminist perspectives on youth justice' p 169.

of women in the criminal justice system has referred to this duty and called for urgent changes.[128]

Conclusions

The review of several rights based cases in the first part of this chapter suggests two things: that rights do not necessarily help young offenders and those subject to civil orders, and that gender-neutral rights do not make the different needs of boys and girls sufficiently visible and yet these different needs are crucial sources of inappropriate treatment. The higher profile for girls in prison in recent years appears to be more the result of campaigning and focused research than the influence of CEDAW or the other Conventions. Even if CEDAW has been the catalyst leading to a policy endorsement of differential treatment where appropriate it is a pity that a specifically gender based convention is the tool: girls and young women are thereby endorsed as a special category and the specific needs of some boys are overlooked.

What a focus on rights might also obscure is that the implementation of rights requires resources but the amount of resources available is dependent on two factors over which rights have little control: the state of the economy and the extent to which there is the political will to spend money on boys and girls who behave badly. Given that policy is determined by the need to keep the taxpayer 'on side' and the electorate 'friendly' these factors are vulnerable to a range of pressures, not least populist punitiveness and a recession.

---

[128] J. Corston, *The Corston Report: A Report by Baroness Jean Corston of a Review of Women with Particular Vulnerabilities in the Criminal Justice System*, London: Home Office, 2007.

Chapter 5

(En)Gendering the fusion of rights and responsibilities in the law of contact

Julie Wallbank

INTRODUCTION

The centrality of fathers' rights activism to developments in family law is such that it has recently prompted an edited collection dedicated to it.[1] As the preface by Carol Smart points out:

> The fathers' movement have taken their experiences. ... and reframed them as issues of justice and inequality ... In framing the issues as ones of justice, they have also turned to law ... to demand 'fairness' while claiming much moral high ground through the emotive vehicle of personal accounts and anecdotes.[2]

This chapter is concerned with how these claims in respect of the injustice, inequality and unfairness are framed in terms of a conjunction of rights and responsibilities. The tightly focused rights-based discourses which were consistently forwarded by fathers demanding justice in the 1990s and continuing into the twenty-first century failed to bring about the desired outcomes for fathers in family law, particularly evident in respect of the call for 50/50 shared residence. In 2004 in the Green Paper *Parental Separation: Children's Needs and Parents' Responsibilities* the government refused to incorporate a presumption of shared residence and flatly rejected that the law relating to residence and contact was biased against fathers. It stated that both parents are equal and that 'no change is needed to the core principles on parental responsibility set out in section 3 of the Children Act 1989'.[3] However, as

---

[1] R. Collier and S. Sheldon, (eds.) *Fathers' Rights Activism and Law Reform in Comparative Perspective*, Oxford: Hart Publishing, 2006.

[2] C. Smart, ibid, p xii.

[3] Department for Constitutional Affairs, the Department for Education and Skills and the Department for Trade and Industry Cm 6273 London: HMSO, July 2004. The judiciary have also repeatedly insisted that parents are equal before the law; see, e.g. *Re D (Intractable Contact Dispute: Publicity)* [2004] 1 FLR 1226; *Re S (Contact: Promoting Relationship with Absent Parent)* [2004] 1 FLR 1279; Re *O (Contact: Withdrawal of Application)* [2004] 1 FLR 1258.

alluded to by Smart's statement above there is now another facet to fathers' claims for justice and equal rights i.e. their personal accounts and anecdotes of the desire to be responsible fathers. In another piece in the same year Smart noted an important move to what she calls a 'three cornered debate between "rights-talk", "welfare-talk" and "care-talk"'.[4]

She argues that the debate about entitlements in family law has often been cast as one of 'rights *v* welfare' and that the three-cornered debate presents a contemporary narrative device available to family professionals and parents in the negotiation of familial disputes. Smart makes it very clear that 'welfare-talk' and 'care-talk' are not interchangeable. '"Care-talk" may have virtually no overlap with "welfare-talk", while it may even, in some contexts, be deployed to support "rights-talk"'.[5] According to Smart a father may assert his rights claim on the emotional case of how much he cares for the child. A mother on the other hand, may resist his rights-based claim by drawing on 'welfare-talk' and how much she cares for the child, where for example she has concerns about the quality of care offered by the father. Smart's thesis is extremely useful for making sense of shifting discursive constructions of fathers' rights claims. The employment of more sophisticated narrative devices such as the ones outlined above have provided disgruntled fathers with augmented and morally superior positioning in respect of their claims. Arguably, they have not been slow to take advantage of the discursive shift. In this chapter I suggest that in addition to the narrative devices outlined by Smart we might add the concept of responsibility as responsible fatherhood is a key attenuate of paternal rights as propounded by the government in the context of the extension of parental responsibility to all unmarried fathers, 'fatherhood, as well as motherhood, always comes with both rights and responsibilities'.[6]

> Our proposal is that legislation around birth registration for unmarried parents should reflect that parenting is a joint undertaking and it should therefore make both parents equally responsible for registering the birth of their child ... The key benefit of an approach that places equal responsibility on both parents to register is that it is in keeping with the Government's desire to promote responsible fatherhood.[7]

It is not my intention to suggest that Smart's three-cornered approach be replaced by the adoption of a framework that examines familial claims

---

[4] C. Smart, 'The ethic of justice strikes back: changing narratives of fatherhood', in A. Diduck and K. O'Donovan, *Feminist Perspectives on Family Law*, London: Routledge-Cavendish, 2006, pp 123–38, p 125.

[5] Ibid, p 126.

[6] Department for Work and Pensions, *Joint Birth Registration: Promoting Parental Responsibility*, Cm 7160 London: The Stationery Office, 2007, p 6.

[7] Ibid, p 15.

through an examination of the combination of rights and responsibilities. Rather, responsibility acts as an umbrella term which encapsulates both 'care-talk' and 'welfare-talk' as will be shown. It also operates at an individual level in respect of the conflicting human rights claims of mothers and fathers and at a more general level in respect of the governance of post-separation family life. This chapter considers the fusion of rights and responsibilities in the law relating to contact.

It will be argued that current social policy and law reforms are premised on an aspirational or imagined model of paternal responsibility. Because parenting remains a highly gendered activity where many mothers still retain the main responsibility for hands on care it is therefore very important to flag up some of the problems with the utilisation of the as yet imagined shared parental rights and responsibilities paradigm. In light of the persistence of the gendered nature of parenting the chapter will also tentatively suggest an alternative way of approaching the resolution of disputes where the rights of parents conflict.

Here, my argument will be based on the notion of parental investment where both parents and children have a mutual stake in the kinds of investments which are made by each of their parents. It will be suggested that when adult rights collide in respect of children, it is crucial to foreground the relative investments made by the parents in relation to the exercise of their responsibilities. In considering the future arrangements for children courts, mediators and conciliators need to take close heed of the pattern of exercised and gendered responsibilities prior to the point of dispute. That is not to say that arrangements for the children would necessarily remain static and merely mimic what has gone before but those which at the outset of the dispute radically depart from the status quo are unlikely to meet with wholehearted approval by both parents and attend to their needs at a very difficult time. It might be more appropriate to provide parents in dispute with desired and realistic future objectives but which start out from the level and kind of investment made by the parent to the child at the pre-dispute stage. I will return to the model in the final section. At this point I will outline the ascendancy of the fusion of rights and responsibilities discourse.

Fathers' rights discourses

Fathers' rights groups have since the early 1990s argued that women's rights in respect of children are now prioritised over men's. They have sought to redress this perceived imbalance and are endeavouring to swing the pendulum back towards recognising the competing rights of the father. Their arguments are in part based upon the idea which began to be emanated in the 1980s that family law has gone too far in protecting women's rights and that the law shows preference for mothers in issues concerning children. One important context in which this idea emerged in recent history was child support. Fathers made the emotional claim that they were the victims of an over-powerful state which was making excessive and unfair demands on their financial resources which undermined their ability to build meaningful relationships with their children due to a lack of funds. The antipathy felt by men's pressure groups towards the Child Support Act was regarded as part of a broad canvas of hostility to the slight but significant shift in the balance of power between women and men. As Collier noted men were constructed as the 'victims' of a feminism which has gone 'too far' in unbalancing hitherto 'equal rights'[8]. Their campaigns against the government were organised in terms of their dwindling rights. Ultimately, fathers' support groups managed to bring about a great number of changes to their benefit and eventually, to the widespread reform of the Act.[9]

Over 10 years later these two themes of victim status and the mobilisation around claims to formal legal rights remain common elements of fathers' discourses as is outlined by Collier and Sheldon.[10] In the edited collection on fathers' rights activism contributors on various jurisdictions discuss the impact that fathers' rights activism has had on law and law reform in relation to residence and contact. On the Canadian jurisdiction Boyd notes that 'fathers' rights advocates succeeded to a significant degree in generating the notion that mothers are favoured in family law'.[11] Their submissions included the conflation of fathers' rights with child welfare, despite the ambiguities in the research on outcomes for 'children of divorce'.[12] However, it is also noted that another feature of fathers' rights discourses was that fathers should have equal rights regardless of the pattern of care that existed within the family which as Boyd notes ascribes formal rights to fathers without any corresponding need to exercise responsibilities towards the child and permits for a facet of control over the mother's decision making.[13]

She concludes that although fathers' rights discourses in parliamentary debates over Canadian contact law reform were mediated by research and a desire to avoid 'gender wars', they did result in government promoting

---

[8] R. Collier, '"Waiting till father gets home ... ": family values and the reconstruction of fatherhood in family law', *Social and Legal Studies*, 1995a, vol. 4, 5–30. See also J. Wallbank, *Challenging Motherhood(s)*, Harlow: Pearson Education, 2001.

[9] For a full discussion of fathers' rights groups claims in relation to the child support legislation see R. Collier, *Masculinity, Law and the Family*, London: Routledge, 1995b; R. Collier, 'The campaign against the Child Support Act', "Errant fatherhood" and "Family men"', *Family Law*, vol. 24, 384–87, 1994. J. Wallbank, 'The campaign for change of the Child Support Act 1991: reconstituting the "absent" father', *Social and Legal Studies*, 1997 vol. 6, 191–216.

[10] Collier and Sheldon, *Fathers' Rights Activism*, p 16.

[11] S. Boyd, 'Robbed of their families'? Fathers' rights discourses in Canadian parenting law reform processes', in Collier and Sheldon, *Fathers' Rights Activism*, p 28.

[12] Ibid, p 29.

[13] Ibid, p 38.

'a package of reforms' which promoted the ideal of shared parenting. Additionally, and rather worryingly the fathers' rights movement in Canada has succeeded in influencing a gender-neutral approach to residence which has been evidenced by increased numbers of joint custody awards and has had a wider cultural effect upon the public and family and legal professionals.[14]

Although the impact of equal rights rhetoric on residence and contact may be viewed as having been considerable in Canada, as outlined at the start of the chapter the UK government has flatly denied that the law of contact was biased against fathers. To some extent that denial rests on the purported gender neutrality of the concept of parental responsibility, thus is arguably clearly influenced by the notion of the equal gender rights of mothers and fathers. However, in England and Wales discourses around the rights and interests of family members are now frequently articulated in terms of a conjunction between rights and responsibilities and that rights, devoid of responsibilities is empty and meaningless as illustrated by the government's position that 'fatherhood, as well as motherhood, always comes with both rights and responsibilities'.[15] In highlighting the importance of the relationship between rights and responsibilities, the government is recognising the problems which are commonly associated with a strictly rights-based approach to family law. At the same time, it is also flagging up the advent of a dominant model for negotiating conflicting rights of adults in respect of family life where responsibility and rights are centralised.

Problematising rights discourse

The Human Rights Act 1998 means that rights-based approaches now feature much more highly in family law and pose a challenge to welfare-based approaches. However, as Harris-Short has argued there has been a strong resistance to rights-based reasoning because of its emphasis on individualism and equality which are seen as potentially threatening to the integrity of the family unit.[16] The fear of rights has been identified as the potential for fathers' rights activists hijacking rights to promote fathers' position at the expense of children and mothers' rights.[17] The debate about the appropriateness of adopting rights-based strategies is not a new one for feminism and the discussions about the utility of rights have thrown up some cogent

[14] Ibid, p 51.
[15] Department for Work and Pensions, *Joint Birth Registration*, p 6.
[16] S. Harris-Short, 'Family law and the Human Rights Act 1998: judicial restraint or revolution?', *Child and Family Law Quarterly*, 2005, vol. 17, 329–62.
[17] J. Fortin, 'The HRA's impact on litigation involving children and their families' *Child and Family Law Quarterly*, 1999, vol. 11, 237–55.

critiques.[18] One of the main feminist criticisms of rights is that they are 'inherently individualistic and competitive' and women's experiences do not necessarily translate well into the language of rights.[19] The emphasis on individual rights permits for the elision of mutual responsibilities, of ideas of dependency and inter-dependency and the importance of relationships, particularly in the familial context.[20] In respect of many of the rights which are commonly associated with families they involve 'not individuals per se but the claims, responsibilities, and boundaries of particular human relationships'.[21] The associated problems with the individualistic nature of rights which flows from traditional Western liberal version of autonomy has led to the development of 'relational autonomy' in order to account for the fact that most people 'live their lives in a complex web of relationships and connection'.[22]

A related point is that rights-based discourses presuppose the existence of a gender-neutral individual who has the power to assert her or his right against the state. The use of rights discourse necessitates an appeal to an 'ethics of justice' approach to family life where the concern is to ensure, as far as possible, parity of the legal rights of women and men in a gender-neutral manner. Following on from Tronto, Sevenhuijsen shows how the ethic of justice, (in this case where primacy is given to the issue of equality of rights between mothers and fathers), is concerned with the central question to the ethic of justice is 'what are the highest normative principles and rights in situations of moral conflict?'.[23] This is made clear in the health care law context by Herring who has cogently critiqued the way that medical

---

[18] Some of the major theoretical discussions appear in the edited collection of J. Bridgeman and S. Millns, *Feminist Perspectives on Law*, London: Sweet & Maxwell, 1998. Among these are E. Kingdom, 'Body politics and rights', in J. Bridgeman and S. Millns (eds.), *Law and Body Politics: Regulating the Female Body*, Aldershot: Dartmouth, 1995, pp 1–21; E. Kingdom, *What's Wrong With Rights? Problems for Feminist Politics of Law*, Edinburgh: Edinburgh University Press, 1991; S. Palmer, 'Critical perspectives on women's rights: the European Convention on Human Rights and Fundamental Freedoms', in A. Bottomley (ed.), *Feminist Perspectives on the Foundational Subjects of Law*, London: Cavendish, 1996, pp 223–42.

[19] S. Palmer, 'Critical Perspectives on Women's Rights, pp 223–42.

[20] For an eloquent discussion of this aspect of rights, see M. Minow and M. Lyndon Shanley, 'Relational rights and responsibilities: revisioning the family in liberal political theory and law', in *Hypatia*, 1996, vol. 11, 4–10.

[21] Ibid, p 9.

[22] J. Herring, 'Relational autonomy and rape' in S. Day Sclater, F. Ebtehaj, E. Jackson and M. Richards (eds), *Regulating Autonomy*, Oxford: Hart, 2009, pp 53–72.

[23] See further S. Sevenhuijsen, *Citizenship and the Ethics of Care: Feminist Considerations about Justice, Morality and Politics*, London: Routledge, 1998, p 107 and J. Tronto, *Moral Boundaries: A Political Argument for an Ethic of Care*, London: Routledge, 1993, who develops the distinction between what she terms 'an ethics of justice' and an 'ethics of care' approach in respect of women's caring experiences.

and legal discourse has developed the notion of consent based upon an 'individualised model of rights' with the result that carers who are often women, and their interests combined with the significance of the work they provide are ignored.[24]

The ideal outcome under an ethic-of-justice approach would be the implementation of generalisable procedural rules in order to secure justice or equal rights between the two parties. As Smart and Neale argue, rights discourse does not attend to the empirical realities of women and men's lives. 'A decision based on the ethic of justice cannot be easily changed or modified. It tends to be made once and for all, even though conditions may change at a later date.'[25] These concerns have been added to in the social policy and gender studies literature that the rights approach is adversarial, conceives persons as autonomous rather than relational and that rights are based on a 'disembodied rationalism'.[26] In practical terms, where the rights model is adopted, law has as its imperative the protection and enforcement of individual rights and does not look at the wider and gendered consequences for the parties. As highlighted earlier the two approaches have been characterised as justice versus welfare and as two opposing and incompatible approaches. However, as Virginia Held has recently made clear although the ethic of care and ethic of justice have frequently been polarised, recent writings have explored the relationship between them and how they might be used together. She states that: 'Few would hold that considerations of justice have no place at all in care.'[27] She does acknowledge however, that care is perhaps the more 'deeply fundamental value'.[28] Her point is that care can occur without justice but that 'there can be no justice without care'.[29] It is care that provides 'the wider and deeper ethics within which justice should be sought'.[30] Although Held's work considerably advances the debate on the ethic of care and justice debates, she, along with previous writers, argues for a re-evaluation and reconstruction of the care ethic in order to bring about a wider social revolution in the relative value ascribed to both ethics.

It is to the credit of feminist contributions on the ethics-of-justice versus ethic-of-care approaches that the problems with the individualistic framework

---

[24] J. Herring, 'Where are the carers in healthcare law and ethics?', *Legal* Studies, 2007, vol. 27, 51–73, p 51.

[25] See further C. Smart and B. Neale, *Family Fragments*, London: Polity Press, 1999, pp 170–71 for an eloquent discussion of the differences between Tronto's two approaches.

[26] D. Curtin, 'Towards an ecological ethic of care', *Hypatia*, 1991, vol. 6, pp 60–74 as discussed in T. Cockburn, 'Children and the feminist ethic of care' *Childhood*, 2005, vol. 12, 71–87, p 73.

[27] V. Held *The Ethics of Care: Personal, Political and Global*, Oxford: Oxford University Press, 2006, p 15.

[28] Ibid, p 17

[29] Ibid.

[30] Ibid.

of rights and their gender neutrality have been highlighted. What has occurred in attempts to challenge the potential of rights-based discourse gaining a firm foothold in respect of family law is a powerful challenge to the ethic of rights by using the ethic-of-care approach.[31]

However, perhaps an unforeseen consequence of the emphasis on the importance of relationships, responsibilities and interdependency is that these ideas have provided a strategic mechanism for fathers' rights groups to advance their claims, as will be discussed below. In addition, social policy and law reform imagines that the conferment of equal status or equal rights will lead, in a manner that remains in the main unquestioned, to the assumption of shared (though not necessarily equal parental responsibilities). I am not suggesting that the combination of rights and responsibilities in family law is a novel phenomenon, nor am I claiming that it is surprising. Rather, what I am suggesting is that the current socio-political climate provides fathers' claims to equal rights with a cogency derived from the moral force of their aspirational responsibilities.

In the fusion of rights and responsibilities, responsibilities are read off from the equality of rights side of the conjunction, based on what Scourfield and Drakeford have called an 'optimistic view of fathering' that 'men are keen to embrace'.[32] In arguing that the Labour government has broken new ground by making 'masculinity policy' which focuses specifically on fathering they suggest that family policy developed to support fathers is founded upon the assumption that men want to spend more time with children. As discussed in the following section, there is evidence to suggest that there is a dissonance between what both women and men say they want in respect of the paternal role, i.e. an increased role in hands-on care for children and what actually happens in practice currently, that men on average spend one month a year less with their children than women.[33] The resulting effect is that the current gendered realities of mothers' and fathers' lives are ignored.

Additionally, it is made difficult for mothers to oppose contact precisely because claims to shared residence or contact are regarded as vehicles by which fathers may exercise the responsibilities which derive from their paternal rights. Moreover, contact with the non-residential parent, usually the father is constructed as almost always in the best interests of the child, that the application for contact is constructed as a manifestation of parental responsibility while at the same time is an assertion of the right deriving from parental status. The exercise of both parents' responsibilities is the model to which post-separated parents should aspire.

[31] See further, Sevenhuijsen, *Citizenship and the Ethics of Care*; Herring, 'Where are the carers'; Smart and Neale, *Family Fragments.*

[32] J. Scourfield and M. Drakeford, 'New Labour and the problem of men', *Critical Social Policy*, 2002, vol. 22, 619–40, p 625.

[33] www.news.bbc.co.uk/1/hi/uk/7175673.stm citing a poll of 1,000 people for the Fatherhood Institute.

The fusion of rights and responsibilities in the law of contact

The fusion of rights and responsibilities is clearly forged in the government's consultation paper on parental separation which preceded the Children and Adoption Act (CAA) 2006: 'both parents have equal status as parents and the court's expectation is that both parents should continue to have a meaningful relationship with their children following separation'.[34] Later, the Green Paper refers to fathers' rights claims for the automatic 50:50 division of the child's time designed to give parents 'equal rights to equal time'.[35] Making short shrift of the claim for what is in effect equal shared residence the government claims that this type of arrangement may not be what children want and that it may have a 'damaging impact on some of them'.[36] However, the paper does state that 'both parents are equal' and 'it is important that parents recognise their responsibilities to promote the welfare of their child and, for their child a meaningful relationship with both parents'.[37]

Although the government is unwilling to advocate shared residence as a legal presumption, it is clear that the expectation is that both parents recognise and respond to the promotion of child welfare through contact. As such, non-residential fathers are hailed to act as responsible parents by assuming contact and residential mothers by facilitating contact. The assumption is that child welfare is best served by the continuing relationship, through contact with the non-residential parent. Contact is in itself seen as a manifestation of parental responsibility deriving from parents' equal rights. The responsible parent is therefore one that facilitates or assumes contact and thus promotes the welfare of the child. However, the construction of the gender-neutral responsible parent may work to the disadvantage of the residential mother. In respect of contested contact case law Smart and Neale have identified a 'double standard at work'.[38] Faced with a mother who is hostile to contact the courts have constructed her as implacably hostile, a phrase which was prominent in case law throughout the 1990s. However, in respect of the father who fails to have contact with his child, no equivalent label for the father such as 'implacably irresponsible' was employed.[39] Despite the construction of the gender-neutral norm of the responsible

---

[34] Department for Constitutional Affairs, the Department for Education and Skills and the Department for Trade and Industry, *Parental Separation: Children's Needs and Parents'* Responsibilities, July 2004, Cm 6273, London: HMSO, p 18.

[35] Ibid p 19.

[36] Ibid.

[37] Ibid.

[38] C. Smart and B. Neale, 'Arguments against virtue – must contact be enforced?' *Family Law*, 1997, vol. 27, 332–36, p 336.

[39] Ibid. For a discussion of the construction of the implacably hostile mother see further J. Wallbank, 'Castigating mothers: the judicial response to wilful women in cases concerning contact' *Journal of Social Welfare and Family Law*, 1998, vol. 20, 357–77.

parent, the enforcement measures recently introduced by the Children and Adoption Act 2006 are likely to affect detrimentally mothers who are constructed as implacably hostile to contact.[40] The CAA 2006 introduced contact activity directions and conditions to s 11 of the Children Act 1989 including parenting programmes, classes and counselling or guidance sessions to facilitate or aid contact.[41] Although the provisions (when in force) apply to both mothers and fathers it is not unlikely that resident parents (usually mothers) will be subject to parenting programmes and classes to help them to understand the benefits of contact.

> As Masson and Humphreys have noted enforcement is biased and one-sided.[42] Moreover, as rightly highlighted by Diduck and Kaganas 'fathers' rights campaigns appear to have had the effect of galvanising the government and the courts into action against mothers whom they see as obstructive.[43]

Contemporary fatherhood is constructed as a mutually beneficial relationship between fathers and their children and has served to propagate the view that both children and non-residential fathers 'suffer' from the enforced denial of this relationship. Further, that fathers are being unreasonably prevented from exercising their parental responsibilities. As such, where fathers successfully demonstrate that the emotional and physical relationship is being denied or obliterated, they are given the opportunity to raise the debate about fatherhood on the terms of lack of contact with children as being a denial of a 'right' to a beneficial and productive relationship. In respect of the application of the welfare principle, the conflation of children and fathers' interests in relation to contact disputes effectively means that the rights of children and fathers potentially become one and the same. Fathers may then find it strategically useful to draw upon the fusion of rights and responsibilities in respect of their claims to contact. The point is made thus by Julian in the *Telegraph's* speakers' corner web blog when addressing the question 'Are we guilty of ignoring fathers' rights?'[44]

---

[40] Under s. 11J of the Children Act 1989 as inserted by s. 4 of the CAA 2006. The court may impose an unpaid work requirement on the defaulting parent and in addition make an order for financial compensation to be paid to any parent financially prejudiced by non-compliance such as the cost of a holiday which has been missed under s 11O-P of the Children Act 1989 as inserted by s 4 of the CAA.

[41] Section 11A(5)(a) of the Children Act 1989.

[42] J. Masson and C. Humphreys, 'Facilitating and enforcing contact: the Bill and the ten per cent' *Family Law*, 2005, vol. 35, 548–55, p 552.

[43] A. Diduck and F. Kaganas, (2nd edn), *Family Law, Gender and the State*, Oxford: Hart Publishing, 2006, p 561.

[44] www.telegraph.co.uk/news/main.jthml?view accessed 5 December 2007.

> All these posts have a common theme – the absence of family rights – equal parental rights to exercise responsibility towards one's children. … I speak as a father who has attempted to act responsibly for over ten years now, whilst being denied all contact.[45]

The theme of fathers being denied the right to exercise responsibilities or to express love for the child is an often repeated one: 'I am writing as a falsely accused father, denied his right to love. … I have irrefutable evidence to prove I was a good caring dad. … .'[46] 'Family Law rewards dysfunction and punishes responsible behaviour. … Equality would render the entire system virtually useless.'[47]

As Collier highlights these representations of fathers as victims of family law were promulgated throughout the 1990s and reached fever pitch in the early twenty-first century with highly publicised campaigns.[48] In addition, another theme is that men are victims of a shift in gendered power towards mothers and away from fathers. Therefore, the claims of aggrieved fathers are mobilised around the ideas that they do not have equal rights with mothers in respect of contact as a result of an institutional bias in favour of mothers and that as a result they are prevented from exercising their responsibilities. Their battle becomes one against family law and also against women, 'marked by an increasingly virulent anti-feminism. … '[49] The Internet has provided a means by which fathers' rights groups can organise themselves and share their grievances amongst 'communities of men'.[50]

The anti-feminist tone of campaigns for law reform in respect of residence and contact draws on a very negative 'depiction of women'[51] set against the often promulgated view that fathers are beneficial to children and as 'sharer[s] of responsibilities'.[52] Smart argues that Fathers 4 Justice's ability to utilise the combination of 'rights', 'welfare' and 'care' talk in the context of the campaign against the 'unfair privileging of mothers' has meant that there has been 'an erasure of narratives of motherhood'.[53] Smart's observation has

---

[45] Ibid, posted 29 November 2006 2:57pm.
[46] Ibid, posted by dad4justice 30 November 2006 9:29pm.
[47] Ibid, posted by Armando Milani 30 November 2006 2:52am.
[48] For a full discussion see further R. Collier, '"The Outlaw Fathers Fight Back": fathers' rights groups, Fathers 4 Justice and the politics of family law reform – reflections on the UK experience', in Collier and Sheldon, *Fathers' Rights Activism.*
[49] Ibid, p 57.
[50] Ibid.
[51] Ibid, p 62.
[52] Ibid, citing S. Boyd, 'Demonizing mothers: fathers' rights discourses in child custody law reform processes', *Journal of the Association for Research in Mothering,* 2004, vol. 6, p 60.
[53] C. Smart, 'The ethic of justice strikes back', in Diduck and O'Donovan, *Feminist Perspectives on Family Law,* pp 127–28.

resonance in respect of the way women have failed to mobilise themselves and to pose counter-narratives to reject the idea that they are somehow privileged by family law. However, although discourses on the management of post-separation life focus on the gender-neutral category of the responsible parent, it can be argued that a very particular discursive construction of motherhood emerges as one who facilitates, compromises and sets aside post-separation conflict. Further, the organisation of fathers' rights groups around the themes of lost responsibilities as a result of the diminution of rights also draws strength from the prevalence and rise in importance of the normative discourses on the effective management of post-separation relationships, particularly in respect of how the responsible mother manages contact.

While the government has refuted that women's rights are prioritised over men's it does stress the importance of the relationship between fathers' rights and responsibilities. In the context of contact fathers' grievances are framed in terms of both a lack of the right to contact and their inability to exercise paternal responsibilities as a result. Fathers' aspirations in respect of their parenting responsibilities have become a major feature of social policy on the family as discussed below. A central feature which has been discussed extensively in the research on contact is the centrality to child welfare of the continuing relationship between fathers and children. I do not wish to expand on that existing body of important literature.[54]

Rather, I am more interested in how developments in policy on paternal responsibilities feed into the debate on contact law reform and the management of intractable contact cases. The 'optimistic view of fathering' has become such that contact must follow separation whenever possible. More importantly, the perceived need to be forward- rather than backward-looking

---

[54] See, e.g. J. Dunn, H. Cheng, T.G. O'Connor, and L. Bridges, 'Children's relationships with their non-resident fathers: influences, outcomes and implications', *Journal of Child Psychology & Psychiatry*, 2004, vol. 45, pp 553–56; B. Rodgers and J. Pryor, *Divorce and separation: The outcomes for children*, York: Joseph Rowntree Foundation, 1998; S. Kraemer, 'What are fathers for?', in C. Burck, and B. Speed, (eds.) *Gender, Power and Relationships*, London: Routledge, 1995, p 202; P. Amato and S. Rezac, 'Contact with non-residential parents, interparental conflict and children's behaviour,' *Journal of Family Issues*, 1994, vol. 15, p 961; P. Amato and J. G. Gilbreth, 'Non-resident fathers and children's well-being: a meta-analysis,' *Journal of Marriage and the Family*, 1999, vol. 61, 557, p 564 as discussed in S. Gilmore, 'Contact/ shared residence and child well-being: research evidence and its implications for legal decision-making,' *International Journal of Law Policy and the Family*, 2006, vol. 20, p 344; P.D. Allison and F.F. Furstenberg, 'How marital dissolution affects children: variations by age and sex' *Developmental Psychology*, 1989, vol. 25, pp 540–49; D.A. Dawson, 'Family structure and children's health and wellbeing: data from the 1988 National Health Interview Survey on Child Health, 53 *Journal of Marriage and the Family*, 1991, vol. 53, pp 573–84; M. Maclean, *Foundations: Together and Apart, Children and Parents Experiencing Separation and Divorce*, York: Joseph Rowntree Foundation, 2004.

in respect of the pattern of care that existed during the parents' relationship may lead to problems in respect of the management of the conflict which may arise as a result of failing to look at the pre-existing exercise of parental responsibilities. In other words, there is a need for any response to difficult contact cases to take into account the pattern of responsibilities that existed before the end of the relationship, while also keeping an eye on the future arrangements. I will pursue this theme in the final section.

The 'fathers' revolution'[55] (again)

In the Green Paper preceding the Children and Adoption Act 2006 the government states its normative project in respect of contact as: 'both parents should have responsibility for and a meaningful relationship with their children after parental separation. ... both parents have equal status. ... The law is gender neutral in intent'.[56] As with the proposals for mandatory joint birth registration to confer and embed the importance of parental responsibilities, the government is keen to stress its gender neutrality in respect of parents. The claim of gender neutrality serves the important discursive function of refuting that the law is biased against fathers and reiterates that fathers and mothers have equal rights. The repeated reference to the responsibilities discourse offers the normative dimension that there should be no rights without the attenuating responsibilities. In some important ways social policy on the fusion of rights and responsibilities echoes the concerns that have been highlighted by feminist accounts of the problem with rights as being individualistic and failing to account for relationships of care. While there is clear appeal in attending to the relationships of care when articulating and instituting rights-based claims there are some concerns about reaching decisions on intractable contact disputes on the basis of the imagined future participation of fathers rather than looking to the pattern of care that existed whilst the adult relationship was intact.

The campaigning organisation Fathers Direct (now the Fatherhood Institute) has noted the emergence of a 'new narrative' arising out of government family policy 'supporting fathers' involvement in the care, education and financial support of their children. ... supporting the sharing of care and earning from the birth is important for gender equality' citing six government ministers who all reference the importance of paternal responsibilities to the welfare of children.[57]

---

[55] G. Brown, Donald Dewar Memorial Lecture at www.hm-treasury.gov.uk/press_74_06.htm.

[56] Department for Constitutional Affairs, the Department for Education and Skills and the Department for Trade and Industry, *Parental Separation*.

[57] Fathers Direct, Family sector leaders joint statement on separated family policy principles. A contribution to the Government review of separated family policy at www.fathersdirect.com, 2006, pp 1–2.

A notable contribution is Gordon Brown's (then Chancellor of the Exchequer) Donald Dewar Memorial Lecture on 12 October 2006 which leaned heavily on the concept of social, governmental and individual responsibility and in respect of fathers had the following to say:

> One priority. … is for a fathers' revolution – with more fathers becoming directly involved in their children's learning and schooling. And this is more important given the threefold increase in one parent families … and too often boys' loss of contact with male role models … And we must do more to encourage dads' role in the home.[58]

The 'fathers' revolution' embraces a 'new' model of responsible fatherhood where fathers are active participants in the socialisation and educational development of their (particularly) male children.

Brown's speech makes direct reference to the benefits of active father participation and it is clear that he sees it as being important in shaping the development of social policy and law on the family. Brown also notes the increase in one parent families and that contact between father and child is perceived as the vehicle by which father's role can be performed. Absent from the discussion about the fragmentation of families is the role that the mother plays in the post-separation context. However, that does not mean that the mother's role in facilitating contact is effaced. Indeed, it can be argued that precisely because of the prevalence of the optimism about the possibilities of and for the father–child relationship and its emphasis upon a particular construction of paternal responsibility, the mother's role in respect of care offered to the child and the facilitation of this vital relationship becomes central. As Williams has argued:

> the usage of terms such as parental responsibility can conflate what might be the goal, that of gender equity, with a *given* which is that gender inequity in relation to the actual exercising of responsibility continues.[59]

Furthermore, where poverty is a feature of family life insufficient attention is paid by the government to the:

> (gendered) relationship between financial deprivation and the ability of parents to fulfil the parenting responsibilities expected of them. It is a

---

[58] G. Brown, Donald Dewar Memorial Lecture.
[59] F. Williams 'Troubled masculinities in social policy discourses: fatherhood', in J. Popay, J. Hearn and J. Edwards (eds) *Men, Gender Divisions and Welfare*, London: Routledge, 1998, pp 63–101.

gendered relationship because ... women still carry the main day-to-day responsibility for the care and upbringing of children.[60]

Also ignored is the body of research which shows that in practical terms women may bear the brunt, in responsibility terms of the management of family life in the subsisting family and the post-separation context.[61] An Economic and Social Research Council report has found that despite dramatic changes in working patterns where women increasingly participate in paid employment, they still assume the greater responsibility for housework and childcare.[62] The following quote summarises the burdens and responsibilities faced by working mothers:

> it is predominantly women who take time off to look after sick children, including 60% of women who earn the same or more then [sic] their partners. Working mothers with children put twice as many hours into housework as their partners despite the possibility of 'role reversal' in earnings. ... Both long working hours, the burden of unpaid housework and childcare responsibilities have increased the time pressures for many women.[63]

Brown's vision for paternal responsibility relies upon a very optimistic and aspirational view of fathering based on the clearly unproven notion that men are keen to assume parenting roles which have been more traditionally per-formed by mothers. This view is highlighted in the Green Paper:

> There is a continuing shift in social attitudes, with more parents, both fathers and mothers, wanting to play active roles in their children's upbringing. More fathers wish to have active, close relationships with their children.[64]

---

[60] R. Lister, 'Children (but not women) first: New Labour, child welfare and gender' *Critical Social Policy*, 2006, vol. 26, pp 315–35, p 327.

[61] See in the legal context, e.g. J. Herring, 'Why financial orders on divorce should be unfair', *International Journal of Law, Policy and the Family*, 2005, vol. 19, pp 218–28 and in the social policy context F. Williams, 'In and beyond New Labour: towards a new political ethics of care' in *Critical Social Policy*, 2001, vol. 21, pp 467–93.

[62] S. Harness, 'Employment, work patterns and unpaid work: an analysis of trends since the 1970s' reported in the press release Mothers on the Run: Despite More Hours at Work, There's Always More to do at Home, www.esrctoday.ac.uk, 2005, p 1, accessed 27 February 2008.

[63] Ibid.

[64] Department for Constitutional Affairs, the Department for Education and Skills and the Department for Trade and Industry, Parental Separation, p 7.

It is difficult to argue against the institution of full and committed parenthood by both parents. However, this positive approach to shared care could well mean that patterns and quality of care and responsibility that existed during the parents' relationship may be ignored in difficult contact cases as ensuring contact in order that men assume their paternal responsibilities is the main aim. Contact is presumed as almost always perceived as benefiting the welfare of the child as well as being the right of the child and parent. The promotion of aspirational fatherhood occurs at the expense 'of the social importance of mothers and mothering'[65] and the family law system 'operates to limit women's ability to voice concerns about fathers care of their children'.[66] Ensuring contact is a forward- and not a backward-looking exercise. An extra burden faced by mothers if the relationship breaks down is the facilitation and accommodation of contact, and mothers are called upon to be self-regulating and conciliatory in order that the non-residential father is able to exercise the desired paternal responsibilities.[67]

Despite the fact that discourses around the importance of increasing father participation have been in the socio-political arena since the early 1990s the evidence suggests that fathers are still not reducing their hours in paid work in order to participate more fully in the home when the family is intact. Fathers who are in a position to realise more easily, than non-residential fathers, their aspirations to participate directly in the upbringing of their children do not seem to be taking up the opportunity.

Drawing upon extensive data from the British Household Panel Survey (1991–2004) a recent study has shown that 'the arrival and presence of children has very little impact on men's working hours'.[68] Indeed, fathers' hours in paid employment rise slightly. Subsequent to birth, men's participation in the labour market slightly increases from 91 per cent being employed full-time without children to 96 per cent after children.[69] Although, fathers tend to work slightly longer hours than other men the increase begins prior to the birth of the first child. Paull acknowledges the argument that suggests the increase may be to compensate for the mother's reduced hours. However, she maintains that the evidence does not support

---

[65] R. Collier, 'Fathers 4 Justice, law and the new politics of fatherhood', *Child and Family Law Quarterly*, 2005, vol. 17, pp 511–35, p 525.

[66] H. Rhoades, 'The "no contact mother": reconstructions of motherhood in the era of the "new father"', *International Journal of Law, Policy and the Family*, 2002, vol. 16, pp 71–94, p 81.

[67] See further J. Wallbank, 'Parental responsibility and the responsible parent: managing the "problem of contact"', in R. Probert, S. Gilmore and J. Herring (eds) *Responsible Parents and Parental Responsibility*, Oxford: Hart Publishing, 2009, pp 295–315.

[68] G. Paull, 'Children and Women's Hours of Work', in *Economic Journal*, 2008, vol. 118, pp 8–27, p 27.

[69] Ibid, pp 13–14.

that position.[70] Another study which examines the relationship between fathers' patterns of paid employment and their familial responsibilities also shows how the 'version of new fatherhood that posits men reducing their hours of work in order to take on more caring work is certainly not evidenced'.[71] Drawing on Margaret O'Brien, Esther Dermott argues that the 'idea of involved, caring fathers may have become culturally embedded' but accounts of fathers radically reducing their hours of work to care for their children 'are exceptional cases rather than substantial movements'.[72]

In contrast, the effect upon mothers is to drive women out of full-time employment with a reduction from four-fifths to one-third where there are pre-school children.[73] It is suggested that what the author calls the 'family gap' referring to what is in effect the difference between women without children and mothers is more significant to women's employment patterns than the gender gap.[74] Moreover, women professionals seeking to accommodate their parenting responsibilities with employment are downgrading to lower-skilled part-time roles.[75] Almost half who downgraded moved to jobs where the average employee did not have 'A' levels, leaving their higher educational achievements left unused. This is described as the 'hidden brain-drain' of professional and managerial women who become mothers.[76]

The research findings offer a disturbing picture of life for working mothers who attempt to balance their employment and home-life responsibilities, whether in subsisting families or the post-separation context. What is also alarming is the lack of public recognition given to women's efforts to contribute to the economy by negotiating and attempting to balance these two sets of demanding requirements. Fathers on the other hand are placing themselves and are being placed by government as central to the social policy agenda on the basis of their importance to children and also upon their constructed desire to be more involved in their children's lives. The fusion of fathers' rights and responsibilities is the vehicle which is elected in order to achieve father participation. When contact law is failing mothers are constructed as the source and site of the solution, therefore adding another layer of already onerous responsibilities. Although discourses forwarding the optimistic view of fathering proliferate, the research shows that

---

[70] Ibid, p 27.
[71] E. Dermott, 'What's parenthood got to do with it? Men's hours of paid work', in *British Journal of Sociology*, 2006, vol. 57, pp 619–34, p 629.
[72] Ibid, citing M. O'Brien *Shared Caring: Bringing Fathers into the Frame*, London: EOC, 2005.
[73] Ibid.
[74] Ibid, p 8.
[75] S. Connolly and M. Gregory, 'Moving down: women's part-time work and occupational change in Britain 1991–2001, *Economic Journal*, 2008, vol. 118, pp 52–76.
[76] Ibid, p 52 drawing upon the Equal Opportunities Commission, *Britain's Hidden Brain Drain – Final Report*, Manchester: Equal Opportunities Commission, 2005.

rather than there being a 'fathers' revolution', in practice there seems to be a good degree of inertia. Questions may therefore be raised about the extent to which patterns of care and responsibilities which existed during a relationship might impact upon the way mothers approach the issue of contact. Additionally, it is also necessary to interrogate the trends in family law which draw upon the notions of collaboration, cooperation and conciliation.

Recognising parental investment in contact disputes

The argument I wish to make here is that parental attitudes to contact are likely to be influenced by the pattern of care-giving and the responsibilities assumed which existed prior to the relationship breakdown. It is crucial therefore that both the relative investments and types of responsibilities assumed by mothers and fathers are taken into account when considering the level, form and degree of contact. The notion of investment I use was in part influenced by Herring's model which he calls 'relationship-based welfare' and is designed to get away from:

> conceiving the problem as a clash between children and parents and in terms of weighing two conflicting interests, and towards seeing it rather as deciding what is a *proper* parent–child relationship.[77]

His model rests on the idea that children's welfare is advanced by living in 'a fair and just relationship with each parent, preserving the rights of each, but with the child's welfare at the forefront of the family's concern'.[78] While providing a model that attends to all parties' interests and simultaneously with child welfare, he acknowledges one of the major problems that 'promotion of the welfare of children has been used to promote the rights in particular of fathers, and the sacrifices … all too often fall on mothers'.[79] He therefore advocates the avoidance of gendered stereotypes in deciding what reasonable expectations are and what constitutes a 'fair relationship'.[80] The decision about what constitutes a 'proper' parent–child relationship draws upon the idea (if not the reality) that the 'proper' father is one who participates and contact is seen as the way in which this much lauded relationship can develop. The fusion of rights and responsibilities has been seized upon by fathers' rights groups in order to show how the law of contact is

---

[77] J. Herring, 'The Human Rights Act and the welfare principle in family law— conflicting or complementary?', *Child and Family Law Quarterly*, 1999, vol. 11, pp 223–35, p 233 emphasis added.

[78] Ibid.

[79] Ibid. citing F. Olsen, 'Children's rights: some feminist approaches to the United Nations Covenant on the Rights of the Child' in P. Alston, S. Parker and J. Seymour (eds) *Children, Rights and the Law*, London: Clarendon, 1992.

[80] Ibid.

profoundly unjust because of the way it prevents them from living out the normative ideal of the 'proper' father. Additionally, problems in respect of contact are also constructed as residing with mothers. Herring's model therefore involves the law in a process of imagining what constitutes a 'fair and just relationship'[81] between the child and each parent, 'preserving the rights of each, but with the child's welfare at the forefront of the family's concern'.[82] While offering a sophisticated and subtly nuanced way of conceiving and responding to family disputes, like social policy and law's emphasis on the ideal post-separation family, the model could be said to be future oriented.

> It is not clear from Herring's model how patterns of care that existed whilst the relationship existed might be taken account of in deciding what constitutes a 'fair and just' relationship. However, he later clarifies his position on relationship-based welfare by unequivocally stating that: 'Herring's approach is less straightforward because it requires an understanding of the nature of the relationship in the past, and the foreseeable future'.[83]

It is likely however, that Herring's relationship-based welfare would involve courts making decisions based on what the 'proper' relationship *should* be rather than accounting for what the relationship *is* and responding on that basis. An example of this danger is provided by *Re S*[84] where the resident mother had provided the consistent primary care for her disabled child. She failed in her appeal against the condition that she be prohibited from moving to Cornwall in order that the child's relationship and contact with the father be preserved which was regarded as in the child's best interests.

Herring recognises that welfare discourses have been used to promote fathers' rights and that gender stereotypes of the expectations of mothers and fathers should not be used. However, the fusion of rights and responsibilities (which is arguably to some extent at least consonant with the relationship-based welfare approach) has meant that the 'proper' parent–child relationship is one which relies on the aspirational view of fatherhood – is imagined and future oriented, with women bearing the brunt of more onerous measures to ensure that contact takes place. Contact is taken as an end in itself and the aim of contact law and new models of dispute resolution are tightly focused on the future rather than the past.

The developing models of resolution and management of contact disputes may exacerbate rather than ameliorate conflict between separating parents.

---

[81] Ibid.
[82] Ibid.
[83] J. Herring (2nd edn) *Family Law*, Oxford: Longman, 2007, p 401.
[84] [2003] 1 FCR 138.

For example, as Trinder has stated although parents will have a wide range of needs in the contact context in-court conciliation as a method of dealing with difficult cases, has the very simple goal of 'reaching an agreement about when and how contact will occur'.[85] In seeking to achieve this goal courts focus on the future rather than the past for fear of being confronted with a wide range of situations that they cannot deal with. Bailey-Harris *et al.* have concluded that judges strive to maintain some form of contact even in cases of serious violence, tending to look to the future rather than back at past mistakes.[86] Additionally, professionals engaged in contact disputes find it important to draw a line under the past and to focus on 'being constructive' for 'the benefit of the child for the future'.[87]

However, by focusing on the need to reach agreement and promoting the ideal responsible parent, the gendered nature of parenting which occurred during the relationship is allowed to be ignored. Mothers and fathers are highly likely, as evidenced by the research, to have very different experiences of the 'business of day-to-day care' of children.[88] Katherine Gieve, an experienced family law practitioner, argues that 'in most families the management, the gathering together of tasks and the holding on to and organising children is done by mothers.'[89] She does however recognise that fathers are capable of assuming the primary carer role and clearly some men will. However, she maintains that gender neutrality suppresses the gendered reality of day-to-day care patterns. Gieve argues that insufficient attention is paid to the relative roles played by mothers and fathers and also to the support that the primary carer may need on the end of the relationship.[90] She strongly advocates that parents' as well as children's needs should be attended to in the resolution of contact disputes and, at the moment, attention to the gendered reality of parental roles and the needs of both primary and non-resident parents are ignored.[91]

Martha Fineman's seminal book also posits a strong argument for the adoption of the 'Mother/Child' dyad as metaphor for representing the

[85] L. Trinder, 'In-court conciliation: brief encounter or permanent resolution', in Thorpe L.J. and R. Budden, (eds) *Durable Solutions: The Collected Papers of the 2005 Dartington Hall Conference*, Bristol: Jordan Publishing, 2005, pp 35–42, p 38.

[86] R. Bailey-Harris, J. Barron and J. Pearce, 'From utility to rights? The presumption of contact in practice', *International Journal of Law, Policy and the Family*, 1999, vol. 13, pp 111–31.

[87] Trinder, 'In-Court conciliation' citing interview data with a District Judge in L.J. Thorpe and R. Budden, (eds) *Durable Solutions*.

[88] K. Gieve, 'Mothers and fathers', in L.J. Thorpe and R. Budden, (eds) *Durable Solutions*, pp 81–101, p 85.

[89] Ibid.

[90] Ibid.

[91] Ibid.

'specific practice of social and emotional responsibility'.[92] She makes clear that fathers as well as mothers can and should assume the nurturing role that is more traditionally associated with motherhood. 'To be a nurturing father is to concede the importance of mothering.'[93] Moreover, she argues that if fathers seek legal rights to children they must act as mothers in the 'stereo-typical nurturing sense of that term – that is, engaged in caretaking'.[94] Consonant with the current social policy aspirational view of contemporary fatherhood practices, Fineman advocates the no-rights-without-responsibilities approach.

She has built on this work by arguing for the centralisation of inevitable dependency in respect of personal relationships and the responsibilities of the state.[95] Her argument is that in the USA the ability to 'take responsi-bility' financially for one's self and family is the 'key qualification for autonomy'.[96] It is therefore a burden borne within the private sphere, invariably by women. The meeting of these dependency needs incurs a 'collective or social debt' precisely because of the inevitability and universality of dependency and the reliance of society upon the work performed in this respect.[97]

Although Jo Bridgeman notes the 'perhaps pragmatic'[98] limitation of Fineman's work for focusing on 'inter-generational dependency in the parent/child and adult child/parent relationships rather than presenting a more radical critique' of the 'nature of inevitable dependencies',[99] Fineman retains a very strong case for looking at the specific practices and responsi-bilities that are assumed in relation to child welfare. In her earlier work she pointed out that fathers' responsibilities to children are all too often cast in terms of their financial duty to provide for their children and that fathers are right to challenge the 'primacy of the economic emphasis'.[100] By casting men primarily as economic providers other connections between children and fathers are also frequently elided.

However, in practical terms the law is often forced to address the question about how to treat gender differences between women and men when women are the primary caretakers and men the primary earners. Writing on the US context Pamela Laufer-Ukeles comes up with a cogent answer:

---

[92] M. Fineman, *The Neutered Mother, the Sexual Family and Other Twentieth Century Tragedies*, London: Routledge, 1995, p 234.
[93] Ibid, p 205.
[94] Ibid, p 235.
[95] M. Fineman, *The Autonomy Myth: A Theory of Dependency*, New York: Routledge, 2004.
[96] J. Bridgeman, book review in *Feminist Legal Studies*, 2006, vol. 14, pp 407–10, pp 407–8.
[97] Fineman, '*The Autonomy Myth*'.
[98] Bridgeman, book review, p 408.
[99] Ibid.
[100] Fineman, *The Neutered Mother*, p 207.

Modern divorce law, in its pursuit of gender neutrality, does not sufficiently address such differences. ... The traditional caretaker role must be affirmatively recognized and revalued to give caretakers the dignity they deserve commensurate with the important societal contributions they provide. Caretaking provides an important and needed contribution to society by supporting dependants, a job which would otherwise fall to the state.[101]

When the relationship between the parents breaks down the primary earner will continue to benefit financially from their financial role in ways which the resident parent may not. In many cases women will have given up the opportunity for a full-time career in order to care for children and will continue to do so as highlighted in the empirical research discussed above. My notion of parental investment is designed to recognise the particular responsibilities which were assumed by each parent during their relationship, rather than merely on the aspirational view of fatherhood and the goal of reaching agreement on future arrangements. The recognition of specific parental investments should be the starting point for resolving contact disputes in order to better account for the relative needs and interests of parents and children when the parent's relationships end.

Moreover, when difficult cases come before the courts judges would be able to articulate their decisions in relation to the relative investments made by both parents and include the recognition that the assumption of economic responsibilities is one form of investment which is made and that it is attributed with a value of its own. However, where either parent's investment has occurred solely at the level of providing the day-to-day care, with one being rather less involved in hands-on caring, that person's concerns about capacity for caring should be listened to and taken seriously in order to protect the interests of children. Additionally, where one parent works full-time and the other cares full-time it is unlikely that a radical shift in these patterns of investment would benefit either parent or the child and make for hostile-free contact. I am not suggesting that future contact should necessarily reflect the pattern of care that existed during the relationship. Rather, that the responsibilities which were assumed during the relationship should provide a starting point for the negotiations as to an appropriate level of contact. In this way, fathers' and mothers' relative investments would be acknowledged and also provide a framework of expectations in respect of their future investments to child welfare and as a way of renegotiating contact arrangements where relationships of care evolve. In short, where contact

---

[101] P. Laufer-Ukeles 'Selective recognition of gender difference in the law: revaluing the caretaker role', *Harvard Journal of Law and Gender*, 2008, vol. 31, no. 1, pp 1–64, p 3.

is disputed courts need to stress to parents the importance of their specific contributions to the child and acknowledge the importance of both the financial support offered and especially the hands-on care of the child. Agreements about future contact arrangements are perhaps more likely to be achieved if patterns of care and investment made during the relationship provide the starting point for negotiation and may help to quell any insecurities experienced by the parties.

However, as the above discussion shows the term investment may in itself raise important gender issues. Arguably, the term 'investment' has inherent in it the idea that one gets a return on the investment made.[102] For example, non-resident fathers have sought to emphasise the link between the financial investments made in respect of child maintenance and contact in order to show themselves as responsible fathers who are prevented from valuable contact because of weak and ineffective contact law. In other words, fathers who are able to show themselves as being financially responsible for their children have argued that weak contact law fails to provide them with the reward of contact with their children. Resident parents, usually mothers, will see the failure to pay child support on separation as evidence of the lack of commitment to the child with fathers forfeiting their right to contact. As Carol Smart has argued 'financial support is taken as a proxy for love particularly where fathers are concerned because the idea that a "good" father is predominantly a good provider is still a powerful motif for many parents'.[103]

The family courts currently treat child support and contact as separate issues but as work such as Smart's shows both mothers and fathers draw upon a 'moral calculus' in respect of the non-resident parent's willingness to continue to provide financial support when the relationship ends.[104] There is no doubt that a primary earner's financial contribution to a child matters and counts for mothers and fathers as an important investment made to the child from which the child benefits. However, whether or not the person responsible for financial support continues or reneges on her or his responsibilities, the person (usually a mother) with primary care will remain primarily responsible for the care and support of the child.

Arguably then, the investment made through the provision of hands-on care has a higher moral value and the everyday gendered work that women often perform must feature highly in contact disputes. Here I am drawing on Selma Sevenhuijsen's work, where she describes the ethics-of-care approach

---

[102] I am particularly grateful to Shazia Choudhry and the various contributors to this edition for this point. As discussed at the Rights, Gender and Family Law conference at Oxford University 26 September 2008.

[103] C. Smart, 'Parenting disputes, gender conflict and the courts', in L.J. Thorpe and R. Budden (eds) *Durable Solutions*, p 107.

[104] Ibid.

to family life. An ethics-of-care approach is inevitably bound to concrete realities and emphasises the moral activity of active caring.[105] Of course as Richard Collier's chapter in this volume shows, fathers also have emotional investments in children and I do not wish to downgrade either the importance for fathers of the emotional relationships they have with children or the significance of emotions in contact disputes. As Collier's work shows, fathers are driven by a wide range of emotions when experiencing relationship breakdown and to a great extent their responses to separation will be driven by a sense of loss or perception of betrayal of the emotional investment they have in their relationships with children. Collier urges a fuller engagement with and reconceptualisation of the gendered male subject in respect of the relationship between how fathers '*emotionally* feel' and how they '*rationally* act'.[106] He convincingly argues for 'rethinking how the issues of emotion and the psychological and sociological dynamics of separation referred to above are dealt with in family justice processes' and how social policy in respect of contact and the gendered realities of separation might be developed.[107] There is undoubted value in this project.

As the above discussion shows there are several, not unproblematic ways of conceptualising investment – as financial support, as emotion, as emotion combined with hands-on care. My own position in respect of investment is that social policy and law should both recognise and respond to the gendered pattern of the investments that existed during the relationship. Where one parent has overwhelmingly committed to one or other kind of investment, the investment of hands-on care should be attributed with the value it deserves. A failure to recognise the value of caring work and to place undue emphasis on fathers' prospective willingness and ability to provide adequate care is likely to exacerbate parental conflict which is neither good for the child or the parents' post-separation relationship. Quite simply, it is unrealistic to conceive it possible that the past can be left behind in contact disputes, nor should it be. My point is that although the aspiration that both parents share the day-to-day hands-on care for the child is a laudable one, the legal responses to contact needs to recognise, value and attend to the gendered realities of mothers' and fathers' lives while the relationship existed.

Although Fineman herself recognises that law is a 'weak tool' with which to bring about her utopian re-visioning of a society where all members are concerned with exercising and sharing responsibility for

---

[105] As highlighted by Jo Bridgeman at Rights, Gender and Family Law conference. S. Sevenhuijsen, *Citizenship and the Ethics of Care: Feminist Considerations about Justice, Morality and Politics*, London: Routledge, 1998.

[106] See R. Collier below, p 136.

[107] Ibid.

children,[108] currently contact law is rather too concerned with the 'utopian re-visioning' of society based upon the aspirational view of fatherhood than with recognising and acting upon the basis of gendered reality of mothers' and fathers' lives.

Conclusion

This chapter has drawn together a range of material to demonstrate how a wide range of discourses support the idea that in the context of family law, and particularly in relation to the law of contact, that there should be no rights without responsibilities. The fusion of rights and responsibilities has allowed fathers to present 'moral claims to fatherhood ... into a new recognisable narrative'.[109] In putting together these moral claims, fathers have been quick to respond to the discredited rights-based approach which featured highly throughout the 1990s and into the twenty-first century.

They have been aided to a great extent by welfare discourses which have lauded the benefits of the father–child relationship and also by social policy which has constructed an aspirational view of fatherhood where fathers claim to desire to be increasingly involved in the practical and emotional aspects of childcare. However, as the research evidence has clearly demonstrated the extent to which fathers are taking up these responsibilities is in some doubt. Rather, what is provided is a utopian vision of gender-neutral patterns of care and responsibilities. It is the case that familial responsibilities remain highly gendered and that the existence of differences in the ways that women and men contribute to family life during the parents' relationship, may well impact upon the way that they come to address the issue of contact at the end of it.

The evolving methods for dealing with disputed contact cases focus on the main aim of reaching an agreement over contact without taking into account the gendered investments made by the parents before relationship breakdown. This is an important omission as it is clear that the relative contributions made by parents during this time will impact on how that role is likely to be fulfilled in the immediate short term. Of course, courts are not just concerned with the short term and they are seeking to lay down contact arrangements which will meet the longer-term interests of children.

While acknowledging that there are many ways of conceptualising the notion of investment (some of which are not altogether unproblematic), I believe that it is imperative for courts to both acknowledge and value the patterns of parental investment which may have been in place for a number

---

[108] Fineman, *The Neutered Mother*, p 232.
[109] Smart, 'The ethic of justice strikes back', in Diduck and O'Donovan, *Feminist Perspectives on Family Law*, p 135.

of years – including the assumption of a mainly financial role, while laying down the normative expectations of parental roles in respect of longer-term and evolving contact arrangements. As I have suggested, although it is very difficult to argue against the fusion of rights and responsibilities, the research shows that this is rather a long way from the reality and the law of contact might better attend to the needs of children and parents by recognising this.

Chapter 6

Fatherhood, law and fathers' rights: Rethinking the relationship between gender and welfare

Richard Collier

INTRODUCTION

'What has been missing from policy and reform discussions', Martha Fineman has suggested, 'is a debate about the nature of fatherhood' and 'the transformation of the role of the father in response to changing expectations, norms and practices'.[1] 'How', she asks, does a 'desire for gender neutrality and the ideal of egalitarianism play a role in the creation of *a new set of norms for fatherhood*'?[2] This chapter seeks to explore these questions in the context of recent debates in England and Wales around post-separation contact. More specifically, focusing on the area of fathers' rights, law and responsibility, it considers the interrelationship between gender, rights and welfare within one particularly high-profile and politically sensitive area of family law. Diverse critics of developments around fathers' rights politics,[3]

---

[1] M. Fineman, *The Autonomy Myth*, New York: The New Press, 2004, p 195.

[2] Ibid, my emphasis.

[3] This critical literature is now vast. For simply a flavour of the debates and concerns: J. Crowley, *Defiant Dads: Fathers' Rights Activism in America*, Ithaca: Cornell University Press, 2008; R. Collier and S. Sheldon, *Fathers Rights Activism and Legal Reform*, Oxford: Hart, 2006; M. Kaye and J. Tolmie, 'Discoursing dads: the rhetorical devices of fathers' rights groups', *Melbourne University Law Review*, 1998, vol 22, p 184: S. Boyd, 'Demonizing mothers: fathers' rights discourses in child custody law reform processes', *Journal of the Association for Research in Mothering*, 2004, vol 6 (1), p 52; H. Rhoades, 'The "non contact mother": reconstructions of motherhood in the era of the new father', *International Journal of Law, Policy and the Family*, 2002, vol 16, p 72; H. Rhoades, 'The rise of shared parenting laws – a critical reflection', *Canadian Journal of Family Law*, 2002, vol 19, p 75; C. Smart, 'Losing the struggle for another voice: the case of family law', *Dalhousie Law Journal*, 1995, vol 18(2), p 173; C. Smart, 'Equal shares: rights for fathers or recognition for children?', *Critical Social Policy*, 2004, vol 24(4), p 484; S. Boyd and C.F. Young, 'Who influences family law reform? Discourses on motherhood and fatherhood in legislative reform debates in Canada', *Studies in Law Politics and Society* 2002, p 43; R. Graycar, 'Law reform by frozen chook: family law reform for the new millennium?', *Melbourne University Law Review*, 2000, vol 24, p 737; R. Collier, 'Fathers 4 Justice, law and the new politics of fatherhood', *Child and Family Law*

troubled by the arguments advanced by, and possible impact of, an increasingly vocal international fathers' rights movement',[4] have suggested that there is a pressing need to articulate what significance adopting a rights-based approach might have upon the idea of welfare and its practical application.[5] Concern has been expressed, in particular, about the implications of fathers' rights activism in terms of its influence on legal policy and practice, and for women and children especially. Within one strand of literature, the resurgence of fathers' claims in the legal arena has been interpreted as something akin to a 'backlash' to feminism, a problematic, troubling and regressive shift in the terrain of family politics.[6]

This chapter seeks to contribute to these debates by considering how an embedding of gender neutrality and ideal of egalitarianism in law has played a key role 'in the creation of a new set of norms for fatherhood' within the context of shifting understandings of fathers' rights and responsibilities around post-separation parenting. Drawing on a rather different literature from that which has informed much of the discussion to date, I shall suggest that the present political and policy debate around fathers' rights has been marked by profound contradictions and tensions. On closer examination, these reflect a deep-seated cultural uncertainty about the nature of contemporary fathering itself.

The structure of the argument is as follows. First, I will briefly ground this discussion of fathers' rights in the context of a broader, and multi-layered, 'fragmentation' of fatherhood in law. This theme is discussed in more detail in the book *Fragmenting Fatherhood: A Socio-Legal Study* and it is explored here in specific relation to these debates around separated fathers.[7] Second,

---

Quarterly, 2005, vol 17, p 511; J.E. Crowley, 'Adopting "equality tools" from the toolboxes of their predecessors: the fathers' rights movement in the United States', in R. Collier and S. Sheldon, ibid. For A. Diduck and F. Kaganas, *Family Law, Gender and the State: Text, Cases and Materials* (2nd edn, Oxford: Hart 2006), the 'fathers' rights campaigns [do] appear to have had the effect of galvanising the government and the courts into action against mothers whom they see as obstructive', p 561.

4 On the idea of a 'movement' see R. Collier and S. Sheldon (eds), ibid, Ch 1; also M. Messner, *Politics of Masculinities: Men in Movements*, London: Sage, 1997; A. Gavanas, *Fatherhood Politics in the United States: Masculinity, Sexuality, Race and Marriage*, Illinois: University of Illinois Press, 2004.

5 See further Ch 1.

6 M. Flood, 'Backlash: angry men's movements', in S.E. Rossie (ed.) *The Battle and Backlash Rage On: Why Feminism cannot be Obsolete*, Philadelphia: Xlibris Press, 2004. Contrast: S. Boyd, 'Backlash and the construction of legal knowledge: the case of child custody law', *Windsor YearBook Access Justice*, 2001, vol 20, p 141; S. Boyd, 'Backlash against feminism: Canadian custody and access reform debates of the late twentieth century', *Canadian Journal of Women and Law*, 2004, vol 16(2), p 255.

7 R. Collier and S. Sheldon, *Fragmenting Fatherhood: A Socio-Legal Study*, 2008, Oxford: Hart.

tracing changing ideas of the 'good' (separated) father in law, I suggest that it is misleading to see the increased political and cultural prominence of fathers' rights groups simply in terms of a backlash to feminism. It is inter-linked, rather, to a redrawing of social and legal understandings of what it means to be a father and what responsibilities and obligations should accrue to that status. In developing this argument, I proceed, third, to highlight some of the issues emerging from recent studies of fathers' rights groups This research, which was conducted in the UK and internationally, concerned the evolution of these debates about law, rights and gender.[8] Fourth, by way of conclusion, I will readdress the question of what a 'new set of norms for fatherhood' might look like by turning to the broader reconfiguration of ideas about men and masculinity within family policy, a theme that, I sug-gest, has much to offer in developing our understanding of the relationship between rights, gender and family law.

Fragmenting fatherhood: a context

Against the backdrop of significant social, economic and cultural change, as well as shifting understandings of scope and purpose of family law and policy,[9] discussion of fatherhood in recent years has been marked by a heightened political debate about fathers' rights and responsibilities in law. The question of what is happening 'to' fathers and fatherhood has become a central feature of more general contestations about the parameters of the (heterosexual) family.[10] Responding to these debates, a body of socio-legal scholarship, drawing on developments in legal and social theory, has sought to explore the way fathers have been understood, constructed and regulated within law.[11] Complementing the now well-established literature on

[8] I will, in the following, also make reference to the preliminary findings of a research project conducted in England Wales that traced the evolution of debates about law reform and fathers' rights since 2002: R. Collier, 'The UK fathers' rights movement and law: report to the British Academy', British Academy rlf/SRF/2005/ 88 (2008) (unpublished). See further R. Collier, *The Man of Law: Essays on Law, Men and Gender*, London: Routledge, 2009 forthcoming.

[9] For discussion, see S. Boyd, 'Legal regulation of families in changing societies', in A. Sarat (ed.), *The Blackwell Companion to Law and Society*, London: Blackwell 2004.

[10] See, e.g. Centre for Social Justice, *The Family Law Review Interim Report*, London, Centre for Social Justice, 2008, on the idea of 'guesting fathers'; I. Duncan Smith, 'Now they want to abolish fatherhood', *Mail on Sunday* (18 November 2007) News 29; N. Dennis and G. Erdos, *Families Without Fatherhood*, London: Institute of Economic Affairs, 1993; For the US context, see: D. Bla-kenhorn, *Fatherless America: Confronting Our Most Urgent Social Problem* New York: Basic Books, 1995; cf C.R. Daniels (ed.), *Lost Fathers: The Politics of Fatherlessness in America* New York: St Martin's Press, 1998.

[11] E.g. Collier and Sheldon, 2008, op cit; N. Dowd, *Redefining Fatherhood*, New York: New York University Press, 2000.

fatherhood in the fields of sociology and social policy, history, popular culture, psychology, gender and family studies,[12] work has explored diverse aspects of the relationship between fatherhood and law. Elsewhere, I have charted significant shifts in how law has approached the responsibilities of fathers within marriage,[13] tracing the emergence of an engaged father discourse that reflects the growing concern at a policy level, in particular over the past decade, to promote father-inclusive practice in the delivery of services.[14] It is in relation to policy developments around men's post-separation parenting and non-residential fathers, however, that it becomes possible to see, in a particularly clear way, how the reshaping of the contours of the 'good' separated father[15] in law has informed a heightened politicisation of fatherhood within the legal area.

These shifts must be placed within the broader context of how law has historically approached fathers. Legal understandings of fatherhood have evolved unevenly over time, interacting in complex ways with the economic, cultural and political contexts in which ideas about parenthood and, importantly, childhood are produced. Considering how ideas about paternal rights and responsibility emerge as distinctive *kinds* of social problems,[16] it is important to note that legal approaches to fatherhood are themselves highly context specific. There is no 'one' way fatherhood has been understood and regulated within English law and social policy and various ways of awarding paternal rights and responsibilities have been foregrounded at different times, in different areas of law. Marriage has of course historically played a central role in how law has sought to attach men to their children.[17]

[12] See further Collier and Sheldon, op cit, Ch 1.
[13] R. Collier, 'Engaging fathers? Responsibility, law and the problem of fatherhood', in J. Bridgeman, C. Lind and H. Keating (eds), *Responsibility, Law and the Family*, Aldershot: Ashgate Publishing, 2008. See further Collier and Sheldon, op cit, Ch 4.
[14] See further J. Page, G. Whiting and C. Maclean, *A Review of How Fathers Can Be Better Recognised and Supported Through DCSF Policy*, London: Department for Children, School and Families, 2008; D. Bartlett, A. Burgess and K. Jones, *A Toolkit for Developing Father-inclusive Practice*, London: Fathers Direct, 2007; A. Burgess and D. Bartlett, *Working With Fathers*, London: Fathers Direct, 2004; The Fatherhood Institute, *The Difference a Dad Makes*, London: The Fatherhood Institute, 2007: K. Stanley, *Daddy Dearest? Active Fatherhood and Public Policy*, London: Institute for Public Policy Research, 2005.
[15] See further, and generally, G.B. Wilson, 'The non-resident parental role for separated fathers: a review', *International Journal of Law, Policy and the Family*, 2006, p 1.
[16] J.I. Kitsuse and M. Spector, 'The definition of social problems', *Social Problems*, 1973, vol 20(4) p 407; N. Rose and M. Valverde, 'Governed by law?', *Social and Legal Studies*, 1998, vol 7(4) p 541. See also: J. Scourfield and M. Drakeford, 'New Labour and the "problem of men"', *Critical Social Policy*, 2002, vol 22, p 619.
[17] C. Smart, '"There is of course the distinction dictated by nature": law and the problem of paternity', in M. Stanworth (ed.), *Reproductive Technologies: Gender, Motherhood and Medicine* (Feminist Perspectives Series) Cambridge: Polity, 1987.

However, a complex amalgam of economic, cultural, technological and political change, as well as shifts in the nature of law's governance,[18] has served to challenge the possibility of relying on marriage as a way of grounding legal fatherhood and the rights and responsibilities that have traditionally accompanied it.

In relation to marriage, more specifically, we have moved from a position whereby, at the end of the nineteenth century, married fathers were invested with sole rights of custody and control over their legitimate children at common law,[19] to one in which, by the mid-twentieth century, fathers were reconstituted primarily as familial 'breadwinners'.[20] The decline, if not demise, of this father-as-breadwinner model has been well-documented,[21] and, in more recent years, encapsulated in the idea of the 'new fatherhood', it has been widely suggested that contemporary fathers are now expected to have, and to desire, a closer, more emotionally involved and nurturing relationship with their children. A significant shift has occurred, in short, described as a move from 'cash to care' in how fathers have been repositioned within law and policy,[22] a development that reflects changing understandings of the place of the father within child welfare and development.[23] It is this new fatherhood ideal that has informed a range of developments relating to men's parenting both within subsisting relationships (for example, in debates around work–life balance) and, importantly, post-separation parenting.

[18] Note, e.g. J. Dewar, 'Family law and its discontents', *International Journal of Law Policy and the family* 2000, vol 14 p 59; J. Dewar, 'The normal chaos of family law', *Modern Law Review*, 1998, vol 61 p 467; R van Krieken, 'The "best interests of the child" and parental separation: On the "civilising of parents"', *Modern Law Review*, 2005, vol 68 (1) p 25; R van Krieken, 'Legal informalism, power and liberal governance', *Social and Legal Studies* 2001, vol 19(1) p 5.

[19] Blackstone's *Commentaries on the Law of England*, 1765 Vol 1: 453; See, e.g. *Re Agar Ellis* (1883) 24 Ch D 317, per Bowen LJ p 338.

[20] Note, e.g. H. Land, 'The family wage', *Feminist Review* 1980 vol 6 p 55; R.W. Connell, *Gender and Power*, Cambridge: Polity Press, 1987, p 106; S. Whitehead, *Men and Masculinities*, Cambridge: Polity, 2002 pp 124–38; S Coltrane, *Family Man: Fatherhood, Housework and Gender Equality*, Oxford: Oxford University Press, 1996; R. Collier, *Masculinity, Law and the Family*, London: Routledge, 1995; R. Collier, 'A hard time to be a father? Law, policy and family practices', *Journal of Law & Society* 2001, vol 28(4), p 520.

[21] R. Crompton, *Restructuring Gender Relations and Employment: The Decline of the Male Breadwinner*, Oxford: Oxford University Press, 1999; see further J. Lewis, 'Individualisation, assumptions about the existence of an adult worker model and the shift towards contractualism', in A. Carling, S. Duncan and R. Edwards (eds), *Analysing Families: Morality and Rationality in Policy and Practice*, London: Routledge, 2002.

[22] B. Hobson (ed.), *Making Men into Fathers: Men, Masculinities and the Social Politics of Fatherhood*, Cambridge: Cambridge University Press, 2002.

[23] M. Lamb, *The Role of the Father in Child Development*, New York: John Wiley, 1997.

In the latter context, the dominant representation of paternal responsibility within the 'new consensus' in family policy[24] that evolved from the late 1980s around the desirability of post-separation contact has drawn explicitly on beliefs about both the father as financial provider and the new father as emotionally engaged, hands-on carer.[25] Studies of what being a 'good' father entails in law have explored the indeterminate nature of the welfare of the child as 'first and paramount consideration',[26] as amended and elaborated as a result of the Human Rights Act 1998,[27] and sought to unpack historical shifts in ideas of parental rights and responsibilities in law.[28] It would be misleading to see this transition from rights to responsibility, however, in terms of a linear interpretation of change, a straightforwardly progressive narrative of 'modernisation'. The reconstruction of fatherhood is more complex – and contradictory – than it may seem at first, an issue with particular significance for understanding the rise of fathers' rights politics in the legal arena.

It is possible, charting how ideas about fatherhood have changed in law and policy, to make two points at this stage. These concern, first, the reconstruction of a set of normative beliefs about fatherhood in law and, second, the implications of these shifts for the political terrain around fathers' rights and responsibilities in the context of post-separation parenting and in relation to the embedding of ideas of gender neutrality and egalitarianism in law referred to by Fineman. In the next section, I explore each of these issues.

Politics, rights and equality – reconstructing the 'good father'

The suggestion put forward by many fathers' rights groups, as well as some theorists of individualisation,[29] has been that this move entailed a simple diminution or displacement of the figure of the father in law. Such an interpretation is misleading however. Normative ideas of fatherhood have been transformed, rather, in ways marked by a refiguring of a nexus of assumptions that had historically constituted fathers as a desirable presence within

---

[24] For discussion see, e.g. S. Day Sclater and C. Piper (eds), *Undercurrents of Divorce*, Aldershot: Ashgate, 1999.

[25] M. O'Brien, *Shared Caring: Bringing Fathers into the Frame*, Manchester: Equal Opportunities Commission, 2005. See also M. O'Brien and I. Shemilt, *Working Fathers: Earning and Caring*, Manchester: Equal Opportunities Commission, 2003.

[26] H. Reece, 'The paramountcy principle: consensus or construct?', *Current Legal Problems* 1996, vol 49 p 267; J. Eekelaar, *Family Law and Personal Life*, Oxford, Oxford University Press, 2006, p 140–44.

[27] S. Choudhry and H. Fenwick, 'Taking the rights of parents and children seriously – confronting the welfare principle under the Human Rights Act', *Oxford Journal of Legal Studies*, 2005, vol 25, p 453.

[28] Note, e.g. Eekelaar, op cit.

[29] U. Beck and E. Beck-Gernsheim, *Individualization*, London: Sage, 2002; U. Beck and E. Beck-Gernsheim, *The Normal Chaos of Love*, Cambridge: Polity, 1995. Contrast the reading of C. Smart, *Personal Life*, Cambridge: Polity, 2007, Ch 1.

families in the first place. This has involved a fragmentation of beliefs about what Sally Sheldon and I have termed,[30] first, the father as *heterosexual* (the sexual father); second, about the father as family *breadwinner* (the worker father, as above); and, third, around the idea of the father as a figure of *authority* within the household (or the father as patriarch). Each of these ideas, and the gendered associations they bring with them, has been subject to extensive critique. Just as a growing sociological literature has questioned the conceptual limits and political ambiguity of the new fatherhood ideal,[31] however, two more specific challenges have served to further challenge and undermine earlier ideas of fatherhood and, in so doing, reshape understandings of paternal responsibility and rights.

First, social and economic shifts in patterns of employment and a restructuring of the workforce (and the workplace) have reshaped cultural ideas of fatherhood in ways, I shall suggest below, mediated by assumptions about class, race and ethnicity. A related commodification of many aspects of masculinity, and cultural problematising of the parenting practices of both sexes, interlinked with changing ideas about children and childhood, risk and anxiety, has further refigured understandings of what constitutes a 'good' (and, especially, a 'safe') father.[32] What has resulted is an ideal of fatherhood informed by contrasting ideas about men and masculinity[33] and marked by both change and continuity. There exists, for example, continuity with earlier times in certain aspects of men's family practices, not least in how traditional gendered divisions remain structured and embedded within many households.[34] A wealth of research evidence attests, however, to how the experience of fathering, and of being fathered, is, for many men, women and children, in certain aspects at least, qualitatively different from earlier moments.[35]

---

[30] Collier and Sheldon, op cit, 2008, Ch 4.

[31] C. Haywood and M. Mac an Ghaill, *Men and Masculinities: Theory, Research and Social Practice*, Buckingham: Open University Press, 2003; C. Smart and B. Neale, '"I hadn't really thought about it": new identities/new fatherhoods' in J. Seymour and P. Bagguley (eds), *Relating Intimacies: Power and Resistance*, Basingstoke: Palgrave Macmillan, 1999.

[32] F. Furedi, *Paranoid Parenting*, London: Allen Lane, 2002; R. Collier, 'Anxious parenthood, the vulnerable child and the "good father": reflections on the legal regulation of the relationship between men and children', in J. Bridgeman and D. Monk (eds), *Feminist Perspectives on Child Law*, London; Cavendish, 2001.

[33] See Scourfield and Drakeford, op cit.

[34] See Wallbank, Ch 5 in this volume.

[35] For simply a flavour of this literature, see: W. Hatten, L. Vinter and R. Williams, *Dads on Dads: Needs and Expectations at Home and Work*, Manchester: Equal Opportunities Commission, 2002; J. Warin *et al.*, *Fathers, Work and Family Life*, London: Family Policy Studies Centre, 1999; Equal Opportunities Commission, *Fathers: Balancing Work and Family*, Manchester: Equal Opportunities Commission, 2003; C. Lewis, *A Man's Place in the Home: Fathers and Families in the UK*, York: Joseph Rowntree Foundation, 2000.

Second, as suggested above, earlier normative assumptions about father-hood[36] have been challenged by techniques around assisted reproduction[37] and the increased centrality of formal equality and gender neutrality in law,[38] developments enmeshed with the decentring of marriage in attaching men to children, as above. Further, changes around law's governance,[39] including a rebalancing in family law of rules, discretion, rights and justice,[40] has occurred alongside the emergence of a heightened commitment in law and policy to promoting social responsibility, to setting out normative expectations, 'radiating messages' about desirable conduct and modifying the behaviour of both parents (and, indeed, children).[41] Research suggests that normative messages about the welfare of the child and 'doing the right thing' have, for both women *and* men, filtered through to the accounts of parents in making sense of their actions.[42]

These developments around parental responsibility, rights and law, beyond the scope of this chapter, are not a recent phenomenon. They track to longer-term shifts within law's governance, part of a wider 'civilising process' in law.[43] They constitute, however, an important backdrop against which changes in the place of fathers' rights politics in the legal arena should be understood. A growing body of empirical and theoretical research on fatherhood suggests men are dealing with this fragmentation, a legal treatment of fatherhood as a bundle of rights and responsibilities (that may be split up and shared between dif-ferent men, and allocated on different bases), in a number of different ways. And what is also becoming clear is that the idea of fragmentation might also capture aspects of the lived *experience* of many contemporary fathers, opening out the possibility of contradiction and tension between various aspects of fathering identity around, for example, what it means to be a good father or a 'family man', a breadwinner, a caring father, a partner, a friend.[44]

---

[36] That is, of the father as, a priori, heterosexual, as family breadwinner and embo-diment of a particular kind of masculinity.

[37] See further Collier and Sheldon, op cit, 2008, Ch 3 and, on the place of father-hood in recent debates around the reform of the Human Fertilisation and Embryology Act 1990, Ch 7.

[38] In the context of England and Wales, a range of legislative and other initiatives that have sought to promote equality, in particular since 1997. Note, e.g. B. Featherstone and L. Trinder, 'New Labour, families and fathers', *Critical Social Policy*, 2001, vol 21(4), p 534.

[39] Above, n 18.

[40] S. Parker, 'Rights and utility in Anglo-Australian law', *Modern Law Review*, 1992, vol 55, p 311.

[41] See further V. Gillies, *Marginalised Mothers: Exploring Working Class Experiences of Parenting*, London: Routledge, 2006; H. Reece, *Divorcing Responsibly*, Oxford: Hart, 2003; R. van Krieken, op cit, 2005.

[42] F. Kaganas and S. Day Sclater, 'Contact disputes: narrative constructions of "good" parents', Feminist *Legal Studies*, 2004, vol 12(1), p 2.

[43] Van Krieken, op cit, 2005.

[44] E. Dermott, *Intimate Fatherhood: A Sociological Analysis*, London: Routledge, 2007.

This brings into the frame issues of emotion, life history and the significance of the psychological, as well as sociological, dynamics of separation. And mapping to recent developments in sociology, in pursuing this theme further, work concerned to question the gaps and silences of the 'grand theories' of family studies sheds some further light on recent developments around fathers' rights. An engagement with recent sociological accounts of personal life, intimacy, identity and subjectivity, I shall suggest in the following section, raises a number of questions about what may be lost if we dismiss the rise of fathers' rights agendas as little more than a manifestation or reassertion of (gendered) power on the part of men.[45] I will here consider, necessarily briefly,[46] what kinds of issues come into view if we reframe the debate about fathers' rights by recasting these questions about 'personal life', emotion and the psychological dimensions of separation.

Fatherhood, law and fathers' rights: recasting the questions

Fatherhood, law and 'personal life'

In the edited book *Fathers Rights Activism and Law Reform in Comparative Perspective*[47] Sally Sheldon and I sought to explore, within an international context, some of the concerns that have been raised about recent developments in the field of fathers' rights politics. The critique that has developed, not least by feminist law and society scholars, has been far-reaching, encompassing a wide range of issues beyond this chapter (see further Featherstone, this volume).[48] The scale, prevalence and gendered nature of men's violence has, in particular, proved an important and contested issue, a 'toxic' question dividing stakeholder organisations in the sector and polarising policy debates about fathers and contact.[49] At the same time, the many grievances fathers'

---

[45] I am not claiming this is not an element or effect of this development. Evidence suggests some individuals, e.g. are indeed committed to an (anti-feminist) 'backlash', and to a reassertion of men's power (a theme that is particularly present on the Internet). However, I suggest, such a reading can itself miss out on what *else* may be happening here: see further below.

[46] See further Collier and Sheldon, op cit, 2008, Ch 5: Collier, op cit, 2009, forthcoming.

[47] Collier and Sheldon (eds), op cit, 2006.

[48] Research questions, e.g. whether non-resident parents, as a group, are unreasonably treated by the family courts. Rather, courts start from the position that contact is in the interests of the child. Non-resident parents are usually successful in getting the type of contact sought: J. Hunt and A. Macleod, *Outcomes of Applications to Court for Contact orders after Parental Separation or Divorce*, London: Ministry of Justice, 2008.

[49] See, e.g. B. Featherstone and S. Peckover, 'Letting Them Get Away With it: Fathers, Domestic Violence and Child Welfare', *Critical Social Policy*, 2007, vol 27(2) p 181; H. Saunders, *Twenty-Nine Child Homicides: Lessons to be Learnt on Domestic Violence and Child Protection* London: Women's Aid, 2004; H. Saunders, *Failure to Protect? Domestic Violence and the Experiences of Abused Women and Family Courts* Bristol, Women's Aid, 2003.

rights groups have with the present substance of the law and system of family justice in England and Wales has been well documented.[50] These complaints transcend, it is important to note, the issue of the (lack of) any statutory legal presumption of contact and equal, shared parenting in law (s 1, Children Act 1989). They encompass, rather, an array of concerns about the lack of openness and structured decision making in family law and the social, economic and psychological costs of separation for many fathers, their families and society, concerns that resonate, to varying degrees, with those of other stakeholder groups, policy makers and politicians.[51] There is, I have argued elsewhere, considerable force to aspects of the critique of fathers' rights groups that has developed in law and other disciplines. This work has raised important questions about the political and conceptual limits of gender neutrality and formal equality, key themes of this book, as well as a failure of imagination around engaging with the legal contours of the private (sexual) family and gendered understandings of care, caring and family autonomy (Herring, this volume).[52]

In what follows I wish to recognise the force of these concerns about the consequences, for women and children in particular, of fathers' adopting a rights-based approach premised upon appeals to welfare and the discourse – if not the material reality – of gender convergence (be it in employment, the caring practices or gendered 'roles' of women and men and so forth). Noting the broader social shifts around fatherhood traced thus far in this chapter, however, questions remain unanswered. Does this then mean that fathers' rights groups are simply 'wrong' in their assessment of the law? Are their claims without foundation? Are they manifestations of a form of 'false con-sciousness', a failure to recognise what is, from one feminist perspective, the material realities of their structural empowerment *as men*? If legal scholars are to engage with fathers' rights politics, what is really going on here, and what might it mean for understanding how concrete demands become intelligible as the pursuit of 'justice' within the legal arena?

The reading presented thus far rejects both the idea that men have been displaced in families, and the notion that a seemingly straightforward pro-gressive modernisation of fatherhood has occurred (and that 'new' fathers are, somehow, better than 'old').[53] Rather, fatherhood has been reconstituted

---

[50] E.g. B. Geldof, 'The real love that dare not speak its name', in A. Bainham *et al.* (eds), *Children and Their Families*, Oxford: Hart, 2003. Note: Fathers 4 Justice, 'Family Justice On Trial: Opening The Door On Closed Courts' (http://fathers-4-justice.org/f4j//index.php?option=com_content&task=view&id=13&Itemid=39 accessed 27 December 2007).

[51] Note, e.g. Families Need Fathers *et al.*, 'Letter to the editor: the government must help the children of divorcees', *The Times* (12 June 2007) p 16; other signatories to this letter included Women's Aid and Fathers Direct.

[52] Fineman, op cit, 2004; M. Fineman, *The Neutered Mother, The Sexual Family, and Other Twentieth Century Tragedies*, New York: Routledge, 1995.

[53] A point made by Haywood and Mac an Ghaill, op cit.

in ways that reflect an uneasy mix of traditional ideas (of a man's role, male authority) and the values and practices associated with the new fatherhood. There are significant limits to interpreting these historical sifts in terms of what I have called elsewhere a 'zero-sum' approach to the power of law. It is misleading, for example, to see legal change in terms of a pendulum swing in power relations between the sexes, whereby a move has occurred from a bias towards the interests of fathers at the end of the nineteenth century, to what, as some would have it, is now a systematic prioritisation of the interests of mothers.[54]

At the same time, however, following the above, it is equally misleading to reduce what has happened in recent years around contemporary fathers' rights activism to no more than a backlash against perceived maternal bias in the substance or operation of law.[55] The emergence of a multi-layered and frequently contradictory father-victim discourse results, rather, from social shifts more complex and intricate than any simple manifestation of 'anti-women' sentiment on the part of (some) men, however resonant that theme undoubtedly is within strands of the father right discourse, particularly on the Internet.[56] As feminist legal scholars have noted, in questioning the 'siren call' of law, family law reform can be more open-ended and uncertain in its effects than such a reading of 'winners' and 'losers' allows.[57] However culturally and politically resonant this language of gender or 'sex war' may be – and it has been adopted vociferously by some fathers' rights groups, as well as some of their opponents – it is of little help in trying to address the very real problems that both parents and children can face in dealing with separation.

Turning to a literature developing at the interface of sociological engagements with family practices and recent studies of identity, subjectivity and masculinity, it is possible however to reconsider some of this complexity as it relates to fathers' rights.[58] One issue increasingly salient within recent

---

[54] R. Collier, 'From "women's emancipation" to "sex war"? Beyond the masculinized discourse of divorce', in S. Day Sclater and C. Piper (eds), op cit.

[55] Collier and Sheldon, op cit, 2008, Ch 1.

[56] Note here the reading of Crowley, op cit, 2008.

[57] See further, on this complexity, A. Diduck and K. O'Donovan, 'Feminism and families: *plus ça change?*', in A. Diduck and K. O'Donovan (eds), *Feminist Perspectives on Family Law*, Abingdon: Routledge-Cavendish, 2006, p 6: also C. Smart, 'Feminism and law: some problems of analysis and strategy', *International Journal of the Sociolgy of Law*, 1986, vol 14, p 109; C. Smart, *Feminism and the Power of Law*, London: Routledge, 1989.

[58] Smart, op cit, 2007; D. Morgan, *Family Connections: An Introduction to Family Studies*, Cambridge: Polity, 1999; L. Jamieson, *Intimacy: Personal Relationships in Modern Society*, Cambridge: Polity, 1998; M. Wetherell and N. Edley, 'Negotiating hegemonic masculinity: imaginary positions and psycho-discursive practices', *Feminism and Psychology*, 1999, vol 9 p 335; R. W. Connell and J. Messerschmidt, 'Hegemonic masculinity: rethinking the concept', *Gender and Society*, 2005, vol 19, p 829; C. Brickell, 'Masculinities, performativity and subversion: a sociological appraisal', *Men and Masculinities*, 2005, vol 8, p 24; S. Frosh, *After Words: The Personal in Gender, Culture and Psychotherapy*, Basingstoke: Palgrave Macmillan, 2002.

socio-legal scholarship concerns the dangers that can inhere in deconstructive attempts within law to 'reveal' or 'unpack' (let us call) the gendered subject(s) of legal discourse.[59] As Carol Smart suggests in her book *Personal Life*, such engagements run the risk of ignoring the significant affective dimensions of social relations, effacing the complexity and interconnectedness of the 'everyday' lives of women, children and men, erasing what she terms the 'real lives' of individuals.[60] This point has a particular bearing on the present discussion as, understood as (distinctive) family practices, in Morgan's term,[61] experiences of both fathering and of being fathered are mediated (inevitably) by a range of factors, such as age, class, geographical location, religion, ethnicity, sexuality, health and disability. One challenge in approaching the relationship between fatherhood and law, therefore, is to avoid a form of analysis whereby 'real people and their lives ... become a kind of grist to a pre-existing theoretical mill ... reduced to ciphers for a culturally and historically specific knowledge-building industry'.[62] Beyond the differences that exist between social groups, what it means to *be* a father can vary enormously between individual men, depending on the specificities of life history and biography, stage of life course and the diverse social contexts that situate specific fathering practices.[63] In relation to men and fatherhood, such an approach can be aligned to broader attempts to develop anti-essentialist engagements with masculinity and ideas of the male subject.[64]

Why is this point significant? Just as the highly conflicted separation of the kind associated with an involvement in fathers' rights politics cannot be seen as typical of the majority of separations,[65] it would be erroneous to dismiss the rise of fathers' rights activism as little more than an extreme and minority activity. Equally, even a cursory engagement with sociological and psychological developments in studies of men and masculinities suggests that reducing the actions of an individual man – and, say, understanding of his engagement with law and the legal process in a specific local context – to a unitary motivation potentially 'misses out' on much. In particular, it effaces

---

[59] For discussion of these issues in relation to the construction of masculinities in law see: R. Collier, 'Reflections on the Relationship Between Law and Masculinities: Rethinking The "Man Question"', *Current Legal Problems*, 2003, vol 56, p 345.

[60] Smart, op cit, 2007.

[61] Morgan, op cit.

[62] Smart, op cit, 2007, p 190.

[63] See further W. Marsiglio, K. Roy and G. Litton Fox (eds), *Situated Fathering: A Focus on Physical and Social Spaces*, Lanham, MD: Rowman & Littlefield, 2005.

[64] Collier, 2009, forthcoming; N. Dowd, *The Man Question: Feminist Jurisprudence, Masculinities and Law*, New York: New York University Press, forthcoming.

[65] A. Blackwell and F. Dawe, *Non-Resident Parental Contact: Based on Data from the National Statistics Omnibus Survey for The Department for Constitutional Affairs: Final Report*, London: Office for National Statistics, 2003; J. Hunt with C. Roberts, *Family Policy Briefing 3: Child Contact with Non- Resident Parents*, Oxford: Department of Social Policy and Social Work, University of Oxford, 2004.

the question, above, of what may be happening to 'real people and their lives' in terms of the affective dimensions of social relations and the inter-connectedness of the everyday lives of women, children and men.[66] It also sidesteps the question of how these emotions and social experiences are dealt with in the legal arena,[67] the many dimensions, conscious and unconscious, that shape personal action.[68]

What might developments around fathers' rights tell us, therefore, about the changing relationship between rights, gender and family law, a central theme of this volume? Drawing on a growing body of work concerned with the evolution of fathers' rights groups, and necessarily in brief, what do we find? The development of fathers' protests around law is interconnected to the broader changes in the content, scope and function of family law referred to above, as well as the rethinking of the father in child welfare and the shifting social, political and economic contexts that frame the development of the substantive law. In the context of debates in England and Wales, for example, the beginnings of the contemporary fathers' rights movement can be located in the aftermath of the Divorce Reform Act 1969 and the Matrimonial Causes Act 1973.[69] Developments since then, and changes in the content and form of the arguments advanced by fathers' groups – remembering that there is no *one* such type of group or organisation[70] – map to shifting ideas about men and masculinities, as well as the evolution of distinctive policy agendas pertaining to fatherhood. Turning to the cultural and political contexts in which these debates have evolved in England and Wales, we find, over the past three decades, a figure appearing in the mist, as it were, the emergence of the 'father as victim' of law. Interlinked to a discourse of masculine crisis that has pervaded numerous cultural artefacts – a theme particularly visible in the

[66] Smart, op cit, 2007. Note also V. Held, *The Ethics of Care: Personal, Political and Global*, Oxford: Oxford University Press, 2006; J. Tronto, *Moral Boundaries*, London: Routledge 1993; S. Sevenhuijsen, *Citizenship and the Ethics of Care*, London: Routledge, 1998.

[67] See, for an alternative view: S.A. Bandes (ed), *The Passions of Law*, New York: New York University Press, 1999; L. Bently and L. Flynn (eds), *Law and the Senses*, London: Pluto, 1996; M. Douglas, 'Emotion and culture in theories of justice', *Economy and Society*, 1993, vol 22(4), p 501. M. Nussbaum, *Hiding From Humanity: Disgust, Shame and the Law*, Princeton, NJ: Princeton University Press, 2004.

[68] Note, e.g. the work of S. Day Sclater, *Divorce: A Psycho-Social Study*, Aldershot: Ashgate, 1999. S. Day Sclater, 'Divorce – coping strategies, conflict and dispute resolution', *Family Law*, 1998, p 150; S. Day Sclater and C. Yates, 'The psycho-politics of post divorce parenting', in A. Bainham, S. Day Sclater and M. Richards (eds), *What is a Parent? A Socio-Legal Analysis*, Oxford: Hart, 1999; J. Brown and S. Day Sclater, 'Divorce: a psychodynamic perspective', in S. Day Sclater and C. Piper (eds), *Undercurrents of Divorce*, Aldershot: Dartmouth, 1999.

[69] With the registered charity Families Need Fathers, for example, formed in 1974.

[70] Collier, op cit, 2005; Collier and Sheldon (eds), op cit, 2006.

UK in the early to mid-1990s – this idea of the father-victim has shaped how morality and equality arguments have been deployed by fathers groups within family law and policy debates. The depiction of the father as victim, drawing on a diverse array of (gendered) representations associated with ideas of equality, justice, heroism and action (in 'fighting' such injustice), has itself become a hallmark of certain fathers' campaigns around law. Such arguments simply scratch the surface, however, of the many layers of fathers' rights politics. I will here make four points, before concluding.

Rights, justice, care

First, there has been a historical shift in the focus of fathers' grievances that links to how fathers' legal claims are increasingly articulated, as Smart has usefully suggested, through both a language of rights and justice *and* via reference to ideas of men's caring, capacity to care and children's welfare.[71] This reflects wider changes in gendered ideas of intimacy, masculinity and men's familial responsibility, aspirations and practices, as well as developments in law itself, noting a move from central concerns around property and finance in the 1970s and early 1980s,[72] to, by the late 1990s, a growing focus on child contact and residence arrangements. I do not wish to suggest (far from it) that financial issues are not still significant, notably in relation to the Child Support Agency (CSA), the protests against which of the early 1990s in some respects pre-figured the events of recent years. Rather, the heightened focus on the father–child relationship maps to wider social shifts over the past fifteen years interconnected to political changes around formal equality, gender neutrality and rights, as well as changing conceptions of childhood.[73] Drawing on these broader cultural shifts around men's capacity and capability to care it is perhaps unsurprising to find that an ethic of care should increasingly inform the fathers' rights discourse. Nor that, given the nature of the substance and process of law, an appeal to justice, equality and 'rights-talk' should run alongside the reconfiguration of the relationship between fathers and care.[74] Indeed, it would be surprising if that were not the case.

---

[71] Smart, op cit, 2004; C. Smart, 'The ethic of justice strikes back', in Diduck and O'Donovan (eds), op cit, p 123.

[72] Note, e.g. D. Allen, *One Step from the Quagmire* Aylesbury: Campaign for Justice in Divorce, 1982; P. Alcock, 'Remuneration or remarriage? The Matrimonial and Family Proceedings Act 1984', *Journal of Law and Society*, 1984, vol 11(3), p 357.

[73] Note, e.g. F. Kaganas and A. Diduck, 'Incomplete citizens: changing images of post-separation children', *Modern Law Review*, 2004, vol 67(6), p 959.

[74] Smart, op cit, 2006.

Theorising fatherhood

Second, these shifts should also not surprise given how, as others have argued, fatherhood is an undifferentiated social phenomenon conceptually, made of up different elements in how men, and what we men do, are understood. Disputes around fathers' rights are pervaded by conflicting ideas. We find ideas about fathers as, variously holders of legal rights; fathers as representatives of both 'traditional' and 'new' forms of paternal responsibility; fathers as victims of law and perpetrators of social harm (below); fathers who simultaneously embrace and resist social change; fathers who protect and are themselves potential risks to women and children.[75] This relates to what Scourfield and Drakeford have termed a reframing of a 'problem of men' in law and social policy, a problem that does not arise from a homogenous set of concerns but from different directions, focusing on a variety of men's behaviour and approached in different ways.[76]

Each of these ideas about fatherhood pervades recent debates in the legal and policy arena around fathers' rights. Thus, as stakeholder groups seek to engage with this new terrain, we find, simultaneously, a bemoaning of the cultural devaluing of fathers in British society,[77] an idea linked directly to the father as victim discourse and the 'engaging fathers' agendas of the present government. And at the same time, a powerful image of the father as perpetrator, the father as a potential source of risk and harm, not least to women and children. The former draws on the ostensibly progressive ideas of men and masculinity that have become resonant in the family law field associated with the 'new fatherhood' ideal. The latter, in contrast, draws on ideas of masculinity more familiar in other policy contexts, for example debates around men, crime and criminality, where fatherhood tends to be configured in rather different ways (as a resource in preventing crime, as an anchor for gendered socialisation, as embodying ideas of authority and control and so forth).[78]

These debates are also, to refer back to the recent sociological engagements with personal life discussed above, pervaded by conflicting ideas about men and masculinities. This is the case, for example, in terms of ideas of men's emotion, anger and the gendered nature of what it means to be (ir)rational when participating in law reform debates. Notions of hysteria and a failure to 'be reasonable' have been historically associated with women rather than men, culturally encoded as feminine.[79] The protests of contemporary

[75] Smart and Neale, op cit.
[76] Scourfield and Drakeford, op cit.
[77] E.g. Burgess, op cit, 1997; see further Burgess and Russell, op cit. Note also the arguments advanced by The Fatherhood Institute.
[78] Scourfield and Drakeford, op cit: see also R. Collier, *Masculinities, Crime and Criminology: Men, Heterosexuality and the Criminal(ised) Other*, London: Sage, 1998.
[79] E. Showalter, *The Female Malady: Women, Madness and English Culture 1830–1980*, London: Virago 1987.

fathers' groups, however, in some ways, can be seen to both embody and, simultaneously, be the antithesis of traditional ideas of masculinity, what it means to be rational, responsible and reasonable. The gendered nature of some fathers' protests appear, on one level, quintessentially masculine, drawing, in a quite instrumental way, on the strategies of other social movements (not least feminism)[80] via a deployment of the male body in space enmeshed with appeals to danger, risk, heroism, struggle and, importantly, violence or the threat of violence.[81] At the same time, however, rather different ideas of men's emotion/distress, anger and rationality have also been deployed, not just by fathers' groups but also in the media and in the arguments of their critics in accounting for the terrain of fathers' rights politics. These men are seen, in their dealings with law, as beyond reason, irrational, irresponsible.

In recognising that men showing emotion (crying tears or otherwise) can attract a redemptive value culturally not accorded to women, the recent protests of fathers' rights groups, in particular Fathers 4 Justice, I would suggest, in fact stand in an ambivalent relation both to the co-parenting discourse and supposedly dominant 'hegemonic' ideas about masculinity.[82] It could be argued that features commonly seen as characteristic of an engagement with fathers' right politics – obsession, the tendency to self-represent, being psychologically 'stuck' in conflict, appealing to 'my rights' and so forth – are rooted in a mode of masculinity that is increasingly seen as culturally anachronistic, at least within certain social contexts. It is a model of masculinity that ill fits, in its association with symptoms, mental disorders and cognitive impairment, the model of the reasonable, rational subject that underscores the 'new responsibilisation' turn in family policy. It ill fits, also, the model of the new, caring father, evoking an appeal to individual rights that, notwithstanding the Human Rights Act 1998, sits uneasily within dominant conceptions of parental responsibility (Featherstone, this volume).

Further, the protests and the emotional imperatives which drive them – a profound sense, for example, of injustice, anger, betrayal, loss – clash starkly, violently, with an official discourse that suggests contemporary divorce, in the evocation of this new responsibility, has evolved into an arena 'beyond politics'. Yet the arguments advanced by fathers' rights activists are, in this

---

[80] Crowley, op cit 2008, 2006.

[81] It is important to not forget in this context the growing debate about what have been termed 'family annihilators', men who kill their children, and often themselves, in an act of revenge directed against their partners: L. Martin, 'Fathers who kill their children', *Observer* (5 November 2006), Focus 20.

[82] Certainly, as a policy engagement much of this is not pitched at the level of rationality and reason demanded by policy makers and politicians, at which some children's and women's groups have arguably been far more adept at engaging with research evidence, rather than the use of personal anecdote.

regard, not so different from those of their critics, who have similarly questioned the limits of this 'new consensus'. Where they differ is in the seeming inability of some groups to transcend a central commitment to the 'private' (sexual) family[83] and to recognise the complexity, and limits, of gender neutrality, formal equality and reach of law reform itself in this area.[84]

Policy

Third, the conceptual issues about the interrelation of rights, justice, care and fatherhood raise questions that have direct bearing, not just on developing understanding of the gendered dynamics of family practices, but also for rethinking how emotion and the psychological and sociological dynamics of separation referred to above are dealt with in family justice processes. As Day Sclater and Richards suggested in 1995,[85] it is important not to underestimate the psychological dimensions of separation, and the significance (for the parties, for children and for the legal system) of highly conflicted adult relations. What might it mean, for example, to recognise that conflict may be an inevitable and enduring aspect of the human condition? That both mothers *and* fathers may, albeit in different, or perhaps, similar ways constitute a potentially vulnerable population in the context of separation? In the case of fathers' rights groups, what does evidence of a common experience of depression and other health problems amongst activists, a finding consistent with what is known about the divorcing population more generally, mean for developing gender sensitive intervention in addressing the psychosocial aspects of separation for highly conflicted fathers?[86] What does a gendered awareness of issues about fathering and men's health raise for the role of CAFCASS (Child and Family Court Advisory Support Service) and other bodies in meeting fathers' needs? How have these issues been addressed – or not been addressed – by relevant bodies in the field (such as The Fatherhood Institute)? How might the development of child-inclusive family law dispute-resolution initiatives, of the kind developed in other jurisdictions, have an impact on fathers' perceptions of conflict?[87]

These issues relate to what I have suggested elsewhere is the need for socio-legal studies to engage more fully with, and to reconceptualise, the

---

[83] Fineman, op cit, 1995: on UK fathers' groups in this regard, Collier, op cit, 2005.

[84] This is not to say law is unimportant. It is to state that law alone cannot solve the problems that parents may face in the process of separation, while recognising that law can undoubtedly alleviate or make those problems worse.

[85] S. Day Sclater and M. Richards, 'How adults cope with divorce – strategies for survival', *Family Law*, 1995, 143 p 145.

[86] Of the kind undertaken, e.g. by father support workers at a local level in the context of supporting and engaging non-resident fathers.

[87] J. McIntosh, 'Enduring conflict in parental separation: pathways on child development' *Journal of Family Studies*, 2003, vol 9, p 63.

(gendered) male subject.[88] That is, for a greater recognition of how life history and individual biography, personal experience, peer groups and social networks are enmeshed with the formation of 'gendered rationalities'[89] that inform how particular individuals encounter law. These arguments support recent sociological calls to acknowledge how what fathers *emotionally* feel and desire may in fact be as important as what they *rationally* think in shaping behaviour.[90] This observation links to and supports recent interventions aimed at promoting a political and policy engagement with the emotional and relational dynamics of separation. It also seeks to recognise that structures beyond law can shape ideas of responsibility[91] and that, as Featherstone argues in this book, a particular model of paternal responsibility has come to encapsulate in its scope a broad range of ideas about fathers in terms of both 'care-talk', welfare, justice and rights-based claims.

In developing further the recognition that fathers may have specific needs, and remembering that fathers are themselves a diverse and heterogeneous group,[92] research further suggests there is more going on 'under the radar' with fathers' rights groups than the high-profile protests of recent years and the collective 'staking out' of rights and equality claims would indicate. Alongside an important service-function (the provision of advice and support), participation in groups can address an emotional need on the part of certain fathers. It may be that, in some instances, this participation is seen as 'harmful', in the sense that it encourages the projection of negative feelings onto former partners and/or the legal system, making a father less able to 'move on' from, and to be stuck in, a highly conflicted position.[93] At the same time, however, Crowly suggests, participation can be experienced as meeting individual 'self-expansion' needs, informing the formation of personal identity at a time of considerable distress and life transition.[94] These can be characterised, borrowing a term from another context, as needs that may be otherwise unmet by the legal system, with a diverse range of local based

---

[88] Collier, op cit, 2002.
[89] A. Barlow, S. Duncan and G. James, 'New Labour, the rationality mistake and family policy in Britain', in A. Carling, S. Duncan and R. Edwards (eds), *Analysing Families: Morality and Rationality in Policy and Practice*, London: Routledge, 2002; A. Barlow and S. Duncan, 'New Labour's communitarianism, supporting families and the "rationality mistake": part I', *Journal of Social Welfare and Family Law*, 2000, vol 22(2), p 23; A. Barlow and S. Duncan, 'New Labour's communitarianism, supporting families and the "rationality mistake": part II', *Journal of Social Welfare and Family Law*, 2000, vol 22(2), p 129.
[90] Haywood and Mac an Ghaill, op cit.
[91] J. Bridgeman, C. Lind and H. Keating (eds), *Responsibility, Law and the Family*, Aldershot: Ashgate Publishing, 2008.
[92] B. Featherstone, 'Taking Fathers Seriously', *British Journal of Social Work*, 2003 vol 33(2), p 239.
[93] Contrast Flood, op cit.
[94] Crowley, op cit, 2008.

groups, providing valuable practical and emotional support, information, advice and assistance to many fathers.

It cannot be assumed, moreover, that all fathers who participate necessarily 'buy in' to the broader critique of law and the legal system propounded by the more high-profile fathers' groups. Nor that personal identity is formed around a commitment to fathers' rights activism. The experience of fathers' groups appears more fluid and complex, with some men dipping 'in and out' of involvement, and, in particular, some groups dependent on the high levels of commitment of a small core of members. Such an approach suggests, in summary, the development of organisational politics around fathers' rights is bound up with broader cultural discourses around gender, equality, rights and responsibilities in ways that provide a grounded context in which renegotiations of personal identity in the process of separation take place.

Impact and politics

Fourth, and finally, it is important to recognise the limits, as well as the extent, of the influence of fathers' rights groups in shaping policy agendas. There appears a degree of consensus among stakeholders, policy makers and academics in England and Wales, as well as within the media, that the events of recent years, in particular following the formation of Fathers 4 Justice in 2002, have (at the very least) shaped the wider cultural context in which debates about law reform take place. The background to the relevant provisions of the 2006 Children and Adoption Act, Pt 1, are, in particular, of relevance here.[95] There is reason to believe some fathers' claims have found a degree of resonance with certain judges, politicians and policy makers. Meanwhile, academics, policy makers and parts of the media have seen recent reforms around the enforcement of contact orders as the direct product of fathers' campaigns, protests that, in this regard at least, can be considered 'successful'. However, this does not mean fathers' groups have necessarily moved centre stage within the networks and communities concerned with

---

[95] The coming into force of the Children and Adoption Act 2006 has renewed discussion around the enforcement measures contained in Pt 1 of the Act. These 'penalties for partners who block access' (*Observer* 27 September 2008) have been widely interpreted, in the media and by academic commentators, as the product of a policy debate and reform process influenced, at least to degrees, by the high profile campaigns of fathers' rights groups. The forthcoming introduction of the Debt and Enforcement powers of the Child Maintenance and Enforcement Commission, meanwhile, alongside the Child Maintenance Options scheme, further reshapes the landscape in which these debates take place. See further J. Wallbank, 'Getting tough on mothers: regulating contact and residence', *Feminist Legal Studies*, 2007, vol 15(2), p 189; F. Gibb, 'Child contact powers could worsen parent wars', *The Times*, 8 December 2008 p 11; J. Wallbank, 'Clause 106 of the Adoption and Children Bill: legislation for the "good father"?', *Legal Studies* 2002, vol 22 (2), p 276; Collier and Sheldon, op cit, 2008, Ch 5.

law reform. A case can be made, indeed, that debates in these arenas, in this jurisdiction at least,[96] have been informed by research, including that of socio-legal scholars, that directly counters some of the key fathers' rights claims.[97]

Recognising the scale of the distress caused by fathers' campaigns – and how gender has undoubtedly informed the targeting of certain individuals – the observations of diverse organisations suggest that the very form of recent protests may have rendered it unlikely that politicians will in the future accord them a 'place at the table' in reform debates.[98] Moreover, these protests appear contradictory in their effect, raising the profile of issues yet, at the same time, proving counter-productive in alienating potential support. At the time of writing, this is a political terrain in flux, with the Conservative Party, in particular, positioning itself as broadly sympathetic to some fathers' claims. There is reason to believe that fathers' protests have prompted a degree of realignment within the sector,[99] and that what may now be occurring is a move away from direct action protest and towards more mainstream political campaigning.[100] In this move, there appears a degree of convergence in the aims and objectives of organisations, at least around some issues,[101] with diverse stakeholders, including the group Families Needs Fathers, increasingly stressing the limits of adversarial proceedings in court and the need, as above, to engage with the emotional dimensions of separation.[102]

---

[96] This is not to say that this terrain has not been shaped by fathers' groups in different ways elsewhere: see Collier and Sheldon (eds), op cit, 2006.

[97] Arenas that have been informed, to degrees, by other voices, some of which could be aligned to (and would align themselves with) certain strands within feminism (including, it has been suggested, at senior government level, where different kinds of arguments have been advanced about policy around 'engaging fathers'): Collier, op cit, 2008 'Fathers' rights'.

[98] Ibid.

[99] Note, e.g. the re-branding on the part of *Fathers Direct* (now *The Fatherhood Institute* as of January, 2008), a change prompted in part by a desire to place distance from 'fathers' rights' groups in the field.

[100] In September 2008 the founder of Fathers 4 Justice, Matt O'Connor, announced, for the second time, the disbanding of the group: D. Jarvis, 'Fathers 4 Justice leader ends fight due to stress', *Sunday Express* 7 September 2008, p 15. Fathers 4 Justice is to be relaunched as a helpline 'for all parents whose family lives are in crisis' (*Independent on Sunday*, 28 September 2008).

[101] While the above is unlikely to mean the end of direct action protest by some fathers and their supporters, it does map to a realignment of organisations and family sector leaders around the need to encourage co-operation and bring together stakeholders. Note, e.g. 'Putting children first' (October 2008, Centre for Separated Families) and other initiatives seeking to share best practice (e.g. 'Kids in the middle', launched in July 2008 by *Relate*, One Parent Families, Families Need Fathers and the Fatherhood Institute).

[102] Note also the comments of Jon Davies, Chief Executive of Families Need Fathers: J. Doward, 'Penalties for partners who block child access', *Observer* 7 September 2008, p 4.

Concluding remarks

I wish, by way of concluding remarks, to make three final related points concerning the conceptual ambiguity and heterogeneity of fatherhood that have particular bearing on discussion of fathers' rights, gender and family law.

First, fathers, like mothers, can experience a profound tension between the ideals of desirable parenting contained in law and their own social experience, the result being a potential sense of disappointment, frustration and, for some, feelings of anger (with law, the legal system) that needs to be managed emotionally (as above). It has been suggested that the ideal of co-parenting contained in law has the potential to fuel conflict between separating parents, in particular where it is perceived to be the product, not of co-operation, but of legal or other coercion.[103] This appears precisely the scenario in some cases involving fathers' rights group activists, where there is a personal history of highly conflicted separation. To look back to that 'bigger picture' of social and legal change, however, for some men an identification with the model of the father as 'hands-on' carer is undercut in a social context in which the father can himself no longer be valued for 'being there' for his children.[104] The result can be a profound sense of loss, pain, injustice and anger with law and the legal system, and former partner, that runs alongside the maintenance of a continuing and considerable faith in the ability of legal reform to ultimately 'solve' the problems that fathers face. It is a faith in law that much socio-legal research suggests may be misplaced. This does not mean, however, that it is any less 'real' or experientially significant, or that the engagements with law that result in highly conflicted cases are any less damaging, for women, children and, indeed, for fathers themselves.

[103] R. Bailey-Harris, J. Barron, and J. Pearce, 'From utility to rights? The presumption of contact in practice', *International Journal of Law, Policy and the Family*, 1999, vol 13, p 111. See also H. Rhoades, 'The rise and rise of shared parenting laws: a critical reflection', *Canadian Journal of Family Law*, 2002, vol 19(1), p 75; C. Smart and B. Neale, 'Arguments against virtue: must contact be enforced?', *Family Law*, 1997, p 332. Both resident and non-resident parents can experience problems with contact, and if the minority who use the legal system are more likely to be those with problems, this does not mean that the majority of parents who do not may not also face real difficulties: V. Peacey and J. Hunt, *Problematic Contact after Separation and Divorce? A National Survey of Parents* London: One Parent Families/Gingerbread, 2008.

[104] Drawing on his own empirical material gleaned from focus groups with fathers, Jonathan Ives has expressed this in terms of layers of meaning: 'fathering ideology has been building up in layers, with the "father as carer" model the most recent addition. If we dig below the surface we find the father as gender role model, a little deeper and we find the breadwinner, and deeper still we find the dominant, patriarchal disciplinarian and moral compass': J. Ives, 'Becoming a father/refusing fatherhood: how paternal responsibilities and rights are generated' (DPhil thesis, University of Birmingham, 2007) p 187.

Second, in approaching contemporary ideas of men's responsibility and rights in family law, it is important to recognise how, just as there is no one model of fatherhood or experience of fathering, normative expectations and practices have been historically mediated by ideas and assumptions about social class, race, ethnicity and sexuality. In approaching these changes around fatherhood, rights and equality in law, it is necessary to note in this regard, as some feminist scholars have argued, the potential disjuncture between the ideas about parenting contained in legal discourse and the diverse material realities of fathering practices. A rich body of historical research has charted the shifting contours of fatherhood from the mid-nineteenth century to the present day.[105] What is clear from such work is that no one model of paternal responsibility was ever, at any historical moment, diffused throughout the social order.[106] Rather, however culturally resonant and embedded in law particular ideas about fatherhood may have been, it cannot be assumed they necessarily map to the social experience of all men, women and, indeed, children.

This means that we cannot extrapolate from a cultural imagery of fatherhood, or from a reading of 'gender in legal discourse', direct knowledge of fathering as a social practice and lived experience in particular communities, a point particularly relevant to our present discussion. Feminist critiques of fathers' rights have drawn attention to how a focus on the deployment of individualistic rights and equality claims can divert attention from law's conceptualisation of the private (sexual) family and the gendered dimensions of care and social dependency. At the same time, however, as suggested, social structures beyond 'the family' impact on ideas of family responsibility, rights and equality in ways that render law just part, albeit a significant part, of how these rights and responsibilities come to be experienced. It cannot be assumed therefore, that all social groups relate to the 'new responsibility' in law in the same way. Research suggests that the privatisation of responsibilities within family law, and rise of this 'new responsibilisation', has had a particularly hard impact on already vulnerable social groups, not least, as the work of Val Gillies shows, some groups of mothers.[107] Yet recognising the diversity of fathers' experiences, it is open to question to what extent policy debates about fatherhood have themselves been informed by

---

[105] See, e.g. J Mangan and J Walvin (eds), *Manliness and Morality: Middle Class Masculinity in Britain and America 1800–1940*, Manchester: Manchester University Press, 1987; J. Tosh, *A Man's Place: Masculinity and the Middle-class Home in Victorian England*, London: Yale University Press, 1999; J. R. Gillis, *A World of Their Own Making: Myth, Ritual and the Quest for Family Values*, Cambridge: Harvard University Press, 1996.

[106] Richards, op cit, p 27.

[107] Gillies, op cit, 2006; see also V. Gillies, 'Meeting Parents' Needs? Discourses of "Support" and "Inclusion" in Family Policy', *Critical Social Policy*, 2005, vol 25 (1), p 70.

problematic assumptions about class, race and ethnicity and social disadvantage[108] in ways that have effaced the very real vulnerabilities of certain groups of men in contemporary British society.

With this in mind we can ask a number of questions. Have these debates about fathers' rights and responsibilities cast some men (white? middle-class?), but not others, as the embodiments of a normative 'new father' ideal? While certain men 'grapple' with and 'juggle' contradictory discourses around masculinity in areas such as work–life balance,[109] others, notably in the context of crime/criminality, tend to be pathologised by law, and subject to law's surveillance, in very different ways. How, in this respect, does an appreciation of what Sayer terms the 'the moral significance' of class[110] and material disadvantage inform collective cultural perceptions of the play of masculinities within the field of fathers' rights politics? Just who is included, and who is excluded, from these debates about fathers, rights and responsibility, and how are some men's actions constituted as irrational, unreasonable, over-emotional and so forth within particular contexts, while others are not? Who is actually being talked to and included in the debates? It is not difficult to see how, just as ideas about respectable femininity have been mediated by class based assumptions, class, race and ethnicity can also inform cultural representations of acceptable masculinity.

Third, and finally, against the backdrop of significant changes in legal ideas of paternal responsibilities, the debates about fathers' rights considered above transcend matters of specific legal decisions, law reforms or policy initiatives. Underscoring the debates I have argued in this chapter are questions about the changing nature and conceptual ambiguity of fatherhood itself, struggles over its meaning and value. What we can trace in this area is a reshaping of norms and expectations around fatherhood and masculinity that is contradictory, marked by ideas of both change and continuity in men's family practices. The shifts that have occurred around fatherhood,

---

[108] Raising the question of how the 'father-inclusive' policy agenda may itself represent a reframing of, rather than challenge to, dominant ideas of hegemonic masculinity, whereby certain negative qualities are projected on subordinated groups of men (with the 'new father' embodying 'virtues' in ways others may be less able to): see K. Henwood and J. Proctor, 'The "good father": reading men's accounts of paternal involvement during the transition to first-time fatherhood', *British Journal of Social Psychology*, 2003, vol 42(3), p 337; note: S. Hall, 'Daubing the drudges of fury: men, violence and the piety of the "hegemonic masculinity" thesis', *Theoretical Criminology*, 2002, vol 6(1), p 35; Scourfield and Drakeford, op cit; Collier, 1998, op cit.

[109] J. Lewis, 'Balancing work and family: the nature of the policy challenge and gender equality', Working Paper for GeNet Project 9: Tackling Inequalities in Work and Care Policy Initiatives and Actors at the EU and UK Levels: www.genet.ac.uk/projects/project9.htm, p 2.

[110] A. Sayer, *The Moral Significance of Class*, Cambridge: Cambridge University Press, 2005.

rights and gender from the late nineteenth-century to the present day are the product of a complex interweaving and inter-discursive nexus of law, medicine, psychology, religion and science. All (in different ways) have been implicated in the production of normative beliefs about 'family life', children and childhood, health and illness, sexuality, social class, good parenting, the 'good divorce' and so forth. While mothers have been subject to levels of surveillance, scrutiny and regulation in ways that fathers have not,[111] ideas about the 'family man' and 'good father' have also been transformed. In recognising the continued importance attached to legally establishing a father figure within certain contexts the *basis* on which fathers should be recognised in law, I have argued elsewhere with Sally Sheldon, has changed considerably.[112] The result is a shifting, complex web of rights and responsibilities in which a renegotiation of men's role has been shaped by a reconfiguration of gender relations occurring in the light of shifting household forms, evolving discourses of parenting, childhood and intimacy, as well as changes in legal norms and modes of governance.

Asking if a 'debate about the nature of fatherhood' might inform, 'policy and reform discussions', Martha Fineman's observation, with which we began, issues of emotion and the psychological complexity of separation are of considerable significance in approaching fathers' rights. Becoming involved in fathers' rights politics connects, research suggests, for some men at least, to the need to address complex emotional needs. This raises the difficult question of what, at a policy level, might be the gains, and the dangers, of seeing separated fathers as a distinctive group of men, individuals who may themselves have specific, if diverse, needs at a moment of life transition. There is, at present, some agreement that few services reach out and support or engage non-residential fathers.[113] How important is it that recent initiatives aimed at supporting contact activities, building on the recognition of 'system failures' in how law responds to the emotional fallout of divorce, address the needs of separating and separated fathers? What are the implications in terms of resources, for policy and practice, of developing an engagement with the gendered nature of these emotional and psychosocial aspects of separation?

---

[111] Kaganas, above Ch 3. See further S. Boyd, *Child Custody, Law and Women's Work*, Oxford: Oxford University Press, 2003: M. Fineman, *The Neutered Mother, The Sexual Family, and Other Twentieth Century Tragedies*, New York: Routledge, 1995; A. Diduck, 'In search of the feminist good mother', 1998 vol 7 (1), *Social and Legal Studies* p 129; M. Fineman and I. Karpin (eds), *Mothers in Law: Feminist Theory and the Legal Regulation of Motherhood*, New York: Columbia University Press, 1995; E. Silva (ed.), *Good Enough Mothering? Feminist Perspectives on Lone Motherhood*, London: Routledge, 1996.

[112] Collier and Sheldon, 2008, op cit.

[113] Page *et al.*, op cit.

I recognise that, for some, the impact of raising these issues in the context of a discussion of fathers rights and law (and thus of a chapter such as this) may be profoundly problematic, in that it might be read as serving to increase popular and academic sympathy for the concerns and arguments of fathers' rights groups. Further, that it may divert academic attention from the deleterious consequences of their actions for women and children. By placing these debates within the broader context of social and legal changes around rights, gender and family law, however, it becomes possible to look to that 'bigger picture' and unpack something of the complexity of what may actually be happening here, and to recognise that these developments raise important questions for legal systems in dealing with separation. These changes tell us much about the shifting relation between rights, gender and family law. This 'transformation in the role of the father' has taken place both in the slipstream of feminism and the women's movement,[114] and in the context of the embedding in law, and heightened cultural salience of, ideas of gender neutrality and formal equality. It is against this backdrop that the terrain of fathers' rights politics has evolved. What is taking place around fathers' rights represents a complex social development that raises important questions about diverse aspects of social life. The reframing of parental responsibility in family law, the forceful legal imperatives of co-parenting and the messages conveyed about active fathering within law and popular culture are, research suggests, reshaping men's expectations of equity and fairness in the process of divorce. Dealing with the implications of these issues raises complex questions for political systems in the development of law and policy around families, as well as important questions for future research.

---

[114] On the influence of feminism in family policy, see Diduck and O'Donovan, op cit.

Chapter 7

Mandatory prosecution and arrest as a form of compliance with due diligence duties in domestic violence – the gender implications

Shazia Choudhry

This chapter is concerned with the impact of rights discourse on the issue of domestic violence and the gender implications that employing such a discourse entails. It will start with outlining how women's organisations harnessed international human rights norms in order to produce international legislation designed to combat domestic violence and simultaneously introduce state responsibility, by way of due diligence mechanisms, in order to measure compliance with their obligations. A brief outline of human rights instruments at the regional and domestic level, the European Convention on Human Rights and the Human Rights Act 1998, will demonstrate how such instruments can and have been used by individual victims of domestic violence to enforce State compliance with their obligations under these instruments. The second part of the chapter examines the effectiveness of mandatory arrest and conviction policies as a means of state compliance with the positive obligations created by international human rights instruments. The pros and cons of these policies will also be examined from the feminist perspective as will the implications that the adoption of such policies hold for women. The chapter will conclude with recommendations concerning the use of such policies in a manner which strikes the right balance between respecting the human rights of women, individuals and society as a whole.

Second wave feminism and international human rights

Domestic violence occurs on a domestic and global level. It has therefore become an issue of both national and international legal concern. The recognition of the issue at the international level was, however, brought about, in large part, by the intensive grass-roots work and lobbying of the international women's movement and thus, as Chesney-Lind[1] has argued, needs to be understood by reference to second wave feminism. This work culminated at the World Conference on Human Rights in Vienna in 1993 where demands by feminist organisations, that domestic violence be

---

[1] M. Chesney-Lind, 'Patriarchy, crime and justice: feminist criminology in an era of backlash', *Feminist* (2006) 1 *Criminology*, 6–26.

recognised as a violation of women's human rights, directly contributed to the adoption of the Declaration on the Elimination of Violence against Women[2] by the General Assembly later that year. It was in this declaration that the United Nations defined the term 'violence against women' as:

> Any act of gender-based violence that results in, or is likely to result in, physical, sexual or psychological harm or suffering to women, including threats of such acts, coercion or arbitrary deprivation of liberty, whether occurring in public or private life.[3]

The declaration also urged States, in Art 4(c), to "exercise due diligence to prevent, investigate and, in accordance with national legislation, punish acts of violence against women, whether those acts are perpetrated by the State or by private persons."[4] The acceptance of the fact that violence against women was global, systematic, and rooted in power imbalances and structural inequalities between men and women was therefore integral to the international recognition of domestic violence as a human rights issue. Following Vienna, the Beijing Declaration and Platform for Action,[5] consolidated these gains by underlining that violence against women is both a violation of women's human rights and an impediment to the full enjoyment by women of all human rights. The result is that a number of international[6]

---

[2] United Nations General Assembly resolution . 'Declaration on the Elimination of Violence against Women'. A/RES/48/104, 20 December 1993.

[3] Committee on the Elimination of Discrimination against Women General Recommendation No. 19, para 7. In addition, General recommendation No. 19 (1992) of the Committee on the Elimination of Discrimination against Women (CEDAW), asserted unequivocally that violence against women constituted a form of gender-based discrimination and that discrimination is a major cause of such violence. This was despite the fact that the Convention does not explicitly refer to violence against women.

[4] Other declarations contain similar requirements as to due diligence: CEDAW, in its General recommendation No. 19 (1992) called on states to act with due diligence to prevent and respond to violence against women. Article 7(b) of the Inter-American Convention on the Prevention, Punishment and Eradication of Violence against Women (1994) (Convention of Belém do Para), requires that states 'apply due diligence to prevent, investigate and impose penalties for violence against women'.

[5] Adopted by 189 countries at the Fourth World Conference on Women in Beijing in 1995.

[6] The International Bill of Human Rights, comprised the Universal Declaration of Human Rights 1948, the International Covenant on Civil and Political Rights 1966 and the International Covenant on Economic, Social and Cultural Rights 1966, sets forth general human rights standards that victims of domestic violence may invoke against their state of citizenship if that state is a party to the above instruments. The same can be done under the Convention on the Elimination of All Forms of Discrimination against Women, 1979, together with its Optional Protocol of 2000, and under the Convention against Torture and Other Cruel, Inhuman, or Degrading Treatment or Punishment, 1984. See Byrnes and Bath, 'Violence against women, the obligation of due diligence, and the Optional Protocol to the Convention on the Elimination of All Forms of Discrimination Against Women – recent developments', *Human Rights Law Review*, 2008, 8(3), 517–33 for an overview of recent successes.

and regional[7] human rights instruments now exist which can be used to assert the rights of battered women against their home countries on the basis that they articulate a state's duty to protect fundamental human rights that are commonly violated in domestic violence cases. Those rights include the right to life, the right to physical and mental integrity, the right to equal protection of the laws and the right to be free from discrimination and tortuous treatment.[8] Thus, states must not only ensure that their criminal *and* civil laws adequately protect the victims of domestic violence but also that they do so on an equal footing with other victims of violence. The first Special Rapporteur on violence against women[9] has thus described the violence against women movement as 'perhaps the greatest success story of international mobilization around a specific human rights issue, leading to the articulation of international norms and standards and the formulation of international programmes and policies'.[10]

However, while such declarations are important for their ability to highlight the need for the development of national policies to combat and eradicate domestic violence, they also have their limitations. International declarations, in the main, carry political weight but they are not, on their own, legally binding instruments. That is, unless they are seen as embodying notions of customary human rights law, which has a legally binding effect upon states.[11]As such, the implementation of such measures is highly dependent upon political will and the commitment of significant resources. This is not always available or, indeed, possible. Furthermore, there has been significant criticism from feminist quarters with regard to the general inability, it is argued, of international human rights law to adequately reflect and

---

[7] The European Convention for the Protection of Human Rights and Fundamental Freedoms 1950, the American Convention on Human Rights 1969, together with the Inter-American Convention on the Prevention, Punishment and Eradication of Violence Against Women 1994 and the African Charter on Human and Peoples' Rights 1981 are the major regional human rights documents that may be invoked by victims of domestic violence.

[8] Advocates and scholars increasingly recognise that domestic violence is a form of torture. Under international human rights law, torture is severe mental or physical pain or suffering that is intentionally inflicted either by a state actor or with the consent or acquiescence of a state actor for an unlawful purpose.

[9] The mandate of the Special Rapporteur on violence against women, its causes and consequences, was established by the Commission on Human Rights in 1994 (Commission on Human Rights resolution 1994/45) and was extended in 1997, 2000 and 2003 (Commission on Human Rights resolutions 1997/44, 2000/45 and 2003/45). This mandate created an institutional mechanism for regular in-depth review and reporting on violence against women around the world.

[10] R. Coomaraswamy, 'The varied contours of violence against women in South Asia', paper presented at the Fifth South Asia Regional Ministerial Conference, Celebrating Beijing +10, Islamabad, Pakistan, 3–5 May 2005.

[11] See A. Vesa, 'International and regional standards for protecting victims of domestic violence' (2004) 12 *Am. U.J. Gender Soc. Policy & Law* 309.

respond to the experiences and needs of women.[12] This issue is further exacerbated by the individualistic language and mainstream understanding of rights which, in turn, are based upon a male model of what it is to be human.[13] Thus, the discourse has been said to have remained blind to structural inequalities and done little to challenge the patriarchal nature of the state.[14] However, these deficiencies have not gone unnoticed by those working within the international human rights arena. The current UN Special Rapporteur on Violence against Women[15] has recently noted:

> The application of the due diligence standard, to date, has tended to be limited to responding to violence against women when it occurs and in this context it has concentrated on legislative reform, access to justice and the provision of services. There has been relatively little work done on the more general obligation of prevention, including the duty to transform patriarchal gender structures and values that perpetuate and entrench violence against women.

As a result, some work has been done on how the human rights discourse can move onto the next level, of challenging and changing the patriarchal nature of the State. This work will be examined in the next section.

Regional and domestic human rights instruments – the European Convention on Human Rights and the Human Rights Act 1998

The ECHR, as a regional instrument, has proved itself to be much more effective than other such instruments in ensuring State compliance with the human rights norms it represents. In brief, the ECHR acknowledges the

[12] See R. Cook (ed.), *Human Rights of Women: National and International Perspectives*, Philadelphia: University of Pennsylvania Press 1994; J. Peters and A. Wolper (eds), *Women's Rights, Human Rights: International Feminist Perspectives*, New York: Routledge, 1995; K. Askin and D. Koenig (eds), *Women and International Human Rights Law*, New York: Transnational Publishers, 1999; H. Charlesworth and C. Chinkin, 'The boundaries of international law: a feminist analysis,' in M. Schill (ed.) *Studies in International Law*, Manchester: Manchester University Press 2000.

[13] C. Bunch. 1995, 'Transforming human rights from a feminist perspective', in *Women's Rights Human Rights: International Feminist Perspectives*, Peters and Wolper, (eds) 1993 pp 11–17.

[14] Asian Pacific Forum on Women, Law and Development, Draft report of the Asia-Pacific Regional Consultation, 'Access to justice: holding the state accountable for violence against women,' 5–6 October 2005, Bangkok, Thailand, p 14.

[15] Y. Erturk, 'Integration of the human rights of women and the gender perspective: violence against women – the due diligence standards as a tool for the elimination of violence against women', Report of the Special Rapporteur on Violence Against Women, its Causes and Consequences, to the United Nations Commission on Human Rights, E/CN.4/2006/61, 20 January 2006 p 6.

right to life in Art 2 and the right to be free from torture and from inhuman or degrading treatment or punishment in Art 3. Article 1 requires all States Parties to secure the rights and freedoms delineated within the ECHR 'to everyone within their jurisdiction' and Art 14 discusses the ECHR's ban on gender-based discrimination, women and men being equally entitled to the aforementioned rights. Finally, Art 8 requires the right to private and family life to be respected. However, it was only very recently, in two highly significant decisions, that the ECtHR was able to finally apply the Convention to the issue. In *Kontrovia* v *Slovakia*[16] the applicant, a victim of domestic violence, brought a claim regarding her inability to obtain compensation from the police department, who had failed to take action with regard to a number of reports she had made concerning the violence of her husband and, which, eventually resulted in her husband killing their two children. This was despite the fact that the domestic courts had found that three of the police officers involved had been in dereliction of their duties under domestic law. In finding that her Art 2 rights had been breached by the failures of the police to act, the ECtHR reiterated the general principles of Art 2[17] and, in particular, the duty, in appropriate circumstances, to a positive obligation on the authorities to take preventive operational measures to protect an individual whose life is at risk from the criminal acts of another individual. Thus a positive obligation to take positive action to prevent a risk to a victim of domestic violence may arise within certain limited circumstances.[18] In addition, the likelihood of a breach will almost certainly occur where the authorities have failed to satisfy, in particular, their own domestic obligations towards such victims, particularly where Arts 2 and 3 are engaged. If this is the case, it is also clear that civil liability for damages ought to be made available to victims under Art 13.

The second case to come before the ECtHR, specifically on the issue of domestic violence, was addressed by the court under Art 8. In *Bevacqua and another* v *Bulgaria*[19] the applicant mother, a victim of domestic violence, found herself in the position of having to agree to shared care of their 3-year-old child (the second applicant) with her violent husband when, instead of dealing with her application for interim custody, she was threatened with prosecution for the abduction of the child. The alleged abduction had, in fact, arisen when she fled the family home with her child for a hostel for victims of domestic violence in another town. Violence

---

[16] (& App No. 7510/04;) 31 May 2007.
[17] Set out in *LCB and Osman* v *the United Kingdom* [1998] 29 EHRR 245.
[18] The European Court of Human Rights used a variant of the due diligence standard in *Osman* v *United Kingdom* to further develop its case law in relation to the obligations of states to provide protection against human rights violations by non-state actors.
[19] App No. (71127/01), 12 June 2008.

against the applicant continued however and, after a series of further proceedings, the applicant was eventually granted custody of the child, the domestic courts having accepted that witnessing such behaviour from the father was a bad example 'for a young boy to witness'[20] Crucially, however, the father was not prosecuted for any of the violence used against the applicant both before and subsequent to this decision. After a detailed examination of the facts, the ECtHR held that by not dealing with the application for interim custody with due diligence and without delay, the authorities' had failed to secure the enjoyment of both applicants right to normal contacts between them and, as a result, a breach of Art 8 had occurred. A number of important points were made in the judgment. First, that the positive obligations under Art 8 could include, in certain circumstances, a duty to maintain and apply in practice an adequate legal framework affording protection against acts of violence by private individuals.[21] Second, there was reliance on a number of international instruments to emphasise the particular vulnerability of the victims of domestic violence and the need for active state involvement in their protection.[22] Finally, and of most significance, was the articulation by the Court of the second applicants (the child's) right to respect to family life and the ability to effectively exercise his right to regular contact with his mother. Of particular note was the clear recognition by the Court of the adverse affects upon his welfare of having to witness the violence between his parents. Thus, victims of domestic violence can rely on these Convention rights via the Human Rights Act 1998 and if, after exhausting all domestic remedies, their situation does not improve, they may also be able to take the matter to the ECtHR.

Further, Convention rights are now, under the HRA, capable of direct enforcement. The vertical effect of the Act is demonstrated by s 6 which states that public authorities can be held liable for the breach of Convention rights. In addition, two private individuals are also capable of bringing a claim against each other by virtue of the horizontal effect of the Act. There are three main ways in which claims could be brought under the HRA which would be advantageous to the victims of domestic violence. First, under the Human Rights Act 1998 public authorities are required to protect victims of violence.[23] This means the government, police, prosecution authorities and courts are required to take positive steps to protect victims of violence. Rights in the domestic violence context should, thus, not be seen as restraining government activity, but rather compelling it. Second, that where

---

[20] See para. 37. It was not specified whether this view was from the point of view of the child's welfare or just simply a bad example. The court went on to simply add that 'The first applicant was therefore better suited to raise the child.'

[21] Ibid, para 65.

[22] *Bevacqua and another* v *Bulgaria* (App No. 71127/01),12 June 2008 para 53.

[23] *Islam (AP)* v *Secretary of State for the Home Department* [1999] 2 All ER 545.

the court must balance the property and privacy interests of the perpetrator and the right to protection of the victim, the Human Rights Act 1998 should be used to require the courts to place most weight on the interests of the victim. Third, the Human Rights Act 1998 requires particular attention to be paid to the interests of children. Growing evidence of the harmful impact of domestic violence on children's welfare can therefore be used to necessitate state intervention in order to protect children.

It is important to recognise at this point in the analysis therefore, that applying a human rights framework *can* bring about concrete protection for the victims of domestic violence. In *Kontrovia*, Art 2 was successfully utilised to ensure that states now have an additional financial incentive to ensure that the positive obligations towards protecting those victims of domestic violence, whose lives are at significant risk, are adequately protected. In *Bevacqua* we saw Art 8 being utilised to ensure that domestic legislatures manage the intersection between child contact and domestic violence in a manner which does not place both the child and adult victims of domestic violence at risk of further danger where this is clearly foreseeable. Thus, as the UN Secretary-General[24] has argued, claims on the state in this respect can 'move from the realm of discretion and become legal entitlements.'[25] Addressing the issue as one of human rights is therefore capable of empowering women, 'positioning them not as passive recipients of discretionary benefits but as active rights holders.'[26]

However, as has been well documented, taking a claim to the European Court of Human Rights is not only extremely difficult and costly but also very slow. This was something that the domestic incorporation of the ECHR via the HRA was supposed to solve. Unfortunately, the oft cited aim of the HRA to 'bring rights home' has not, as the author has noted elsewhere,[27] materialised within the context of domestic violence. What is particularly striking is the total lack of reference to human rights when discussing the issue by both the executive and the judiciary. For example, the National Action Plan on Domestic Violence[28] published by the Home Office and the most recent guidelines on sentencing in domestic violence cases[29] make no

---

[24] See the United Nations General Assembly, Report of the Secretary General, 'In depth study of all forms of violence against women', A/61/122/Add.1, 6 July 2006, pp 17–18.

[25] Ibid, p 18, para 39.

[26] UN Report, 'In depth study of all forms of violence against women,' p 18, para 40.

[27] See S. Choudhry and J. Herring. 'Domestic violence and the Human Rights Act 1998: a new means of legal intervention' [2006] *Public Law*, 752–84; S. Choudhry and J. Herring, 'Righting Domestic Violence' (2006) 20 *International Journal of Law, Policy and the Family*, 1–25.

[28] Home Office, *Domestic Violence – A National Report*, March 2005.

[29] Issued by the Sentencing Guidelines Council, Overarching Principles: Domestic Violence, Definitive Guideline, December 2006.

reference to human rights at all. Similarly, court decisions on domestic violence have paid little or no attention as to how the Human Rights Act 1998 affects the issues raised.[30] In only one official document[31] produced by the National Policing Improvement Agency on behalf of the Association of Chief Police Officers, was the need for positive action towards victims of domestic violence, as a direct effect of the HRA, explicitly mentioned. It is not surprising therefore that anecdotal evidence from those working within women's organisations demonstrates that there is very little knowledge of how to use the HRA and international instruments effectively. Tania Pouwhare, a women's rights activist working at the Women's Resource Centre in London summed up these concerns in a recent interview:[32]

> I mean, the idea that we're working with human rights issues is absolutely correct but in terms of using the instruments, that's the tricky bit. ...
> We just don't have the kind of skills to be able to say 'here's a situation, right, this is how we use the Human Rights Act' or 'this is how we're going to use the Optional Protocol'. What I would really like is a guide that gives an example and then it [tells you how to file your claim]. So if you don't know how it works, you tend to think it's about capacity, because I haven't got enough time to sit down and [work it out].

Thus, although the HRA has the potential to be used as a powerful legal and political tool to combat domestic violence, the understanding of how individual victims of domestic violence can readily access, understand and utilise it to their immediate advantage has been limited within the UK. One further issue, which could also be regarded as problematic, is one which is caused by the communitarian nature of the ECHR. This element of the document requires that the interests of the individual to be balanced against the interests of the state and/or wider interest of the community. It is this balance which may, consequently, set up a particular conflict when applied to the specific context of domestic violence and which may cause further concern from the feminist point of view.

---

[30] Only in relation to the committal proceedings that will concern Art 6 rights of the defendant. See *Mubarak* v *Mubarak* [2001] 1 FCR 193, 203 and 207, CA; *DPP* v *Tweddell* [2001] EWCA Admin 188 [2002] 1 FCR 438; *Clibbery* v *Allan* [2002] EWCA Civ 45 [2002] 1 FCR 385 [2002] 1 FLR 565.

[31] The National Policing Improvement Agency, 'Guidance on investigating domestic abuse', 2008.

[32] See G. Grabham and R. Hunter, '"It's another way of making a really big fuss" human rights and women activism in the United Kingdom: an interview with Tania Pouwhare' (2008) 16 *Feminist Legal Studies* 97–112, pp 104–5.

Mandatory arrest and prosecution policies as a means of state compliance with human rights – an assessment of the gender implications

The purpose of this chapter is thus not to outline the detailed application of the HRA and the ECHR to UK domestic violence provisions[33] but rather, to examine the gender implications of one of the ways that it has been suggested that the state could comply with its positive obligations towards the victims of domestic violence: by implementing a mandatory prosecution and arrest policy. However, before doing so it is necessary to consider the prevalence of domestic violence within the UK today and the current police and prosecutorial response to it.

The extent of the problem

Although domestic violence is chronically under-reported, research[34] estimates it accounts for 16 per cent of all violent crime and that it will affect one in four women and one in six men in their lifetime. Further, 77 per cent of victims of domestic violence are women and domestic violence has more repeat victims than any other crime. On average there will have been 35 assaults before a victim calls the police.[35] Other research has found that one incident of domestic violence is reported to the police every minute.[36] On average, two women a week are killed by a current or former male partner and nearly half of all female murder victims are killed by a partner or ex-partner.[37] It is also apparent that the problem is not confined to adult women. A recent survey found that 16 per cent of the teenage girls that were questioned (whose average age was 15) had been hit by their boyfriends. A further 15 per cent had been pushed and 6 per cent forced to have sex by their boyfriends.[38] Domestic violence can also be measured in terms of its costs to wider society. A recent Home Office study[39] estimated that the total annual costs of domestic violence to the Criminal Justice

---

[33] S. Choudhry and J. Herrring, 'Domestic violence and the Human Rights Act 1998' and 'Righting domestic violence'.

[34] 'Crime in England and Wales 2006/2007', produced by the Research Development and Statistics Directorate within the Crime Reduction and Community Safety Group in the Home Office

[35] Ibid.

[36] Elizabeth Stanko, 'The day to count: a snapshot of the impact of domestic violence in the UK' (2000) 1 *Criminal Justice* 2.

[37] Claire Flood-Page and Joanna Taylor (eds), Crime in England and Wales 2001/2002: supplementary Vol (London: Home Office, 2003), p 12.

[38] NSPCC *Teen Abuse Survey of Great Britain*, London: NSPCC, 2005.

[39] Walby, *The Cost of Domestic Violence*, London: DTI Women and Equality Unit, 2004. See also Brand and Price, 'The economic and social costs of crime', Home Office Research Study 217, London 2000.

System, health services, social services, housing and civil legal aid amounted to £3.1 billion each year. The cost to the economy was found to be a further £2.7 billion.

A more recent concern has been the effect of domestic violence upon children. Research has demonstrated that children can experience domestic violence not only as direct victims but also as witnesses. At least 750,000 children a year witness domestic violence[40] and in London 30 per cent of domestic violence murders are witnessed by children.[41] Children who live with domestic violence are at increased risk of behavioural problems, emotional trauma, and mental health difficulties in adult life[42] Nearly three-quarters of children deemed to be 'at risk' live in households where domestic violence occurs and 52 per cent of child protection cases involve domestic violence[43] One of the effects of domestic violence between adults is thus that experiencing domestic violence directly or indirectly as a child can constitute child abuse. Current child protection policies reflect this fact in that a 'failure to protect' may result in social services involvement and possible removal of the child from the family. Thus, an additional conflict has been set up, between the victim mother and the victim child.[44] Further, if we recall that children's interests are accorded at the very least, priority at the European[45] and international[46] level and, as a maximum, *paramountcy* at the domestic level it is clear that the individual interests of a parent victim of domestic violence could easily be overridden by the interests of the child, if those interests are threatened by choices made by that parent – choices which can range from a failure to leave an abusive relationship or to co-operate in action taken against the perpetrator.

---

[40] Department of Health, *Secure Futures for Women: Making a Difference*, London: Department of Health, 2002.

[41] Metropolitan Police, Findings from the Multi-Agency Domestic Violence Murder Reviews in London, London: Metropolitan Police, 2003, 10.

[42] A. Mullender, *Children Living With Domestic Violence: Putting Men's Abuse of Women on the Childcare Agenda*, London: Whiting and Birch, 1995; M. Hester, C. Pearson and N. Harwin, N. (2000; new edn 2007) *Making an Impact: Children and Domestic Violence*, London: Jessica Kingsley, 2007.

[43] Department of Health, *Secure Futures for Women*; E. Farmer and M. Owen, *Child Protection Practice: Private Risks and Public Remedies*, London: HMSO, 1995.

[44] For a review of the tension this has created, see: R. Smith, 'The wrong end of the telescope: child protection or child safety?' (2002) 24 *Journal of Social Welfare and Family Law*, 247–61.

[45] See, e.g. *Suss* v *Germany* App No. para 43 and *Zawadka* v *Poland* (2004) 38 EHRR 15 para 44.

[46] UN Convention on the Rights of a Child, Art 3.

The police response

The police are the statutory agency that is most often told about domestic violence by victims.[47] The importance of this is highlighted when we recall that only a minority of incidents of domestic violence are reported to the police, with estimates varying between 23 per cent[48] and 35 per cent.[49] The response of the police is thus crucial and despite the fact that a number of policies and initiatives have been implemented, which encourage proactive investigation and arrest,[50] (and thus represents a 'discretionary' rather than 'mandatory' arrest policy) recent evidence given to the Home Affairs Select Committee demonstrates that problems in attitude with rank-and-file police officers continue which has undoubtedly had a negative effect upon victim reporting of domestic violence.[51] Of those incidents reported, typically only 26 per cent of incidents result in arrest and 7 per cent of incidents result in charge.[52] A report by the Independent Police Complaints Commission (IPCC)[53] in July 2007 highlighted a range of problems with the police response to a range of domestic homicide cases: namely, a lack of awareness of the circumstances likely to trigger domestic violence, a failure to recognise factors in a perpetrator's history that showed a need for intelligence in order to assess risk and a complete lack of risk assessment or review on an escalation of violence. As a result, the Select Committee concluded that 'failure by the police adequately to assess the risk of harm to victims has, in a number of cases, resulted in homicides which might have been prevented.'[54] The government has thus set a National Delivery Plan Target for the Association of Chief Police Officers to train all frontline officers in domestic violence by 2008.[55]

---

[47] Followed by medical services, legal advisers, counsellors and community and religious leaders. See D. James-Hanman, *Domestic Violence and the Asian Community*, London Borough of Hounslow, Equal Opportunities Unit, 1990.

[48] Stanko, 'The Day to Count'.

[49] S. Walby and J. Allen, Domestic Violence, Sexual Assault and Stalking: Findings from the British Crime Survey, Home Office Research Study 276, 2004.

[50] See The National Policing Improvement Agency, *Guidance on Investigating Domestic Abuse*, 2008, pp 29–30 which reminds officers of the need for positive action to be taken towards victims of domestic violence under the HRA but still provides for situations where, although there are grounds for arrest, an arrest may not be appropriate.

[51] House of Commons, Home Affairs Committee, 'Domestic Violence, Forced Marriage and Honour Killings', Sixth Report of Session 2007/8, Vol 1, para 192–203.

[52] Ibid, para 194 given by Chief Constable Brian Moore, ACPO lead for domestic violence.

[53] IPCC Learning the Lessons Bulletin, 'Domestic violence', 1 June 2007 available at: www.learningthelessons.org.uk/bulletins/bulletins_one.htm.

[54] House of Commons, Home Affairs Committee, 'Domestic Violence, Forced Marriage and Honour Killings,' para 191.

[55] Ibid, para 199.

The prosecutorial response

How successful are we at dealing with those offenders that are actually charged? Although there is no national figure, in areas in which the attrition process has been tracked, it is extremely low, at around 5 per cent.[56] This is comparable to the conviction rate for rape, which is 5.7 per cent. The reasons for such low prosecution and conviction rates are multiple and complex, however, it is clear that inconsistent application of CPS policy by prosecutors[57] and problematic attitudes and processes within the court system[58] have played a part. Notwithstanding these issues, it is also clear that the difficulty of cataloguing sufficient evidence of abuse to mount a prosecution plays a significant role, as does the high rate of retraction of statements by victims. The CPS recently reported, in evidence to the Home Affairs Select Committee[59] that a 'snapshot' of domestic violence case statistics recorded by them showed that the proportion of victims who retracted their statement was 28 per cent in 2006 compared with a rate of 10.8 per cent for all cases handled by the CPS.[60] The CPS has acted to counterbalance this, in line with its current policy[61] by, in particular, prosecuting cases despite retraction by the victim, where there is sufficient evidence to do so. Thus, current CPS policy states that:

> Generally, the more serious the offence because of, for example, the presence of children, or the level of violence used or the real and continuing threat to the victim or others, the more likely the CPS are to prosecute in the public interest, even if the victims do not wish the same.[62]

If this is the case, the CPS will then consider three options: to apply to the court to use the victim's statement as evidence without the victim having to

---

[56] In areas in which the attrition process has been tracked, for example in the Northumbria Police Force area, where, out of a total of 2,402 domestic violence incidents, perpetrators were arrested, charged and convicted in only 120 incidents (5 per cent), Hester and Westmarland, Criminal Justice Matter, (2007) cited in para 267 of the House of Commons, Home Affairs Committee, 'Domestic Violence, Forced Marriage and Honour Killings'.

[57] See paras 2.44, 3.28, 7.27, 7.3, 7.5 and 7.68 of the HM Inspectorate of Constabulary (HMIC) A Joint Inspection of the Investigation and Prosecution of Cases Involving Domestic Violence, 2004.

[58] Such as a reduction in the availability of legal aid, inadequate sentencing of offenders and ignorance from magistrates and judges. These issues thus account for further attrition once cases reach the courts. See House of Commons, Home Affairs Committee, 'Domestic Violence, Forced Marriage and Honour Killings', paras 283–305.

[59] Ibid, paras 270–72.

[60] Crown Prosecution Service Annual Report and Resource Accounts, 2006–7.

[61] CPS guidance: 'Policy for Prosecuting Cases of Domestic Violence', 2005.

[62] Ibid, para 5.13.

give evidence in court, to proceed with the prosecution by helping the victim to attend court by the use of special measures[63] or to compel the victim to give evidence in person in court.[64] As such, current CPS policy would appear to be in the 'soft' no-drop category and there is evidence that it has had some success. The CPS has recently reported[65] that it decided to continue with the prosecution of 49 per cent of cases where statements were retracted by the victim in 2006.This represents an increase from 19 per cent in 2002. A range of other evidence is currently being employed by the CPS to prosecute cases: such as using 999 tapes, photographs, evidence from other people who may have witnessed the violence and the encouragement of the victim. In addition, the establishment of the first Specialist Domestic Violence Courts (SDVCs) in 2005 along with Multi-Agency Risk Assessment Conferences (MARACs) and Independent Domestic Violence Advisers (IDVAs) will enable domestic violence cases to be fast-tracked, and to be heard by specially trained magistrates, with support for victims from specialist staff, including IDVAs.

Why use mandatory policies at all?

Aside from a good method of compliance with human rights obligations, such policies hold other benefits. Mandatory arrest and prosecution sends a clear and powerful message to perpetrators that their behaviour is criminal and will not be tolerated by the rest of society.[66] Of particular weight is the argument that such policies show the victim that domestic violence is not an individual and 'private' issue, requiring her to take sole responsibility to end the behaviour, but rather it is a societal problem attracting state responsibility.[67]

---

[63] An application has to be made to the Court under the Special Measures Youth Justice and Criminal Evidence Act 1999. Measures include: the use of screens in the courtroom to shield a victim or other witness from the defendant; giving evidence away from the courtroom through a live television link; clearing the public gallery in sexual offence cases or cases involving intimidation, giving evidence through an intermediary and giving video-recorded evidence.

[64] This is, however, rarely used. Note, however, the policy also states that 'an experienced prosecutor will only make that decision after consultation with the police and with the safety of the victim and any child or vulnerable person as a prime consideration. In cases involving same-sex relationships, where relevant we will also consider the consequences of potentially "outing" the victim by the court process.' Para. 5.16 of CPS guidance: 'Policy for Prosecuting Cases of Domestic Violence', 2005.

[65] Crown Prosecution Service Annual Report and Resource Accounts, 2006–7.

[66] Jessica Dayton, 'The silencing of a woman's choice: mandatory arrest and no drop. Prosecution policies in domestic violence cases' (2003) 9 *Cardozo Women's Law Journal*, 281, 284–85.

[67] See Donna M. Welch, 'Comment, mandatory arrest of domestic abusers, panacea or perpetuation of the problem of abuse?' (1994) 43 *DePaul Law Review*, 1133, 1153.

In addition, mandatory arrest policies can also provide victims with essential 'breathing space' and the time and opportunity to access non-law enforcement services, such as counselling and alternative housing in order to form a plan for their future safety.[68] Such policies also have the added advantage of illustrating how the balance, required by the Convention, between the interests of the individual and the interests of the community may result in certain conflicts within the context of domestic violence. However, what is arguably of most significance about these policies is their potential to transform the patriarchal nature of the state. Yakin Erturk,[69] the current UN Special Rapporteur on domestic violence, has recently argued that each of the different powers of the state has a role to play in changing patriarchal values. Prosecutors as exercisers of state power are representatives of the state and can thus be defined as state actors. Any action consequently taken by prosecutors is therefore state action and is part of the character of the state.[70] The effects of prosecutorial action are thus twofold, according to Erturk: *consequential*, in that condemnations of patriarchy may lead to changes in socio-cultural norms and *intrinsic*, in that strong statements made by prosecutors through their actions against violence against women will make that society less patriarchal.[71] It is, however, as Madden Dempsey[72] argues, the intrinsic value of prosecutions that are of most significance when assessing their effectiveness in relation to combating domestic violence because this will require an examination of the extent to which prosecutorial actions have transformed the character of the state into being less patriarchal.

In human rights terms, the discretionary arrest and 'soft' prosecution policy that is currently in place in the UK certainly goes some way towards complying with the positive obligations of the state in such cases. A mandatory or preferred arrest and 'hard' prosecution policy would go even further by taking the discretion out of the police response when confronted with a domestic violence call-out and, out of the CPS's hands when there is a real chance of prosecution, despite a withdrawal of the victim's co-operation. Although this would not, as the evidence above indicates, provide a one-stop solution to the depressingly high rate of attrition for domestic violence related crimes, such policies could potentially hold significant *intrinsic* feminist

---

[68] Donna Wills, 'Domestic violence: the case for aggressive prosecution' (1997) 7 *UCLA Women's L.J.* 173, 181.

[69] Y. Erturk, 'Integration of the human rights of women and the gender perspective: violence against women – the due diligence standards as a tool for the elimination of violence against women' Report of the Special Rapporteur on Violence Against Women, its Causes and Consequences, to the United Nations Commission on Human Rights, E/CN.4/2006/61, 20 January 2006.

[70] Madden Dempsey, 'Toward a feminist state: what does "effective prosecution" of domestic violence mean?' (2007) 70 *Modern Law Review* p 908, 910.

[71] Erturk 'Integration of the human rights of women' p 20.

[72] Madden Dempsey, 'Toward a feminist state', p 910.

value as Madden Dempsey[73] has recently argued. Such intrinsic value is, however, capable of realisation only if, first, they can be regarded as feminist in character and, second, that they become habituated within the prosecutorial and police process and thus within the state itself. One important qualification is made in her analysis however, and which is of particular relevance to the question of which type of mandatory prosecution and arrest policies would satisfy these criteria. Any such prosecutorial policies need to distinguish between what she terms domestic violence in its strong sense, which tends to sustain or perpetuate patriarchy and domestic violence in its weak sense, which does not tend to sustain or perpetuate patriarchy. The classic example of 'strong' domestic violence would, according to Madden Dempsey,[74] be 'wife beating' but may also include 'domestic abuse' consisting of a refusal to allow access to money, friends and generally possessive behaviour. Examples of 'weak' domestic violence would include 'a slap by a woman on her male partner's cheek to convey offence, the actions of a victim of domestic violence in its strong sense who engages in violent retaliation against his or her abuser and 'domestic conflict' such as the loss of temper and play fighting. Interpreting mandatory policies to apply only to cases of domestic violence in its strong sense and categorising an abused woman's violent resistance as domestic violence in its weak sense thus enables prosecutors to retain discretion to dismiss charges in such cases despite the existence of mandatory policies.'[75] Madden Dempsey thus offers a way in which mandatory policies can be assessed against one of the major aims of feminism, the reduction of state patriarchy. However, other concerns have also been expressed about the effectiveness of such policies from feminist quarters and these concerns will also need to be examined before we can conclude whether either type of policy is feminist enough in both nature and character to effect any intrinsic *and* consequential change. It is first necessary to define the different types of arrest and prosecution policies that are currently being utilised.

Types of mandatory policies

Mandatory prosecution policies can vary in both form and process, but can essentially be divided into what has been termed 'hard or 'soft' no-drop policies.[76] 'Hard' policies require prosecutors to pursue cases regardless of

---

[73] Madden Dempsey, 'What counts as domestic violence? A Conceptual Analysis' (2006) 12 *William and Mary Journal of Women and the Law*, 301.

[74] Ibid, p 381 although she uses the term 'structural inequality' as opposed to the term patriarchy used in her later work in the MLR above.

[75] 'Toward a Feminist State', p 935.

[76] N. Mordini, 'Mandatory state interventions for domestic abuse cases: an examination of the effects on victim safety and autonomy' Winter, (2004), 52 *Drake L. Rev.* 295.

the victims' withdrawal of complaints or protests with some requiring victims to testify by issuing summons and threatening prosecution in response to a victims' refusal to co-operate. 'Soft' no-drop policies encourage victims to participate but allow prosecutors some discretion in determining the extent to which the victims' participation is required. Some of these policies may require that the prosecutor consult with the victim prior to making charging decisions, in at least the very serious cases. In both cases, however, the victim's decision-making ability is removed at the point at which charges are brought. She will then take on the position of witness in the case, and the state replaces her as the complaining party. Of particular note, is that if a mandatory arrest policy is also in place, the victim's decision-making ability ends with the phone call to the police; a phone call which she may not have even made.[77]

Arrest policies can be divided into three categories.[78] Mandatory arrest, where police officers must arrest if certain specified circumstances exist.[79] Preferred arrest, where arrest is encouraged if certain specified circumstances exist and discretionary arrest where the law enforcement officer is given the discretion to decide whether or not to make an arrest in certain specified circumstances. Alternative models such as legislation enacted in Austria, Germany and Norway can also give the police more than just the power to arrest by, for example, allowing for the removal of the perpetrator for two weeks[80] and some jurisdictions in the US have enacted 'primary' or 'predominant aggressor' laws. These laws seek to ensure that police officers receive guidance in assessing who is the 'real' offender both in the relationship and in a particular situation, and encourage them to use information about the history of abuse to assist them in distinguishing between defensive and offensive injuries.

Assessing the arguments

The main arguments against policies requiring victims to participate in the arrest and prosecution of their abusive partners have centred on the lack of respect they have for the individual autonomy of the victim and an invasion of her privacy by ever increasing state intervention in familial activities.

---

[77] Ibid.
[78] As categorised by D. Hirschel, E. Buzawa, M. Pattavina, D. Faggiani and A. Reuland in 'Explaining the Prevalence, Context and Consequences of Dual Arrest in Intimate Partner Cases'. Report funded by the National Institute of Justice (Agency of the US Department of Justice) 25 July 2008.
[79] E.g. in Alaska where there is probable cause to believe that a crime of domestic violence was committed within the past 12 hours.
[80] E. Buzawa and C. Buzawa, *Domestic Violence: The Criminal Justice Response*, London: Sage, 2003.

Further, some decisions by the victims of domestic violence can seem to be in conflict. For example, many victims of domestic violence do not necessarily want the relationship to end but do want the violence to stop. Some may feel that it is for the very benefit of the family that the relationship continues and that separating from the violent partner may cause greater harm to the children and their family life than remaining. Forcing such women to co-operate in the arrest and prosecution of their violent partner may not therefore adequately respect the complicated nature of such relationships. Hoyle and Saunders[81] have thus argued that 'the pro arrest approach assumes a position opposite to that of the victim choice model approach: that victims have little agency and that the police and policy makers know what is best for them'. Any arguments that these policies can be justified in the longer-term interests of the autonomy of the victim can thus be seen as deeply problematic not least because it could be viewed as extremely patronising but, most importantly of all, that it may lead to the opening up of floodgates concerning other areas of interest to women. Thus, the argument goes, once autonomy is conceded in one context, it is only a matter of time before further inroads are made into the autonomy of women in other contexts. The preservation of individual autonomy for women can thus, be seen, rightly, as integral to the ability of women to make their own decisions about their own lives and bodies. However, arguments based on the 'privacy' of a domestic violence victim can be viewed as equally problematic when we recall that the 'ideology of privacy'[82] was generally regarded as *enabling* the continuation of domestic violence and was thus one of the first arguments that feminist campaigners sought to dismantle in the early history of the campaign for state intervention in domestic violence. Furthermore, we have seen that where children are involved, the individual autonomy of the victim cannot override the interests of children if those interests are sufficiently threatened. Children (unless of sufficient understanding) are unable to exercise true autonomous choices and are thus dependent upon their parents to make their choices for them. It must be accepted therefore that a victim's autonomy is, and ought to be, at the very least, subject to the interests of any children if those interests are threatened. To do otherwise would surely run counter to current child protection policies and would fail to respect the individual rights of any children in respect of their right to live a life free from violence. Once this is accepted, we must also then accept that victim autonomy within the context of domestic violence has to be qualified to some extent. Implementing mandatory policies of arrest and prosecution as

[81] C. Hoyle and A. Saunders, 'Police responses to domestic violence: from victim choice to victim empowerment' (2000) 40 *British Journal of Criminology* 14.
[82] See for a discussion of the concept generally K. O'Donovan, *Family Law Matters*, London: Pluto, 1993.

part of a human rights framework does not alter this position – victim autonomy must be qualified if the rights and interests of others are as a result being breached by a disproportionate and unjustified level. Applying a human rights analysis will, however, have some effect on the type of policy that is being proposed. Mandatory arrest, as an essentially short-term measure (in that the consequences will be a removal of the perpetrator from the scene of a violent incident) particularly where children are involved, may not necessarily result in a disproportionate infringement of the rights of the victim, where she does not wish the perpetrator to be arrested. State intervention in this context can be seen not only as legitimate and justified, in pursuance of the preservation of law and order but also as a proportionate measure in the heightened situation of a violent incident. However, blanket 'hard' mandatory *prosecution* policies may, depending upon the individual circumstances of a victim of domestic violence, be regarded as a disproportionate interference in her rights by not allowing for enough consideration to be given to the wishes and long-term circumstances of the victim, even though they could be regarded as possibly justifiable in the long-term interests of society. Where the absolute articles are involved, Arts 2 and 3, the Convention requires that the State must step in to ensure that all potential or actual victims of violence which is at a level to breach these articles are *adequately* protected. However, what is regarded as adequate is not specified. It may be the case therefore that a 'soft' rather than 'hard' mandatory prosecution policy may be sufficient to satisfy the positive obligations that have been created under these articles. It may also be that the 'softer' pro arrest and conviction policy represents a more appropriate balance between respecting the autonomy of the individual victim and the interests of the state and wider society. In this way the consequential value of publicly condemning the violence *and* the intrinsic value of prosecuting 'strong' domestic violence with or without the victim's participation can also be maintained.

Other arguments have centred on concerns regarding the general effectiveness of such policies in response to a number of studies examining their impact. On the plus side, one study[83] that examined the impact of a newly implemented mandatory police charging policy in London, Ontario, over a 10-year period found that the implementation of the policy resulted in a dramatic increase in police-laid charges in cases of domestic violence. In 1979, the year prior to the introduction of the policy, police officers laid charges in only three per cent of the occurrences involving spousal assault. By 1983, the figure had risen to 67 per cent and by 1990 to 89 per cent. The study also assessed the extent and severity of violence used by males 12

---

[83] P. Jaffe, H. Hastings, D. Reitzel and G. Austin, 'The impact of police laying charges', in N. Hilton (ed.), *Legal Responses to Wife Assault* Newbury Park, CA: Sage Publications, 1991

months before police intervention and 12 months after police intervention. In the majority of cases, a significant reduction in the level of violence was reported after police intervention and the laying of a charge by police. The most famous study into mandatory arrest policies was, however, undertaken by Sherman and Berk[84] in Minneapolis, USA. They found that arrested abusive partners manifested significantly lower levels of subsequent violence than those who were only given a warning or ordered to leave the premises. Further, compared to arrest, the temporary separation of the victim and offender resulted in two-and-a-half times the number of repeat incidents. Victim interviews also indicated that fewer repeat incidents occurred after arrest than after the use of any other police intervention strategy. However, replication studies conducted in six other American cities produced conflicting results.[85] While in some cases arrest had a crime-reduction effect, particularly for those perpetrators who were employed, married and had earned a secondary school diploma, it was concluded in other instances that arrest actually had a long-term criminogenic effect, increasing the violence among unemployed, unmarried, and minority abusers. These findings raised concerns that the impact of the implementation of mandatory arrest policies could be dependent upon the divergent backgrounds of victims. How desirable is it, however, for these issues to be taken into account at the point of arrest? Furthermore, do they, erroneously, take the focus away from the victim and towards the perpetrator? Ought decisions to arrest be based, as Herschel and Hutchinson[86] on 'victim safety immediately after the arrest, justice and proportionality' rather than theories relating to long-term impacts and differences amongst perpetrators?

One particularly concerning consequence of mandatory arrest policies that has widely been reported has been the increase in dual arrests of both victim and perpetrator[87] with evidence of perpetrators manipulating the criminal justice system by involving the police themselves, self-inflicting wounds and making counter allegations.[88] However, the reliability of these findings has

---

[84] L. Sherman and R. Berk, 'The specific deterrent effects of arrest for domestic assault' (1984) 49 *American Sociological Review*, 261–72.

[85] J. Garner, J. Fagan, and C. Maxwell, (1995) 'Published findings from the spouse assault replication program: a critical review', 11(1) *Journal of Qualitative Criminology*, 3–28.

[86] D. Hirschel and I. Hutchinson, (2003) 'The voices of domestic violence victims: Predictors of victim preference for arrest and the relationship between preference for arrest and re-victimisation', 49(2) *Crime and Delinquency*, 313–36.

[87] R. Tolman, and A. Weisz, (1995) 'Co-ordinated community intervention for domestic violence: the effects of arrest and prosecution on recidivism of woman abuse perpetrators', 41(4) *Crime and Delinquency*, 481–95, 493.

[88] Buzawa and Buzawa, *Domestic Violence: The Criminal Justice Response* 135–38; M. Martin, 'Double your trouble: dual arrest in family violence' (1997) 12 *Journal of Family Violence*, 139–57; S. Miller, 'The paradox of women arrest for domestic violence' (2001) 7 *Violence Against Women*, 1339–76.

recently been questioned[89] on the basis that these studies were limited by their use of a single department, departments in a single state, and/or the size and composition of their sample. Further, past studies into the issue did not compare the police response in domestic to non-domestic violence cases or examine the many factors that influence the police's decision to arrest. The first large-scale and most recent study[90] to examine the police response to intimate partner violence and the issue of dual arrest in 19 US States, conducted by the National Institute of Justice (NIJ), found that although dual arrest rates were higher for intimate partner (1.9 per cent) and other domestics (1.5 per cent) than for acquaintance (1.0 per cent) and stranger (0.8 per cent) cases, the overall dual arrest rate was in fact only 1.3 per cent. However, the study also found that it was the existence of *mandatory* arrest laws (but not preferred arrest laws) that significantly increased the likelihood of dual arrest. Furthermore, prosecutorial decision-making and court outcomes indicated that cases in states with mandatory arrest provisions are more likely *not* to end up in conviction than cases that take place in states with discretionary arrest laws. Meanwhile attempts have been made to deal with the issue. In the US a number of jurisdictions have enacted legislation which requires law enforcement officers to determine the 'principal aggressor' in domestic violence situations through effective evidence gathering and taking into account whether one person has acted in self-defence.[91] Similarly, in the UK, current ACPO guidance[92] stipulates that officers should examine whether the victim may have used justifiable force against the suspect in self-defence and attempt to identify the principal aggressor in a counter-allegation situation. Officers are also told to avoid making dual arrests without conducting a full investigation as to who is the primary aggressor. Unfortunately, research on these issues has not taken place in the UK and is clearly needed in order to assess not only the incidence of dual arrests but also whether current police policy is in any way mitigating the issue.

Leaving aside the interpretation of the results of such studies there is also some doubt as to whether it will ever be possible to ever accurately measure the deterrence value of such policies, as recidivism after an initial arrest and prosecution could be attributable to a number of factors. Thus, as Faubert

---

89 Hirschel, Buzawa, Pattavina, Faggiani and Reuland in 'Explaining the prevalence, context and consequences of dual arrest in intimate partner cases,' p 21.

90 Ibid. Phase I examined all assault and intimidation cases in the year 2000 National Incident-Based Reporting System (NIBRS). This database contains 577,862 police records from 2,819 police departments in 19 states. Based on findings in Phase I 25 police departments were selected in four states for more intensive examination.

91 J. Radford, (2003) 'Professionalising responses to domestic violence in the UK: Definitional difficulties' 2(1) *Community Safety Journal*, 32–39, 38.

92 The National Policing Improvement Agency, 'Guidance on investigating domestic abuse,' 2008, pp 34–35.

and Hinch[93] have noted, where an abusive partner assaults his spouse after having been arrested, it should not be assumed that the arrest itself, isolated from other factors, is the sole cause of the behaviour. Abusive behaviour subsequent to arrest may be attributable to the difficulties associated with marriage breakdown, separation, and divorce. In summary, therefore, studies on the deterrent effect of mandatory charging and arrest policies can be regarded at best as inconclusive and, at worst, an impossible goal to achieve. In terms of the effect on arrests it is apparent that mandatory or preferred arrest policies have had a significant impact on police behaviour. The NIJ study[94] also revealed that mandatory and preferred arrest laws are having the intended effect of producing higher domestic violence arrest rates in states who implemented these policies as compared to states with discretionary arrest laws. In mandatory arrest states, with other factors held constant, the odds of arrest in intimate partner incidents increase by 97 per cent compared to discretionary arrest states. In preferred arrest states the increase was even higher: about 177 per cent.[95] However, the same study found that these policies had the opposite effect on prosecutorial decision-making and court outcome. Cases in states with mandatory warrantless arrest provisions were more likely *not* to end up in conviction than cases that took place in states with discretionary arrest laws.[96] The authors conclude however that this may be more of an indicator of prosecutors dismissing cases in order to handle an increase in caseload created by the higher number of arrests.[97]

What these studies demonstrate therefore is the need for greater vigilance when drafting and implementing such policies and the proper direction of resources to ensure that, not only, victims but also law enforcement agencies are adequately supported throughout the process by being given the necessary training and resources. It is also clear that mandatory arrest and prosecution policies, like all legal measures attempting to deal with the problem of domestic violence, cannot be operated in isolation and need to be 'joined up' with the work of other agencies in order to be truly effective.[98] What these studies do not demonstrate, however, is a compelling

---

[93] J. Faubert and R. Hinch, 'The dialectics of mandatory arrest policies', in T. O'Reilly-Fleming (ed.), *Post-Critical Criminology*, Scarborough, Ont.: Prentice-Hall, 1996, pp 230–51.

[94] Hirschel, Buzawa, Pattavina, Faggiani and Reuland in 'Explaining the prevalence, context and consequences of dual arrest in intimate partner cases'.

[95] Ibid, p 8.

[96] Ibid, p 168.

[97] Ibid.

[98] The establishment of Multi-Agency Risk Assessment Conferences (MARICs) and Specialist Domestic Violence Courts and Advisers are an example of such an approach.

argument for their withdrawal. Thus as Drumbl[99] has argued, the complete absence of any arrest policy is a non-solution, returning the onus to the victim to lay charges herself has been proven only to perpetuate the cycle of violence:

> The simple fact that pro-arrest policies have rough edges does not mean they should be jettisoned ... The real challenge is thus to render these policies sufficiently flexible and contextual so that they can effectively meet the needs of the victim as well as of society more generally.[100]

The way in which the legal process is managed and the high attrition rate in most cases of domestic violence have also been said to have had a further effect of silencing and disempowering women. Landau[101] has thus questioned the utility of continued reliance on such polices in Canada when weaknesses in the ways in which police officers and prosecutors carry out their duties has the overall effect of silencing and disempowering female victims of violence to an even greater degree than before the introduction of the policies. She found, for example, that police rarely documented independent, material evidence of an assault and that, in the vast majority of cases, the only evidence in the file was the statement taken from the victim even though there were witnesses to the assault in over 50 per cent of the cases. Lack of case preparation by the Crown was also cited as a problem with the present system. In fewer than 30 per cent of the cases studied did the victim report meeting with the Crown attorney before the case came to court. Almost 60 per cent of the women reported meeting the Crown for the first time on the day of the trial. As a result she suggests that funds ought to be redirected to shelters, legal aid and social assistance. These issues are certainly in evidence within the UK with victims reporting significant delay in the criminal justice system with uncertainty about dates of trial a major source of frustration and stress.[102] Once in court, survivors of domestic violence have similar experiences to other victims involved in criminal prosecutions in that they find their credibility undermined with tactics including the minimisation and denial of the violence, exploiting

---

[99] M.A. Drumbl, (1994) 'Civil, constitutional and criminal justice responses to female partner abuse: proposals for reform' (1994) 12 *Canadian Journal of Family Law*, 115–69.

[100] Ibid para 68.

[101] T. C. Landau, (2000) 'Women's experiences with mandatory charging for wife assault in Ontario, Canada: a case against the prosecution' (2000) 7 *International Review of Victimology*, 141–57.

[102] M. Hester, J. Hanmer, S. Coulson, M. Morahan and A. Razak, *Domestic Violence: Making it Through the Criminal Justice System*, University of Sunderland: Northern Rock Foundation and International Centre for the Study of Violence and Abuse, 2003, p 4.

myths about domestic violence and capitalising on the victim's social isolation.[103] What particularly exacerbates the situation in the UK is that prosecutors do not generally meet with victims prior to trial for fear of accusations that the witness has been coached. There is also evidence of inadequate or inappropriate sentencing, such as fines, being handed down in some domestic violence cases.[104] An evaluation[105] of the first Specialist Domestic Violence Courts (SDVCs) in Croydon and Gwent found that, out of all the sentences handed down by the SDVC in Croydon over an eight-month period, a financial penalty was handed down in 43 per cent of cases and by the Gwent SDVC in the same period, a financial penalty was handed down in 24 per cent of the cases.

However, these issues are capable of being dealt with and, once again, do not provide a compelling argument for the wholesale abandonment of mandatory arrest and prosecution policies. The CPS has put in place measures[106] to support vulnerable victims and witnesses in criminal courts. It has also adopted minimum service standards for victims, which include keeping victims informed about the progress of their case, and consulting with victims, where possible, on bind-overs and bail conditions. Multi-agency Witness Care Units (WCUs) had been established in every CPS Area through the 'No Witness, No Justice' programme and in domestic violence cases, Witness Care Officers (WCOs) ensure that a single point of contact provides tailored support to victims and witnesses from the point of charge through to the finalisation of a case.[107] In addition, SDVCs have been established precisely to ensure the fast tracking of domestic violence cases. However, regular monitoring and evaluation of the implementation of these policies needs to take place to ensure this support is actually being provided. Judges should ensure that the Bar code of conduct is complied with and prosecutors should intervene on behalf of witnesses to challenge and rebut unjust criticisms and offensive statements. Finally, as the Home Affairs Select Committee recently recommended, accredited training should be 'developed and made compulsory for all lawyers, magistrates and judges undertaking domestic violence cases, including in child contact cases'.[108]

---

[103] Ibid Hester *et al.*; L. Ellison, *The Adversarial Process and the Vulnerable Witness*, Oxford: Oxford University Press, 2001, p 87.

[104] House of Commons, Home Affairs Committee, 'Domestic violence, forced marriage and honour killings', Evidence 336.

[105] Evaluation of Domestic violence pilot sites at Gwent and Croydon 2004/05, Interim Report, CPS September 2004, p 24.

[106] House of Commons, Home Affairs Committee, 'Domestic violence, forced marriage and honour killings,' para 273.

[107] The WCO provides a range of other support, including referral to specialist domestic violence organisations, identifying vulnerable and intimidated witnesses and arranging for Victim Personal Statements to be taken.

[108] House of Commons, Home Affairs Committee, 'Domestic violence, forced marriage and honour killings', para 309.

Although research has not been conducted into victim's views of such policies in the UK other jurisdictions provide some evidence of support from them. Jaffe *et al.*[109] found that victim satisfaction with police response to incidents of domestic violence increased dramatically following the implementation of a mandatory charge/arrest policy in London, Ontario. Between 1979 and 1990, victim satisfaction with police response increased from 48 per cent to 65 per cent. Moreover, 87 per cent of the victims in the study indicated that they would call the police again. There was also an increase in satisfaction with Crown attorneys from only 31 per cent of victims in 1979 to 65 per cent in 1990.[110] This satisfaction also seemed to correspond with a reduction in the rate of withdrawn or dismissed charges from 38.4 per cent in 1979 down to 10.9 per cent in 1990. The results of a study conducted by Plecas, Seggar, and Marsland[111] of 74 female victims of domestic violence in Abbotsford, British Columbia also indicated widespread support among victims for the implementation of a mandatory arrest policy. Specifically, 86 per cent of victims stated that they agreed with the policy, with support for the policy persisting in spite of the fact that 30 per cent of the victims reported suffering financially following the offender's arrest, and 43 per cent of offenders reassaulted their victim within the 27-month follow-up period. Although sceptical of the effectiveness of such policies Landau[112] nevertheless found that the majority of victims of domestic violence in her study were also supportive of such policies. When asked specifically whether they wanted the police to lay charges in their case, 60 per cent of victims responded affirmatively. The most common reason identified by the women in support of charging was that it would teach the abuser not to repeat the violence and that it was a crime to assault someone. Significantly, 80 per cent of the women interviewed agreed with the policy to lay charges against the wishes of *other* women.

Conclusion

It would seem therefore that, in the absence of detailed research in the UK on the impact of such policies, provided enough support is given to both victims and those involved in the legal process, they are capable of having a significantly positive impact, not only upon the protection for victims of domestic violence but also upon the successful arrest and prosecution of perpetrators. There is also evidence that such policies have the support of victims. Although the research has not demonstrated a case for their

[109] P. Jaffe *et al.*, 'The impact of police laying charges'.
[110] Ibid, p 82.
[111] D. Plecas, T. Segger and L. Marsland, *Reticence and Re-Assault among Victims of Domestic Violence*, British Columbia: Ministry of the Attorney General for the Province of British Columbia, 2000.
[112] Landau, 'Women's experiences with mandatory charging'.

withdrawal it has shown that some types of mandatory policies have had some negative effects and these issues need to be taken into account during the drafting process. In terms of the gender implications, there are as many feminist arguments against these policies as there are for them, which have led, inevitably, to those supporting criminal justice system interventions parting ways with those who do not. Notwithstanding such disagreements, despite the evidence that some women may experience charging and prosecution policies as fundamentally disempowering, such policies have, as Light and Rivkin[113] have commented, nevertheless, gone a long way toward sensitising the justice system's approach to violence against women in relationships by increasing awareness and knowledge about the extent, seriousness and dynamics of family and sexual violence and about victims' reluctance to participate in the justice system. The point that also needs to be made, from a human rights perspective, is that a human rights framework, within the context of domestic violence has provided the victims of domestic violence with an essential tool with which their rights to protection can be enforced and mandatory policies are just one example of how this can be done. Furthermore, understanding violence against women as a human rights concern does not preclude other approaches to preventing and eliminating violence, such as education, health, development and criminal justice efforts. Rather, it calls for the strengthening and accelerating of state initiatives in these areas in order to prevent and eliminate violence against women. It has also ensured that domestic violence has become a global, national and local concern and, most importantly of all, that it has received the attention that it deserves from the rest of society.

[113] L. Light and S. Rivkin, 'Power, control and violence in family relationships: a criminal justice response', in M. Russell, J. Hightower and G. Gutman (eds), *Stopping the Violence: Changing Families, Changing Futures*, Vancouver: British Columbia Institute on Family Violence, 1996, pp 175–84.

Chapter 8

The limitations of equality discourses on the contours of intimate obligations

Lisa Glennon

INTRODUCTION

Family law has not been immune to the influence of rights-based arguments and values shaping its development. The articulation of 'rights' can be seen most clearly in the context of the parent–child relationship. The Human Rights Act has been invoked directly to negotiate the boundaries of this relationship and, in particular, rights-based arguments have been used by fathers to underpin claims to enforceable contact with, and shared residence of, their children.[1] This has undermined the predominance of welfarism under s 1 of the Children Act 1989 and has led to questions concerning the balancing exercise between the competing rights of parents and children.[2] However, it is not just the parent – child relationship which has been affected by claims of equality and rights. The relationship between adult partners, both in terms of structural organisation and internal meaning, has been shaped by the emergence of rights-based agendas. While there has been little direct usage of the Human Rights Act 1998, the law governing the interaction of adult partners has been influenced by two facets of equality, that is, the desire to achieve equality between, and equality within, adult relationships.[3] The purpose of this chapter is to highlight the contour of these agendas which are fuelled by the liberal ideals of choice, equality and individual autonomy. It will be argued that they have reinforced the reliance in legal policy on the structural form of relationships at the expense of a more

---

[1] See J. Wallbank, '(En)Gendering the fusion of rights and responsibilities in the law of contact', Chapter 5, in this volume.

[2] See S. Choudhry, J. Herring and J. Wallbank, 'Welfare, rights, care and gender in family law', Chapter 1, in this volume. See also S. Choudhry and H. Fenwick, 'Taking the rights of parents and children seriously: confronting the welfare principle under the Human Rights Act' (2005) 25 *Oxford Journal of Legal Studies*, 453–92; S. Harris-Short, 'Family law and the Human Rights Act 1998: judicial restraint or revolution?' (2005) 17 *Child and Family Law Quarterly*, 329–62.

[3] This distinction was made by the Law Commission of Canada in their report – Beyond Conjugality: Recognizing and Supporting Close Personal Adult Relationships, 2001.

function-based analysis which would consider the performance of familial caregiving as a valued activity in its own right and not merely through the lens of the relationship form in which it takes place.

Structural equality 'between' adult relationships

Policy-based initiatives in the area of adult relationship obligations have focused primarily on the need to achieve equality *between* relationships, regardless of sexual orientation. Most notably, discourses surrounding same-sex partnership recognition have been based on the assimilationist agenda of ensuring parity with opposite-sex couples. This discourse began when the judiciary, with the help of the Human Rights Act, broke down the functional distinctions between opposite- and same-sex relationships. In *Ghaidan* v *Godin-Mendoza*,[4] the question before the court was the extent to which a same-sex partner could claim succession rights in the rented accommodation of his deceased partner under the Rent Act 1977. In an earlier decision, which pre-dated the implementation of the Human Rights Act,[5] the House of Lords held that a same-sex partner could succeed to such a tenancy by qualifying as a member of the tenant's family,[6] but that he could not be classed as a de facto spouse under the gender-specific provision of 'living with the original tenant as his or her husband or wife'.[7] This differential treatment, which had practical as well as ideological consequences,[8] was considered in light of the Human Rights Act 1998 in *Ghaidan* v *Godin-Mendoza*.[9] The House of Lords held that the gender-specific interpretation of living together 'as husband or wife' infringed Art 14 of the European Convention on Human Rights and that there was no objective or reasonable justification for the difference in treatment between same-sex couples and their functional comparators, unmarried opposite-sex cohabitants. Thus, the statutory category of those who 'live together as husband and wife' was interpreted to include same-sex couples. In reaching this decision the court accepted that both opposite- and same-sex relationships can be marriage-like in nature, with the result that any difference in treatment between the two was based upon sexual orientation which had no objective or reasonable justification. Baroness Hale said:

[4] [2004] UKHL 30.
[5] *Fitzpatrick* v *Sterling Housing Association* [2000] 2 FLR 271.
[6] Under para 3(1) of Sch 1 to the Rent Act 1977.
[7] Under para 2(2) of Sch 1 to the Rent Act 1977 which states that 'a person who was living with the original tenant as his or her wife or husband shall be treated as the spouse of the original tenant'. Of note, this has now been amended by the Civil Partnership Act 2004 (Sch 8, para 13) to include 'a person who was living with the original tenant as if they were civil partners'. See n 24.
[8] A family member is only entitled to succeed to a, less secure, assured tenancy as opposed to a statutory tenancy which is enjoyed by de facto and de jure spouses.
[9] [2004] UKHL 30.

> Homosexual couples can have exactly the same sort of inter-dependent couple relationship as heterosexuals can ... Some people, whether heterosexual or homosexual, may be satisfied with casual or transient relationships. But most human beings eventually want more than that. They want love ... And many couples also come to want the stability and permanence which go with sharing a home and a life together, with or without the children who for many people go to make a family. In this, people of homosexual orientation are no different from people of heterosexual orientation.[10]

This had important consequences. The judicial willingness, first, to accept that same-sex relationships can embody normative familial characteristics[11] and, second, to use their interpretative duties under the Human Rights Act to include same-sex couples within the statutory category of de facto spouse created a climate where the legal distinctions between opposite- and same-sex couples were erased. Although the decision in *Ghaidan* related to a specific statutory provision, it called into question the legitimacy of other provisions which conferred rights on unmarried opposite-sex but not same-sex couples.[12] Indeed, given that Convention jurisprudence requires 'convincing and weighty' reasons to justify differences based on sexual orientation,[13] it may have been difficult to justify differential treatment in similar cases between, what had been judicially accepted as, functionally synonymous legal categories. Thus, the success of the analogy-based litigation strategy used in *Ghaidan* not only brought the issue of same-sex partnership rights within the mainstream political agenda, but it also helped to shape the assimilationist policy response. This came in the form of the Civil Partnership Act 2004 which was designed to give same-sex couples the choice to opt-in to a formalised state-sanctioned relationship structure. The Consultation Paper preceding the Act made this intention clear:

> Same-sex couples face many problems in their day-to-day lives because there is no legal recognition of their relationship. In many areas, each partner in the couple is treated as a separate individual; they are denied rights and responsibilities that could help them to organise their lives together. Opposite-sex couples have the choice to marry and have the relationship recognised by law. Same-sex couples have no such choice.[14]

---

[10] Ibid, p 142.
[11] *Fitzpatrick* v *Sterling Housing Association* [2000] 2 FLR 271.
[12] R. Bailey-Harris and J. Wilson, '*Mendoza* v *Ghaidan* and the rights of de facto spouses' (2003) 33 *Family Law*, 575–79.
[13] *Karner* v *Austria* (2004) 38 EHRR 24, p 42.
[14] DTI, Women and Equality Unit, 'Civil partnership: a framework for the legal recognition of same-sex couples', 2003, p 10.

Given this, the Act created a civil partnership registration scheme for same-sex couples only,[15] thus pursuing a streamlined rights-based agenda to close the gap between opposite- and same-sex couples by giving the latter 'the benefits of marriage in all but name'.[16] As such, the policy discourse on homosexuality shifted from protecting the individual rights of gays and lesbians[17] to recognising the partnership status of same-sex relationships. This evolutionary progression corresponded with the 'standard sequence' of steps, identified by Waaldijk, usually involved in the legal recognition of homosexuality.[18] However, it also had a more unintended effect on policy development. It was during the passage of the Civil Partnership Bill through the House of Lords that direct concerns were raised about the legal position of unmarried/unregistered relationships and, in particular, the economic hardship suffered by cohabitants 'owing to the current lack of any coherent legal remedies addressing their financial and property disputes' on relationship breakdown.[19] In response, the Law Commission was asked to undertake a

[15] Thus preventing other homesharers, such as siblings, and also opposite-sex cohabitants from registering their relationship. This exclusionary approach was criticised as an opportunity missed to consider the legal status of unmarried cohabitants more generally. See, e.g. the Law Society, Response to the Civil Partnership Consultation Paper, 2003, p 1. As I have argued elsewhere, however, the assimilationist and exclusionary approach of the Civil Partnership Act can be justified for strategic reasons such as improving the status of gay and lesbian relationships in legal and social consciousness, see L. Glennon, 'Strategising for the future through the Civil Partnership Act' (2006) 33(2) *Journal of Law and Society*, 244–76. Indeed, I have also argued that the attempts during the passage of the Civil Partnership Act to allow those in non-sexual caregiving relationships to also register under the scheme arose not from concern about the welfare of such family members, but to deflect attention from the express legal recognition of same-sex partnerships, see L. Glennon, 'Displacing the conjugal family in legal policy – a progressive move? (2005) 17 *Child and Family Law Quarterly*, 141–63.

[16] *Wilkinson* v *Kitzinger* [2006] EWHC 2022 (Fam), [88].

[17] This included equalising the age of consent for homosexual and heterosexual activity under The Sexual Offences (Amendment) Act 2000; outlawing discrimination in the workplace on the grounds of sexual orientation under The Employment Equality (Sexual Orientation) Regulations 2003 and abolishing s 28 (s 122 of the Local Government Act 2003 repealed s 2A of the Local Government Act 1986 (known as s 28) which prohibited local authorities from intentionally promoting homosexuality or publishing material with the intention of doing so or from promoting teaching in schools of the acceptability of homosexuality).

[18] See K. Waaldijk, 'Standard sequences in the legal recognition of homosexuality – Europe's past, present and future' (1994) 4 *Australasian Gay and Lesbian Law Journal*, 50–72; K. Waaldijk, 'Taking same-sex partnerships seriously: European experiences as British perspectives' (2003) *International Family Law*, 84–95 and K. Waaldijk, 'Civil developments: patterns of reform in the legal position of same-sex partners in Europe' (2000) 17 *Canadian Journal of Family Law*, 62–88.

[19] Law Commission of England and Wales, *Cohabitation: The Financial Consequences of Relationship Breakdown*, 2007, Law Com No. 307, para 1.18.

review of the law in this area[20] and proposals were published in 2007.[21] Thus, the debates around same-sex partnership recognition and, in particular, the deliberate exclusion of opposite-sex couples from the civil registration scheme, politicised the issue of cohabitation law more generally. Indeed, it was the perceived prioritisation of same-sex couples (by offering an exclusive civil registration scheme) that created a certain amount of urgency around the government's decision to initiate a review of cohabitation law. Although, not surprisingly, once the dust settled over the Civil Partnership Act, this sense of immediacy certainly waned.[22]

Not only have these policy debates fed off each other, but they have common ideological underpinnings. They are both constructed against the notion of marriage as the ideal intimate connection and they also appeal to the liberal values of equality, choice and individual autonomy. The Civil Partnership Act took a formal equality approach to relationship recognition. It followed the assimilationist policy of prior judicial decisions[23] and sought to eradicate family law distinctions based upon sexual orientation.[24] This involved extending the normative relationship framework in substance, if not in form, to same-sex couples thus reinforcing the primacy of a formalised partnership structure to govern the regulation of adult relationships. At the same time, it safeguarded the privileged position of marriage by limiting registration to same-sex couples and thus not offering opposite-sex partners an alternative legal structure. The policy of the Act is also informed by the liberal ideals of choice and individual autonomy, not only in extending the

---

[20] The Law Commission's Ninth Programme of Law Reform stated that 'Parliamentary debate on the Civil Partnership Bill highlighted the case for fundamental legislative reform for cohabitants', Law Commission for England and Wales, Ninth Programme of Law Reform, 2005, para 3.5.

[21] Law Commission of England and Wales, *Cohabitation*.

[22] In March 2008, the Justice Minister announced that 'for the time being' no further action would be taken in relation to the Law Commission's proposals on cohabitation law. The decision on their implementation was postponed pending research into the cost and efficacy of provisions in Scotland (under the Family Law (Scotland) Act 2006) which gave rights to cohabitants similar to those proposed by the Law Commission, Hansard HC, vol 472, col 123WS (6 March 2008). In response to this impasse, Lord Lester of Herne Hill (backed by Resolution) has introduced a Private Members Bill in the House of Lords on the rights of unmarried cohabitants. The Cohabitation Bill was introduced to the House of Lords on 11 December 2008 and is due to have its second reading in March 2009.

[23] *Fitzpatrick* v *Sterling Housing Association* [2000] 2 FLR 271; *Ghaidan* v *Godin-Mendoza* [2004] UKHL 30.

[24] Indeed, as well as creating a civil partnership scheme, the Civil Partnership Act 2004 also amended existing legislation (such as the Rent Act 1977 and the Inheritance (Provision for Family and Dependants) Act 1975) which refers to persons 'living together as husband and wife' to include those 'living together as if they were civil partners'.

right to consensual partnership recognition to same-sex couples, but also in respecting the autonomy of opposite-sex couples who have chosen not to marry. As made clear in the Consultation Paper:

> The Government believes that opposite-sex couples do not have the same need for a civil partnership registration scheme. Opposite-sex couples already have the opportunity of obtaining legal (and socially recognised) status for their relationship by entering into a marriage, whether religious or civil. Some couples choose not to marry and that is entirely a decision for them.[25]

Indeed, the policy framework within which the Act was created was careful not to blur the ideological distinction between those who formalise their relationships and those who do not. For example, the Consultation Paper rejected a piecemeal approach to issues of family law policy which could, for example, construct functional definitions of legally significant relationships based upon a purposive approach to individual instances of legislative intervention.[26] It was concluded that such a presumptive approach would undermine the autonomy of individuals in unformalised relationships as it carried the:

> danger of imposing rights and responsibilities on couples who did not want them (that is those who prefer to arrange their lives separately and would not choose to make a formal legally-recognised commitment to each other, in a comparable way to those opposite-sex couples who choose not to marry).[27]

On this view, the deliberate intention of regulatory avoidance is imputed to the decision not to marry or enter into a civil partnership, thus preserving the bright line distinction between formalised and unformalised relationships.[28]

---

[25] DTI, Women and Equality Unit, *Civil Partnership: A Framework for the Legal Recognition of Same-sex Couples*, 2003, para 2.7.

[26] The reasoning of the House of Lords in *Fitzpatrick v Sterling Housing Association* [2000] 2 FLR 271 is an example of this type of approach.

[27] DTI, Women and Equality Unit, *Civil Partnership*, Annex A, para 3.2.

[28] However, this essentialist view is undermined by studies which continue to show that the majority of unmarried cohabitants mistakenly believe that they have rights and responsibilities under common law (the 'common law marriage myth'). In the recent British Social Attitudes Report, 53 per cent of unmarried cohabitants falsely believed that common law marriage exists, Barlow, Burgoyne, Clery and Smithson, 'Cohabitation and the law: myths, money and the media', in A. Park *et al.* (eds) *British Social Attitudes: the 24th Report*, 2008, pp 40–42.

Equality 'within' adult relationships

The Law Commission's subsequent consideration of the legal consequences of unmarried/unregistered cohabitation[29] was similarly underpinned by the ideals valorised in a liberal democracy. In pursuit of equality, the Commission sought to achieve a 'fairer means of resolving the property and financial disputes that can arise between cohabitants on separation' than that provided by the current operation of trust law principles.[30] Thus while the Civil Partnership Act was concerned with structural equality *between* same- and opposite-sex relationships, the Law Commission's review of cohabitation law sought to minimise the economic detriment one party may suffer as a result of a cohabiting relationship and thus achieve a measure of equality *within* relationships. By focusing on the obligations between the partners *inter se*, this had the potential to achieve a more substantive version of equality than the formal equality agenda of the Civil Partnership Act. However, this was undermined, to some extent, by the clear priority of the Law Commission to ensure that the ancillary relief system, which governs the distribution of spouses' assets on divorce, maintained its practical and ideological superiority.[31] Indeed, the Commission rejected the extension of this system to cohabitants because:

> cohabitants have not given each other the legal commitment, or accepted the status, of marriage or civil partnership. We therefore believe that it is necessary to find a middle ground between, on the one hand, the law that currently applies to cohabitants and, on the other, the law that applies to spouses and civil partners on their separation.[32]

Under the Commission's proposals, therefore, financial relief is limited to eligible cohabitants[33] who have not disapplied the statutory scheme[34] and who have made 'qualifying contributions to the relationship giving rise to

---

[29] Law Commission of England and Wales, *Cohabitation*. As previously noted, these proposals have now been shelved pending further research. See n 22.

[30] Ibid, para 2.93.

[31] This system also applies to civil partnership dissolution, Civil Partnership Act 2004, Sch 5.

[32] Law Commission of England and Wales, *Cohabitation*, para 4.2.

[33] The Law Commission proposed that cohabitants who had a child together should, without more, be eligible to apply for financial relief under the scheme. Under the proposals, cohabitants without children would become eligible only when their cohabitation satisfied a minimum duration requirement (the Commission recommended that the requisite time-period should be set by statute but suggested a period of between two and five years), ibid, para 3.63.

[34] Ibid, para 2.94.

certain enduring consequences at the point of separation'.[35] Thus, to gain a remedy, the applicant would have to show that the respondent had retained a benefit, or that they had suffered a continuing economic disadvantage as a result of the contributions to the relationship. The important point for present purposes is that these financial remedies are very different from those available to divorcing spouses under the ancillary relief system:

> Simply cohabiting, for however long, would not give rise to any presumed entitlement to share in any pool of property. Nor would the scheme grant remedies simply on the basis of a party's needs following separation, whether by making orders for maintenance or otherwise.[36]

Thus, while the proposed scheme was concerned with issues of individualised justice between separating cohabitants, this had to be balanced against the competing policy objective of ensuring that the justice meted out was less than that provided to spouses and civil partners on divorce/dissolution. It is thus an example of a 'Marriage Minus' approach to the construction of relationship obligations,[37] that is, where the resulting obligations are designed to 'subtract from the marriage ceiling'.[38] As well as appealing to traditional family values rhetoric regarding the prioritisation of marriage as the most stable family framework, this approach, which seeks to create an 'entirely self-standing'[39] scheme for cohabitants, can also be justified by the libertarian desire to respect the autonomous choice of unmarried cohabitants to avoid legal regulation.[40] Indeed, the Commission attempted to find a balance between ensuring that the contributions and sacrifices made in an intimate relationship are fairly distributed between the parties on separation, whilst taking account of the 'importance of preserving individuals' freedom to conduct their private relationships on their own terms'.[41]

---

[35] Law Commission of England and Wales, *Cohabitation*, Executive Summary, para 1.13.

[36] Ibid, para 1.18.

[37] N. LaViolette, 'Waiting in a new line at City Hall: registered partnerships as an option for relationship recognition reform in Canada' (2002) 19 *Canadian Journal of Family Law*, 115–72, pp 122–23.

[38] Ibid.

[39] Bridge, 'Money, marriage and cohabitation' (2006) 36 *Family Law*, 641–46, p 641.

[40] Although it is clear that a significant number of cohabitants still believe that cohabitation for a period of time confers the same legal rights as married couples, see Barlow, Burgoyne, Clery and Smithson, 'Cohabitation and the law: myths, money and the media', pp 40–42.

[41] Law Commission of England and Wales, *Cohabitation*, para 2.93.

It is clear, therefore, that the ideological context of these recent policy discourses is based on the idea of the autonomous individual making rational choices about relationship form and consensual obligations.[42] Notions of individual autonomy cuts both ways in these debates, creating the equality-based argument that all should have the choice to opt-in to a state-sanctioned relationship structure (regardless of sexual orientation)[43] and, at the same time, providing the justification for not extending spousal obligations to those who remain outside of the preferred formalised boundaries.[44] An additional commonality between these policy discourses is that they are both limited to the highly conformist strategy of determining accessibility to prevailing family law norms. The Civil Partnership Act gave same-sex couples the opportunity to opt-in to marital obligations 'in all but name',[45] while the Law Commission was concerned with whether, and how, family law norms could be applied to non-marital relationships. These are ultimately questions of *accessibility* as prevailing norms are not disturbed but either simply extended, or modified to apply, to alternative family structures.

It is interesting that while policy discourses have drawn from the marital model, to either extend marital obligations to civil partnerships, or to use them as a ceiling when constructing obligations between unmarried partners, the precise content of these obligations as they arise on divorce has been under judicial scrutiny where the courts have pursued the goal of gender equality. As a comparative reference point, therefore, spousal obligations are a moving target. Seeking to achieve equality *within* relationships at the point of divorce, these judicial developments have pursued a similar goal to that of the Law Commission in its review of cohabitation law. And, once again, relationship status features heavily in this distributive model. While the lack of a formalised relationship status between unmarried cohabitants resulted in the Law Commission's diluted version of familial obligations, the institutional form of marriage has determinative consequences on divorce. As will be discussed in the next section, the status of marriage not only gives divorcing spouses access to a discretionary-based regime to govern the distribution of their property and finances, but it also operates within the principles to strengthen the claimant's entitlement to share in the capital assets.

---

[42] See A. Barlow and S. Duncan, 'Family law, moral rationalities and New Labour's communitarianism: part II' (2000) 22 *Journal of Social Welfare and Family Law*, 129–43.

[43] The Civil Partnership Act 2004.

[44] Law Commission of England and Wales, *Cohabitation*.

[45] *Wilkinson* v *Kitzinger* [2006] EWHC 2022 (Fam) [88].

Economic obligations on divorce

Marital obligations, in economic terms, are seen most clearly at the point of divorce where the courts have wide discretionary powers, under the Matrimonial Causes Act 1973, to distribute the full range of the parties' assets in order to achieve a fair outcome. Speaking in the US context, Fineman notes that:

> dependency is no longer assumed to be the justification for allocation of marital wealth to women; rather it is the contribution they have made to the family which justifies their partnership share at dissolution.[46]

A similar assessment can be made of the evolution of ancillary relief principles in the UK where the courts, in their quest for gender equality, have initiated a shift from a welfare-based rationale for economic redistribution on divorce to an entitlement-based model.[47] The judicial 'principles' which have evolved since the House of Lords' decision in *White* v *White*[48] are premised on the need to achieve a 'generally accepted standard of fairness' between the parties.[49] Prior to the House of Lords decision in *White*, the claimant's award on divorce was limited to satisfying his/her 'reasonable requirements',[50] which were assessed in light of the available wealth and the marital standard of living. Although this 'relative' approach resulted in a more generous award than satisfying bare economic necessity, the notion of 'reasonable requirements' created a 'glass ceiling'[51] beyond which an award could not go. In *White*, the House of Lords disparaged this needs-driven approach in big-money cases and laid down principles, informed by a gender equality agenda, which have underpinned the law ever since. First, the non-discrimination principle which states that:

> whatever the division of labour chosen by [the parties] ... if, in their different spheres, each contributed equally to the family, then in principle it did not matter which of them earned the money and built up the assets. There should be no bias in favour of the money-earner and against the home-maker and the child-carer.[52]

---

[46] M.A. Fineman, *The Neutered Mother, the Sexual Family and other Twentieth Century Tragedies*, New York: Routledge, 1995, p 158.

[47] J. Eekelaar, 'Back to basics and forward into the unknown', (2001) 31 *Family Law*, 30–34.

[48] [2001] AC 596.

[49] Ibid, 599.

[50] *O'D* v *O'D* [1976] Fam 83; *Page* v *Page* (1981) 2 FLR 198; *Preston* v *Preston* [1982] Fam 17.

[51] E. Hess, 'Assessing the quantum of periodical payments after *McFarlane*' (2006) 36 *Family Law* 780–84, p 780.

[52] [2001] AC 596, 605.

In addition, to avoid such gender-based discrimination, judges were directed to check their provisional views against the yardstick of equal division and as a general guide, equality should be departed from only if there were good reasons for doing so.

This was taken even further by the House of Lords in the joint appeals of *Miller* v *Miller*; *McFarlane* v *McFarlane*.[53] Contrary to the opinion of Thorpe LJ that academic classifications were unnecessary,[54] the House sought to clarify the law by categorising the bases of economic redistribution on divorce. Thus, the Lords articulated three 'strands' of fairness to a redistributive ancillary relief award where the ultimate objective is 'to give each party an equal start on the road to independent living'.[55] In reaching a fair outcome between the parties, the award should meet financial needs;[56] provide compensation for a spouse who has suffered economic disparity due to the manner in which the marriage was conducted;[57] and share the financial fruits of the marital partnership through the equal sharing principle.[58] While subsequent decisions have cast doubt on whether these three strands should be regarded as 'separate heads of claim',[59] what is clear is that the marital relationship is now subject to the norm of equal sharing on divorce. Under the equal sharing principle, when the marriage partnership ends each partner is 'entitled to an equal share of the assets of the partnership, unless there is a good reason to the

---

[53] [2006] UKHL 24.
[54] *Parlour* v *Parlour* [2004] EWCA Civ 872, [106].
[55] [2006] UKHL 24, [144], *per* Baroness Hale.
[56] Ibid, [11]; [138–39], *per* Lord Nicholls and Baroness Hale.
[57] Ibid, [13]; [140], *per* Lord Nicholls and Baroness Hale. In the *McFarlane* case, Mrs McFarlane was awarded ongoing compensation over and above her financial needs to take account of the economic disadvantage she had suffered as a result her career sacrifices. She gave up her successful career as a lawyer (where she, at one point, had earned more than her husband) during the couple's 16-year marriage to look after their three children. On the other hand, her husband's career as an accountant had gone from strength to strength and he was earning around £750,000 per annum.
[58] Ibid, [16–17]; [141–43], *per* Lord Nicholls and Baroness Hale.
[59] *RP* v *RP* [2006] EWHC 3409 (Fam), [60]. Indeed, it is worth noting that the precise interaction between these strands is unclear and remains the subject of continued jurisprudential analysis. It seems though that the courts are wary of treating the three strands as a 'series of statutory tests' the passing or failing of which would lead to 'particular and set results', *H* v *H* [2007] EWHC 459 (Fam), [41], *RP* v *RP* [2006] EWHC 3409 (Fam), [58], [60]. Instead the courts have emphasised the discretionary nature of the judicial exercise where the primary objective is to achieve fairness 'which requires an individual assessment of each case', *B* v *B* [2008] EWCA Civ 543, [24]. The recent heavy emphasis on judicial discretion is somewhat of a retreat from the earlier Court of Appeal decision in *Charman* v *Charman* [2007] EWCA Civ 503 where the court sought to give clear guidance on *Miller;McFarlane* and, in particular, the equal sharing principle.

contrary'.[60] There is now a much stronger presumption of capital sharing on divorce which is based on the notion of marriage as a collaborative partnership. Indeed, rather than viewing the claims of a caregiver as seeking an award from the independently owned assets of the wealthier spouse, the marital relationship is now viewed as a joint endeavour to which both spouses contribute in equally valuable, albeit different, ways. It has been said that this recognises the value, in economic terms, of domestic contributions within marriage,[61] a view which is confirmed by the fact that the equal sharing principle is not confined to long marriages. Thus caregiving contributions to a marriage are deemed to have instantaneous value, giving rise to an immediately realisable entitlement to share in the accumulated assets on divorce. Indeed, the House of Lords rejected the 'accrual over time' approach[62] suggested in the earlier case of *GW* v *RW*[63] where Mostyn, QC opined that it would be 'fundamentally unfair' to find that:

> a party who has made domestic contributions during a marriage of 12 years should be awarded the same proportion of the assets as a party who has made the domestic contributions for a period in excess of 20 years.[64]

This was rejected by the House of Lords where Lord Nicholls made it clear that 'a short marriage is no less a partnership of equals than a long marriage'.[65] Referencing the gender equality agenda, Lord Nicholls observed that to hold otherwise and:

---

[60] [2006] UKHL 24, [16] *per* Lord Nicholls. It seems that the equal sharing principle was regarded by the House of Lords as a starting point for the distributive exercise (once the parties' assets had been established), rather than an end-of-assessment yardstick. This was confirmed by the Court of Appeal in *Charman* v *Charman* [2007] EWCA Civ 503 where the court referred to Lord Nicholl's use of the phrases 'the equal sharing principle' (*Miller;McFarlane*, [20]) and 'sharing entitlement' (*Miller;McFarlane*, [29]) which, according to the Court of Appeal 'describe more than a yardstick for use as a check,', *Charman*, [65]. Unhelpfully, however, in *B* v *B* [2008] EWCA Civ 543 the Court of Appeal appeared to suggest that the principle should be applied as a yardstick, [50–60], although emphasised that this decision depended on the unusual facts of the case and thus should not be regarded as establishing any new point of principle [57], [60].

[61] A. Barlow, 'Configuration(s) of unpaid caregiving within current legal discourse in and around the family' (2007) 58 *Northern Ireland Legal Quarterly*, 251–67, p 252.

[62] Ibid, p 258.

[63] [2003] 2 FLR 108.

[64] Ibid, [43].

[65] [2006] UKHL 24, [17].

confine the *White* approach to the 'fruits of a long marital partnership' would be to re-introduce precisely the sort of discrimination the *White* case was designed to negate.[66]

Thus, the general principle to be applied is that each spouse is, *prima facie*, entitled to share in the assets acquired for the benefit of the family and other assets which have been acquired during the marriage regardless of the length of time it has taken to accumulate them.[67] This means that awards in short marriage cases are no longer limited to the pre-*White* restitutionary position of simply getting the wife back on her feet, or to compensate her for any financial disadvantage arising as a result of the marriage.[68] In the *Miller* case itself, Mrs Miller was made a capital award of around £5 million after a marriage which lasted less than three years. This award was made primarily because the husband had acquired substantial assets during the marriage which, based upon the idea that marriage is an equal partnership, the wife was entitled to have some share. As such, the award totalling £5 million, which was less than one-sixth of the value of the husband's total worth, was not deemed to be inappropriate.

Placing economic value on familial caregiving

It is clear, therefore, that the judicial search for 'fairness' on divorce has, since *White*, embraced a gender equality discourse that has sought to eradicate discrimination between the contributions of the breadwinner and the caregiver.[69] The result has been, according to Barlow:

---

[66] Ibid, [19]. Case citations omitted.

[67] *Miller;McFarlane*, [157]-[158]. In *Charman* v *Charman* [2007] EWCA Civ 503, the Court of Appeal interpreted "the sharing principle" to mean that 'property should be shared in equal proportions unless there is good reason to depart from such proportions,' [65]. One reason to depart from equal division is that certain assets do not fall within the classification of 'matrimonial property'. Indeed, in *Charman* v *Charman* [2007] EWHC Civ 503, the Court of Appeal held that the equal sharing principle 'applies to all the parties' property but, to the extent that their property is non-matrimonial, there is likely to be better reason for departure from equality', [66]. However, the delineation between matrimonial and non-matrimonial property is not entirely clear. In *Miller;McFarlane*, Lord Nicholls confined non-matrimonial property to assets which were acquired by gift or inheritance, [21] while Baroness Hale took a more restrictive approach and also viewed "business/investment assets which were generated solely or mainly by the efforts of one party" as non-matrimonial property, [149–53]. On the distinction between matrimonial and non-matrimonial property, see also *Rossi* v *Rossi* [2006] EWHC 1482 (Fam); *S* v *S* [2006] EWHC 2793 (Fam).

[68] Of course, cases of limited financial resources will still have to focus primarily on meeting the parties' needs, *Miller;McFarlane* [2006] UKHL 24, [55] *per* Lord Nicholls.

[69] Barlow, 'Configuration(s) of unpaid caregiving', p 259.

a move away from the language of a welfare-style dependency construction of a wife's needs towards a new entitlement basis, with entitlement having been earned through unpaid caregiving.[70]

Indeed, the parties' respective contributions are at the core of this distributive model. The norm of equal sharing is underpinned by the presumed equality of contributions to the marriage, the origins of which can be traced back to the non-discrimination principle.[71] As a result, both parties are *entitled* to enjoy the financial fruits of the joint venture in a quasi-proprietorial award where homemaking generates 'an entitlement earned through the contributions'.[72] Based on the equivalence of the parties' homemaking and financial contributions to the family, this approach would seem to appeal to care ethicists who wish to take 'seriously the labor of care in which women traditionally have been engaged'.[73] Certainly it would seem that the aspirational ideal of gender equality has improved the currency of care work by deeming it to be functionally equivalent to market work in terms of its value to the family, and giving the caregiver an entitlement to share in the assets on divorce which is in stark contrast to the preceding jurisprudence which limited the claimant's award to her 'reasonable requirements' in cases where there were surplus assets over needs.[74] Indeed, one could say that the underlying rationale of this agenda is, in the words of Williams, to remedy the effects of 'domesticity'.[75] Williams' conception of 'domesticity' refers to the continued organisation of market and family work which precipitates the gendered performance of breadwinner and primary caregiving roles:[76]

---

[70] Ibid, p 257. In making this point Barlow refers to the observations of John Eekelaar in 'Back to basics and forward into the unknown' (2001) 31 *Family Law*, 30–34.

[71] *White* v *White* [2001] AC 596, 605.

[72] J. Eekelaar, 'Asset distribution on divorce – the durational element' (2001) 117 *Law Quarterly Review*, 552–60, p 553.

[73] E. Feder Kittay, 'Dependency, difference and the global ethic of longterm care' (2005) 13(4) *Journal of Political Philosophy*, 443–69, p 453.

[74] See *Page* v *Page* (1981) 2 FLR 198; *Preston* v *Preston* [1982] Fam 17.

[75] J. Williams, 'Do wives own half: winning for wives after *Wendt*' (2000) 32 *Connecticut Law Review*, 249; J. Williams, *Unbending Gender: Why Family and Work Conflict and What To Do About It*, New York: Oxford University Press, 2000; J. Williams, 'From difference to dominance to domesticity: care as work, gender as tradition' (2001) 76 *Chicago-Kent Law Review*, 1441.

[76] Williams, 'From difference to dominance', p 1442. Recent studies in the UK context also reveal that domestic labour remains a gendered activity even though 'women have substantially increased their participation in paid employment', R. Crompton and C. Lyonette, 'Who does the housework? The division of labour within the home', in A. Park *et al.*, (eds) *British Social Attitudes: the 24th Report*, 2008, pp 53–80, p 74. Despite this, the study reveals that 'men's participation in domestic work has yet to catch up', ibid.

domesticity's peculiar organization of market work and family work first marginalizes mothers from market work, then limits their access to entitlements based on family work. The result is a system that is inconsistent with our commitment to gender equality, and leads to the widespread impoverishment of mothers and the children who depend on them.[77]

The judicial pursuit of gender equality seeks to rectify this by placing 'economic value on unpaid caregiving within marriage at the point of divorce'.[78] However, on closer inspection, these principles, which seemingly provide a functional account of family organisation, do not give an inherent value to the performance of care work. While they may seek to remedy the effects of the 'complex system of gender norms' involved in 'domesticity',[79] they do not give intrinsic positive value to caregiving contributions *per se*, but rather to the institutional form in which they are carried out. It is the fact of marriage, and not more functional indices such as the presence of children, which gives rise to the claimant's entitlement to share in the capital assets. This can be seen in the universal application, whether as a starting point or a yardstick,[80] of the equal sharing principle. In the words of Lord Nicholls:

> Marriage ... is a partnership of equals ... This is now recognised widely, if not universally. The partners commit themselves to sharing their lives. They live and work together. When their partnership ends, each is entitled to an equal share of the assets of the partnership, unless there is good reason to the contrary.[81]

Such a status-based approach to dividing the parties' assets on separation was firmly rejected by the Law Commission for unmarried couples.[82] Bridge, then Law Commissioner, said:

> Simply cohabiting with another person, for however long, in the absence of the specific legal commitment made on marriage or registration of a civil partnership, does not seem to us to justify the degree of interference with the parties' existing property rights which is implicit in a regime of equal sharing.[83]

---

[77] Williams, 'Do wives own half', p 253.
[78] A. Barlow, 'Configuration(s) of unpaid caregiving', p 252.
[79] K. Abrams, 'Cross-dressing in the master's clothes' (2001) 109 *The Yale Law Journal*, 745–82, p 750.
[80] See n. 60.
[81] [2006] UKHL 24, [16].
[82] Law Commission of England and Wales, *Cohabitation*.
[83] Bridge, 'Money, marriage and cohabitation', p 643.

As a result, the Commission concluded that:

> Cohabiting relationships differ widely in terms of duration, commitment and degree of economic interdependence. Case law on the [Matrimonial Causes Act] has advocated the treatment of a divorcing couple as a 'partnership of equals' to which the yardstick of equality may be applied. This approach may generate enormous awards even after very short marriages, and we believe that there would be significant public disquiet if cohabitants were to be treated equally.[84]

This is correct. It certainly would be inappropriate to extend this scheme with its strong presumptions of capital sharing to unmarried cohabitants. However, an even more fundamental question is whether it is appropriate for all married couples. While the pursuit of gender equality equalised the value of financial and non-financial contributions in *White*, this potentially functional approach has been morphed into one which is based not on contributions, but on the status of marriage as a 'partnership of equals'.[85] This leap from placing economic value on caregiving contributions to establishing a norm of equal sharing based on institutional status essentialises the interdependencies associated with marriage. However as, Duclos notes:

> marriage is not a monolith, although we are socialized to think of it as such. It is an extremely complex social, economic, legal and religious institution with deep emotional (but certainly not the same) significance to most individuals.[86]

One must ask therefore whether it is appropriate to apply a principle of economic distribution which is based upon the 'supposed functionality' of marriage?[87] In the *Miller* case, for example, there were no children of the relationship, and no significant relationship-generated disadvantages suffered by Mrs Miller after a marriage lasting less than three years, yet she was awarded a large capital sum based on the accrual of assets by her husband

---

[84] Law Commission of England and Wales, *Cohabitation*, para 4.9. Citations omitted.

[85] [2006] UKHL 24, [16] *per* Lord Nicholls; [141] *per* Baroness Hale.

[86] N. Duclos, 'Some complicating thoughts on same-sex marriage' (1991) vol. 1:1, *Law and Sexuality*, 31–61, p 44. In terms of social attitudes, it seems that the 'centrality of the formally married couple has diminished', S. Duncan and M. Phillips, 'New families? Tradition and change in modern relationships' in A. Park *et al.*, (eds) *British Social Attitudes: the 24th Report*, 2008, 1–28, p 25. Indeed, this report observed that 'for many, marriage does *not* have normative centrality, and unmarried cohabitation is seen as its equivalent', ibid, p 7 (emphasis in original).

[87] Duncan and Phillips, 'New families?', p 26.

during the marriage.[88] However, an approach based on the Law Commission's proposed principles for unmarried cohabitants would, it is argued, have produced a more appropriate result to the facts of the case. Under the proposed scheme, there would have been no presumptive award in relation to the 'property acquired during the relationship'.[89] Rather, Mrs Miller would have to prove that she had made qualifying contributions which, at the end of the relationship, either gave rise to a retained benefit in the hands of the respondent, or to her economic disadvantage.[90] The award would, therefore, focus on the functional characteristics of the relationship with the purpose of ensuring that the consequences of the parties' actual contributions and sacrifices were fairly distributed between them on separation.[91] It is submitted that a restitutionary approach of this nature is a more appropriate model to apply to childless relationships, married or not, than the current system where relationship form has become over-determinative in the distribution of the parties' assets.

Thus, while one could say that the partnership ethos of the equal sharing principle has ethic of care dimensions by focusing on the intertwined relationships involved in the common goal of married life and by placing economic value on familial caregiving, this view is undermined by several factors. First, the default sharing rule for the distribution of the accrued capital assets, the equal sharing principle, is based on the institutional form of the relationship and the presumed interdependency of the marital partnership. Second, over-reliance on relationship form affects how future caregiving contributions are viewed, and valued, once this relationship has come to an end.[92] The partnership rationale of the equal sharing principle terminates on divorce and the notion of the parties' unity in a common project is replaced by the idea of two individuals asserting competing rights, set against the normative expectations of autonomy and self-sufficiency. Caregiving after divorce leads to financial support obligations based on the caregiver's relationship-generated financial needs and/or economic disadvantage, alongside the non-residential parent's obligation to meet the

---

[88] Mrs Miller was a high-earning professional who gave up her job (earning £85,000 per annum) on marriage. As indicated, there were no children of the relationship and Mrs Miller was 33 years of age at the time of the parties' separation.

[89] Bridge, 'Money, marriage and cohabitation', p 644.

[90] Law Commission of England and Wales, *Cohabitation*. Qualifying contributions are defined by the Law Commission as 'any contribution arising from the cohabiting relationship which is made to the parties' shared lives or to the welfare of members of their families', ibid, para 4.34.

[91] Bridge, 'Money, marriage and cohabitation', p 644.

[92] See L. Glennon, 'Obligations between adult partners: moving from form to function?' (2008) 22 *International Journal of Law, Policy and the Family*, 22–62, p 40.

children's needs through ongoing maintenance. In *VB* v *JP*,[93] the President of the Family Division stated:

> on the exit from the marriage, the partnership ends and in ordinary circumstances a wife has no right or expectation of continuing economic parity ('sharing') unless and to the extent that consideration of her needs, or compensation for relationship-generated disadvantage so require. A clean break is to be encouraged wherever possible.[94]

The issue, for our purposes, is not assessing the quantum of these awards but questioning whether this conceptual framework places sufficient *positive* value on ongoing familial care work. It seems, unfortunately, that it does not. Meeting the caregiver's financial needs is a welfare-based award which re-casts the primary caregiver as a supplicant. This reflects the 'negative (burdensome) features of care',[95] and 'child support, by definition, aims to provide for children and not for the mother who cares for them'.[96] Compensatory notions of financial support are also problematic as they are speculative and, even if available,[97] quantify economic obligations created by caregiving in terms of lost market opportunities. In seeking to remedy the caregiver's impoverished economic position this 'elevates the male gender role of market work above the female role'.[98] Indeed, in a similar vein,

---

[93] [2008] EWHC 112 (Fam).

[94] Ibid, [59]. Indeed, courts have thus far rejected the argument that a caregiver is entitled to share in a spouse's future earnings post-divorce on the basis of their ongoing contributions to the welfare of the family. See, for example, *H* v *H* [2007] EWHC 459 (Fam) where Charles J rejected the assertion that the post-divorce contributions of the primary caregiver warrants a conclusion 'that a proportion of the husband's future income continues to be attributable to the wife's domestic contribution and thus a fruit of the marital partnership', [87].

[95] M. Fine and C. Glendinning, 'Dependence, independence or inter-dependence? Revisiting the concepts of "care" and "dependency"' (2005) 25 *Ageing and Society*, 601–21, p 604.

[96] C. Starnes, 'Mothers, myths and the law of divorce: one more feminist case for partnership' (2006) 13 *William and Mary Journal of Women and the Law*, 203–33, p 221.

[97] Case law after *Miller;McFarlane* suggests that a restrictive approach is being taken to compensation claims with courts holding that a wife who sacrificed 'ordinary' career prospects is likely to be adequately compensated by an equal division of the family's resources on divorce, *CR* v *CR* [2007] EWHC 3334 (Fam). In addition, courts have refused to treat the compensation strand as a separate head of award but rather have taken such claims into account as part of their general assessment in reaching a fair outcome or within a 'generous assessment of needs', see *RP* v *RP* [2006] EWHC 3409 (Fam), [60]; *Lauder* v *Lauder* [2007] EWHC 1227 (Fam), [79]; *VB* v *JP* [2008] EWHC 112, [59].

[98] P. Laufer-Ukeles, 'Selective recognition of gender difference in the law: revaluing the caretaker role' (2008) 31 *Harvard Journal of Law and Gender*, 1–36, p 30.

Abrams notes that the model of spousal support which views the caregiving labour of one spouse as compensable because it allows the other spouse to concentrate on their career:

> does not give women's caregiving labor its own independent status. It is compensable only upon divorce, and even then it is characterized as dependent or derivative, something that is of value because it assists the market worker.[99]

Similarly, the function-based strands of 'fairness' which meet the claimant's needs and/or provide compensation, conceptualise caregiving in market terms by considering the extent to which the relationship prevented the caregiver from acting as an autonomous individual and impinged upon their ability to live up to the 'ideal worker norm'.[100] This remedial framework does not adequately capture the true value of caregiving work. It looks outward to what has been lost in market terms, and not inwards to what has been gained in familial terms. Caregiving is thus seen as a distraction from market work, a distraction which undermines the caregiver's 'full social citizenship'.[101] As Kittay says:

> While lip service is sometimes paid to the notion that caring for children or caring for an elderly or ill family member is 'work,' such caring lacks both the social standing and the income production of what is generally acknowledged as 'work' within our society.[102]

In short, therefore, the bases of economic distribution on divorce, whether seen as 'separate heads of claim'[103] or fused together in the overall objective of meeting fairness,[104] do not view care work, by and of itself, as a 'value-creating enterprise'[105] either in social terms or within the privatised context of the relationship in which it takes place.

In addition, the remedial construction of the obligations created by caregiving after divorce also gives rise to the very credible criticism, outlined by Ferguson, that as the financial circumstances of the claimant caregiver are due to the structural inadequacies of the market, it is insufficient to look to

---

[99] Abrams, 'Cross-dressing in the master's clothes', p 765.

[100] J. Williams, 'Do wives own half', p 254.

[101] Kittay notes that '[s]ocially approved ways of obtaining income provide not only access to resources, it is also key to full social citizenship, which presumes participation in income-producing social contributions', E. Feder Kittay, 'A feminist public ethic of care meets the new communitarian family policy' (2001) 111 *Ethics*, 523–47, p 528.

[102] Ibid.

[103] *RP v RP* [2006] EWHC 3409 (Fam), [60].

[104] *B v B* [2008] EWCA Civ 543.

[105] Abrams, 'Cross-dressing in the master's clothes', p 765.

privatised, or personal, solutions by placing financial responsibility on a former spouse.[106] In other words, why should responsibility for the economic disparity arising between the parties on separation be attributed to the wealthier spouse?[107] Eekelaar answers this by appealing to the values of justice[108] as he frames the question in terms of 'whether it is fair and just to require the better-off person to alleviate these disparate consequences to *some* degree'.[109] Eekelaar thinks that it is:

> the very reason for imposing the requirement is that the social consequences of the separation bear more harshly on one person rather than the other. If the disadvantaged party were able to overcome them by her own efforts, there would be nothing to compensate. The obligation remains personal, because it does not attempt to make the obligor contribute towards improving the lot of the disadvantaged group generally.[110]

However, while agreeing with the sentiment behind this, it is submitted that 'personalising' or 'privatising' these obligations can be shored up on other bases. Seeking to justify the personal nature of the obligations on the grounds that the payer has not been similarly disadvantaged by the relationship only takes us so far and does not get away from the fact that the disadvantage is caused by the structure of the market and the ideal of the 'unencumbered worker'.[111] For Eekelaar, the obligation remains personal because of its limited nature. That is, the obligor is not being asked to 'contribute towards improving the lot of the disadvantaged group generally'.[112] However, while this limited responsibility does ensure a 'personal obligation', it fails to address the core question posed by Ferguson of why the obligation is personal in the first place? Eekelaar accepts that 'the greater disadvantages to which a woman may be exposed compared to those which men may be

---

[106] L. Ferguson, 'Family, social inequalities and the persuasive force of interpersonal obligation' (2008) 22 *International Journal of Law Policy and the Family*, 61–91.

[107] Ibid, pp 73–74.

[108] J. Eekelaar, 'Partners, parents and children: grounds for allocating resources across households', paper delivered at the 13th World Conference of the International Society of Family Law, Vienna, 16–20 September 2008. Paper on file and referenced with the kind permission of the author. See also J. Eekelaar, *Family Law and Personal Life*, Oxford: Oxford University Press, 2006, p 52.

[109] Eekelaar, 'Partners, parents and children', emphasis in original.

[110] Ibid.

[111] M. A. Fineman, 'Why marriage' (2001) 9 *Virginia Journal of Social Policy and the Law*, 239, p 270.

[112] Eekelaar, 'Partners, parents and children'.

exposed on the termination of the partnership are mostly socially caused'.[113] The fact that these consequences are disproportionately felt by the parties is sufficient, for Eekelaar, to impose a personal compensatory obligation. For Ferguson, however, account must be taken of the fact that the financial circumstances of the impoverished spouse result from her 'economically-disadvantageous decisions'[114] of prioritising family work over market work as well as 'structural economic disadvantages (e.g. [the] undervaluation of women in the workplace)'.[115] As these are based on 'social – structural – inequalities',[116] the interpersonal remedy of spousal support is wholly insufficient and acts as a distraction from the need to address the 'root causes'[117] of social inequalities such as 'the role of the markets'.[118] However, if through an ethic of care lens, care work were to be considered as an activity of intrinsic value, a different rationale emerges for imposing interpersonal obligations on divorce/separation.

An ethic of care approach: the 'parenting partnership'[119]

Bridge observes that a key question which arises when determining the principles to govern orders for financial relief between separating couples is 'how the nature of the relationship with which [the] scheme is concerned should affect the selection of principles'.[120] However, looking beyond structural indicators, an ethic of care approach to dividing the parties' assets on relationship breakdown would focus on 'the inevitable human dependences and interdependences too often ignored in theories that begin with adult moral agents pursuing their own conception of the good'.[121] Indeed, Herring observes that:

> an ethic of care approach ... seeks to move away from an atomistic picture of individuals, with rights that compete against each other, to a model that emphasises the responsibilities of people towards each other in mutually supporting relations.[122]

---

[113] Ibid.
[114] Ferguson, 'Family, social inequalities', p 74.
[115] Ibid.
[116] Ibid, p 73.
[117] Ibid, p 82.
[118] Ibid. p 84.
[119] C. Starnes, 'Mothers as suckers: pity, partnership, and divorce discourse' (2005) 90 *Iowa Law Review*, 1513–52, p 1547.
[120] Bridge, 'Money, marriage and cohabitation', p 642.
[121] Kittay, 'Dependency, difference', p 453.
[122] J. Herring, 'Where are the carers in healthcare law and ethics' (2007) 27 *Legal Studies*, 51–73, p 68.

With this in mind, when constructing obligations between partners on separation, an ethic of care approach would do more than merely seek 'a fair solution between competing individual interests and rights'.[123] It would encourage caregiving (both retrospective and prospective) to be considered as a valued activity in its own right, thus de-emphasising the institutional form in which it takes place.

Adopting such an approach would have important consequences. First, as I have argued elsewhere, familial caregiving, in particular caring for children, could emerge as the primary basis upon which to theorise the parties' rights and duties which is different to the current model where the structure in which families interact determines the contour of their resulting obligations.[124] On this point, I do not wish to suggest that relationship form is irrelevant. However, rather than being determinative, I believe that it should take its place as just one factor of the case, alongside function-based indicators such as relationship duration and the presence of children, to be considered within a unified statutory scheme which governs wealth distribution between separating couples, both married and unmarried.[125] It seems that such an approach would reflect the emerging view that 'in terms of everyday life and commitment, many people see cohabitation and marriage as more or less equivalent, rather than alternatives'.[126] This is not to suggest, however, that all cohabitants view their relationship as 'marriage-like'. Indeed, there will be cohabitants, perhaps most likely those without children, for whom cohabitation is a conceptually distinct living arrangement from marriage. This view could be held by one or both parties to the relationship.[127] Notwithstanding this, it is argued that the economic consequences of the relationship should be fairly apportioned between the parties on separation. However, this is not to be achieved by creating a status of cohabitation which carries presumptive economic consequences once a particular durational threshold has been attained. Rather, a function-based approach would look at the content of each relationship (both married and unmarried) and the parties' respective investment(s) in it.

The primary objective of this functional model would be to consider the actual interdependencies between the parties and on this note, it is submitted

---

[123] Ibid, p 68 citing V. Held, *Ethics of Care*, p 15. See also J. Herring, 'Why financial orders on divorce should be unfair' (2005) 19 *International Journal of Law, Policy and the Family*, 218–28.
[124] Glennon, 'Obligations between adult partners', p 45.
[125] Ibid, pp 44–45.
[126] S. Duncan and M. Phillips, 'New families? Tradition and change in modern relationships', p 8.
[127] See, e.g. the work of Smart and Stevens who identified the different types of commitment (from the 'contingently committed' to the 'mutually committed') which can be found in the continuum of cohabiting relationships, C. Smart and P. Stevens, *Cohabitation Breakdown*, London: FPSC/Rowntree, 2000.

that the presence of children denotes a more accurate mode of differentiation between relationships.[128] On this model, the equal sharing norm (that is, the presumptive equitable distribution of assets accumulated during the relationship) would apply on the proof of mutual dependency, such as the presence of children where parenthood has arisen in the context of a relationship. One could say that this is akin to the partnership model of resource allocation, but rather than being based on the marital partnership ideal, it is based on the 'partnership of parents'[129] which continues after the marital partnership has been dissolved and can apply to non-marital contexts where a child(ren) has been born to the relationship.[130] Economic obligations at the end of a relationship where no children are present may be adequately dealt with under restitutionary principles of a similar nature to the economic advantage/disadvantage model proposed by the Law Commission.[131] In other words, while the partnership model would refer to the parental as opposed to the marital partnership, the financial consequences of other intimate relationships would be governed by restitutionary-style principles designed to equalise between the parties any net economic advantage derived by contributions and sacrifices made during the relationship.

Second, this approach would also encourage a different value to be placed on caregiving which takes place *after* the parental relationship has broken down. This is particularly important where the capital resources are small at the time of the divorce/separation and thus limited assets are available for distribution under the partnership principles. On the breakdown of the marital unit, the desire for self-sufficiency sees the former spouses as autonomous individuals. However, this ignores the relationality of the post-separation family. Where dependent children exist at the time of the divorce/

---

[128] See Glennon, 'Obligations between adult partners', p 45.

[129] Starnes, 'Mothers as suckers', p 1547.

[130] Evidence shows increasing public support for greater financial remedies between cohabiting parents (see S. Athur, J. Lewis, M. Maclean, S. Finch and R. Fitzgerald, 'Settling up: making financial arrangements after divorce or separation', 2002), and for treating married and unmarried couples the same where there are children (see E. Cooke, A. Barlow and T. Callus, 'Community of property: a regime for England and Wales?', Nuffield Foundation, 2006, pp 24, 32–33). The recent British Social Attitudes Report also reveals public support for giving unmarried cohabitants more extensive legal rights based upon the functions of the relationship: 'the public's perception of what separating partners should be entitled is not simply informed by the status of their relationship but strongly relates to its length, as well as the nature and level of investment in it made by the less well off partner,' Barlow, Burgoyne, Clery and Smithson, 'Cohabitation and the law: myths, money and the media' in A. Park *et al.*, (eds) *British Social Attitudes: the 24th Report*, 2008, p 46.

[131] Law Commission of England and Wales, *Cohabitation*.

separation, the parties remain connected through their 'unfinished partnership' as parents[132] contrary to the individualistic philosophy of the clean break ideal and notions of self-sufficiency. As previously highlighted, current constructions which conceptualise the post-divorce contributions of the primary caregiver through a welfare-based consideration of their financial needs and/or compensatory entitlement pay insufficient attention to 'the benefits of caretaking'.[133] As aptly put by Laufer-Ukeles:

> the performance of caretaking duties is not about what is foregone, it concerns an affirmative familial choice with its own benefits. The primary caretaker's different role in the marriage is not just about supporting the working spouse and sacrificing one's own earning potential for him. It is also a choice to raise children; earning potential is foregone and the benefit of raising a child is gained.[134]

With this in mind, Laufer-Ukeles proposes that, on divorce, caretaker support payments should be made to the primary caregiver to 'allow her to smoothly maintain' the caregiving role which was adopted during marriage.[135] This is an interesting attempt to centralise the value of caregiving in that financial support after divorce is based, not on compensating the caregiver for lost market opportunities, but to facilitate the continued performance of caregiving due to its value to the family, and society.[136] As Laufer-Ukeles explains:

---

[132] Starnes, 'Mothers, myths and the law of divorce', p 231. See also Glennon, 'Obligations between adult partners', pp 40, 45.

[133] Laufer-Ukeles, 'Selective recognition of gender difference in the law', p 59.

[134] Ibid, p 59. Of note, Laufer-Ukeles proposes that the primary caretaker presumption should apply in custody disputes. In other words, that primary caretakers have the benefit of the presumption of custody at divorce and thus this issue is 'determined by the past actions of the parents as opposed to the speculative future actions of the parents in a straight best interest analysis', ibid, p 48.

[135] Ibid, p 63. This, however, does not equate to income equalisation. Indeed, as opposed to the 'partnership/income splitting model' of spousal support, this framework contains the 'incentive for the caregiver to return to work when feasible', ibid, p 64. Although if the court deems that this is not reasonably possible due to the caregiver's age or the length of time out of the labour market, caretaker support payments could continue even after minor children have left home, ibid.

[136] In a similar vein, Hale LJ (as she then was) observed in *SRJ* v *DWJ (financial provision)* [1999] 2 FLR 176 that 'It is not only in the [child's] interests but in the community's interests that parents, whether mothers or fathers and spouses, whether husbands or wives, should have a real choice between concentrating on breadwinning and concentrating on homemaking and child-rearing, and do not feel forced, for fear of what might happen should their marriage break down much later in life, to abandon looking after the home and the family to other people for the sake of maintaining a career', 182.

> If a parent constrained her market labor for the sake of caretaking before the divorce, and, therefore a familial value judgment was implicitly made before the divorce regarding the importance of caretaking, such caretaking should be facilitated after divorce.[137]

Using this conceptual framework which considers the provision of care as an activity of intrinsic value, a different interpretation of caregiving and a modified justification for financial support could emerge. As I have argued elsewhere,[138] if it is accepted that a parent has a moral and legal duty to care for his/her child beyond the provision of material support,[139] then the ongoing contributions of the primary caregiver confer a positive benefit on the non-residential parent, either in whole or in part, by divesting the latter of their moral and legal duty of care.[140] While this is a different analysis from that provided by Laufer-Ukeles, it shares the common goal of seeking to place *positive value* on the performance of the care work which, as Starnes points out, includes:

> planning and preparing family meals, editing ... school English papers, transporting children to ballet and swimming and soccer practice, raising money for football helmets, cleaning, laundering, tutoring, baking, shopping, and stocking underwear draws.[141]

Importantly, Starnes continues:

> If a mother performed these labors for an employer no one would question whether the employer received a benefit. When she performs similar labors for her family, her actions also confer benefits, regardless of whether they are actually necessary. The point here is certainly not that mothers *should* do these things, but only that doing them confers a benefit.[142]

---

[137] Laufer-Ukeles, 'Selective recognition of gender difference in the law', p 63.

[138] Glennon, 'Obligations between adult partners', pp 47–48.

[139] See A. Bainham, 'Contract as a right and obligation', in A. Bainham, B. Lindley, M. Richards, and L. Trinder (eds) *Children and their Families: Contact, Rights and Welfare*, Hart Publishing, 2003, pp 74–75.

[140] This notion is supported by the fact after relationship breakdown, non-residential parents are likely to undertake less, not more, care work. Indeed, studies show that despite their increased labour force participation, women still bear primary responsibility for housework and childcare both during the relationship and on its breakdown (which, in this context, also involves managing the post-separation relationships), see J. Wallbank, '(En)Gendering the fusion of rights and responsibilities in the law of contact', Ch 5 in this volume. See also Crompton and Lyonette, 'Who does the housework?'.

[141] Starnes, 'Mothers, myths and the law of divorce', p 225.

[142] Ibid. Emphasis in original.

Indeed, that is the core point of this modified justification for financial support: that the performance of caregiving confers a benefit on the children, the family and, more specifically, the non-residential parent. However, I do not wish to suggest that this model of support can, or should, only apply to full-time homemakers. This interpretation of caregiving justifies some degree of 'caretaker support payments'[143] even if the caregiver works full-time or part-time because the responsibilities and contributions of the primary caregiver extend beyond the provision of care as a full-time homemaker.[144] As Starnes points out, caregiving includes 'both direct care of children and more tangentially related activities that maintain the home in which children live'.[145] Starnes also points out, quite correctly, that, contrary to the myth that 'mothering is [just] for babies',[146] these contributions extend beyond caring for very young children.[147]

Further, as this model is constructed in terms of the positive value of caregiving, it helps to answer the critique of Ferguson regarding the imposition of personal obligations.[148] It is not the caregiver's dependency that is being remedied or compensated, rather the obligations reflect the benefits that the caregiving bestows on the non-residential parent. However, this is not to suggest that there should be no societal responsibility for familial caregiving. But in the context of parental separation, to the extent that there is a private third-party beneficiary of the care work who, depending on the circumstances, has the financial means to contribute to the costs of caregiving, this should be reflected in the financial award on divorce/separation. Indeed, on one view, it is this feature of childcare that allows a distinction to be made between this form of familial caregiving and others, such as caring for an elderly or disabled family member. Economic responsibility for these other forms of familial care work should, as Fineman suggests, fall outside the private realm of the

---

143 Laufer-Ukeles, 'Selective recognition of gender difference in the law', p 56.
144 Of course, this obligation could be capitalised at the time of divorce should resources permit it.
145 Starnes, 'Mothers, myths and the law of divorce', fn 9. Starnes refers to the following definition of primary childcare provided by the US Bureau of Labor Statistics: 'physical care; playing with children; reading to children; assistance with homework; attending children's events; taking care of children's health needs; and dropping off, picking up, and waiting for children', ibid, citing the Bureau of Labor Statistics, US Dept of Labor, USDL No. 05–1766, American Time-Use Survey, Technical Notes (2004).
146 Starnes, 'Mothers, myths and the law of divorce', p 224.
147 Ibid.
148 Ferguson, 'Family, social inequalities'.

family.[149] As work which accommodates the 'inevitable dependency' created by old age, disability and illness,[150] this is a matter of social concern which should be subsidised by the state. However, starting from the premise that a parent has a legal and moral duty to care for their child(ren), it is submitted that childcare can be distinguished on the grounds that there is a private beneficiary of the primary caregiver's work. Thus, in these circumstances, it is not inappropriate to impose privatised obligations of support between parents *inter se* by looking to the absent parent to contribute towards the cost of this care. In response to this argument, Eekelaar acknowledges that 'a child's carer may be relieving the father of a burden' but continues that this 'can be seen as an element of his duty to the child' and thus satisfied by child support obligations.[151] It is respectfully submitted, however, that child support is an insufficient conceptual framework through which to recognise the contributions of the primary caregiver because the latter is little more than a vicarious beneficiary. It should also be emphasised, however, that placing a positive value on these contributions as suggested should not be taken to mean automatic income equalisation between the parents after separation. Neither is a causation-style argument being made that the better-off spouse has been allowed to accumulate wealth due to the care provided by the caregiver. Indeed, this would be a reversion to conceptualising care work purely in market terms. Instead, this proposal simply seeks to view caregiving as a positive and valued contribution to the family, and to the non-residential parent which justifies some form of 'caretaker support payments'[152] for the primary caregiver.[153] In practical terms, these payments would, of course, meet the carer's financial needs and, as Eekelaar argues, go towards bridging the relationship-generated economic disparity between the parties. The difference, however, lies in the justification for imposing these obligations. Rather than simply reflecting a 'welfare-style dependency' model,[154] personal obligations of support would be justified on the grounds that the contributions of the primary caregiver are intrinsically valuable to

---

[149] Fineman, 'The neutered mother'; M. A. Fineman, 'Cracking the foundational myths: independence, autonomy, and self-sufficiency' (2000) 8:1 *Journal of Gender, Social Policy and the Law*, 13; M. A. Fineman, 'Why marriage' (2001) 9 *Virginia Journal of Social Policy and the Law*, 239; M. A. Fineman, *The Autonomy Myth: A Theory of Dependency*, New York: New Press, 2004.

[150] Fineman, 'The neutered mother', p 8.

[151] Eekelaar, 'Partners, parents and children'.

[152] Laufer-Ukeles, 'Selective recognition of gender difference in the law', p 56.

[153] However, to the extent that there is no other parent who can make these payments, responsibility should vest in the state.

[154] Barlow, 'Configuration(s) of unpaid caregiving', p 257. See Eekelaar, 'Back to basics', p 32.

the welfare of the family, including the non-residential parent by relieving them (at least partially) of their parental duty of care.

On a final note, it is worth saying that this approach involves revisiting the policy goals which frame the construction of adult relationship obligations. In this respect it is interesting to consider the social policy goals articulated by Eichner. In pointing to the limitations of a liberal democracy which is premised solely on the individualistic ideals of liberty and equality,[155] Eichner argues that, when devising the state's approach to relationships between adults, these important social goals must be accompanied by principles relating to the human condition.[156] She continues:

> although a liberal democracy should give significant pride of place to the goods of individual liberty and equality, it must also pay attention to an array of other goods and principles relating to human dependency and human development that are necessary to a robust democracy and that too often have been excluded from standard liberal accounts.[157]

In a similar vein, the full-range of ideals sought to be achieved in the quest for gender equality, such as the restructuring of the labour market to encourage more egalitarian parenting patterns should not be jettisoned. However, these objectives should not be viewed in zero-sum terms either as they can take their place alongside other important ideals relating to human dependency such as 'furthering caretaking and human development'.[158] As Eichner notes, there may be conflict between these ideals but:

> it is only by considering this richer range of goods and principles, and by seeking more nuanced approaches that ameliorate the tension among them, that the appropriate relationship between families and the state can be brought into focus.[159]

Thus I am not suggesting that we should lose sight of the need to encourage more egalitarian parenting practices, or the need to restructure the market in order to better facilitate market and care work. All of these elements should

---

[155] M. Eichner, 'Marriage and the elephant: the liberal democratic state's regulation of intimate relationships between adults' (2007) 30 *Harvard Journal of Law and Gender*, 25–66, p 31.

[156] Ibid, pp 31–32.

[157] Ibid, p 32.

[158] Ibid.

[159] Ibid. See also M. Eichner, 'Principles of the law of relationships among adults' (2004) 41(3) *Family Law Quarterly*, 433–53.

be pursued in a 'multi-level' approach to achieve gender equality, but in a way that does not demote the intrinsic personal and societal value of caregiving.[160] Unfortunately, however, the current construction of support obligations created by care work does nothing to improve the 'value and prestige of caregiving',[161] but rather portrays it as a distraction from more important market work. As an alternative, therefore, the role of the primary caregiver should be viewed, not in remedial terms, but as a positive benefit to the family.

CONCLUSION

As Eichner observes, one of the most significant questions which the state has to address is whether to '*recognize* relationships between adults for the purpose of assigning rights and responsibilities *between these adults*'.[162] However, in response to this question, discourses in the UK have evolved in a way which disconnects questions about 'relationship functions' from value-neutral questions about 'relationship structures'. In other words, policy initiatives have focused on the *accessibility* of family law norms, while at the other end of the spectrum, jurisprudential developments continue to transform the *content* of these marital norms through the interpretation of ancillary relief principles. The organisation of these debates, in particular, the disconnection between questions of *content* and *accessibility*, is an ill-conceived matrix as relationships remain compartmentalised into structures which pre-determine the content of the parties' legal obligations. This can be seen in both policy- and practice-based developments where the Law Commission's review of cohabitation law deliberately sought to develop a 'Marriage Minus' system,[163] and the judicial evolution of 'fairness' on divorce which has placed the *status* of marriage at the centre of default capital sharing. The result is that familial caregiving is not considered as a valued activity in its own right, but is conceptualised through the lens of the relationship form in which it takes place. As such, it can be said these mutually informing equality discourses, whilst having transformative potential, have failed to generate a root and branch approach to family law development which would strip back the assumptions upon which current norms are based and encourage a deeper connection between the functions which a

---

[160] See M. Eichner, 'Dependency and the liberal polity: on Martha Fineman's the autonomy myth' (2005) 93 *California Law Review*, 1285, pp 1302–3.
[161] Ibid, p 1296.
[162] Eichner, 'Marriage and the elephant', p 49. Emphasis in original.
[163] LaViolette, 'Waiting in a new line at City Hall', pp 122–23.

family (family members) perform(s) and the obligations to which it (they) are subjected.

By contrast, a preferable approach to the construction of legal obligations between adults would de-emphasise relationship form and encourage a more direct consideration of relationship functions. In this way, the focus on actual interdependencies, such as those arising through shared parenthood, would encourage a more direct and positive value to be placed on familial caregiving. It would also allow more accurate demarcations to replace the current bright line distinctions drawn between the married and the unmarried which prevents a proper evaluation of the mutual dependencies which can arise in couple-based relationships of varying forms.[164] Such an approach, it is submitted, would help to bring legal ideology into line with the emerging social view, revealed in the recent British Social Attitudes Report, that 'most people seem to place the emphasis on successfully 'doing' family in practice, whatever situation people find themselves in, rather than on the supposed functionality of different family forms'.[165]

---

[164] Indeed, research shows that spouses and cohabitants 'are not two separate tribes, but overlap in the way they express their mutual commitment', see M. Maclean, and J. Eekelaar, 'Taking the plunge: perceptions of risk associated with formal and informal partner relationships, social contexts and responsibilities to risk network', 2005, SCARR Working Paper 2005/7.

[165] Duncan and Phillips, 'New families?', p 26.

Chapter 9

Public norms and private lives: Rights, fairness and family law

Alison Diduck[1]

No area of law has remained untouched by the Human Rights Act 1998. While the Act has resulted in the virtual overhaul of some laws and only subtle change to others, it is true to say that all lawyers must now be human rights lawyers. Nevertheless, it was thought at the end of the twentieth century that family law would be one of those areas of the law least affected by the HRA and the rights language and rights consciousness it fostered. Writing in 2005 about the impact of the HRA 1998 on family law, Harris-Short found this to be true. She reviewed appellate level case law and observed that 'the prediction that two key factors – the prevailing mistrust of rights and the difficult questions of public policy which arise in family disputes – would result in a cautious and minimalist approach to the 1998 Act in mainstream family law, is borne out by the post-implementation case law'.[2] Her work was part of larger project on judicial reasoning and the Human Rights Act and presents a clear picture of the way in which appellate courts conceived of and applied convention rights in family law cases.

This chapter aims to do something similar. It is also part of a larger project in which I and colleagues intend to examine more broadly the judicial role in family law disputes and it is an examination of the place of rights discourse in family law. I am not interested, however, in those cases in which Convention rights have been invoked or even claimed, whether vertically or horizontally. Instead, I am interested in those cases in which the HRA has not been pleaded by the parties or referred to by the court at all, but in which nevertheless we can see evidence of its 'culture' or 'values' influencing

[1] My thanks go to Shelley Day Sclater, Michael Freeman, Felicity Kaganas, George Letsas, Myriam Hunter-Henin, Colm O'Cinneide, Dawn Oliver and David Seymour, all of whom read drafts of this chapter and offered valuable comments for its improvement. Thanks also to participants at University of Sussex Responsibility and Family Law Conference July 2008 and to the editors of and other contributors to this volume who engaged at a workshop held in Oxford in critical and congenial discussion of this chapter.
[2] S. Harris-Short, 'Family law and the Human Rights Act 1998: judicial restraint or revolution?', *CFLQ* 2005, vol. 17(3), 329–62, p 360.

judicial reasoning. Specifically, I wish to examine whether values underlying the HRA can claim some influence on the exercise of judicial discretion in family law decision making. This exercise is, at this point, only an observational one, but my observations will be made in the belief that as the values that influence judicial discretion shift from time to time they often advert to as much as shape the norms around which family living is to revolve.

I focus my attention here on the way in which the House of Lords has treated claims for property division or financial provision when intimate partners separate. For married or civilly registered partners, these claims are decided in England and Wales on the basis of the factors enumerated in the Matrimonial Causes Act 1973 with its judicially created objective of 'fairness'. Unmarried/unregistered cohabitants have no statutory or common law basis upon which to claim financial provision and their property claims are based in property and trust law, to which this version of fairness has been held not to apply.[3]

Fairness is the crucial concept here. A positivist or non-family lawyer might be forgiven for smiling about the apparent confirmation it provides for the belief that family law is not 'real' law. It is, so the belief goes, an unprincipled body of case law aimed at managing irrational private disputes.[4] Most family lawyers know, however, that while the meaning of 'fairness' might change from time to time and be contingent upon the facts of an individual case,[5] it does not lack a principled foundation. It is and probably always has been assessed according to principles derived from established norms about 'family' living:

> The guidelines (to be laid down by appellate courts on the relative weights to be given to various factors in different circumstances in ancillary relief claims), not expressly stated by Parliament, are derived by the courts from values about family life which it considers would be widely accepted in the community.[6]

---

[3] *Stack v Dowden* [2007] UKHL 17.
[4] J. Dewar, 'The normal chaos of family law', *Modern Law Review* 1998, vol. 61:4, 467–485. Of course judicial statements like the following by Thorpe LJ did not help dispel this view: 'The function of the Family Division judge is not so much to state principles as to reflect the relevant circumstances of the particular case in the discretionary conclusion.' *Atkinson v Atkinson* [1995] 2 FLR 356, p 361.
[5] *White v White* [2001] 1 AC 596. Political and legal philosophers are also unable to agree upon the meaning of fairness. See, e.g. J. Rawls, *Justice as Fairness: A Restatement*, 2nd edn, Boston: Harvard University Press, 2001; R. Dworkin, *Sovereign Virtue: The Theory and Practice of Equality*, Harvard University Press, 2000; J. Wolff, 'Fairness, respect, and the egalitarian ethos', *Philosophy and Public Affairs*, 1998, vol. 27(2), 97–122; T. Hinton, 'Must egalitarians choose between fairness and respect?', *Philosophy and Public Affairs*, 2001, vol. 30(1) 72–87.
[6] *Piglowska v Piglowski* [1999] 2 FLR 763 per Lord Hoffmann, p 785.

According to Lord Hoffmann then, the normative foundation of fairness in family law lies in community values of 'family life'. Given that families and family life are said to be undergoing great change in Britain today, it may not be surprising to observe occasional shifts in those values, or at least in how they are perceived by the courts. At one time courts may have read them as 'traditional' family values such as protection of the collective welfare and the breadwinner's responsibility to support reasonably his dependants. More recently, however, courts have implied that those values about family life accepted in the community include public, democratic values such as equality and non-discrimination between separating partners. Indeed, awards seem now to be conceptualised, assessed and expressed in a language of entitlement rather than welfare and dependence.[7] It seems, in other words, that while equality and non-discrimination have not been claimed as *rights* between separating partners, the House of Lords has adopted them as *values* to give meaning to fairness between those partners.[8]

Whether the House of Lords is imputing them or acknowledging them, judicial articulation of these values in family living and therefore in the fair determination of family law disputes is new. These values, like the rights which they may be said to underlie, are regarded traditionally as 'belonging' to the realm of public law[9] or politics: they were 'originally conceived as rights and freedoms vis à vis the State and other public authorities'.[10] If courts are, in fact absorbing into private, specifically, family law, public rights values, it marks a significant shift in judicial discourse in the area of ancillary relief. It marks, in particular, a shift away from the belief that families are 'intimate or solidaristic associations' in which the 'values and aims of the participants coincide' and 'spontaneous affection and generosity'[11] ought better than rights to govern relations among members, and therefore are collectivities in which the promotion of non-discrimination, rights and democracy is suspect.

Family law: family norms? Part I

In the UK family law is traditionally understood as the paradigm example of private law. The orthodox view is that it is concerned with relationships

---

[7] J. Eekelaar, 'Back to basics and forward into the unknown', *Fam Law* (2001), 30–34, p 32.

[8] On the philosophical link between fairness and equality, see Dworkin, Wolff and Hinton, above n 5.

[9] Y. Dotan, 'The "public", the "private" and the legal norm of equality', *Canadian Journal of Law and Society*, 2005, vol. 20(2), 207–21, p 210.

[10] Ibid. p 207.

[11] S. M. Okin, *Justice, Gender and Family*, USA: Basic Books, 1989, p 28, quoting M. Sandel *Liberalism and the Limits of Justice*, Cambridge: Cambridge University Press, 1982, p 30–31, 33.

between private individuals rather than with relationships between individuals and the state or other public institutions. More than that, it is concerned with relationships between intimates or former intimates. Family law as private law regulates those relationships that are said properly to be beyond – indeed to be protected from – the public, state or legal gaze. On this view, family relationships are the relationships that provide the bulwark *against* an intrusive state and the public norms by which it is regulated.[12] It is at least partly for this reason that legal 'intrusion' into cases of domestic violence was resisted for so long.

The orthodox view continues: When it does intervene in intimate relationships, law must apply rules and/or principles appropriate to those relationships which are different from those developed for or in response to other, less personal, complex or, indeed, irrational relationships. Family law's rules and principles must respect at the same time the parties' privacy, their individuality, the unity 'the family' represents and the collective endeavour of support and succour for which it supposedly aims. They must respect both *the family* and the individuals who comprise it. These rules or principles, in other words, must respect the norms of *family living*, a concept which condenses any potential conflict between the interests of 'family' as a normative fiction and those of the differently placed and always gendered individuals within it. And so, when courts are called upon to resolve family financial disputes, because they have no clear statutory rules, they have a number of values from which to choose in order to give meaning to the principle of fairness. Traditionally, they adopted a welfare rather than a rights-based approach to fairness:[13]

> The Family Court takes the rights and obligations of the parties all together – and puts the pieces into a mixed bag. Such pieces are the right to occupy the matrimonial home or to have a share in it, the obligation to maintain the wife and children and so forth. The court then takes out the pieces and hands them out to the two parties – some to one party and some to the other – so that each can provide for the future with the pieces allotted to him or her. The court hands them out without paying any too nice a regard to their legal rights or equitable interests but simply according to what is the fairest provision for the future, for mother and father and the children.[14]

[12] This view comes, of course, from a common law perspective. In the continental tradition, family law's acknowledged political objectives render it 'neither to the public sphere, nor entirely included in the private one'. M R Marella 'The non-subversive function of european private law: the case of harmonisation of family law', *European Law Journal*, 12:1 78–105, p 79.

[13] See, e.g. Harris-Short, 'Family law and the Human Rights Act'; Dewar, 'Normal chaos', 1998.

[14] *Hanlon* v *Law Society* [1981] AC 124 p 147 per Lord Denning.

We see these traditional family values reflected also in this decision about post-separation family living:

> The statutory design [of the MCA 1973] was to give the judge exercising the power of equitable distribution the widest discretion to do fairness between the parties, reflecting considerations and criteria laid out within the section. Parliament might have opted for a community of property system or some fraction approach. It opted instead for a wide judicial discretion that would produce a bespoke solution to fit the infinite variety of individual cases [...] The purpose of this statute was to make fair financial arrangements on or after divorce in the absence of agreement between the former spouses. Beyond that the power was not introduced to reorganise proprietary rights within families.[15]

In these two decisions we see the English courts inserting into fairness elements of the orthodox view of family living and family law. In the first, Lord Denning refers to the 'mixed bag' of (presumably moral) rights and obligations including maintenance of dependants, and the court's responsibility to distribute them fairly 'without too nice a regard for legal rights'. In the second, Thorpe LJ reiterates that the court's role is to make fair financial arrangements 'in the absence of agreement between the former spouses', reinforcing the view that law's jurisdiction arises only when the unity of the family – in this case agreement – breaks down. In both, the courts emphasise the idiosyncratic nature of the remedies; fairness is personal, discretionary and allows for 'bespoke' solutions.[16] One of fairness' underlying values, it seems here, is its very privacy, intimacy or subjectivity. Further, the Court of Appeal commended this state of affairs both normatively and constitutionally:

> The statutory basis upon which the financial affairs of divorcing couples are decided has now been in place for a quarter of a century. It has been well tried, its operation is well understood by practitioners and it has in my estimation served society well. If a fundamental change is to be introduced it is for the legislature and not the judges to introduce it. Not only is the legislative process the democratic process but it enables the

---

[15] *Dart v Dart* [1996] 2 FLR 286 p 294 per Thorpe LJ.

[16] In *Cowan v Cowan* [2001] 2 FLR 192 p 210, Thorpe LJ reflected upon his erstwhile commitment to individual solutions over principled ones, and concluded that there is 'an attainable middle ground between the two extremes.' See also the Court of Appeal in *McFarlane* and *Parlour* in which the court eschewed recourse to principles over pragmatic case by case solutions and commentary on that approach: J. Miles, 'Principle or pragmatism in ancillary relief: the virtues of flirting with academic theories and other jurisdictions', *IJLPF*, 2005, vol. 19, 242–56.

route of future change to be surveyed in advance of adoption by extensive research and consultation.[17]

Family law and family living in these judgments are envisioned as quite properly both socially and constitutionally idiosyncratic and private. Family disputes require bespoke solutions in which discretion is exercised based upon accepted norms about family life around privacy, obligation, dependency and property rights. Fairness' reach is thus limited to the parties *inter se* rather than encompassing also the way in which family living and family law engage public institutions, political values, the state and civil society.[18] That broader reach, which would take into account 'sensitive issues of public policy, including complex socio-economic considerations', was regarded traditionally as the responsibility of Parliament rather than the courts.[19] And, all in all, this approach was said in 1996 by the Court of Appeal to have 'served society well'.[20]

There is another view of family living and family law, however. This view acknowledges the intimate relationship between public and private responsibility for individual and social well-being. It is feminist in orientation and offers a view of the economic consequences of forming and ending

---

[17] *Dart* v *Dart* p 301.

[18] See on this J. Herring, 'Why financial orders on divorce should be unfair', 2005, *Intl J of Law, Policy and the Family*, vol. 19, 218–28; A. Diduck, 'Shifting familiarity', *Current Legal Problems*, 2005, vol. 58, 235–54; A. Diduck, 'Relationship fairness' ch 5 in S. Wong and A. Bottomley (ed.) *Changing Contours of Domestic Life, Family and Law: Caring and Sharing*, Oxford: Hart, 2009. In the continental tradition the family is assumed to be ruled by the solidarity principle while its contrast, the market, is based on individualism, but this formulation leads interestingly to the conclusion that the family is therefore a 'public rather than a private affair' (Marella 'The non-subversive function' p 85) and family law is 'conceived as a medium of the political economy.' Marella 'The non-subversive function' p 79.

[19] Harris-Short 'Family law and the Human Rights Act', p 329.

[20] There are (at least) three ways of interpreting the court's position here. The first is to say that out of deference to Parliament and out of respect for what was assumed to be the accepted values of privacy and the subjectivity of family values, the courts exercised judicial restraint such that they were not prepared to engage in their own or a principled, objective moral evaluation of what fairness in these disputes entails. The second is that the courts always engage in moral evaluations in exercising their discretion in ancillary relief cases, but they also always have employed a misguided test for fairness in doing so. That test arguably presupposed a flawed conception of family which hid power and exploitation behind altruism and sacrifice and submerged equality and agency beneath privacy and solidarity. A third possible view is that the courts in these statements are expressing both: there is expressed here a troublesome idealisation of 1) families, 2) the public-private divide and 3) the appropriate constitutional restraints on the judicial role. I am grateful to George Letsas for discussion on these observations.

relationships that overtly implicates gender, the social and the political.[21] It reinforces the idea that obligation arises not only from law and private individual choices but also from the moral and social conditions in which that law and those choices are expressed.[22] On this view of family living and family law those 'values about family life' that give meaning to fairness include also values that animate public and political life.

This view promotes the legitimacy and importance of factors such as social and economic policy, legal principle and social conditions/context when assessing fairness in family financial disputes. It also increases the legitimacy of including in assessments of fairness that other bastion of public discourse: rights. We see examples in Canada and South Africa where Charters of Rights have encouraged the increased influence of rights discourse, if not rights themselves, in family law.[23] In Canada it has meant, argues Young,[24] the 'publicisation' or constitutionalisation of family law such that Charter values have begun to play a role in changing aspects of family law both substantively and constitutionally. Substantively, Young argues that in Canada the concern of the Supreme Court seems not to be with rights in a formalistic or individual sense in family law, but with an idea of equality that embraces a sense of social justice and human dignity.[25] This approach has had a clear if uneven effect upon gender equality questions. Constitutionally, it means that the court is adopting more of a reforming role than it traditionally takes.

Young first suggests that the increase in the number of family law cases to reach the Supreme Court of Canada is evidence of the publicisation of family law there. There is merit to this argument and to its applicability in England and Wales. Because the House of Lords, like the Supreme Court of Canada, hears only cases of important public policy, traditionally family law cases, particularly property/finance cases, tended to stop at the Court of Appeal. *Piglowski*[26] and *Fitzpatrick*[27] in 1999 were the beginning of the Lords' recent interest in families. Before that we have to look back to *Rosset*[28] to see them taking an interest in family matters, and even then it was, arguably, more the interests of financial institutions that were of concern. Since then, all within eight years or so, we have seen the House of Lords decide

[21] Diduck, 'Shifting familiarity'; Diduck, 'Relationship fairness'.
[22] D. Cooper, *Challenging Diversity, Rethinking Equality and the Value of Difference*, Cambridge: Cambridge University Press, 2004.
[23] A. H. Young, 'The changing family, rights discourse and the Supreme Court of Canada' *Canadian Bar Review*, 2001, vol. 80, 749–92; J. Sloth-Nielsen and B. Van Heerden, 'The constitutional family: developments in South African family law jurisprudence under the 1996 constitution', *IJLPF*, 2003, vol. 17, 121–46.
[24] Young, 'The changing family'.
[25] Young, 'The changing family'.
[26] *Piglowski* v *Piglowska* 1999.
[27] *Fitzpatrick* v *Sterling Housing Association* [2001] 1 AC 27.
[28] *Lloyds Bank* v *Rosset* [1991] 1 AC 107.

White,[29] *Ghaidan*,[30] *Bellinger*,[31] *Miller*,[32] *Stack*[33] and *M*[34] and in its role as the Privy Council *MacLeod* v *MacLeod* case from the Isle of Man regarding the impact of pre- and post-nuptial agreements on ancillary relief claims.[34a]

Young[35] also points in Canada to changes in the nature of the court's decision making as evidence of the publicisation of family law. Whereas courts traditionally restricted their role in family law cases to interpreting doctrine and statutes and to fashioning bespoke solutions to individual problems, she identifies a new concern to articulate broader principles and policy. According to Young, judges now grapple with policy questions that are not explicit in the statute; they find the parties' issues *to be* or to reflect matters of policy. They are happier to use non-judicial sources to identify that policy and the context in which it is expressed. Rather than search for pragmatic individualised solutions based only upon the common law, they rely upon evidence of social conditions, social trends and broader principles. They see their constitutional role differently: the Supreme Court of Canada no longer follows social change, but is leading it. There is merit to the argument that on this measure also, a similar form of public-isation of family law may be occurring in England and Wales: perhaps one of the (unintended?) consequences of the HRA is that it has boosted judges' confidence to be less deferential in approach and also to tackle moral and policy issues expressly and openly in family law.

Let us consider the most recent House of Lords decisions on family finance/property matters in the light of these observations. *White* v *White* is the watershed. It is a clear attempt to give a principled rather than pragmatic meaning to fairness. Moreover, the principle, the *meaning* of fairness derives from (social) policy rather than simply from the words of the statute and it derives from public, rights values rather than exclusively from traditional family values such as that which gave rise to the now discredited 'reasonable requirements' principle. While acknowledging that fairness exists in the 'eye of the beholder', Lord Nicholls states also that, at its heart, is non-discrimination between the husband, the wife and their respective family roles. Under the heading 'equality' he states:

> Self-evidently, fairness requires the court to take into account all the circumstances of the case. [...] But there is one principle of universal application which can be stated with confidence. In seeking to achieve a

---

[29] *White* v *White* [2001] 1 AC 596.
[30] *Ghaidan* v *Godin-Mendoza* [2004] UKHL 30.
[31] *Bellinger* v *Bellinger* [2003] UKHL 21.
[32] *Miller* v *Miller*; *McFarlane* v *McFarlane* [2006] UKHL 24.
[33] *Stack* v *Dowden* [2007] UKHL 17.
[34] *M* v *Secretary of State for Works and Pensions* [2006] 2 WLR 637.
[34a] [2008] UKPC 64.
[35] Young, 'The changing family'.

fair outcome, there is no place for discrimination between husband and wife and their respective roles.[36]

He then created the 'yardstick of equality' by which all financial orders must be measured. While fairness was still to be determined by judicial discretion, the court added new values or factors to the mix to give it meaning: public, rights-based ones, importantly said to be 'universal'. And crucially, substituting, *in fairness*, the values of non-discrimination and equality for the 'traditional' family principles of breadwinner/dependant, resulted here in a vastly increased award for the claimant wife. *White* was decided just as the HRA was coming into effect, arguably when rights consciousness was only emerging in English law. Six years later, in *Miller* v *Miller; McFarlane* v *McFarlane* the court took the opportunity not only to affirm but to fine tune the way in which principles of non-discrimination and equality underpin fairness in family matters.

Fairness, confirmed Lord Nicholls in 2006, is grounded in social and moral values[37] that appear to add a new dimension to the values about family life widely accepted in the community. Like those first identified in *White*, they go beyond the traditional confines of 'family' and the words of the statute as Lord Hoffmann stated in *Piglowska* seven years earlier. First, fairness means that like cases must be treated alike. Second, it means that parties' needs must be met; third that it includes an element of compensation, and fourth that there is, in marital living, an expectation of equal sharing. In these elements of fairness we see references both to traditional family values (meeting needs) and to rights-based values of equality, from the Aristotelian notion of formal equality to a more nuanced version of substantive equality (compensation). Non-discrimination also has an important place in the principle of fairness according to Lord Nicholls. There should, he states, be no discrimination in its application on the basis of length of the marriage, the gender roles undertaken in the marriage or the type of assets to be considered, and thus he adds further to the mix of normative considerations. Baroness Hale also affirms the need for principle in family law cases[38] and that this principle must be based upon a fairness that reflects equality and non-discrimination. She uses social science research and other non-judicial sources liberally to support her view of fairness as contextualised substantive equality. Importantly, both Mrs Miller and Mrs McFarlane received far greater awards after these rights-based values were introduced as a part of fairness than they would have received under the traditional family value of 'reasonable requirements'.

---

[36] *White* v *White* p 8.
[37] *Miller;McFarlane*, para 4.
[38] Ibid, paras 122–23.

Most recently we have the third case I wish to consider here. In *Stack* v *Dowden* the parties cohabited without marriage for almost 20 years. They had four children together and bought the family home in joint tenancy. While Stack and Dowden were, without doubt, a 'family' and while their dispute was about the family home, this case did not fall within the traditional boundaries of family law. Because they were not married, Stack and Dowden were subject neither to the MCA nor to the norms of family living, including fairness, which are said to underlie it. They were treated as legal strangers to whom the House of Lords applied 'ordinary law'[39] which meant that it focused upon the parties' intentions in order to determine how to allocate beneficial ownership of their home. It applied norms about private property ownership and the rationality of contractual transactions to identify those intentions. Lord Neuberger in particular felt that any implication of intention to the parties based upon their formerly intimate relationship was inappropriate:

> I am unimpressed, for instance, by the argument that, merely because they have already lived together for a long time sharing all regular outgoings, including those in respect of the previous property they occupied, the parties must intend that the beneficial interest in the home that they are acquiring, with differently sized contributions, should be held in equal shares. Particularly where the parties have chosen not to marry, their close and loving relationship does not by any means necessarily imply an intention to share all their assets equally.[40]

Recall though, that Stack and Dowden represented a new socially acceptable form of family living. Indeed, Baroness Hale referred to social science research to position them in this way.[41] The Court thus could not ignore their family relationship entirely.[42] Their quasi-familial status meant that while neither fairness nor an assumption of marital equality was deemed an appropriate principle to import into the 'ordinary' law[43] applicable to them, Stack and Dowden's familial interdependence could not be disregarded entirely in identifying their intentions with regard to beneficial ownership of their home.

> [T]he interpretation to be put on the behaviour of people living together in an intimate relationship may be different form the interpretation to be put upon similar behaviour between commercial men. To put it at its

---

[39] *Stack* v *Dowden* para 44 per Baroness Hale.
[40] Ibid, para 132.
[41] Ibid, paras 44–48.
[42] Ibid, Lord Hope para 3; Lord Walker para 27; Baroness Hale paras 68–70; Lord Neuberger paras 107 and 137.
[43] Ibid, Lord Neuberger para 144.

highest, an outcome which might seem just in a purely commercial transaction may appear highly unjust in a transaction between husband and wife, or cohabitant and cohabitant.[44]

And:

the domestic context is very different from the commercial world […] Many more factors than financial contributions may be relevant to divining the parties' true intentions.[45]

Stack and Dowden's case thus lies on the boundary of family law/not family law. It is about the determination, according to ordinary (property and trust) law, of a post-separation *family* asset. While neither 'old' (welfare-based, meeting of dependant's needs) nor 'new' (non-discrimination and equal sharing) family norms could be applied to that determination, neither could they be ignored. In 'divining the parties' true intentions' the House of Lords could rely on presumptions neither about transactions between married couples nor about those between 'commercial men'. Traditionally, neither could it apply rights principles to the dispute, for the HRA is as difficult to apply in the ordinary law of property and trust as it is in family law. It is tempting to say, therefore, that the House of Lords looked only to the facts of the case, in their social and personal context, and made a pragmatic decision regarding those two individuals and that equality or other rights-based values or principles had little influence on them. But the contrast between a pragmatic decision and a principled one, is as we have seen, potentially spurious. Judges must always engage in some form of moral or principled evaluation and the moral value or principle they choose to underpin their reasoning will usually determine which facts or context they deem relevant. If we unearth, therefore, some of the different underlying values or interests protected by the principle of equality, we may see that protecting the parties' apparently 'real' intentions as opposed to those that otherwise would have been implied by reason only of their family status actually does invoke a form of the principle of equality.

Equality, as we saw in *Miller* has different interpretations, different nuances, different underlying values. It could mean consistency or sameness of treatment, it could mean non-discrimination and it could mean substantive equality achieved by way of compensation for economic disadvantage. Establishing the substance of equality is always problematic. Like fairness, it is an indeterminate or at least disputed concept and for this reason it is important that we identify and examine the way in which it takes shape from case to case. In *White* it took the form of non-discrimination and formal

---

[44] Ibid, Baroness Hale, para 42.
[45] Ibid, para 69

equality, in *Miller/McFarlane* it took the form of redress of disadvantage while in *Stack*, we see the House of Lords attaching importance to the parties' life choices. They may in this way be promoting a type of equality linked to respect for individual autonomy as an expression of human dignity. Indeed, in 2002 the Supreme Court of Canada did just that in when it found no breach of the Charter's equality guarantee by a matrimonial property law which applied to married couples and not to cohabiting couples.[46] It held that dignity was the underlying value to be protected by substantive equality and autonomy was a fundamental expression of dignity. The dignity of cohabitants, the Court said, was protected by respecting their decisions not to marry and thereby not to subject themselves to the matrimonial property regime. Protecting their dignity by protecting their autonomous life choices, therefore, was a way to interpret and give meaning to the value of substantive equality. The House of Lords in *Stack* may be protecting a form of equality not as sameness, nor as the equal sharing that is said to inhere in the marital relationship, but as one which respects individual dignity and autonomy.[47] Further, it is saying that this form of equality is an important value in 'ordinary' law, or at least when ordinary law is applied to family disputes. In *WIC Radio Ltd and Rafe Mair* v *Kari Simpson*, decided by the Supreme Court of Canada in June 2008, the Court agreed that the Charter of Rights and Freedoms was relevant in private law cases, in this case, defamation. The Court said at para 2: 'This is a private law case that is not governed directly by the Charter. Yet it was common ground in the argument before us that the evolution of the common law is to be informed and guided by Charter values.'

Three cases obviously do not constitute a trend, but they do raise questions about shifts in judicial method, reasoning and language in family law. The broad discretion in ancillary relief cases always allowed courts to rely upon pragmatism to accommodate the idiosyncracies of individual families as well as upon principles and values both public and private. These cases may suggest, however, that the essence and therefore the nature of those public values have shifted, perhaps from patriarchy to democracy. Rights appear in these cases as a legitimate or even mandatory discourse through which to engage in the discretionary exercise.

Let us examine further the case for this new form of publicisation or politicisation of determinations of fairness. Because it agreed to hear them,

---

[46] *Nova Scotia Attorney General* v *Susan Walsh and Wayne Bona* [2002] 4 SCR. 325. See now, however, *R* v *Kapp* 2008 SCC 41, in which the Supreme Court of Canada clarified that while dignity was an essential value underlying the s 15 equality guarantee, it was, on its own, an 'abstract and subjective notion' that makes it difficult to employ as a legal test. Paras 21–22.

[47] See further R. O'Connell, 'The role of dignity in equality law: lessons from Canada and South Africa', *International Journal of Constitutional Law*, 2008, Advance Access (Internet) published 21 March 2008.

the House of Lords in *White*, *Miller* and *Stack* (and now *MacLeod*) designated these issues of family finances and family living as matters of public
policy and public importance. Family living and disputes about family living,
this says, are not only of importance to family members, they are of social
and public importance. Further, the rules and values applicable to family
living are important not only to those particular family members embroiled
in dispute, they too are matters of public concern and importantly, are
transferable across families. Indeed, these cases suggest that values informing
family living and justice in resolving family disputes are no longer located
within or informed exclusively by the parties' personal circumstances and
traditional welfare based norms about 'the family', but also by social and
political conditions and social and political norms such as equality, non-
discrimination and autonomy which are said to be 'self-evident' or 'universal'. Finally and importantly, it is also interesting that the House of Lords
utilised extra-judicial materials to locate the parties' personal financial
circumstances in their social context and was willing to forge social policy in
its decisions. It seems in these cases to be stepping back from traditional
judicial deference to the 'common law tradition' with its conservative
constitutional role.

Family law: family norms? Part II

Perhaps, however, there is another explanation for these decisions. Oliver,[48]
for example, would say that the separation of public law and private law is
artificial, but even if we were to conceive of these areas of law as separate,
they have much in common. Both are influenced by principles of democracy
which flow from state and international organs, domestic and international
legislation and the common law. Moreover, these democratic principles
'attach increasing weight and importance to upholding the dignity, autonomy, respect, status and security of individuals against the exercise of
power'[49] whether by the state or by private individuals. 'These values are at
once individualistic and social'[50] and it therefore makes no sense to label
some as public and some private.

In a similar vein, political philosophers have argued that (variants of)
equality, non-discrimination and dignity are inherent values in any democracy,[51] whether or not they are enumerated as such in a rights document.

---

[48] D. Oliver, *Common Values and the Public Private Divide*, London: Butterworths,
1999. Continental lawyers are also struck by the way in which the public/private
divide is constructed in the common law.

[49] Ibid, p 273.

[50] Ibid.

[51] Dworkin 2000, for example, calls the value 'equal concern'; see also A. Sen,
'Equality of What?' in *The Tanner Lectures on Human Values* S. M. McMurrin
(ed.) 1980 Vol. 1 Cambridge: CUP pp 195–220.

Many public lawyers agree and declare that the judicial role has always been to promote those values in the common law.[52] They would see no reason to distinguish between an individual's dispute with a public body and her dispute with another individual in the applicability of those democratic values whether they are invoked by a legal right or not. Sandra Fredman sees the HRA as encouraging this perception:

> From the bland view of democracy as requiring deference to legislators, courts have begun to see human rights as constitutive of democracy rather than ranged against it. With this has come the emergence of equality as a central democratic principle ... [53]

She acknowledges that when judges attempt to apply the principle in law they are making a political decision but says that it is not an undemocratic one. It is deliberative decision-making of which value and principle are an integral part and in which they become able to evolve in an open and reasoned manner.[54]

It is not only public law scholars who question the (family's place in the) public–private law divide. Family law scholar John Eekelaar[55] believes that the legitimate legal regulation of people's personal lives must incorporate the values of friendship, truth, respect, responsibility and rights. On this view, the House of Lords in *White, Miller/McFarlane* and *Stack* has simply interpreted the 'family values' that give meaning to fairness as now properly including rights values. Lind[56] states that, particularly in a multicultural society, there never has been a single family norm or set of family norms by which to assess family living and family disputes. He sees only different multicultural and gender norms we live personally which always carry over into the public where they then require some public, normative teeth by which they can be assessed. On this view, family living has always been both public and private and so it has always been legitimate to apply public standards to various 'family values' in order to give meaning to indeterminate concepts like fairness.

Yet another view is that judges always have attended to 'public' values in exercising their discretion in family law disputes. The patriarch–dependant

---

[52] See S. Fredman, 'From deference to democracy: the role of equality under the Human Rights Act 1998', *LQR*, 2006, 53–81; Baroness Hale of Richmond, 'Maccabaean lecture in jurisprudence 2007 A minority opinion?', 2007, paper on file with the author.

[53] Fredman, 'From deference to democracy', p 53.

[54] Ibid, p 81.

[55] J. Eekelaar, *Family Law and Personal Life*, Oxford: Oxford University Press, 2006.

[56] C. Lind, 'Unanswerable dilemma? – legal regulation for cross-cultural family norms', in P. E. Andrews and S. Bazilli (eds), *Law and Rights: Global Perspectives on Constitutionalism and Governance*, 2008, Lake Mary: Vanderplas Publishing.

relationship that came to form the 'traditional' or 'ideal' family is derived from a public, political norm and certainly can claim some effect upon the exercise of judicial discretion in ancillary relief cases over the years. Even the principle of equality has a history in ancillary relief. The value of formal equality that informed the clean break amendment to the MCA in 1984 assuredly had a wider effect on courts' perceptions of fairness than only when they considered the then new section 25A. Finally by way of example, John Dewar sees interpretive trends in family law as always shifting, from family law's original reliance upon rules to its reliance in the mid-twentieth century upon discretion to its shift back now to rules, perhaps resulting from a perceived need to find some principled basis for itself.[57]

We could also say that family practices themselves are what are shifting; they are now more public, democratic and rights conscious,[58] and so have changed those values about family life that would be widely accepted in the community. Family law, on this view, is only properly attending to this social shift.

While there is probably some truth to all of these alternative readings of the recent House of Lords cases, it is still the case that something seems to have changed since the inception of the HRA. The change is subtle, but important. First, the cases say that the public values that ought to inform family living are derived from human rights rather than exclusively from 'traditional family' values. Second, the court did not adjudicate these disputes on the basis of family privacy, idiosyncracy or subjectivity. It made clear that the arrangements people make in their personal lives both are contingent on their public lives and have public and policy rather than simply personal meaning and consequences. Finally, the court is now openly articulating its decisions in the *language* of rights principles. Perhaps the HRA has given it a type of constitutional 'permission' to do so.

Boyd argued in 2000 that even then the Charter of Rights and Freedoms had an impact on the way in which judicial discretion was exercised in family law cases in Canada.[59] Judges adopted an approach by which they

---

[57] Dewar 'Normal chaos', p 473.

[58] See on this A. Giddens, *The Transformation of Intimacy*, Cambridge: Polity, 1992. There is evidence, furthermore, that attitudes to marriage are changing so that mutuality, self-fulfilment and equality are now cited by many as important elements of a successful marriage: see J. Reynolds and P. Mansfield, 'The effect of changing attitudes to marriage on its stability', 1999, Lord Chancellor's Department Research Series No. Vol. 1, London: The Stationery Office; and respondents to a survey by the National Family and Parenting Institute were frustrated that issues such as traffic, street lights, public transport, low wages and racism which affected the family practices they expressed outside the home were not included in questions about the quality of their family relationships: see National Family and Parenting Institute, 'Is Britain family-friendly?' The parents' eye view', 1999, London: National Family and Parenting Institute.

[59] S. Boyd, 'The impact of the Charter of Rights and Freedoms on Canadian family law' 2000, *Canadian Journal of Family Law*, vol. 17, 293–331.

developed the common law and made court orders under statutes in the context of private litigation in a manner consistent with the fundamental values enshrined in the Charter, including equality. While we see the House of Lords now considering the social context and social history of the family disputes before them, and also articulating some decisions in rights language, it may be too early yet to say whether the same approach has been adopted in England and Wales. The Court of Appeal, for example, has demonstrated that its interpretation of the principles articulated in *White* and *Miller/ McFarlane* may differ from the Lords'. In the rarely used form of a 'post-script' to its decision, in *Charman* v *Charman*[60] the Court called for a review of the newly interpreted discretion under Matrimonial Causes Act on the basis that *White* and *Miller/McFarlane*'s principled, contextual approach to its interpretation may have been inappropriate, first, on a constitutional basis: 'There is a limitation on the resources of even the judges of the House of Lords to conduct wide-ranging comparative studies as a prelude to establishing a new principle, or perhaps to abandoning an existing principle in what is essentially a social policy field.'[61]

Second, the Court of Appeal was unsure of the applicability or at least universality of the principle of equality in all family law cases. In the case law established before 2000:

> the applicant's reasonable requirements became the focus of the case, throughout its preparation and in its final determination. This method brought predictability and clarity, characteristics that were refined by a mechanism for capitalising the applicant's future spending requirement, a mechanism inferentially sanctioned by this court in its decision in *Duxbury* v *Duxbury* (Note) [1992] Fam 62, [1987] 1 FLR 7. The emphasis on the applicant's reasonable requirements as the yardstick of the award satisfied the anxiety of judges and others that we should not be drawn into the extravagance of some American states, particularly California, where very large awards were commonplace. This judicial preference for moderation ruled essentially for a generation from the mid-1970s to the year 2000. It suited the society of its day.[62]

Conceding the necessity of reform of the judicial preference for moderation in determining the amount of wives' awards, the Court goes on:

> Was the need for reform met by the decision of the House in *White*? The decision deprived practitioners and judges of the old measure of

---

[60] [2007] EWCA Civ 503, para 114.
[61] Para 122.
[62] Para 106.

reasonable requirements, offering instead the cross check of equality to ensure fairness and to banish discrimination.

Of course these innovations were well founded on profound social change, particularly in the recognition that marriage is a partnership of equals and that the role of man and woman within the marriage are commonly interchangeable. In the majority of cases the innovations resulting from *White* were timely and beneficial.

However a social change that was not perhaps recognised in that decision was the extent to which the origins and the volume of big money cases were shifting [...] These socio-economic developments coincided with a retreat from the preference of English judges for moderation. The present case well illustrates that shift. At trial Mr Pointer achieved for his client an award of £48m. Before us he freely conceded that he could not have justified an award of more than £20m on the application of the reasonable requirements principle. Thus, in very big money cases, the effect of the decision in *White* was to raise the aspirations of the claimant hugely. In big money cases the *White* factor has more than doubled the levels of award and it has been said by many that London has become the divorce capital of the world for aspiring wives. Whether this is a desirable result needs to be considered not only in the context of our society but also in the context of the European Union of which we are a singular Member State ... [63]

More recently, in *B* v *B*[64] the Court of Appeal played down the significance of the principles enunciated in *White* and *Miller/McFarlane, as principles*, by returning to the idea that no two family law cases are ever alike. Marginalising both principle and the role of precedent, Wall, LJ states 'since each case requires its own particular resolution, the concept of fairness becomes, essentially a matter of judgment'.[65] He repeats several times in this case the importance of exercising objective 'judgment' of the particular facts in ancillary relief cases. Consider his words in the following passage:

One of the frustrations of family law, as well as one of its fascinations, is that no two cases are ever the same. Since the essence of any judicial discretion lies in its application to particular facts, and since each case requires its own particular resolution, the concept of fairness becomes, essentially a matter of judgment. In this context I am reminded of the wise words of Ormrod LJ, in *Martin* v *Martin* [1978] Fam 12 at 20, [1977] 3 All ER 762, [1977] 3 WLR 101; words spoken more than 30

---

[63] Paras 114–116.
[64] [2008] EWCA Civ 543.
[65] Ibid, para 54, per Lord Justice Wall.

years ago on 10 March 1977, but still, in my judgment, as applicable today as when they were first uttered:

' ... It is the essence of such a discretionary situation that the court should preserve, so far as it can, the utmost elasticity to deal with each case on its own facts. Therefore, it is a matter of trial and error and imagination on the part of those advising clients. It equally means that decisions of this court can never be better than guidelines. They are not precedents in the strict sense of the word. There is bound to be an element of uncertainty in the use of the wide discretionary powers given to the court under the Act of 1973, and no doubt there always will be, because as social circumstances change so the court will have to adapt the ways in which it exercises discretion. ... '[66]

After approving these words and acknowledging that the *White* and *Miller/McFarlane* non-discrimination and equality principles may have required the courts to 'adapt' the ways in which they exercise discretion, he says later:

But what remains unchanged, and will remain unchanged for as long as these matter are governed by s 25 of the 1973 Act, is that the outcome of every case is a matter of judgment. This case is no exception to that universal rule. As Hughes LJ has stated, and I repeat, this appeal raises no new point of principle. The profession should therefore resist the temptation to treat it as a precedent. What it is, and this in my view is its only value, is a demonstration of the manner in which this court has exercised its judgment in relation to particular facts.

In the instant case, both the district judge and the circuit judge, in my judgment, mistakenly sought to give effect to what they wrongly thought to be the need to achieve equality. In so doing, their decisions were plainly wrong and the outcome was, as a consequence and in each case, unfair. What this court proposes to put in its place is, in my view, both pragmatic and fair.[67]

The court here appears to be resiling from the idea that universally applicable principles of family living underlie fairness, and to prefer instead a universally applicable rule that fairness in every case is individual. But it also seems to have tempered this idea with a concurrent change in the language used to describe its role in determining that fairness. It seems that judges no longer must exercise discretion in making these decisions, they must exercise judgment. This change in language may have no jurisprudential

[66] Para 54.
[67] Paras 57, 59.

significance,[68] intended or otherwise, but is curious. To form a judgment about something popularly implies reaching a considered decision about it; a judgment is constrained by rules and is deliberate. It is authoritative, objective and the result of reflective wisdom. To exercise discretion about something, on the other hand, implies exercising a freedom to act on one's own; while judicial discretion must be exercised responsibly and within the bounds imposed by law, it connotes a more free-ranging exercise of choice than does exercising judgment. In using the word judgment rather than discretion, the Court of Appeal may here be conceding some degree of reflective, even principled objectivity to its role, even as it reinforces its right to determine the principles at play.

Conclusions

It is easier for me to conclude that there is a new rights discourse emerging from the courts than to assess its benefits or otherwise for women and the children in their care, indeed for all who traditionally have been disadvantaged in family law decision-making. This question is particularly acute if we agree that in adopting this approach the courts are indeed presiding over a change in the 'underlying vision and purpose of family'[69] and that the change is occurring in a time of the neo-liberal privatisation of responsibility within a pervasive climate moral uncertainty. The effect of the new discourse therefore may be to find a new way to anchor a 'family' that has broken away from its moorings, bringing potential (moral) chaos in its wake.[70] If so, the next step must be to evaluate critically that new anchor and its effect. There are risks, particularly for women, in relying too heavily upon individualism and rights at a time of the increased privatisation of families and family responsibilities while government is transforming public into private goods.[71] Further, while (some contestable concept of) equality remains only rhetorical at the social level, presupposing (some equally contestable concept of) it in intimate relationships may result in profound unfairness for those whose social disadvantage cannot be acknowledged or

---

[68] In Dworkinian terms, for example, the court seems to be promoting a shift from courts exercising a 'weak' discretion in which authoritative standards or principles 'cannot be applied mechanically but demand the use of judgment' to a 'strong' discretion in which a judge is bound only by certain standards of rationality, fairness and effectiveness rather than by standards or principles set by an authority. See R. M. Dworkin 'The model of rules', 1967–68, *The University of Chicago Law Review* Vol. 35, 14–46, p 32, 33–34.

[69] Young, 'The changing family'.

[70] I am grateful to Shelley Day Sclater for this observation.

[71] Dotan, 'The "public" and the "private"'. See also Diduck, 'Shifting Familiarity'; M. A. Fineman, *The Autonomy Myth*, New York: The New Press, 2004; B. Cossman and J. Fudge (eds), *Privatization, Law and the Challenge to Feminism*, Toronto: University of Toronto Press, 2002.

accounted for in ancillary relief. More generally, there are risks for women of assessing their claims consequent upon private, intimate living according to liberal, individualistic norms formulated for public, political living,[72] risks that come with judicial activism as the method by which this happens and risks in absorbing rights values rather than rights into the law.[73] In all of these ways at least, the shifts in judicial discourse from *Martin* v *Martin* to *White* and *Miller/McFarlane* to *B* v *B* offer a point of departure for further analysis that is crucial to formulations of economic fairness for women in family law.

---

[72] See, e.g. R. Hunter (ed.), *Rethinking Equality Projects in Law: Feminist Challenges*, Oxford: Hart Publishing, 2008.

[73] A. Diduck, 'The publicisation of family law: risks and reflections', 2008, unpublished paper presented at RCSL Gender Working Group conference Milan, Italy.

Chapter 10

The identification of 'parents' and 'siblings': New possibilities under the reformed Human Fertilisation and Embryology Act

Caroline Jones

INTRODUCTION

The reported need for, or 'right' to, information about the 'truth' regarding one's genetic origins has significant purchase in twenty-first century Anglo-Welsh legal discourse, both within and outside the specific context of donor conception. In terms of genetic links, what could at one time only be inferred can now usually be proved, and on the basis of these findings relationships can be ascribed/created or denied. However, what is less clear is the extent to which the 'fact' of genetic relatedness should (in)form the basis of legal – and indeed social or kin – relationships between progenitors and offspring[1] (these terms are used deliberately here to abstract genetic 'facts' from the legal and social meaning often ascribed to them, although it is acknowledged that these terms are not unproblematic). Within family law two issues are frequently run together: the 'right' to be a parent and the 'right' to know one's genetic origins.[2] In the context of assisted conception these issues are perhaps more accurately expressed as the claims to be legally recognised as a parent of a specific child, and for access to identifying information about one's gamete donor(s); as although further non-identifying information has also been sought, for example in the case of *Rose*,[3] this has not proved to be the focal point of most debates.

Initial analysis of the Human Fertilisation and Embryology Act 2008 (the 2008 Act), amending the 1990 Act of the same name, points towards the central role of consent provisions in both the construction of legal parenthood and in relation to gaining access to further information about one's genetic origins. This approach arguably lends support to the thematic

---

[1] See, e.g. M. Strathern, *Kinship, Law and the Unexpected: Relatives Are Always a Surprise*, Cambridge: Cambridge University Press, 2005; S. Boyd 'Gendering legal parenthood: bio-genetic ties, intentionality and responsibility' (2007) 25 *Windsor Yearbook of Access to Justice*, 63–94.

[2] I am grateful to Jonathan Herring for this point.

[3] *Rose and Another* v *Secretary of State for Health and Human Fertilisation and Embryology Authority* [2002] EWHC 1593, [2003] 2 FLR 962.

unification of these disparate issues. However, upon closer examination, the complexities of these new provisions and the relevant Parliamentary debates point towards gendered dimensions at play, which are downplayed by the gender-neutrality of the statute and rights discourse in general. The focus of this chapter, therefore, is the examination of key issues pertaining to the interest(s) in knowing one's genetic origins, in the wider sense provided for by the 2008 Act. I use the term 'interest' here as my intention is not to add to the burgeoning literature debating donor-conceived children/persons' purported 'right' to know[4] per se, but rather to consider why identity, and in particular genetic information, is highlighted in this context; and also to consider what interests and crucially whose are promoted and protected by the legislative provisions. The fixation with the need for 'truth' around paternal ties rather than with maternal connections remains. Interestingly however, there is an identifiable inversion of the trend to protect a 'recipient family' (of donor gametes) from incursions by their donor(s)[5] to that of shielding the donor's family (read 'legal' family) from interference by donor offspring, and by extension their family members. Furthermore, the grounds upon which this protection is justified – at least in the relevant Parliamentary debates – is largely gender specific. Therefore, while significant aspects of the 2008 Act are couched in gender-neutral terms, it is clear that the impetus for these changes occurred within highly gendered contexts.

---

[4] S. Besson, 'Enforcing the child's right to know her origins: contrasting approaches under the Convention on the Rights of the Child and the European Convention on Human Rights' (2007) 21 *International Journal of Law, Policy and the Family*, 137–59; J. Eekelaar, *Family Law and Personal Life*, Oxford: Oxford University Press, 2007, pp 54–75; C. Smart, *Personal Life*, Cambridge: Polity Press, 2007, pp 122–32; A. Lalos, C. Gottlieb, and O. Lalos, 'Legislated right for donor-insemination children to know their genetic origin: a study of parental thinking' (2007) 22 *Human Reproduction*, 1759–68; J. Wallbank, 'The role of rights and utility in instituting a child's right to know her genetic history', *Social and Legal Studies*, 13(2), 2004, 245–64; S. Maclean, and M. Maclean, 'Keeping secrets in assisted reproduction – the tension between donor anonymity and the need of the child for information' (1996) 8 *Child and Family Law Quarterly*, 243–51; J. Fortin, '*Re F*: the gooseberry bush approach' (1994) 57 *Modern Law Review*, 296–307 – but more recently see J. Fortin 'Children's right to know their origins: too far, too fast?', Allan Levy Memorial lecture, 27 November 2007, University of London. For a discussion of the role of birth certificates in this context, see E. Blyth, L. Frith, C. Jones and J. M. Speirs, 'The role of birth certificates in relation to access to biographical and genetic history in donor conception', *International Journal of Children's Rights*, 17, 2009, 207–233; A. Bainham, 'What is the point of birth registration?' (2008) 20 *Child and Family Law Quarterly*, 449–74.

[5] E. Haimes, 'Recreating the family? Policy considerations relating to the "new" reproductive technologies' in M. McNeil, I. Varcoe and S. Yearley (eds), *The New Reproductive Technologies*, London: Macmillan Press Ltd, 1990, 154–72; C. Jones, *Why Donor Insemination Requires Developments in Family Law. The Need for New Definitions of Parenthood*, New York: Edwin Mellen Press, 2007, pp 22–26, 241–42.

The interest in knowing one's genetic origins

[S]ociety as a whole is much more conscious of the importance to an individual of being able to see himself in a wide genealogical and genetic context than was the case 20 years ago.[6]

Baroness Warnock's comment, made during the House of Lords' debates on the statutory instrument that ended donor anonymity[7] (prospectively), indicated a clear shift away from the approach favoured by the Warnock Committee in 1984, where it was argued that 'absolute anonymity' for donors should be maintained to ensure continued donation and to protect the recipient family.[8] While her comment acknowledges a societal shift in favour of recognition of the importance to many individuals (not only donor-conceived people) of their wider genealogical history, which is often read in genetic terms, it also begs the question of why the emphasis on this context has come to the fore now? Further, the concept of 'identity' is often utilised in legal debates in this field but it is not always defined, usually because it has not formed the focal point of attention in given commentaries.[9] Does the focus on genetic ties inevitably lead to an essentialisation of identity? Also,

[6] Baroness Warnock, *Hansard* House of Lords, 9 June 2004: col 354.

[7] The Human Fertilisation and Embryology Authority (Disclosure of Donor Information) Regulations, SI .

[8] HMSO, *Report of the Committee of Inquiry into Human Fertilisation and Embryology*, Cmnd 9314, 1984, para 4.22; discussed in Jones, *Why Donor Insemination Requires Developments in Family Law*, pp 223–25; see also Blyth *et al.*, 'The role of birth certificates'.

[9] E.g. Fortin, '*Re F*: the gooseberry bush approach', pp 297–98, discusses the child's right to know, framing her discussion around the 'truth' of parentage and difficulties arising in that case due to the lack of focus on the 'psychological need [of the child] for information about her origins' in light of consideration of the provision of information regarding her 'genetic background'. Consequently, notions of identity *per se* go unexplored. Similarly, in Wallbank, 'The role of rights', pp 259–60, the focus is firmly on 'genetic identity' and the separation of this 'information' from social roles of parenthood, rather than the exploration of different models of identity. Mr Justice Scott Baker in *Rose*, para 33, suggests that information about the claimants' donors 'goes to the very heart of their identity'; which in para 45 he defines more widely: 'Respect for private and family life requires that everyone should be able to establish details of their identity as individual human beings. This includes their origins and the opportunity to understand them. It also embraces their physical and social identity and psychological integrity.' Finally, Besson, 'Enforcing the child's right to know her origins' (LexisNexis transcript), does acknowledge 'identity is a complex concept' without legal definition; citing in support Freeman's definition that '[identity is] what we know and what we feel. It is an organizing framework for holding together our past and our present and it provides some anticipated shape to future life', M. Freeman, 'The new birth right? Identity and the child of the reproductive revolution' (1996) 4 *International Journal of Children's Rights* 273–97, 290. Freeman's definition most closely accords with the discussion in this chapter.

the potential significance of wider genetic links remains under-explored. For these reasons, I begin with a consideration of these issues, with one caveat in mind – there is no scope to produce an exhaustive analysis of all the relevant factors here, if indeed a comprehensive list could be drafted – but further contextualisation of these matters is crucial to the assessment of the recent provisions.

Genetic identity: technology and genealogy

To say that there is a single definitive set of reasons as to why notions of genetic identity have come to the fore in social consciousness and legal discourse at this point in time would be overambitious and perhaps rather naïve, particularly as the reason(s) that specific individuals might seek access to this information are inevitably subjective and largely unreported.[10] Clearly there is a danger of over-generalising here.[11] However, writing in 1988, Katherine O'Donovan suggested three possible strands driving interest in accessing this information: the desire for knowledge of the medical history of one's ancestors, the psychological need for identity (i.e. the bloodline), and material/legal interests in property.[12] Eight years later Michael Freeman argued that the second reason had proved the most influential, certainly in academic literature in this field and, to date, his analysis holds true.[13]

As outlined in the introduction, the increased availability of reliable technology that can usually prove whether or not someone is genetically related to another individual has also had an impact; although quite what legal, social and cultural meaning might or should be ascribed to that data is another matter. Nevertheless, it would be erroneous to suggest that the importance ascribed to the 'truth' of one's parentage or genetic origins is simply a late-twentieth/early twenty-first century development hinging on technological advances in DNA testing. In tandem with the rise of DNA testing[14] is the emergence of vast swathes of genealogical data available electronically. Indeed, after 'shopping and porn', tracing one's family history

---

[10] Obviously there are some reported accounts; take for example, that of Joanna Rose in *Rose*, para 7; also David Gollancz, 'Time to stop lying', *Guardian*, 2 August 2007 and D. Gollancz, 'Memorandum to the Joint Committee on the Human Tissue and Embryos (Draft) Bill', *Human Tissue and Embryos (Draft) Bill Volume II: Evidence*, 2007, Ev 44, 366–68; see further Blyth *et al.*, 'The role of birth certificates'; and Bainham, 'What is the point of birth registration?'.

[11] I am grateful to John Eekelaar for reiterating this point during the Oxford workshop.

[12] K. O'Donovan, 'A right to know one's parentage?' (1988) 2 *International Journal of Law and the Family*, 27–45, pp 29–33.

[13] Freeman, 'The new birth right?', p 277.

[14] Smart, *Personal Life*, cites in excess of 550,000 websites advertising paternity testing, p 126, fn 13.

has been dubbed the 'third most popular activity on the web'.[15] Carol Smart has written of her participation in the 'social movement' of genealogy, noting the 'huge rise in interest in family lineage among ordinary people (as opposed to local or family historians)', which she indicates is due to 'the workings of an active family imaginary in the population at large'.[16] Clearly, interests in genealogical roots are wider than an acute focus on 'genetic identity' alone – what might this mean for the conceptualisation of 'identity'?

'Identity': a reflexive project?

In his analysis of self-identity, history and modernity, Anthony Giddens notes that in medieval Europe 'lineage ... and other attributes relevant to identity were all relatively fixed';[17] whereas in the late modern age he argues that 'self-identity [has] becom[e] a reflexively organised behaviour'.[18] Hence, in Giddens' model:

> Self-identity is not a distinctive trait, or even a collection of traits, possessed by the individual. It is the self as reflexively understood by the person in terms of her or his biography. Identity here still presumes continuity across time and space: but self-identity is such continuity as interpreted reflexively by the agent.[19]

Giddens argues that self-identity is both fragile and robust. Its fragility stems from the biography which the 'individual "supplies" about herself', which is only one "story" among many other potential stories that could be told about her development as a self; wherein identity is found 'in the capacity to keep a particular narrative going. ... A stable sense of self-identity presupposes the other elements of ontological security'.[20] Nonetheless, it is usually sufficiently robust to survive even significant changes in the person's social environment. He is also clear that the 'content' of self-identity is socially and culturally influenced, using the example of differential naming practices as potential indicators of kinship.[21] Giddens' analysis is useful here as it points to the arguable lack of 'fixity' in any given individual's identity, and to its contextual construction.

Two points emerge from this approach. Writing in the 1980s, O'Donovan urged caution over the identification of donors due to the biological/genetic

---

[15] *Guardian*, 27 December 2008, Family section, p 4.
[16] Smart, *Personal Life*, p 36.
[17] A. Giddens, *Modernity and Self-Identity. Self and Society in the Late Modern Age*, Cambridge: Polity Press, 1991, p74.
[18] Ibid, p 5.
[19] Ibid, pp 52–53.
[20] Ibid, pp 54–55.
[21] Ibid, p 55.

essentialism of identity that would likely ensue, to the detriment of the recognition of the importance of social parenting.[22] One might refer to this as the 'geneticisation' of identity.[23] However, Giddens' approach indicates that seeking and/or gaining access to information about one's genetic origins does not necessarily lead to the geneticisation of identity. Rather, in his model this information is part of a wider reflexive project. Therefore, some individuals may reify – or be perceived as reifying this information – whereas for others it may hold less importance, now or over the passage of time,[24] while others may show little or no interest whatsoever. Second, if knowledge of one's genealogical background, including genetic ties, is ascribed importance within society (albeit not by all social actors) then it follows that at least some individuals will wish to have access to that information as part of the reflexive narrative construction of their self-identity. Therefore, to simply reject out of hand the reported need/desire or 'right' of some donor-conceived individuals for access to information about their donors (be it of the non- or identifying variety) is erroneous. To do so would in effect bar these individuals from legitimately seeking access to information we assume others can readily obtain, and would arguably stifle the reflexive construction of their identities, potentially threatening their ontological security. Therefore, to be clear, the provision of this information alone does not serve to reify genetic notions of identity; as O'Donovan remarked, identity and the search for one's origins are socially constructed.[25]

These observations highlight one of the problems with Giddens' theorisation of identity. As Carol Smart has persuasively argued, by emphasising 'choice' in the construction of self-identity (for example, in this context 'choosing' to seek further information about one's donor(s), it is easy to overlook relationships of power, be they based on gender, class, race or generational difference, which may limit the so-called options available to a specific individual.[26] In the context of donor-conception these power

---

[22] K. O'Donovan, 'What shall we tell the children? Reflections on children's perspectives and the sexual revolution', in D. Morgan and R. Lee (eds), *Birthrights: Law and Ethics at the Beginnings of Life*, London: Routledge, 1990, pp 96–114.

[23] Although see Sally Sheldon's analysis of the decision in *Leeds Teaching Hospital NHS Trust* v *A and others* [2003] EWHC 259 for an alternative reading of the emphasis on the 'truth' of paternal origins, S. Sheldon, 'Fragmenting fatherhood: the regulation of reproductive technologies', *Modern Law Review* 68, 2005, 523–553.

[24] There is undoubtedly a need for further research into temporal issues in this context, as discussed during the Genetics and Identity Politics of Parenthood and Family: We are family? workshop, 19–20 February, Genomics Forum, Innogen, University of Edinburgh.

[25] O'Donovan, 'What shall we tell the children?', p 111, although she was also clear that this does not render the search any less real.

[26] Smart, *Personal Life*, pp 106–7.

relations include generational control, if a child is not informed of the mode of its conception (as no such duty exists in Anglo-Welsh law), and state-sanctioned limits on possible access to non- or identifying information.

Smart theorises that 'embeddedness' – the sense that family relationships exist across time and after death – 'can either offer ontological security or be experienced as psychologically and emotionally suffocating'.[27] Consequently, embeddedness is not imbued with good or bad qualities, but acts to:

> reflect the tenacity of these bonds and links, sometimes even to the extent that family members and close kin or friends can feel as if they were part of one. ... Blood relationships in particular seem to be unique in possessing these haunting powers.[28]

Nonetheless, Smart's observations should not be mistaken for pointing to a fixed notion of self-identity. Rather, she highlights the contradictions in this field of study accordingly:

> It has become conventional wisdom that familial roots which can locate a person emotionally, genetically and culturally are essential for ontological security and a sense of self. Yet, at the same time, in a kind of parallel universe, it is argued that in post-modern conditions we make our own selves and biographies ... [29]

Smart's intention is not to determine which approach is correct, but to consider how families (and others) thread together these connections in making sense of their personal lives. Indeed, reflecting on findings from previous empirical studies, she cogently argues against this dichotomous division:

> In the 'essential roots' narrative there is a presumption that there is something real located in the past, from which flows authenticity and real meaning. Here the past is reified and its role in providing ontological security is seen as automatic. In the 'choice' narrative the individual is seen to navigate his or her own meanings from a buffet of equally useful values, motifs and practices. In this version the past becomes a commodity rather than being a part of the self. ... neither of these versions captures the complexity and layers of the process of biography building.[30]

---

[27] Ibid, p 45.
[28] Ibid. Smart notes genetic ties are a 'slightly more abstract notion', p 46.
[29] Ibid, p 81.
[30] Ibid. p 106–7. On the contradictory elements in this field, particularly in relation to paternity, see T. Freeman and M. Richards, 'DNA testing and kinship: paternity, genealogy and the search for the "truth" of genetic origins', in E. Fatemeh, B. Lindley and M. Richards (eds), *Kinship Matters*, Oxford: Hart Publishing, 2006, pp 67–95.

As outlined above, Smart argues that to capture the 'nuance, difference and complexity' of the process of developing one's self-identity we must also consider how factors including gender and other power relations affect the stories that can be and are told.

What might this analysis mean for donor-conceived individuals?

Four points can be made at this juncture.

> While it was once entirely normative to treat paternity as a matter of pragmatics rather than biological truth, it is now almost impossible to keep secrets about biological paternity; those who seek to do so are increasingly identified as being outside appropriate moral boundaries.[31]

First, in Anglo-Welsh legal discourse the focus on genealogical information or genetic origins has traditionally and still tends to fall on paternity[32] rather than maternity, despite the rising number of IVF cycles and associated potential disruption of assumed maternal-genetic bonds through the use of donor eggs or embryos (albeit by 2005 only accounting for approximately 1 per cent of all births in the UK[33]). Interestingly, the Warnock Committee approached egg and sperm donors alike in as much as anonymity and the exclusion of legal rights and obligations was recommended for both groups; further, it suggested that it should be possible for the words 'by donation' to be added after the father's or the mother's name respectively where donor gametes were used.[34] However, upon analysis, subtle but important differences emerge. While the Committee recommended that the birth mother 'should, *for all purposes*, be regarded in law as the mother of that child' (emphasis added), the discussion of fathers went further. Legislative change to enable them 'to be registered as the father' was recommended, with the recognition that 'this can be criticised as legislating for a fiction … [as] the register of births has always been envisaged as a true genetic record'.[35] A robust defence of this approach in relation to fathers was considered

---

[31] Ibid. p 122.
[32] See, e.g. Freeman and Richards, 'DNA testing and kinship', although they acknowledge the capacity and use of this technology to trace 'female bloodlines', p 68. Diduck and Herring also make this point: A. Diduck, '"If only we can find the appropriate terms to use the issue will be solved': law, identity and parenthood", (2007) 19 *Child and Family Law Quarterly* 458–80; J. Herring, *Family Law*, Pearson Longman, 3rd edn, 2007.
[33] Freeman and Richards, 'DNA testing and kinship', p 81.
[34] HMSO, *Report of the Committee of Inquiry*, para 4.25, 6.8. The wording of this recommendation indicated this should be a matter of parental choice, and it was not taken up in the 1990 Act.
[35] Ibid.

necessary and appropriate, yet the report was silent on the significance of the genetic 'truth' of mothers.

More recently the gender-neutral language adopted in relation to declarations of parentage[36] masks the fact that as yet no reported cases have concerned the disputed maternity of a specific child, whereas there have been a significant number of paternity cases.[37] Child support legislation and the emergence of accurate DNA testing have undoubtedly proved influential in this sphere.[38] In addition, the Human Fertilisation and Embryology (Deceased Fathers) Act 2003, amending s. 28 1990 Act, provided for the symbolic recognition of deceased fathers on their child/ren's birth certificate/s. Clearly this naming carried no legal consequences, but it cannot be readily explained on the basis of the privileging of progenitor–child relationships alone, as it also permitted men whose wives or partners conceived with embryos created with donor sperm before their death, but implanted afterwards, to be registered as the resulting child's father. Therefore, it was not the genetic link per se which was ascribed significance (at least, not in all instances), but the 'presence' of a father's name on the birth certificate and a recognition of his intention to parent. Interestingly, due to the provisions of s 27 1990 Act whereby only the birth mother can be registered as the child's legal mother, no such accommodation for the posthumous recognition of genetic or intending mothers (where donated eggs were used) was made; there was no gap to be filled, but more problematically for this analysis, nor was there the potential for recognition of her intention to parent either. When the 2008 Act is enacted this situation will be ameliorated as s 46 extends the current provisions pertaining to male partners to 'intended female parents'. Nonetheless, while either or both maternal and paternal genetic origins may be significant to donor-conceived individuals (depending on which gametes were donated), it is the paternal line that has been consistently privileged.

Second, the development of systems facilitating access to non- and identifying information about gamete donors will not necessarily transform power relations that exist along gendered or generational lines.[39] John Eekelaar, in his nuanced analysis of truth and identity, argues in favour of the child's best interests justifying the determination of the genetic truth of their identity, indicating that where a man seeks the truth it is 'hardly equivalent to the interest of a child to know who its father is, for the interest does not affect the man's identity as it does the child's'.[40] He later adds that

[36] s 55A Family Law Act 1986, as amended.
[37] A LexisNexis search on July 11 2008, and repeated in February 2009, yielded 52 cases regarding a possible declaration of paternity under the Family Law Act 1986.
[38] Herring, *Family Law*, p 358.
[39] Smart, *Personal Life*, p 131.
[40] Eekelaar, *Family Law and Personal Life*, pp 64–65.

it cannot 'be plausibly claimed that a parent needs to know his or her child in order to form a fuller picture of his or her own identity'.[41] At least part of his reasoning stems from concern over the disparity of inter-generational power relations, whereby:

> Adults can create legal truths which are at odds with physical truth … Access to 'physical truth' then, is an important way in which the new generation can challenge these adult powers … this knowledge or its prospective availability, allows the individual to confront the world as it is on his own terms, and influence solutions according to his perception of his interests given the physical truth.[42]

He concludes that children's interests here 'are always stronger than those of the adults, because in children they give rise to claims in justice, whereas for adults they form the basis for attempts at exercising power, sometimes beyond the grave'.[43] 'Physical truth', as Eekelaar describes it, has a particular salience. Therefore the issue is not so much the existence of 'family secrets', of which there may be many,[44] but the perception of which truths matter.[45] As DNA testing can now usually prove paternity or maternity (although as outlined above, the focus is usually on paternity) the drive for truth may appear more forcefully in discourse around kinship and family.

These are interesting observations, particularly as this analysis could extend beyond the social parent(s) as the only adult(s) withholding information (i.e. situations where the parents have informed the child but further data about the donor is not available, see *Rose*), and point towards the possibilities for resistance by donor-conceived individuals. However, two cautionary notes must be made. Although I agree that the interests of the children are stronger, I would suggest that putative parents might well derive important facets of their biography building/self-identity from the knowledge that they do/not have a genetic link with a particular individual (irrespective of whether we would discursively label that as a parent–child or progenitor/offspring relationship in light of the preceding discussion), therefore these concerns ought not be as readily dismissed as Eekelaar suggests.[46] Also,

---

[41] Ibid. p 66.

[42] Ibid. p 74.

[43] Ibid. p 76.

[44] Smart, *Personal Life*, Ch 5.

[45] I am grateful to Jonathan Herring for this point.

[46] See, e.g. the interview with a sperm donor by B. Morrison, 'First person', the *Guardian*, 11 March 2006, Family section, p 3; and for an academic analysis, see J. M. Speirs, 'Secretly connected? Anonymous semen donation, genetics and meanings of kinship', unpublished PhD thesis, University of Edinburgh, 2007, especially p 114, pp 223–224. There is, of course, the wider family context to consider, of both donors and donor-conceived individuals, but detailed consideration falls outside the focus of this chapter.

inter-generational power relations are not the only ones present here – we must also pay attention to gender, race, class and even religious interests.[47] As Smart makes clear:

> The drive to truth[48] ... presumes that openness will create equality of knowledge among people who then became equally positioned in relation to each other. However, the parties themselves may not be on an equal footing, so this kind of openness may bring with it forms of vulnerability as well as different forms of regulation of personal life ... I am suggesting changing the rules ... does not transform relations of power between classes, genders and generations. These new truths are simply played out on the existing social landscapes.[49]

This is not a reason to reject the push for truth. On the contrary, it is a call to consider the recent legislative changes within a broader context, to pay attention to the specificities of power relations at different junctures, rather than to assume that small changes will easily dismantle more entrenched power relations.

Third, as detailed further below, the 2008 Act makes provision for donor-conceived individuals conceived under the regulatory framework of the 1990 Act to seek access to information about their donor(s) and (some of) their genetic half-siblings. This approach not only seems to parallel current practice by some donor-conceived individuals,[50] but also recognises the wider remit of genealogical roots beyond those 'merely' of the progenitor(s). However, as Smart has highlighted, sociological and anthropological research into sibling relationships has been the exception rather than the

---

[47] See, e.g. the Progress Educational Trust conference on 'Is the embryo sacrosanct? Multi-Faith Perspectives', London, 19 November 2008.

[48] Smart cites Fortin, '*Re F*: the gooseberry bush approach', as indicative of this drive.

[49] Smart, *Personal Life*, p 131.

[50] Freeman and Richards, 'DNA testing and kinship', p 83, note the informal use of DNA testing by donor-conceived people to ascertain whether or not they are genetically related in circumstances where identifying information is not accessible or forthcoming. See UK DonorLink, the pilot voluntary contact register set up in 2003, funded by the Department of Health (www.ukdonorlink.org.uk/). In the USA, the Donor Sibling Registry has, since 2000, facilitated thousands of donor-conceived half-siblings and/or donors with each other (www.donorsiblingregistry. com/). I am grateful to Carol Sanger for highlighting the significance of the registry during the Oxford workshop. See further, T. Freeman, V. Jadva, W. Kramer and S. Golombok, 'Gamete donation: parents' experiences of searching for their child's donor siblings and donor', *Human Reproduction* 24, 2009, pp 505–16. For media coverage of UK and US stories, respectively, see S. K. Templeton, 'Hi, our boys share a sperm-donor father', *Sunday Times*, 5 October 2008; T. Allen-Mills, 'Hi there, I'm your sperm donor sis', *Sunday Times*, 5 March 2006.

norm.[51] Perhaps this legislative shift indicates a need to address these kinship relations more centrally in academic research?

Fourth, and finally, there remains the question of whether or not there is a right not to know information about one's genetic or genealogical roots – whether in general, or specifically in relation to gene-linked disorders?[52] I return to this below when considering the central role of consent in delineating whose information can be sought. My focus therefore is not so much on what the system ought to do, but on what it has done in the 2008 Act, and how some themes intersect along gendered and other lines.

The 2008 Act

Following a lengthy process of consultation, drafting, pre-legislative scrutiny and debate,[53] the 2008 Act, amending the 1990 Act of the same name (albeit retaining substantial elements of the original regulatory framework), was granted Royal Assent on 13 November 2008. At the time of writing it is anticipated that the statute will be enacted in three stages starting with the new parenthood provisions in April 2009, followed by amendments to the 1990 Act in October 2009, with the revised parental orders set to take effect from April 2010.[54]

As alluded to briefly above, there are significant changes afoot in relation to the recognition of an intention to parent – put simply, more people will be 'identifiable' in law as parents. Perhaps most controversially for some parties, but in my view a welcome step, there is finally a mechanism for the recognition of women intending to parent together with their female partners, without having recourse to adoption; further, this extends to posthumous recognition.[55] Where donor sperm is used, s 42 places women in civil partnerships on a par with married women insofar as their female partners will be recognised as the legal parent of the child unless their partners prove that they did not consent to the procedure.[56] Further, where the woman undertaking 'treatment' is partnered but not married or in a civil partnership, the

---

[51] Smart, *Personal Life*, pp 46–47.
[52] See further G. Laurie, *Genetic Privacy. A Challenge to Medico-Legal Norms*, Cambridge: Cambridge University Press, 2002; R. Gilbar, *The Status of the Family in Law and Bioethics. The Genetic Context*, Aldershot: Ashgate, 2005.
[53] C. Jones, 'Exploring the routes from consultation to (in)forming public policy' in M. Freeman (ed) *Current Legal Issues in Law and Bioethics*, Oxford: Oxford University Press, 2007, pp 257–285.
[54] Information derived from the Human Fertilisation and Embryology Authority website, www.hfea.gov.uk/en/1752.html (accessed February 2009).
[55] Sections 42–47 2008 Act.
[56] Section 35 addresses the meaning of 'father' when the mother was married at the time of implantation.

'agreed fatherhood' and 'agreed female parenthood' conditions are identical (save, of course, for the gendered terminology), rendering consent pivotal in the construction of legal parenthood.[57]

Clearly there are important distinctions in the terminology here – the female partner will become a legal 'parent' not a 'mother' – and as a number of commentators have previously noted, granting formal equality in legislative provisions does not necessarily accord with equal status in practice.[58] One further comment on the parenthood provisions remains: a woman in a lesbian relationship cannot become a legal mother or parent solely by virtue of the provision of her eggs for use by her female partner.[59] Doing so renders her a 'mere' donor, and without the requisite status via a civil partnership with the child's mother, or satisfaction of the 'agreed female parenthood' conditions or adoption she will be – in law at least – a stranger to the resulting child. It is clear that Anglo-Welsh legal discourse still cannot countenance the possibility of two mothers,[60] irrespective of the biological and technological possibilities that the separation of conception and gestation might otherwise allow. Therefore, whilst on the face of it the 2008 Act provides formal equality between women and men, by simply mapping female parenthood conditions onto the social father formula it fails to address the biological differences between the sexes in reproduction[61] – in lay terms, three into two won't go.

Information disclosure: wider access to genetic origins?

Whilst the new parenthood provisions clearly widen the scope for recognition, the 2008 Act also has significant ramifications for the 'identification' of donors and siblings. Section 24 of the 2008 Act replaces s 31 1990 Act with new ss 31 to 31ZG. In summary, once enacted, the changes to the register of information will be as follows: first, a reduction in the age at which a donor-conceived individual can seek information about their donor, from 18 to 16, albeit identifying information will not be provided until they

[57] See ss 37 and 44 2008 Act respectively.
[58] A. Diduck, "If only we can find the appropriate terms to use the issue will be solved"; C. Jones, 'Parents in law: subjective impacts and status implications around the use of licensed donor insemination', in A. Diduck and K. O'Donovan (eds), *Feminist Perspectives on Family Law*, Oxford: Routledge Cavendish, 2006, 75–99; L. Smith, 'Is three a crowd? Lesbian mothers' perspectives on parental status in law' (2006) 18 *Child and Family Law Quarterly* 231.
[59] Section 47 2008 Act.
[60] Unlike the fragmentation of fatherhood, see further Sheldon, 'Fragmenting Fatherhood'. On the issue of multiple mothers in surrogacy, see further J. Wallbank, 'Too many mothers? Surrogacy, kinship and the welfare of the child' (2002) 10 *Medical Law Review* 271–98.
[61] See also Diduck, 'If only we can find the appropriate terms to use the issue will be solved'.

are 18.[62] Second, at 16 a donor-conceived person will be able to seek information about the number, sex and year of birth of their 'donor-conceived half siblings', conceived using gametes of the same donor – but not information regarding the 'donor's *legal* children' (emphasis added).[63] Third, however, the HFEA has some discretion *not* to release this information in 'special circumstances' where disclosure would be likely to lead to the identification of the donor (where this information is not accessible by the donor-conceived person) or any of the 'donor-conceived half siblings'.[64] Fourth, regarding consanguinity, at 16 a donor-conceived person can seek information as to whether or not they are genetically related to someone they intend to marry, enter a civil partnership or intimate physical relationship with (or indeed are already having), providing that person consents to the request.[65] Fifth, at 18, donor-conceived individuals can seek *identifying* information about their 'donor-conceived genetic siblings' (provided neither is the donor's legal child), although all 'siblings' must consent to the disclosure. There is a further caveat that disclosure must not lead to the donor's identity being released, unless they have also consented or provided gametes at a time when the regulations require this information be provided.[66]

However, the changes do not only concern donor-conceived individuals. The sixth point sees the introduction of *some* reciprocity following the prospective removal of donor anonymity in April 2005; that is, the HFEA has the *power* – but not a *duty* – to inform donors that identifying information has been sought by an applicant, but they cannot disclose the identity of that person.[67] Seventh, all donors who have provided gametes under the auspices of the 1990 Act can seek information about the number, sex and year of birth of children born as a result of their donations; again the HFEA can, in 'special circumstances' refuse to provide this information if it would lead to the identification of any of these children.[68]

---

[62] Section 31ZA 2008 Act. Identifying information will only be given in circumstances where gametes were donated at a time when it was a requirement to provide this data to any resulting children, or where the donor has subsequently voluntarily relinquished their anonymity.

[63] Section 31ZA(2)(b) 2008 Act. Note the language cited here is from the explanatory notes, whereas the statute provides the rather more opaque phraseology 'other persons of whom the donor is not the parent but would or might, but for the relevant statutory provisions, be the parent'. The statute does later refer to 'donor-conceived genetic siblings' (s. 31ZE).

[64] Section 31ZA(6) 2008 Act.

[65] Section 31ZB 2008 Act.

[66] Section 31ZE 2008 Act.

[67] Paragraph 152 of the explanatory notes for the 2008 Act suggests that: 'In practice, the HFEA would try to forewarn the donor before identifying information is given to the donor-conceived applicant. This might not be possible in all cases, for example if the donor has moved and has not updated their address.'

[68] Section 31ZD 2008 Act.

Discussion: what is significant about these changes?

At first glance the statute indicates the facilitation of a *wider* disclosure of information (both non- and identifying) than provided under the 1990 Act as amended, thereby seemingly entrenching the linkage between donor-conceived individuals' welfare and the 'right' to or interest in knowledge of their genetic origins.[69] However, detailed examination of these provisions clearly illustrates that although the 2008 Act may be couched in the language of widening access, in practice this may prove to fall short of the mark.

As donor-conceived individuals cannot seek access to any information about their gamete donors until they are 16, the 2008 Act seems to retain most of the protection accorded to 'families-by-donation' originally provided by donor anonymity.[70] That is, the spectre of the donor infringing the family life of the recipients is, at least symbolically limited, as even where the individual knows[71] he or she is donor-conceived they cannot seek further information until they reach the statutory minimum age. Further, they cannot seek identifying information (where available or applicable) until they reach the age of majority. Therefore, any possibility of a donor-conceived individual seeking to meet with their donor is precluded during childhood, thereby ensuring the (donor recipient) family remains protected from intrusion at that time.[72]

The recognition of the potential interests of donor-conceived individuals in their wider genealogical origins is evidenced by the fact that it will be possible to seek information about genetic (half-)siblings, although restrictions will be imposed. Hence, once again individuals will only be able to seek identifying information about these 'siblings', conceived through the use of the same donor's gametes, once they reach the age of majority. However, the statute makes clear that identifying information will not extend to the donor's legal children. This is an interesting inversion of the traditional concern to protect the recipient family from the spectre of the donor – here, it is the donor's 'legal' family, and in particular his or her children, that are protected from (perceived) unwarranted intrusion by those who happen to be their genetic (half-)siblings but legal strangers. This is likely to reflect a concern to protect donors (notably their 'privacy'), and to ensure continued

---

[69] Jones, *Why Donor Insemination Requires Developments in Family Law*, pp 221–42; Wallbank, 'The role of rights and utility'.

[70] Haimes, 'Recreating the family?'.

[71] As outlined above, there is no right to be informed that they were conceived with donor gametes, see Bainham, 'What is the point of birth registration?'.

[72] Although an interesting question is raised regarding families where the same donor was used to conceive two or more siblings, where the eldest child might seek access to this information and/or to contact the donor (where applicable) while his or her siblings have not yet reached majority. The explanatory notes are silent on this issue. This example suggests that the 'protection' afforded to the recipient family is more vulnerable to challenge than perhaps initially thought under the auspices of the legislation.

donation (as the spectre of the potential effect of adverse reporting can readily be appreciated, even if one does not agree with the scaremongering). Certainly, in the relevant Department of Health documentation, the purported respective rights of donors, their families, and donor-conceived individuals and their families are juxtaposed, therefore this section might ameliorate some of those concerns.[73]

The gender-neutral language used in the 2008 Act masks the gendered debate behind these and associated provisions. For example, early in the review process of the legislation in this field[74] the Science and Technology Committee produced a report on the issues it suggested required attention. Despite the fact it was clear the Committee had intended to reflect on the anonymity of *all* gamete and embryo donors (the section was entitled 'donation of gametes and embryos'), nevertheless there was slippage into discussion of donor *insemination* alone without explanation.[75] Indeed, in the same section, it recommended that 'if children born following *donor insemination* have a right to know their genetic parents' that donors ought also to have access to non-identifying information about the children so conceived.[76] Given the context of this statement, one might question whether the Committee's recommendation regarding 'donors' was actually focused on the purported 'rights' of male progenitors alone? When one considers their coverage of the reported depletion of 'sperm stocks' in other jurisdictions that had removed donor anonymity[77] – and their silence on egg or embryo stocks/donation – the impetus behind the Committee's proposals seems highly gendered indeed.

Furthermore, this slippage is also evident in the explanatory notes for the Human Tissue and Embryos (Draft) Bill 2007. In the explanation of the (then proposed) power to inform donors when identifying information has been sought by a donor-conceived individual it refers to donors throughout as 'him', noting difficulties 'if the donor has moved and not updated his address' (although in relation to a different aspect of the same clause it later correctly uses 'his or her').[78] Is the notification of male donors a means by

---

[73] Department of Health, *Summary of Responses to the Donor Information Consultation – Providing Information About Sperm, Egg and Embryo Donors*, 2003, available from: http://www.dh.gov.uk/en/Consultations/Responsestoconsultations/DH_4071838; discussed in Jones, *Why Donor Insemination Requires Developments in Family Law*, pp 228–31.

[74] See further Jones, 'Exploring the routes from consultation to (in)forming public policy'.

[75] House of Commons Science and Technology Committee, *Human Reproductive Technologies and the Law*, Fifth Report of Session 2004–5, March 2005, HC 7–1, paras 146, 151.

[76] Ibid, para 151.

[77] Ibid, paras 152–55.

[78] Department of Health, *Human Tissue and Embryos (Draft) Bill Explanatory Notes*, 2007, Cm 7087, para 138. These issues have been resolved in the explanatory notes for the 2008 Act, which adopts 'his or her' where appropriate.

which to protect their legal families in a way which is not debated in relation to egg donors? (Certainly in the parliamentary debates examples abound on paternity issues,[79] despite the earlier removal of anonymity for egg *and* sperm (and embryo) donors).[80]

Interestingly, in the 2004 debates on the removal of donor anonymity, the ways in which egg and sperm donors were discussed differed considerably. Donors in general were spoken of in terms of the 'fear' that if donor anonymity was removed 'donors will be deterred by what has been rather dramatically described as the threat of a knock on the door in 18 years' time',[81] albeit in the context of the preceding discussion one might assume the comments here were primarily aimed at sperm donors. Egg donors were considered especially vulnerable:

> Where egg sharing is concerned, the number of women willing to donate eggs on an identifiable basis may be affected even more by the risks involved. They expose themselves to the suggestion that they are undergoing treatment for infertility, and the procedure may not be successful. They could be unsuccessful in conceiving and discover later that the child had been born to another couple using eggs that they had donated. They may not want to be in that position and they want to avoid the risk of that happening.[82]
>
> [M]any such women fail themselves to conceive with IVF and they then face the unhappy prospect of meeting a child 18 years later who is genetically half theirs but who they had never known existed. Again, that is a further stress on a childless couple who are likely already to feel deprived. Of course it is possible that some may be pleased with the news, but I fear that more will be most distressed.[83]

I have yet to find references to concerns expressed that male donors might feel 'deprived' as they remain childless at the point of the mythical knock on the door eighteen years on. Furthermore, as the figures provided by Melanie Johnson at the time of these debates indicated that 830 women were donating eggs altruistically and 317 via egg sharing schemes, the concern was not

---

[79] This is a separate issue from that of the removal of the reference to the child's purported 'need for a father' as an aspect of the welfare of the child provisions, which sparked extensive debate.

[80] By way of illustration see, e.g. Lord Jenkin of Roding, *Hansard HL*, November 19 2007, col 684–85; Lord Ahmed, November 21 2007, col 844; Lord Northbourne, November 21 2007, col 849; Lord Darzi of Denham, December 10 2007, col 52; Earl Howe, December 10 2007, col 91–92.

[81] Baroness Andrews, *Hansard HL*, June 9 2004, Vol 666, col 348.

[82] Mr Lansley, Standing Committee on Delegated Legislation, 28 May 2004, col 8.

[83] Lord Turnberg, *Hansard HL*, June 9 2004, Vol 666, col 361; see also Earl Howe col 351.

entirely borne out in the evidence of current practice at the time.[84] That is not to undermine concerns about the potential for pressure (indirect or otherwise) to be exerted on women to participate in egg sharing schemes, which is a significant issue but one that falls outside the focus of this chapter. Rather this chapter highlights the ways in which egg donors are portrayed as requiring protection because of the perceived likelihood that their treatment will fail and they will be faced with the evidence of another woman's success if/when the resulting child seeks them out in adulthood. Clearly, women are not portrayed as wishing to know about the numbers of children conceived through the use of their gametes, in ways that are believed to be entirely appropriate with regard to male donors to the extent that some reciprocity of information is now justifiable (albeit on a non-identifying basis, and indeed in relation to *all* donors). As I indicated in the previous section access to such information may indeed be of relevance to some donors in the narrative construction of their self-identity.

Further, this provision points to the mixed messages contained in the 2008 Act, whereby *some* genetic (half-)sibling ties are accorded significance and information/contact is arguably promoted through the register, yet others who – genetically speaking – are equally 'related', fall outside the facilitative processes of the statute. In legal discourse these particular genetic ties are privileged and rendered unknowable, unless the donor him- or herself *chooses* to make them known.[85] Therefore, as Smart suggested in her analysis, the push for 'truth' will not necessarily ensure that all parties fall on an equal footing. It is the *donors* who hold some control over information in this example, again illustrating the potential for the intergenerational exercise of power *per* Eekelaar's analysis; although given the rise of social networking sites and other genealogical tools it is clear that in future it will not necessarily prove easy to prevent disclosure of this kind of data.[86] These technologies may, in fact, provide avenues for resistance by donor-conceived individuals/siblings.

Three other observations are worthy of note. One, as there is no duty in Anglo-Welsh law to inform donor-conceived individuals of the mode of their conception, unless they are told by their legal parents (or others), or have an inkling or curiosity that they wish to satisfy via recourse to the HFEA, they

---

[84] Standing Committee on Delegated Legislation, 28 May 2004, col 8. There is now a suggestion that more women might enter into egg sharing schemes where the surplus eggs are donated for research, which clearly does call into question issues around financial pressures/incentives. I am grateful to Martin Richards for this information.

[85] This assumes contact is made between the donor-conceived individual(s) and the donor, and that the donor has, in fact, 'legal' children of his or her own (it also assumes these were conceived by the use of the donor's own gametes and were not adopted or indeed donor-conceived).

[86] See DonorLink and the US-based Donor Sibling Registry, noted above.

will not be able to avail themselves of the wider information potentially accessible under the statutory provisions.[87] The 2008 Act does nothing to ameliorate this situation, therefore Smart and Eekelaar's comments regarding the intergenerational exercise of power remain salient under the new scheme.

Second, disclosure of identifying information about one's genetic (half-) siblings is centred around mutual consent. Consequently, if the other parties are unaware of the circumstances of their conception, or do not place significance on knowledge of their wider genetic origins, then a donor-conceived person's search for information and/or contact could be frustrated at a very early stage. Their interest or 'right', if it can be typified as such, to wider genealogical information is therefore arguably rather tentative to say the least, and indeed in some cases it may amount to nothing irrespective of the strength of their wishes. Merely facilitating the possibility of information-sharing does not ensure that this will in fact occur. This may be taken by some to indicate a 'right' not to know one's genetic origins (assuming one has been informed of the mode of conception), as without seeking further information no identifying data about one's donor or genetic (half-)siblings will be forthcoming. However, this is a rather precarious situation. As the recent examples of mothers who have sought out the genetic (half-) siblings of their donor-conceived children show,[88] this facet of the statute may indeed be vulnerable to resistance by some parties who will seek information via alternative means. It is not clear, therefore, that it can be correctly described as a 'right' of the donor-conceived child – rather, it is another example of the potential for intergenerational power to be exercised.[89]

Third, the provision of information, identifying or otherwise, is subject to the discretion of the HFEA in 'special circumstances' where there is evidence that it will lead to the identification of others who ought not to be identified. There is potential protection of the anonymity of both donors and donor-conceived persons here, whether in vertical applications (i.e. when one seeks information about the other where identifying information is not applicable; this will cover *all* cases where donors seek information about children conceived through the use of their gametes), or in horizontal ones (between donor-conceived genetic (half-)siblings), due to the age of the applicant or a lack of mutual consent. Depending on the specific situation in question one

---

[87] See also Bainham, 'What is the point of birth registration?'.

[88] Freeman and Richards, 'DNA testing and kinship'; T. Freeman, V. Jadva, W. Kramer and S. Golombok, 'Gamete donation'; Templeton, 'Hi, our boys share a sperm-donor father'; Allen-Mills, 'Hi there, I'm your sperm donor sis'.

[89] Clearly this intergenerational exercise of power might also work in the opposite direction, where a donor-conceived child might utilise technology to undo the legal protection afforded by 'anonymity'. See, e.g. the report of a 15-year-old boy who traced his sperm donor via an Internet database, A. Karpf, 'On one boy's search for his father', the *Guardian*, Family Section, 12 November 2005.

can readily see whose interests are being promoted and protected, but until it is enacted it is difficult to envisage how this provision will be interpreted and applied by the HFEA – will it prove to be an oppressive measure or a linguistic nicety paying lip-service to the protection of the anonymity of the parties concerned? Either way, its inclusion in the 2008 Act highlights the state's continued interest in controlling the information flow about and between these parties.

Conclusion

This chapter has examined the interests in knowing one's genetic origins in the context of assisted conception, in light of the provisions of the 2008 Act. Despite the apparent widening of access to both non- and identifying information about one's gamete donor(s) and genetic (half-)siblings, and the far-reaching changes in relation to legal parenthood, it has been argued that the new framework does not place all parties on a level playing field. It has been shown that the state continues to regulate the release of information. It is also clear that a number of provisions are grounded in gendered matrixes; whereby the mapping of legal mothers and female parents onto the social father model illustrates a failure to take into account the biological differences between the sexes in reproduction; the protection of donors appears to focus on concerns over the privacy of male donors and their families (and the need for continued donation); and the drive for some reciprocity of information focuses on the 'fear' of male donors of the mythical 'knock on the door' and the perceived need for some knowledge of the outcome of their donations, in contrast to the protection of 'vulnerable' egg donors who are not portrayed as wishing to access this information in the same way. Furthermore, whilst genetic (half-)sibling ties between donor-conceived individuals are promoted, those with the donor's 'legal' children (if any) are – as far as possible – rendered unknowable, and the family is thereby protected from interference.[90] The 2008 Act therefore sends out mixed messages about the importance of access to and knowledge of one's wider genetic origins. It remains to be seen whether the discretion granted to the HFEA will be utilised in ways that deny, protect or promote further knowledge of specific donor-conceived individual's wider genetic heritage.

---

[90] Although, as noted above, this is subject to resistance through the use of web sources and DNA testing.

Chapter 11

Children with exceptional needs: Welfare, rights and caring responsibilities

Jo Bridgeman

All children are inevitably dependent upon others – physically, emotionally and financially. Children need to be cared for. Critically ill children and children with severe disabilities or complex needs have magnified needs according to their physical or mental health or impairments: 'The much more extreme dependence of those with disabilities goes on forever, cannot be commodified to anything like the extent to that of normal children, and is much more extreme in any case.'[1] Parents are entrusted with the primary responsibility for the care of children but depend upon others, professionals, family members, volunteers, or other parents of children with similar needs, to support them in fulfilment of their caring responsibilities, creating a web of dependencies, reliance and trust. In this chapter I explore gendered caring responsibilities through consideration of the welfare, rights and care of children with exceptional needs; that is, children who are dependent upon the care provided by others due to critical illness, complex needs or severe disabilities. I first consider the impact of the welfare principle upon decisions about the care of children with exceptional needs, then the rights of children with exceptional needs and those who care for them before exploring the intensive, and gendered, nature of caring responsibilities for children with exceptional needs. My aim is to develop understanding of the complex nature of caring responsibility in human life in which children depend upon their carers, carers depend upon others to support them in fulfilment of their caring responsibilities and the state depends upon others to fulfil responsibilities to those in need of care.

Welfare and the care of children with exceptional needs

The welfare of children with exceptional needs is considered most frequently in the legal literature in the context of questions about the provision of future life-sustaining medical treatment. The courts have been asked to

---

[1] Roger Goettlieb, 'The tasks of embodied love: moral problems in caring for children with disabilities' (2002) 17 *Hypatia*, 225–36, p 227.

determine whether invasive treatment for critical illness should be provided,[2] life-sustaining treatment withheld[3] or withdrawn[4] from babies and very young children with severe disabilities, and whether a separation operation should be performed upon conjoined twins.[5]

Treatment decisions are made by the child's parents (more accurately, the person(s) with parental responsibility) with the support and advice of the treating healthcare professionals. It is no surprise that, in these extremely difficult cases, parents and professionals may have different opinions about the course of action which is in the best interests of the child. Conscientiously and carefully made, different conclusions may be reached about best interests depending upon the factors selected as well as the weight given to them which may differ depending upon values, beliefs, perspective or experiences. Doctors have medical training, a professional role and responsibility, they focus upon the medical diagnosis and prognosis and draw upon their experiences of treating children. Parents will be focused upon the needs of their child to whom they are emotionally attached and with whom they share a past and hopes for the future.

In the event that the treating doctors disagree with the child's parents, the decision can be referred to the court. Where decisions about medical treatment are made by the court under the Children Act 1989 (for example, a s 8 specific issue order), s 1 applies to require that 'the child's welfare shall be the court's paramount consideration'. In practice, whilst courts do refer to the welfare checklist they tend not to apply it systematically preferring a more holistic approach and one which treats the welfare principle and best interests test as synonymous.[6] Whether the responsibility of the child's parents or the court, treatment decisions must be made in the best interests of the child, broadly conceived.[7] The interests relevant to determination are widely construed, reaching beyond the medical to include whether the

---

[2] *Re T (a minor) (wardship: medical treatment)* [1997] 1 WLR 242; *An NHS Trust v A and others* [2007] EWHC 1696 (Fam).

[3] *Re J (a minor) (wardship: medical treatment)* [1990] 3 ALL ER 930; *Re J (A Minor) (Child in Care: Medical Treatment)* [1992] 3 WLR 507; *Royal Wolverhampton Hospital NHS Trust v B*, 7 September 1999; *A National Health Service Trust v D* [2000] 2 FLR 677; *Re C (a minor) (wardship: medical treatment)* [1989] 2 All ER 782; *Re L (Medical Treatment: Benefit)* [2004] EWHC 2713; *Portsmouth NHS Trust v Wyatt & Others* [2004] EWHC 2247;*Wyatt & Another v Portsmouth Hospital NHS & Another* [2005] EWCA Civ 1181.

[4] *C (a Baby)* [1996] 2 FLR 43, *C (a minor) (medical treatment)* [1998] 1 FLR 384; *An NHS Trust v MB* [2006] EWHC 507; *K (a minor)* [2006] EWHC 1007.

[5] *Re A (Children) (Conjoined Twins: Surgical Separation)* [2001] 2 WLR 480.

[6] *Re A (Children) (Conjoined Twins: Surgical Separation)* [2001] 2 WLR 480, Ward LJ p 512 quoting Lord Hailsham of St Marylebone LC in *Re B (a minor) (wardship: sterilisation)* [1988] AC 199, p 202.

[7] And decisions to withhold or withdraw treatment will only be reached where the child's life, viewed from the perspective of the child, is considered to be intolerable, *Portsmouth NHS Trust v Wyatt & Others* [2004] EWHC 2247, para 24.

proposed treatment is to 'the emotional, psychological and social benefit'[8] of the child. The current practice of the courts for assessment of best interests is to draw up a balance sheet[9] in which the actual benefits from the proposed course of conduct are set against any burdens, as are possible benefits and disadvantages with an estimate of their probability to arrive at a sum of certain and possible benefits against certain and possible disadvantages.[10]

Where issues surrounding the care of children with exceptional needs are considered by the judiciary,[11] it is a medical model of critical illness or disability which frames the approach of the court. The focus is upon the child's abnormality, dysfunction and pathology and the extent to which these can be overcome by the application of medical expertise and intervention.[12] This model locates expert knowledge with the medical professionals rather than with the parents who care for the child. As a consequence, medical professionals are handed the power and, in effect, the decision-making responsibility.[13] As a result, the judgments of the courts in cases concerning the medical treatment of children with exceptional needs can easily be subjected to the criticism that too much weight is given to the views of the medical profession and not enough to the views of others involved in caring for the child, particularly the child's parents.[14] In cases of children with exceptional needs, this tendency might be to avoid the counter-criticism made of the application of the welfare principle, that 'the interests of others, or, perhaps, untested assumptions about what is good for children, actually drive the

---

[8] *Re Y* [1997] 2 WLR 556, p 562.

[9] The practice originated in a case concerning the sterilisation of an adult male with Down's syndrome, *Re A (Male Sterilisation)* [2000] 1 FLR 549.

[10] *Wyatt & Another* v *Portsmouth Hospital NHS & Another* [2005] EWCA Civ 1181, para. 56 referring to the judgment of Thorpe LJ in *Re A (Male Sterilisation)* [2000] 1 FLR 549.

[11] Including cases in which the welfare principle does not apply, such as; judicial review of medical treatment which is delayed *R* v *Central Birmingham Health Authority, ex parte Walker; R* v *Secretary of State for Social Services and another, ex parte Walker*, QBD, 3 BMLR 32, 24 November 1987 (accessible via http://web. lexis-nexis.com/professional/); *R* v *Central Birmingham Health Authority ex parte Collier*, CA, 6 January 1988 (accessible via http://web.lexis-nexis.com/professional/); or refused *R* v *Cambridge District Health Authority, ex parte B* [1995] 1 FLR 1055; or negligence cases where it is alleged that the child has suffered brain damage immediately prior to, during, or shortly after, delivery.

[12] Jane Brett, 'The experience of disability from the perspective of parents of children with profound impairment: is it time for an alternative model of disability?' (2002) 17 *Disability and Society* 825–43, 828.

[13] Ibid, 829.

[14] John Eekelaar, 'Beyond the welfare principle' (2002) 14 *Child and Family Law Quarterly* 237–49, 238, in his terminology, '*the lack of fairness* objection'; Jonathan Herring, 'The Human Rights Act and the welfare principle in family law – conflicting or complementary?' (1999) 11 CFLQ, 223–35; Jonathan Herring, 'Farewell welfare?' (2005) 27 *Journal of Social Welfare and Family Law*, 159–71.

decision'.[15] As Jonathan Herring notes in 'Farewell welfare?', the best interests principle is one of the few legal principles to be found correctly stated in the media, and one which is easily understood by the public.[16] Perhaps, we can surmise, because journalists and the public include amongst them parents who themselves seek to secure, sustain and foster the best interests of their children. Yet, this understanding has not prevented critical comment being made about the decisions of parents as to the best interests of their child in extreme circumstances. Parents have been criticised for putting their own interests above those of their child by pressing for continued treatment as have those who refuse treatment or have reached the difficult decision that it is in their child's best interests for treatment to be withdrawn. This tendency can also be discerned in the case law where parents' views have been dismissed on the basis that they are unable to judge the interests of their child; either too emotionally attached to appreciate the child's lack of potential[17] or too concerned about the burden upon themselves of caring for the child. And it is repeated in some academic commentary upon the case law. For example, there was much critical academic commentary of the Court of Appeal's agreement with the mother of baby C, born suffering from a life-threatening liver defect, biliary atresia, that a liver transplant operation was not in his best interests. Andrew Bainham suggested that it was a 'seriously retrograde decision' 'not very far removed from nineteenth-century notions of the natural rights of parents'.[18]

In the Court of Appeal, Butler-Sloss LJ held that Connell J, at first instance, had erred in that, having concluded that the mother's refusal of consent was unreasonable, he determined the best interests of the child by reference to the medical evidence alone. Consequently, Connell J had failed to weigh in the balance the 'deep-seated concern of the mother as to the benefits to her son of the major invasive surgery and post operative treatment, the dangers of failure long term as well as short term, the possibility of the need for further transplants, the likely length of life, and the effect upon her son of all these concerns'.[19] As Butler-Sloss LJ understood it, the mother 'was focusing ... on the present peaceful life of the child who had the chance to spend the rest of his short life without the pain, stress and upset of intrusive surgery against the future with the operation and treatment taking

---

[15] What John Eekelaar terms the '*lack of transparency* objection', ibid 237.

[16] Jonathan Herring, 'Farewell welfare?' (2005) 27 *Journal of Social Welfare and Family Law* 159–71, p 168.

[17] *A National Health Service Trust* v *D* [2000] 2 FLR 677.

[18] Andrew Bainham, 'Do babies have rights?' (1997) 56 *Cambridge Law Journal* 48–50, 50; Michael Freeman, 'Can we leave the best interests of very sick children to their parents?' in Michael Freeman (ed.), *Law and Medicine, Current Legal Issues 2000*, Oxford: Oxford University Press, 2000, pp 257–68.

[19] *T (A Minor)* [1996] EWCA 1378, Butler-Sloss LJ.

place'.[20] Butler-Sloss LJ then drew upon the evidence of consultant paedia-trician, Dr P, to support her conclusion that it was not in C's best interests for consent to be given to the transplant operation against the judgment of his mother. It is at this point in her judgment that views about commitment and care were introduced and concern expressed as to the:

> effect of coercing, (as Dr P put it) this mother into playing the crucial and irreplaceable part in the aftermath of major invasive surgery not just during the post-operative treatment of an eighteen month-old baby but also throughout the childhood of her son. She would inevitably be the primary carer, ... and would be expected to care for him for many years through surgery and continuing treatment while she, on her present view, believed that this course was not right for her son. The total commit-ment of the caring parent, in Dr P's view, was essential to the success of the treatment.[21]

And then to give further support to her conclusion, her Ladyship added her own comments speculating as to the consequences for the mother of the court giving the consent sought:

> [P]assing back the responsibility for the parental care to the mother and expecting her to provide the commitment to the child after the operation is carried out in the face of her opposition is in itself fraught with danger for the child. She will have to comply with the court order, return to this country and present the child to one of the hospitals. She will have to arrange to remain in this country for the foreseeable future. Will the father stay in Country AB and work or come with her to England, giving up his job and having to seek another job? If he does not come she will have to manage unaided. How will the mother cope? Can her professionalism overcome her view that her son should not be sub-jected to this distressing procedure? Will she break down? How will the child be affected by the conflict with which the mother may have to cope?[22]

The evidence of Dr P and judicial speculation were emotively combined in the judgment of Waite LJ:

[20] *T (A Minor)* [1996] EWCA 1378, Butler-Sloss LJ. A similar position was adopted by the parents of an 18-month-old child who refused their consent to a bone marrow transplant for their child because of the pain and suffering caused by earlier treatment, her quality of life at the time compared with ongoing treatment and suffering resulting from treatment and the risk of immediate death from the treatment, *An NHS Trust* v *A and others* [2007] EWHC 1696 (Fam).

[21] *T (A Minor)* [1996] EWCA 1378, Butler-Sloss LJ.

[22] *T (A Minor)* [1996] EWCA 1378, Butler-Sloss LJ.

Dr P maintained a very clear view that – even assuming that the operation proved wholly successful in surgical terms – the child's subsequent development could be injuriously affected if his day to day care depended upon the commitment of a mother who had suffered the turmoil of having her child being compelled against her will to undergo, as a result of a coercive order from the court, a major operation against which her medical and maternal judgment wholeheartedly rebelled.[23]

As Marie Fox and Jean McHale observe in their comment on the case, the judges of the appeal court attempted to embrace caring responsibilities. But, in their efforts to do so, I believe, the judiciary came to misrepresent the mother's position with regard to the care of her son. Marie Fox and Jean McHale note the 'unresolved tensions in this portrayal of the mother'; if she was 'exceptionally devoted' it was surely not the case that she was refusing to care for her son should he undergo a life-saving operation?[24] The decision of the mother, grounded in the experiences of caring for her son after his first operation, was explained in terms of her future care of her child. While his dependence upon her care is explicitly recognised in the judgments of the Court of Appeal, mother and son are understood as two separate, unconnected beings.[25] Dependency, commitment and care are explained in terms of individualism, separation, danger, conflict and injury.

Whilst welcoming a care-based approach to welfare determinations, Marie Fox and Jean McHale rightly observe that, in this case, the Court of Appeal had failed to develop a clear framework for care-based determinations:

Given the limitations of rights arguments and their capacity to exacerbate conflict, rooting the determination of the boundaries of treatment in an ethics of caring seems to us to be legitimate and to offer a more promising approach. Nevertheless, if a paradigm of caring is to function as a framework for deciding such cases the courts need to be explicit about what this means ... Certainly, in cases involving young children, judicial guidance and clarification would be necessary as to the meaning of caring and the weight to be ascribed to the views of carers. In Re T itself, reference is made to the importance of caring without such articulation and there are unanswered questions as to why such

---

23 T (A Minor) [1996] EWCA 1378, Waite LJ.
24 Marie Fox and Jean McHale, 'In whose best interests?' (1997) 60 *Modern Law Review* 7009–7709, 705.
25 Despite the comment about their unity: 'This mother and this child are one for the purpose of this unusual case and the decision of the court to consent to the operation jointly affects the mother and son and it also affects the father', T (A Minor) [1996] EWCA 1378, Butler-Sloss LJ.

stress was laid in this particular case on the part played by the 'caring parents'.[26]

Jonathan Herring has argued that the law adopts an 'individualistic' approach to the welfare principle which means that 'the child and his or her welfare are viewed without regard for the welfare of the rest of his family, friends and community. The claims of other members of the family and of the community are only relevant to the extent that they directly affect the child's welfare.'[27] He develops 'relationship-based welfare' which understands that healthy relationships are central to children's welfare and that it is not generally in the best interests of the child to always, and in all instances, put their interests first, especially where that is at great cost to the parent. 'Relationship-based welfare', Jonathan Herring suggests, 'provides a means of holding onto the welfare principle while respecting the rights and interests of others involved in the child's life.'[28] Relationship-based welfare would, he argues, enable us to form a fuller picture of the welfare of the child bringing in to the determination relationships and caring responsibilities, both past and future. And, I would add, consideration of the circumstances in which and extent to which parents do put the interests of their child first.

It is more usually welfare and rights that are considered together than care and rights. For example, seeking to answer the question, 'can we protect children and protect their rights?', Andrew Bainham concluded that 'what welfare and rights based approaches have in common is that they are both grounded in value judgment and require the courts to adjudicate between competing values.'[29] Acknowledging that determinations of welfare and rights are both indeterminate and value-dependent, he argues that the benefit of a rights-based approach is that it brings into the equation the interests of the adults concerned, which a welfare assessment, as noted above, should not do. And, second, Andrew Bainham continues, a rights framework would ensure that all the competing interests pertinent to the decision are weighed, interests which a welfare assessment might overlook.[30] I now turn to explore whether a rights-based approach secures a more comprehensive assessment of the competing interests than is achieved by the welfare principle.

---

[26] Marie Fox and Jean McHale, 'In whose best interests?' (1997) 60 *Modern Law Review*, 7009–7709, 708.

[27] Jonathan Herring, 'The Human Rights Act and the welfare principle in family law – conflicting or complementary?' (1999) 11 *Child and Family Law Quarterly*, 223, 233.

[28] Jonathan Herring, 'Farewell welfare?' (2005) 27 *Journal of Social Welfare and Family Law*, 159–71, 166.

[29] Andrew Bainham, 'Can we protect children and protect their rights?' (2002) *Family Law*, 279–89, 281.

[30] Ibid, p 285.

The potential of rights and the care of children with exceptional needs

Whilst academic commentators have attempted to assess the consequences for welfare determinations of our obligations under the Human Rights Act 1998, in the case law considerations of rights are juxtaposed rather than integrated into decision-making. Given that the welfare principle applies, by virtue of the Children Act 1989 s 1, to decisions of the court in relation to children's upbringing, it is perhaps no surprise that the judiciary have limited their examination of the rights of the child, keeping rights discourse in the shadows of welfare determination. Jonathan Herring has observed that 'most leading exponents of children's rights include a powerful element of paternalism or welfarism within their descriptions of such rights', bringing welfare into the shadows of rights-based analysis. Jonathan Herring considers the work of John Eeklelaar, Michael Freeman and Jane Fortin noting that all have emphasised that children's rights should be employed to protect children from harm and that in many instances a children's rights approach and a children's welfare approach would lead to the same conclusion: the point of departure being whether the child's autonomous decision should be respected even if the exercise of that autonomy appears to be contrary to their best interests.[31]

One case which supports the view that both a children's rights approach and a children's welfare approach would lead to the same conclusion without the former offering a more comprehensive assessment of the competing interests, is the case of David Glass. The ECtHR considered whether the decisions and actions of the doctors and hospital management at Portsmouth NHS Trust were compatible with the ECHR. David, now a young man, was born with severe physical and mental impairments: he has cerebral palsy, hydrocephalus, epilepsy, curvature of the spine and a dislocated hip, limited sight and limited cognitive function. David is cared for at home by his mother with the help of his sisters and aunts, with the assistance of community paediatricians and episodes of hospital care. The incident which later took David and his mother to Strasbourg was an infection, which he developed after undergoing a tonsillectomy performed to assist his breathing, for which he was hospitalised on a number of occasions. Having formed the view that David was dying and should be treated to enable him to die with dignity, diamorphine (which in the alleviation of pain depresses respiratory function) was administered against his mother's wishes and a 'Do Not

---

[31] Jonathan Herring, 'Farewell welfare?' (2005) 27 *Journal of Social Welfare and Family Law*, 159–71, 165 giving as examples John Eekelaar, 'The interests of the child and the child's wishes: the role of dynamic self-determinism' (1994) 8 *International Journal of Law and the Family* 42–63; Michael Freeman, *The Rights and Wrongs of Children*, 1983 and Jane Fortin, *Children's Rights and the Developing Law*, 2003.

Resuscitate' order (DNR) placed on his notes without her knowledge. His medical treatment thus involved both the provision, against his mother's wishes, of medication to alleviate distress which would have the effect of hastening death and the intention to withhold certain forms of resuscitation, without his mother's knowledge or consent. His mother resuscitated him, whilst family members prevented doctors from stopping her, and David was discharged later the same day. They were told that the hospital would only be able to offer palliative care in the future and that David would have to go elsewhere if he required active treatment. Judicial review proceedings of this decision were brought,[32] although that case merely affirmed that decisions about the best interests of the child should be brought before a Family Division judge in s 8 proceedings or in the exercise of the court's inherent jurisdiction.

Before the ECtHR, it was argued that the actions of the hospital amounted to a breach of Arts 2 (right to life), 6 (right of access to court), 8 (right to respect for private and family life), 13 (right to an effective remedy) and 14 (right not to be discriminated against in the enjoyment of Convention rights). Conceiving narrowly of the issue, the complaint of breach of Art 8 was held to be admissible, the remainder manifestly unfounded.[33] Central to the case was the legal advice given to doctors caring for David that permission of the High Court was necessary if they were to treat against his mother's wishes but that no court had ever required doctors to treat contrary to their clinical judgment. As a consequence of this advice, the doctors believed that the law permitted them to treat David, as they saw fit, contrary to his mother's wishes. The ECtHR concluded that administration of diamorphine without the consent of his mother or the court amounted to a breach of the child's, David's, right to physical integrity and hence, respect for private life.[34] As the doctors had acted in what they assessed to be David's best interests their actions had a legitimate aim but administration of diamorphine without the consent of his mother or the court was not necessary in a democratic society, given the ability of the hospital to seek a declaration of the court beforehand or in an emergency.[35]

There are a number of points to be made about this cautious conclusion: first, it is notable that the court found that it was the child's right to have a decision made about their treatment either by their parent (or adult with parental responsibility) or the court. This approach gives to parents, of a child who lacks the capacity to give or refuse consent, the power to consent on their behalf, giving permission to doctors to invade the physical integrity

---

[32] *R* v *Portsmouth Hospitals NHS Trust, ex parte Glass*, 50 BMLR 269 and *R* v *Portsmouth Hospitals NHS Trust, ex parte Glass* [1999] 2 FLR 905.

[33] ECHR, *Decision as to the Admissibility of Application no. 61827/00 by David and Carol Glass against the United Kingdom*, 18 March 2003, (2003) 37 EHRR CD66.

[34] *Glass* v *United Kingdom* [2004] 1 FLR 1019, para 70.

[35] Ibid, paras 77–83.

of a child without committing a battery.[36] Adopting this approach and focusing upon the legitimate invasion of the boundaries of the individual meant that very fundamental issues of the dependency of a child upon his mother or, importantly in this context, for this is where the wrong lies, of his mother upon the healthcare professionals involved in his care, were avoided. The court declined to consider the Art 8 rights of David's mother, as mother, as the person with primary responsibility for her child or as the carer upon whom David depended for both his survival and his well-being. Furthermore, the majority declined to consider whether placing a DNR on his notes without the knowledge of his mother (let alone her consent) was a breach of his, or her, Art 8 rights.[37] In other words, the ECtHR only went so far as to hold that English Law properly understood – that is, the decision to give or refuse consent to treatment for a child rests with the child's parent or, in the case of professional disagreement with the parental decision, the court – is compliant with the ECHR.[38] What if the focus had been upon the care of a vulnerable and dependent child whose well-being, personal integrity and dignity depended upon the mother who cared for him and had experience gained through that care yet whose ability to care depended upon others? Or if the court had acknowledged the responsibilities of his mother and of the professionals upon whom she depended for medical expertise?

Preceding the consideration of David Glass's treatment by the ECtHR and shortly before incorporation of the ECHR into English Law, Cazalet J considered children's rights in the context of the question whether it would be lawful to withhold mechanical ventilation from baby D, a baby with irreparable and worsening lung disease. Cazalet J was of the opinion that withholding life-sustaining treatment would not infringe his Art 2 'right to life' if this course of action was in his best interests. Furthermore, that withholding treatment positively respected the child's right to die with dignity protected under Art 3.[39] In his commentary upon the case, Andrew Grubb expresses the view that the conclusion may be correct in light of the subsequent case of *NHS Trust A* v *M; NHS Trust B* v *H*.[40] This case, brought very soon after the Human Rights Act 1998 came into force, tested whether the principles

---

[36] Jonathan Montgomery, 'Children as property?' (1988) 51 *Modern Law Review* 323–42, 334.

[37] Judge Casadevall dissented considering the DNR to be an aggravating factor exacerbating the distress of Carol Glass.

[38] Jo Bridgeman, 'Caring for children with severe disabilities: boundaried and relational rights' (2005) 13 *International Journal of Children's Rights* 99–119.

[39] *A National Health Service Trust* v *D* [2000] 2 FLR 677. Andrew Grubb has suggested that the case cited *D* v *UK* (1997) 24 EHRR 423 did not establish that Art 3 gave a right to die with dignity, rather it prevented the state from causing suffering of a level which amounted to inhumane treatment, Commentary, (2000) 8 *Medical Law Review* 339–342.

[40] *NHS Trust A* v *M; NHS Trust B* v *H*, 25 October 2000.

established by the House of Lords in *Bland*[41] by which artificial nutrition and hydration could lawfully be withdrawn from patients in a permanent vegetative state remained good law as consistent with, principally, Art 2 of the ECHR.[42] Butler-Sloss P (as she then was) reasoned that although the purpose of withdrawal of artificial nutrition and hydration was to bring about the patient's death, the prohibition upon the intentional deprivation of life required a positive act. The decision to withdraw artificial nutrition and hydration which is no longer in the patient's best interests did not amount to a violation of the negative obligation to refrain from intentionally depriving the patient of his or her life.[43] Article 2 also imposes a positive obligation upon states to safeguard life. Butler-Sloss P concluded that a clinical decision to withhold treatment, as not in the best interests of the patient and supported by a competent body of professional opinion, did not infringe this right. The positive obligation to safeguard life did not extend to treatment which is no longer in the best interests of the patient because it is futile.[44]

Undoubtedly the most strident advocacy of the rights of a child in the context of medical treatment was that Laws J in *R v Cambridge District Health Authority ex parte B*.[45] His Lordship was asked whether the decision of the health authority not to fund further, experimental, treatment of 10-year-old Jaymee Bowen, who was suffering a relapse of acute myeloid leukaemia, was lawful. Laws J held that the decision of the health authority to refuse to fund further treatment had a material effect upon her chances of life and thus required 'substantial objective justification on public interest grounds'. Jaymee had first been treated for acute lymphoblastic leukaemia at the age of 5 and had undergone two courses of chemotherapy, total body irradiation and a bone marrow transplant. The health authority declined to fund further treatment on the grounds that it was not in her best interests, rather that she should now receive palliative care. Further, that the proposed treatment which was experimental, expensive, and carried a small chance of success would not be an effective use of limited resources given competing claims upon them. His Lordship concluded that their decision had not been objectively justified because, in his understanding, the view that it was not in her best interests was based upon the clinical evidence and paid insufficient attention to her father's views, the health authority had not explained what treatment might be unavailable if Jaymee was treated, nor had it stated its priorities or given an account of the health authority budget or its budget for extra-contractual funding. Expressing her rights in forceful terms, 'Of all human rights, most people would accord the most precious place to the right

---

[41] *Airedale NHS Trust v Bland* [1993] AC 789.
[42] Dame Butler-Sloss P, as she then was, also considered briefly compatibility with Arts 3 and 8.
[43] *NHS Trust A v M; NHS Trust B v H*, 25 October 2000, para 30.
[44] *NHS Trust A v M; NHS Trust B v H*, 25 October 2000, paras 36–37.
[45] *R v Cambridge District Health Authority ex parte B* [1995] 1 FLR 1055.

of life itself',[46] Laws J concluded that 'where the question is whether the life of a 10-year-old child might be saved, by however slim a chance, the responsible authority must in my judgment do more than toll the bell of tight resources. They must explain the priorities that have led them to decline to fund the treatment.'[47]

Despite attempts to identify the inevitable connectedness in rights claims on the basis that the enjoyment of a right imposes a duty upon another and reframing rights as relational,[48] and the case being made for a right to care,[49] there remains an incongruity between the foundational premises and values of the ethics of rights and the ethics of care. As Jonathan Herring has forcefully argued:

> We are not self-sufficient but interdependent; not isolated individuals but people in relationship; not people with rights clashing with those who care for us and for whom we care, but people who live with entwined obligations and interests with those we love. We are not easily divided up into carers and cared for. We are in mutually supportive relationships. We need then a legal and ethical approach that promotes just caring: respects it; rewards it; and protects those rendered vulnerable by the caring role – an approach which has relationship at its heart.[50]

Rather than understanding individuals as separate, reaching out from choice, obligation or relationship, the question which needs to be posed is: what insights do we get from an approach which gives central place to dependency, caring relationships and responsibilities and what implications does that have for the law?

---

46 Ibid, 1056.
47 Ibid, 1065. While Laws J quashed the health authority's decision not to fund Jaymee's treatment, that afternoon the Court of Appeal allowed the health authority's appeal against the order. An anonymous benefactor donated the money required for the proposed course of treatment. The health authority funded further care and routine treatment as she went into remission; Jaymee died 15 months later in May 1996, (Carol Midgley, 'She wanted to come back as a butterfly', *The Times*, 23 May 1996).
48 Martha Minow and Mary Lyndon Shanley, 'Revisioning the family: relational rights and responsibilities' in Mary Lyndon Shanley and Uma Narayan (eds), *Reconstructing Political Theory: Feminist Perspectives*, Polity Press: Cambridge, 1997, 84–108.
49 Robin West, 'The right to care', in Eva Feder Kittay and Ellen K. Feder, *The Subject of Care: Feminist Perspectives on Dependency*, Rowman & Littlefield, Lanham, 2002, pp 88–114.
50 Jonathan Herring, 'Where are the carers in healthcare law and ethics?' (2007) 27 *Legal Studies* 51–73, 73.

Gender, Responsibility and Care

In 'Cracking the Foundational Myths: Autonomy and Self-Sufficiency'[51] Martha Fineman advances the argument, which she develops in *The Autonomy Myth*,[52] for a 'theory of collective responsibility for dependency'.[53] In these works she argues that the myths of autonomy, individualism and economic self-sufficiency, prevalent in the USA and echoed in UK policy and law, mask the reality of universal, inevitable dependency, recognition of which would offer the basis for recognition of our collective dependency. Her thesis is premised upon the extent to which the work of caring for dependants has been hidden in the private sphere of the family enabling caring work to be understood as a private family matter. The key elements of her critique are that:

> This reliance on what I have termed the 'assumed family' distorts analysis and policy. The assumed family is a specific ideological construct with a particular population and a gendered form that allows us to privatize individual dependency and pretend that it is not a public problem. Furthermore, the gendered nature of this assumed family is essential to the maintenance and continuance of our foundational myths of individual independence, autonomy and self-sufficiency. This assumed family masks the dependency of society and all its public institutions on the uncompensated and dependency work assigned to caretakers within the private family.[54]

Placing responsibility for dependency within the family, and primarily to women within the family, is unjust because it renders the person providing care a derivative dependant, dependent in turn upon others.[55] Separation of family and market and the view that the values, norms and relationships within each are different means that the implications of public policy for the family are not considered nor vice versa.[56] Martha Fineman argues that society as a whole depends upon the work of caring for individuals and thus incurs a societal or collective debt to the care provider.[57] The theory of collective responsibility for dependency which she advocates would require

---

[51] Martha Fineman, 'Cracking the foundational myths: autonomy and self-sufficiency' (2000) 8 *American University Journal of Gender, Social Policy and the Law*, 13–29.

[52] Martha Fineman, *The Autonomy Myth: A Theory of Dependency*, The New Press, New York, 2004.

[53] Martha Fineman, 'Cracking the Foundational Myths', p 16.

[54] Ibid, p 14.

[55] Ibid, p 20.

[56] Ibid, p 14.

[57] Ibid, p 18.

recognition of the universality and inevitability of dependency and acknowledgement of the value of caring, establishing entitlements to support.[58] The entitlements would include financial recompense, the provision of equipment and support and necessitate structural changes which would enable people to both care for dependants and have access to paid work. In other words, recognition of the inevitability of dependency and society's collective responsibility for it would result in practical measures of support for carers and recognition of the caring aspects of our identities. Martha Fineman, like other feminists before her such as Eva Feder Kittay,[59] argues that failure to recognise the inevitability of dependency is central to the enduring inequality of women and the devaluing of dependency work with damaging consequences for carer and cared for alike.

While the challenge which Martha Fineman presents, for society, policy and law to recognise and respect dependency, is to be welcomed, her thought-provoking thesis raises a number of unanswered questions many of which are eloquently articulated by Helen Reece in her review including;[60] how can family privacy and individual decision-making in the caring relationship be protected if caring work is to attract entitlements? Would the opportunity to both care and participate in paid work evolve into the expectation to do both given the current dominance in UK government policy of the dual-worker model of the family? However, reflecting upon her thesis in the context of caring for children with exceptional needs raises three primary issues about the nature of caring responsibilities. First, that the care of children with exceptional needs is intensive and may be enduring and the difficulties which carers face may be added to by discriminatory attitudes and environments. Second, the derivative dependency of carers is not confined to dependency upon another, or the state, for financial support; rather, it includes dependency upon others for support in the provision of care. Third, Fineman's argument that care incurs a societal debt is premised upon the view of the cared for themselves being economically productive (or contributing in some tangible way to the public benefit) at some point in their lives, whether later in the case of children, previously in the case of the elderly or on other occasions in the case of the temporarily ill. A 'broader sense of obligation' is needed, she suggests, because care produces citizens, workers, producers and consumers.[61] In other words, the thesis is premised upon the primacy of the economically productive citizen.

---

[58] Ibid. p 16.
[59] Eva Feder Kittay, *Love's Labor: Essays on Women, Equality and Dependency*, New York: Routledge, 1999.
[60] Helen Reece, Review article, 'The autonomy myth: a theory of dependency' (2008) *Child and Family Law Quarterly*, 109–24.
[61] Martha Fineman, 'Cracking the foundational myths' p 19.

It is suggested above that when children with exceptional needs appear in the case law, their stories are constructed in terms of a medical model which focuses upon the individual pathology of the child. The individualistic approach means the focus is upon the child rather than upon their dependencies and relationships of care but when parents do appear, the story is of personal tragedy to which they have responded with heroic efforts. For example, in the negligence case of *Smithers* v *Taunton and Somerset NHS Trust*, Cox J commented that:

> As a result of his disabilities Lewis requires, and will for the rest of his life continue to require, help with every aspect of his daily living. He is therefore totally dependent upon his parents for all activities. The fact that Lewis has continued to maintain a good standard of health and to avoid infections or other complications, despite these severe disabilities, is mainly due to the devoted care and attention provided by his family, who deserve in consequence the highest praise.[62]

Yet still, the responsibility for meeting the needs of the child is the individual, personal, responsibility of the parents, often reported with admiration, an undercurrent of expectation and frequently without any question.

Her research with families of disabled children has enabled Janice McLaughlin to identify the ways in which 'care is valued or disvalued, how contexts channel care towards particular actors and how barriers within society confine both care practices and those involved in care into a marginalised and secluded private sphere'.[63] In other words, the ways in which children with exceptional needs are considered to be, and treated as, the private responsibility of their parents. Which, in practice, means their mothers:

> Families with young children with disabilities experience a variety of refusals to care and rejections from both formal actors and agencies. Through these refusals care is drawn inwards as a private, family matter where parents, in reality often the mothers, are the central actors. The minimalist approach that parents find within formal care provision keeps care in the private sphere and articulates public responsibilities towards care as a burden on the state and society, which mothers should take responsibility for.[64]

---

[62] *Smithers* v *Taunton and Somerset NHS Trust* [2004] EWHC 1179, paras. 2 and 55.
[63] Janice McLaughlin, 'Conceptualising intensive caring activities: the changing lives of families with young disabled children', Sociological Research Online, vol 11, Issue 1, www.socresonline.org.uk/11/1/mclaughlin.html, para 1.3.
[64] Ibid, para 5.1.

Children with exceptional needs will be more dependent upon their parents to meet their needs, which may be enduring and may require intensive caring. Informal networks available to mothers of children without these special needs such as 'play dates', playgroups, nurseries, sporting and artistic activities may not be accessible to children with exceptional needs. While the UK may offer health and social services, studies of parents whose children have exceptional needs report the additional skills they have developed to negotiate, access and manage these services. In addition to the difficulties in securing services which meet the needs of their children, parents of children with exceptional needs may face additional difficulties in caring for their children presented by discriminatory attitudes and environments.

The derivative dependency of carers in Martha Fineman's theory is financial dependency, upon either their husbands, or the state. Whilst the more extensive nature of caring for children with exceptional needs does have a financial impact, there is a further important sense in which the carer is dependent. That is, that the carer will also be dependent upon others who participate in caring for the child. This might be a dependency upon support workers or care workers who assist in the daily care of a child whose needs must be met 24 hours a day, 7 days a week. Parents need to trust that these care workers will care for their child with love, respect and affection – the activity of care needs a caring attitude. It may be a range of community healthcare professionals such as physiotherapists, speech and language therapists or community nursing services upon which parents depend in order to maximise the well-being of their child. In other circumstances, and these are the instances we see in the case law, it is the dependency of the parents upon healthcare professionals whose specialist skills are required in a time of crisis. Parents need to depend upon these professionals to care for their child informed by the experiences of parents gained as they care. Carol Glass, mother of David, must have acutely felt the refusal of care of the doctors upon whom she had to rely to provide life-saving medical treatment to her son. One of the reasons given by the parents of Ashley X that their profoundly disabled daughter should undergo a hysterectomy, removal of breast buds, appendectomy and high-dose oestrogen therapy to restrict her height and weight, was that they had been unable to find unrelated caregivers they considered were 'qualified, trustworthy, and affordable'.[65] While her father explained that the guiding principle for the decision was her best interests, and led to discussion of her right to dignity, understanding of the privatisation of caring responsibility and the dependency of parents upon others in caring for a child with exceptional needs adds a further dimension to examination of this case.

Third, Maxine Eichner has suggested that collective responsibility should be understood as the responsibility of the state to the vulnerable,

---

[65] http://ashleytreatment.spaces.live.com/blog/.

rather than as a societal debt incurred through the care of the productive citizen of the past or the future.[66] In the context of caring for children, primarily by women, there is a further dimension to the caring work, that of mothering. The current dominant ideology of mothering is that of intensive mothering which is 'exclusive, wholly child centred, emotionally involving, and time-consuming'.[67]

In *The Cultural Contradictions of Motherhood*, Sharon Hays identifies the features of the construction of intensive mothering to involve the allocation to mothers of the role as primary carer of the child as necessary for appropriate child rearing (mother can delegate some care, but to other women rather than to the child's father). Child rearing requires time, energy and resources, is focused upon child development, responding to the needs of the child and is 'child-centred, expert-guided, emotionally absorbing, labor-intensive, and financially expensive'. The cultural contradiction is that the values of mothering stand in stark contract to the norms of the rational actor.[68] Mothering is other-directed, caring, unselfish, grounded in love for the child, whilst the values of the market are individualism, efficiency and personal achievement.[69] Hays argues that the ideology of intensive mothering prevails influencing the mothering of working ('double shift' workers) and stay-at-home ('outsiders')[70] mothers alike. As Terry Arendell suggests this ideology offers 'the normative standard, culturally and politically, by which mothering practices and arrangements are evaluated.'[71] Mothering is understood as the task of 'raising children to become successful independent adults, making their contribution to society through work and raising their own family'.[72] And as Pamela Fisher explains, what is considered 'normal' is defined as autonomy, independence and financial self-sufficiency and the good, or successful, mother ensures her children develop the qualities and skills required.[73] If intensive mothering is the dominant ideology presenting contradictions for all women, it has particular complexities for the mothers of children with exceptional needs, whose caring activities are of greater

---

[66] Maxine Eichner, 'Dependency and the liberal polity: on Martha Fineman's *The Autonomy Myth*', (2005) 93 *California Law Review*, 1285–1321.
[67] Terry Arendell, 'Conceiving and Investigating Motherhood: The Decade's Scholarship' (2000) *Journal of Marriage and the Family*, 1192–1207, 1194.
[68] Sharon Hays, *The Cultural Contradictions of Motherhood*, New Haven: Yale University Press, 1996, 8–9.
[69] Ibid, p 97.
[70] Ibid, p 149.
[71] Terry Arendell, 'Conceiving and investigating motherhood: the decade's scholarship' (2000) *Journal of Marriage and the Family*, 1192–1207, 1195.
[72] McLaughlin, 'Conceptualising intensive caring activities' para 9.1.
[73] Pamela Fisher, 'Experiential knowledge challenges "normality" and individualized citizenship: towards "another way of being"' (2007) 22 *Disability & Society* 283–98, 285.

intensity and duration, and whose child may not develop to fulfil the ideal of the economically productive citizen.

Pamela Fisher explains how the parents in her study, caring for children with disabilities, develop different narratives to articulate their experiences:

> The parents in this study did not generally subscribe to the idea that the entrepreneurial, autonomous self provides the only blueprint for achieving 'the good life'. Instead, they were embracing alternative 'ways of being' and challenging the narrow parameters of individualized citizenship that emphasises entrepreneurial success in the public sphere. Many saw lives based on mutuality and interdependence not as a form of second class citizenship but as a way of being in which relationships and meanings develop in alternative patterns that challenge the boundaries that define normality according to narrow measures of self-sufficiency.[74]

Not only does society have obligations to those who are unable to look after themselves but we should not see the value of a human being solely in terms of economic productivity or their contribution to the greater good, rather, as Kittay has argued, in terms of valued relationships.[75]

[74] Ibid, 294.
[75] Kittay, *Love's Labor*.

Chapter 12

Relational autonomy and family law

Jonathan Herring

INTRODUCTION

Autonomy has achieved a 'sacred status'[1] not only among lawyers, but within the wider society. The themes of independence, self-determination and choice play a major role in public debates and popular culture. Many of the heroes of our day: Jack Bauer, James Bond, Jason Bourne fight alone against the wicked powers that be: they are the epitome of the isolated autonomous man. The themes of independence, autonomy and choice resonate in public policy statements from the government.[2] This chapter will consider the role played by autonomy in family law. It will argue against placing weight on autonomy as it is popularly understood, and instead argue in favour of using the notion of relational autonomy.

Autonomy at its most simple is a recognition that individuals should be allowed to make decisions for themselves. Joseph Raz defines it in this way:

> The ruling idea behind the ideal of personal autonomy is that people should make their own lives. The autonomous person is a (part) author of his own life. The ideal of personal autonomy is the vision of people controlling, to some degree, their own destiny, fashioning it through successive decisions throughout their lives.[3]

Such an understanding of autonomy is central to a liberal conception of the self. As Helen Reece puts it:

---

[1] M. Chen-Wishart, 'Undue influence: vindicating relationships of influence' in J. Holder and C. O'Cinneide (eds), *Current Legal Problems*, Oxford: Oxford University Press, 2007, p 231.

[2] To give one example, when considering the plight of older people within our society the government produced a paper, Department of Health, *Independence, Well-Being and Choice*, London: TSO, 2005.

[3] J. Raz, *The Morality of Freedom*, Oxford: Oxford University Press, 1986, p 369.

within liberalism, what is arguably most essential to the individual's identity is the individual's capcity to choose his or her own roles and identities, and to rethink those choices.[4]

This individualist conception of autonomy is linked to a whole set of other ideas: self-sufficiency, self-sovereignty, moral independence, self-government, pluralism and liberty.[5] The freedom to able to make decisions as to how you live your life is seen as a central part of 'Western political culture'.[6] Amel Alghrani and John Harris have claimed that:

> one of the presumption of liberal democracies is that the freedom of citizens should not be interfered with unless good and sufficient justification can be produced for so doing … The presumption is that citizens should be free to make their own choices in the light of their own values, whether or not these choices and values are acceptable to the majority. Only serious danger, either to other citizens or society, is sufficient to rebut this presumption.[7]

To many people the right to autonomy or self-determination is one of the most important rights an individual has.[8] Indeed it might even be seen as the source of all rights. Without autonomy we cannot choose how to exercise our other rights and they become worthless or, even worse, tools that others can use against us.

A central role of the law is, therefore, to protect individuals' autonomy from invasion from the state or from others. This means that the rights attached to individualistic autonomy are all about fighting off unwanted intrusions into a person's freedom of choice[9] Justice Brandeis has identified the 'right to be let alone' as the most valuable right belonging to 'civilized men'.[10] Jo Bridgeman, before criticising the concept, explains individualistic autonomy in this way:

> all individuals exercise their autonomy and pursue their own ends within the shadow of the possibility of conflict arising from a clash of interests individually desired. Criminal and civil laws place limits upon the selfish

---

[4] H. Reece, *Divorcing Responsibly*, Oxford: Hart, 2003, p 13.
[5] M. Fineman, *The Autonomy Myth*, New York: New Press, 2004, p 263.
[6] R. Dworkin *Life's Dominion*, London: Harper Collins, 1993, p 166.
[7] A. Alghrani and J. Harris, 'Reproductive liberty: should the foundation of families be regulated?' (2006) 18 *Child and Family Law Quarterly*, 191, 192.
[8] J. Griffin, *On Human Rights*, Oxford: OUP, 2007, Ch. 1.
[9] A. Donchin, 'Understanding autonomy relationally', (2001) 26 *Journal of Medicine and Philosophy*, 365.
[10] *Olmstead* v *United States*, 277 US 438, 478 (1928) (Brandeis, J, dissenting).

pursuit of individual interest and seek to protect the individual from invasion of the boundaries of their bodies.[11]

So seen a central purpose of the law is to leave individuals free to pursue their autonomy, while providing means to resolve disputes when individual rights clash.

Family law and autonomy

Family law, at least until recently, has placed relatively little weight on the idea of autonomy and it is easy to see why. It fits uncomfortably with what are commonly thought to be the central themes of family law: the responsibilities of parents; the state interest in upholding marriage; the enforcement of obligations between spouses. None of these are readily reconcilable with the freedom to forge one's life story which is at the heart of individualist models of autonomy. However, in recent times we have seen an increasing emphasis within family law on autonomy and with it the importance of self-sufficiency and self-determination. We can see this in calls for no fault divorce; greater use of mediation; pressuring parties to resolve contact disputes themselves;[12] enforcement of pre-marriage contracts; and for a privatisation of child support. The state's role is limited to assisting the parties to reach an agreement. Typical is the recent White Paper on Child Maintenance which declares:

> We want to move to a child maintenance system that promotes greater parental responsibility and enables and empowers parents to make their own arrangements for child maintenance.[13]

The reasons for this shift towards autonomy are complex, but I suggest they include the following.

First, it fits in well with the government's continued attempts to reduce expenditure. The legal aid budget, particularly as it relates to family matters, has been a cause of concern for the New Labour government and there have been consistent restrictions on the access to legal aid and legal aid lawyers.[14] Conveniently this can readily be tied in with autonomy-based language and the claim that couples should seek to resolve their family disputes themselves through mediation, rather than involve lawyers and the courts. When combined

---

[11] J. Bridgeman, *Parents, Young Children and Healthcare Law*, Cambridge: Cambridge University Press, 2007, p 11.

[12] See e.g. *Re A-H (Children)* [2008] EWCA Civ 630.

[13] Department of Work and Pensions, *A New System of Child Maintenance*, London: DWP, 2007, p 32.

[14] A. Macdonald, 'Legal aid reform – beyond "no more money"' (2007) 37 *Family Law* 130.

with references to the wickedness and greed of lawyers, the severe restrictions on legal aid have gone through with little objection from the general public.

Second, the government is feeling the heat from complaints about the way courts and state bodies make decisions in relation to family matters. This is true particularly of the court's response to applications by non-resident fathers for contact with their children and the operation of the Child Support Agency. The outrageous campaigns of men's pressure groups in these areas have embarrassed the government and courts. In both cases the responses have involved attempts to shift decision making away from state agencies or courts and towards the couples themselves.[15] These render the decisions less susceptible to public scrutiny and less likely to cause criticism of the government.

Third, there is a growing acceptance of the argument that family disputes are essentially private disputes that matter primarily to the couple themselves. This can be seen in the increased use of mediation and the encouragement to use parenting plans. This may reflect a human rights era with an emphasis on private life. In particular there is a general distrust of the state's interference in private and sexual matters. The message to the state from many quarters is: 'don't go there'. John Eekelaar has written powerfully of the need for the law to respect the 'a sphere of personal interaction' by not regulating the intimate aspects of life.[16] One explanation is that this is a matter of freedom: people should be free to divorce when they wish; couples should be free to contract what agreements they wish; parents should be free to raise their children as they wish.[17] Hence, although family law emphasises the responsibilities of parenthood and the importance of child welfare, it is generally assumed that it is best for children to be raised by their parents, unless there is evidence that they are suffering significant harm.

In some quarters the increased emphasis on autonomy has evoked a strong reaction against what is seen as increased individualism within society generally. Mary Ann Glendon writes:

> [T]he legal imagery of separateness and independence [in US family law] contrasts everywhere with the way most functioning families operate and with the circumstances of mothers and young children in both intact and broken homes. Yet the law holds self-sufficiency up as an ideal, suggesting that dependency is somehow degrading, and implicitly denying the importance of human inter-subjectivity.[18]

---

[15] Adoption and Children Act 2002; Child Maintenance and Other Payments Act 2008.

[16] J. Eekelaar, *Family Law and Personal Life*, Oxford: Oxford University Press, 2007, p 82.

[17] N. Woolcock, 'It's no nanny state, more an extended family, minister says', *The Times*, 26 November 2004.

[18] M. Glendon, *The Transformation of Family Law*, Chicago: University of Chicago Press, 1989.

Helen Reece has written of the emphasis on the 'responsible post-liberal' individual as at the heart of the proposed reforms to the Family Law Act 1996. Her observations are just as pertinent to some more recent legislation such as the Children and Adoption Act 2006. She explains:

> The responsible post-liberal individual is judged, not by what he does but by how profoundly he has thought about what he does. The old view of responsibility was clear-cut; there just were certain actions that you should or should not take: 'good behaviour is simple. It is about easy things. The choice may be difficult but the distinction is easy. Stealing is wrong; lying is wrong; telling the truth is right.' The new form of responsibility is no longer about discrete decisions – responsible behaviour has shifted to a way of being, a mode of thought. Faced with the decision whether to tell a lie, we can no longer say with confidence that the responsible individual is the one who tells the truth. Now, the individual shows his responsibility by the attitude with which he approaches the decision, the extent to which he reflects on the implications of what he chooses.[19]

So autonomy still plays a central role: this is your decision and you must make it; but the government may offer advice and encouragement to help you make it.

Family law against autonomy

I will now argue that autonomy as it is commonly understood should not be seen as a value of fundamental importance in family law. At the heart of my argument is the claim that individualistic autonomy regards freedom to live as one chooses; a separation from others; and respecting an individual's choice is simply inconsistent with family life as it is understood and experienced by most. As Pamela Scheininger puts it:

> Because the law is conceived of in its application to the isolated individual rather than in its application to the individual's various associations and relationships, the law does not accurately reflect the reality of human existence. The legitimacy of the law is thus challenged. Individual persons do not operate as independent, separate entities, but as interdependent, connected parts of larger groups. In failing to deal with laws as they affect human relationships, lawmakers ignore a fundamental aspect of our humanity ... [20]

[19] H. Reece, 'Divorcing responsibly' (2000) 8 *Feminist Legal Studies* 65.
[20] P. Scheininger, 'Legal separateness, private connectedness: An impediment to gender equality in the family' (1998) 31 *Columbia Journal of Law and Social Problems* 283.

Taking marriage as an example, Robin West writes: 'Marriage just is, through and through, anti-individualistic. That is precisely its moral strength, and no small measure of its immense appeal.'[21] To develop the argument that there is an inherent antagonism between autonomy and family law I make four points.

First, the separation of the interests of individuals is simply impossible in family law. Under the traditional liberal approach, the freedom of autonomy of an individual in the family context must be weighed against the claims of their partner or children or perhaps some state interests.[22] This, however, is predicated on the basis that we *can* separate out the interests of a parent and a child. But, as I have argued elsewhere one cannot separate out the interests of a parent and a child or the interests of intimate partners. They are inter-twined.[23] To harm a child is to harm the person caring for the child; and to harm the carer is to harm the child. Katherine Baker has described the basis of the right to marry as:

> the right to be considered as part of a unit, to have another person's needs, wants and desires determine one's own needs, wants and desires. It is a right rooted not in self-expression or autonomy but almost in their opposite. It is a right rooted in the human flourishing that comes from relationship. After all, what seems sacred, or at least awe-inspiring and worthy of protection is not that two people make the promise, but that they actually keep it, by being able to subordinate the 'I' to the 'We'.[24]

Second, family life practices inevitably raise important social and community issues. It is not possible to consider the significance of family practices in isolation from those practices. Quite simply many family disputes are not essentially private matters. An important example is that of care work. As Martha Fineman has pointed out in her book *The Autonomy Myth* care for those who are unable to look after themselves is one of the most important jobs within society. She demonstrates how this care of dependants has been delegated to 'families' and thus been rendered unacknowledged in the public. Women in particular have, as a result, had their crucial societal contribution unrecognised and unrewarded. Fineman argues:

---

[21] R. West, 'Universalism, liberal theory, and the problem of gay marriage' (1998) 25 *Florida State University Law Review*, 705, 729.
[22] M. Eichner, 'Principles of the law of relationships among adults' (2007) 41 *Family Law Quarterly*, 433.
[23] J. Herring, 'The Human Rights Act and the welfare principle – conflicting or complimentary?' (1999) 11 *Child and Family Law Quarterly*, 223.
[24] K. Baker, 'Family, the law, and the constitution(s)', available at SSRN: http://ssrn.com/abstract=1106423, p 16.

> [T]he family in [the traditional 'separate spheres' understanding of society] is positioned as a unique and private arena. I argue that this is an incorrect and unsustainable conception. The family is contained within the larger society, and its contours are defined as an institution by law. Far from being separate and private, the family interacts with and is acted upon by other societal institutions. I suggest the very relationship is not one of separation, but of symbiosis. It is very important to understand the roles assigned to the family in society – roles that otherwise might have to be played by other institutions, such as the market or the state.[25]

Third, if autonomy is about developing and living out a vision for one's own flourishing, for many, if not all, that involves being in relationships with others. As seen earlier, many regard the primary role of the state must be to refrain from intervention in the intimate aspects of life. The best way for love to flourish and the relationship to grow is for the state to keep well out. John Eekelaar has supported a very moderate version of this argument, calling for respect of the intimate sphere. We need to respect 'the value of having space to develop one's personality and personal interaction free from external gaze ... love itself demands such a space if it is to sustain a lifelong partnership'. However, his view is significantly tempered by his later emphasis that although the personal sphere is privileged, it is not 'licensed for irresponsibility' and 'respect for the privileged sphere may ... demand intervention where harm is inflicted within it'.[26]

Others see a more active role for the state in fostering policies that bolster and support relationships. This might be through support for marriage or other relationships based statuses or through support for relationships of dependency. The state is required to create the conditions where a person can exercise their autonomy by entering a relationship which receives support and protection by society; and ensures a person is not disadvantaged by entering such a relationship. As Jennifer Nedelsky argues, the state must attend to:

> conditions that foster people's capacity to form caring, responsible and intimate relationships with each other – as family members, friends, members of a community, and citizens of a state.[27]

Margaret Brinig and Steven Nock argue that the availability of state supported forms of relationship provides benefits for society and the individuals:

---

[25] Fineman, *The Autonomy Myth*, p xviii.
[26] Eekelaar, *Family Law and Personal Life*, 82.
[27] J. Nedelsky, 'Property in potential life? A relational approach to choosing legal categories' (1993) 6 *Canadian Journal of Law and Jurisprudence*, 343, 343.

The normative expectation of permanence and unconditional love is the basis for collective trust that the relationship in question will function in its prescribed way. For couples, that means that others will trust that they will pursue intimacy in socially recognised (i.e., normative) ways. For parents, that means trusting that they will provide an environment within which children can flourish. In return for conforming to community norms, that is, people in relationships are given various legal and other supports that further encourage and promote the relationship.

Such arguments raise a host of issues. While public support and recognition of a relationship is, I believe, important, whether that needs to be in the form of a legal status, or even in the form of state-approved status may be questioned. Indeed for some families, no doubt, the support and approval of their community or faith is of far greater significant than any legal or state recognition.[28] Nevertheless, I suggest, the state has a role in fostering the circumstances in which dependent relationships receive recognition and support. While marriage as it is presently understood is far too narrow (and too broad) for that role,[29] I agree with Martha Minow and Mary Lyndon Shanley who argued:

> while loving and committed relationships might presumably exist without the state, there are in fact no family or family-like relationships that are not shaped by social practices and state action.[30]

The social practices and state action are likely to reflect the values of the society and in a patriarchal society to reflect patriarchal values. So the power of the state to structure and affect intimate relationships can be used to both good and bad ends.

Finally, privileging individualist autonomy can operate in a way that disadvantages women. It promotes the unattached unencumbered person as the norm. In advocating autonomy as the ideal, the obligation and responsibility of carework is downplayed. Indeed it is seen as antagonistic to the autonomous ideal. As women undertake the majority of carework it disadvantages them. As Pamela Laufer-Ukeles puts it:

> Revaluing nurture work does not mean that women must or should perform such work; rather, it is in the interest of society that such work be given proper accord. Gender makes a difference, and ignoring that difference creates unfairness. This unfairness must be addressed. An

---

[28] J. Eekelaar and M. Maclean, 'The Significance of Mariage: Contrasts between White British and Ethnic Minority Groups in England' (2005) 27 *Law and Policy* 379.

[29] M. Minow and M. Lyndon Shanley, 'Relational rights: Revisioning the family in liberal political theory and law' (1996) 11 *Hypatia* 4.

[30] Ibid.

alternative to the gender neutral paradigm of divorce law must be identified. Gender difference in the context of divorce should be recognised by advocating support for the different and important contribution of caretaking. Such recognition will begin to address the hardships caretakers face at divorce.[31]

In most, if not all, intimate relationships parties invest in varying ways and extents to the relationship. Putting central value on the autonomy of the parties to leave the relationship and pursue their own life goal will disadvantage the party who has invested more in it and has suffered economic or social disadvantage as a result. In most relationships, especially where there are children, that will be women. Carol Gilligan argues:

> Women's place in man's life-cycle has been that of nurturer, caretaker, and helpmate, the weaver of those networks of relationships on which she in turn relies. But while women have thus taken care of men, men have, in their theories of psychological development, as in their economic arrangements, tended to assume or devalue care. When the focus on individuation and individual achievement extends into adulthood and maturity is equated with personal autonomy, concern with relationships appears as a weakness of women rather than as a human strength.[32]

Do these arguments mean that we should abandon the notion of autonomy in family law or more generally? No. As Marilyn Friedman argues:

> Although women still have occasion to fear men's autonomy, it seems that many women have good cause to welcome our own.[33]

There is much debate over whether, in the light of such comments, feminists should support or oppose rights.[34] I do not want to enter that debate. I will assume for now that if only because the current legal and political climate is rights-soaked, the politically most astute course of action is to retain the language of rights.[35] So, what I will do next is to consider whether it is possible to rework the notion of autonomy in a way which will protect women's interests more effectively and chime with the reality of women's lives.

---

[31] P. Laufer-Ukeles, 'Selective recognition of gender difference in the law: Revaluing the caretaker role' (2008) 31 *Harvard Journal of Law and Gender*, 1.
[32] C. Gilligan, *In a Different Voice*, Cambridge: Harvard University Press, 1982, p 17.
[33] M. Friedman, 'Autonomy, social disruption, and women', in C. MacKenzie and N. Stoljar, *Relational Autonomy*, Oxford: Oxford University Press, 2000, p 47.
[34] See Chapter 1 this volume.
[35] S. Mendus, 'Human rights in political theory' (1995) 43 *Political Studies*, 10.

Relational autonomy

Relational autonomy is based on a reconfiguration of the concept of individualistic autonomy.[36] Lorraine Code argues that for supporters of individualized autonomy:

> Autonomous man is – and should be – self-sufficient, independent, and self-reliant, a self-realizing individual who directs his efforts towards maximizing his personal gains. His independence is under constant threat from other (equally self-serving) individuals: hence he devises rules to protect himself from intrusion. Talk of right, rational self-interest, expedience, and efficiency permeates his moral, social, and political discourse. In short, there has been a gradual alignment of autonomy with individualism.[37]

At this point it should be emphasised that most supporters of the traditional liberal view of autonomy reject such a description of autonomy. Some people may choose to live their life in an unattached way; other, fortunately, choose to live a relational life. The criticisms made of liberal autonomy, it is said, are better directed at the choices people make, rather than the concept of autonomy itself. This objection has much validity. But, autonomy must be seen in the context of the broader social and legal picture. Mary Becker writes: 'patriarchy values power, control, autonomy, independence, toughness, invulnerability, strength, aggressiveness, rationality, detachment (being non-emotional), and other traditionally masculine attributes that have proven effective in the battle against other men'.[38] Once put in the context of other values that society and law values autonomy can be said to play its part in promoting individualism. Individualism ignores the complex web of relations and connections which make up most people's lives. The reality for everyone, but in our society particularly women, is that it is the values of inter-dependence and connection, rather than self-sufficiently and independence, which reflect their reality. People do not understand their family lives as involving clashes of individual rights or interests, but rather as a working through of relationships. The muddled give and take of everyday family life where sacrifices are made and benefits gained, without them being totted up on some giant familial star chart, chimes more with everyday family life than the image of independent interests and rights.

[36] I have written further on relational autonomy in J. Herring, 'Relational autonomy and rape', in S. Day-Sclater, F. Ebtehaj, E. Jackson and M. Richards, *Regulating Autonomy: Sex, Reproduction and Family*, Oxford: Hart, 2009. The following section uses some of the ideas in that chapter.

[37] L. Code, 'Second Persons', in L. Code (ed.) *What Can She Known? Feminist Theory and the Construction of Knowledge*, Ithaca: Cornell University Press, p 78.

[38] M. Becker, 'Patriarchy and inequality: Towards a substantive feminism' (1999) *University of Chicago Legal Forum*, 21.

Those feminists who object to the traditional understanding of autonomy, often turn to the concept of relational autonomy. The starting point for an approach based on relational autonomy is that a relational life is inevitable. From our earliest days our character and understanding of ourselves is fixed by our relationships with others.[39] We all at some points in our lives have been dependent on others for our survival and many people are dependent on us. For many people their self-definition of themselves is based on relationship, be it as a mother, a Muslim or a Millwall Football Club fan.[40] Our sense of self is a mixture of interlocking and sometimes conflicting social identities.[41] We are not in reality free to 'live our lives as we choose' because we are constrained by the responsibilities, realities and relationships which embed our lives.[42] Hence Allan Johnson[43] has called our culture's insistence that we are separate and autonomous as patriarchy's 'Great Lie'.

Our decisions are not just 'ours' they usually affect those we are in relationship and their decisions will affect others. Linda Barclay notes that 'our ongoing success as an autonomous agent is affected by our ability to share our ideas, our aspirations, and our beliefs in conversation with others. It is unlikely that any vision or aspiration is sustained in isolation from others.'[44]

Not just is a relational life inevitable, it is good. Dependency is inevitable and without relationships the needs of dependants cannot be met. Relationships of care and dependency need to be supported, nurtured and upheld, not hidden and downplayed.[45] Of course not all relationships are good. As women know all too well relationships and social structures can be oppressive. A central aspect of relational autonomy must be in protecting people from the harms that abusive relationships can cause.[46]

Eva Feder Kittay has argued that one must always 'construe oneself and other as selves that are always selves-in-relationship'.[47] But as she recognises there is a difficulty in balancing the need to retain the worth of individuals, with the values of relationships. She argues:

[39] S. Carle, 'Theorizing agency' (2005) 55 *American Universities Law Review*, 307.
[40] E. Barvosa-Carter, 'Mestiza autonomy as relational autonomy: Ambivalence and the social character of free will' (2007) 15 *Journal of Political Philosophy*, 1.
[41] A. Donchin, 'Autonomy, interdependence, and assisted suicide: respecting boundaries/crossing lines' (2000) 14 *Bioethics*, 187.
[42] J. Nedelsky, 'Reconceiving autonomy: sources, thoughts and possibilities' (1989) 1 *Yale Journal of Law and Feminism*, 7–36.
[43] A. Johnson, *Gender Knot*, Philadelphia: Temple University Press, 1997, p 30.
[44] L. Barclay, 'Autonomy and the social self', in C. Mackenzie and N. Stoljar (eds), *Relational Autonomy*, New York: Oxford University Press, 2000, pp 52–71.
[45] M.Verkerk, 'A care perspective on coercion and autonomy' (1999) 13 *Bioethics*, 358.
[46] M. Chen-Wishart, 'Undue influence: vindicating relationships of influence'.
[47] E. Feder Kittay, 'Searching for an overlapping consensus: a secular care ethics feminist responds to religious feminists' (2007) 4 *University of St Thomas Law Journal*, 468–88.

Total self-sacrifice, the annihilation of the self in favor of the cared for, is neither demanded by the practice of care nor is it justifiable, for one can see that a relationship requires two selves, not one self in which the other is subsumed and consumed. A care ethic is not a mere reaction to individualism, but it tempers individualism by insisting that the relationships in which we stand help to constitute the individual we have become, are now and will be in the future.[48]

It is with this in mind that her references to understanding people as 'selves in relationship' is particularly valuable. As Elizabeth Frazer and Nicola Lacey argue:

The notion of the relational self, in contrast to both atomistic and intersubjective selves, nicely captures our empirical and logical interdependence and the centrality to our identity of our relations with others and with practices and institutions, whilst retaining an idea of human uniqueness and discreteness as central to our sense of ourselves. It entails the collapse of any self/other or individual/community dichotomy without abandoning the idea of genuine agency and subjectivity[49]

Another aspect of relational autonomy is that it sees obligations are arising through relationships, which may not be readily tied to voluntarily. Hence the obligations attached to parenthood arise not from a specific choice of an individual, but from the relationship that develops.[50] It might be thought that the responsibilities and obligations that are emphasised by relational theorists are inconsistent with the value of autonomy. But the obligations of a relationship enable the relationship to work and flourish. They recognise the vulnerability that is created by intimate relationships and seeks to protect that vulnerability.

This chapter will now consider two particular issues to consider what an approach based on relational autonomy may have to offer family law.

Pre-marriage contracts

There is much debate among family lawyers in the UK at the moment over whether we should enforce pre-marriage contracts.[51] The courts have

---

[48] Ibid.
[49] E. Frazer and N. Lacey, *The Politics of Community: A Feminist Critique of the Liberal Communitarian Debate*, Hemel Hempstead: Harvester Wheatshear, 1993, p 178
[50] R. Leckey, 'Contracting claims and family law feuds' (2007) 57 *University of Toronto Law Journal*, 1.
[51] J. Morley 'Enforceable prenuptial agreements: their time has come' (2006) 36 *Family Law*, 772. For a useful general discussion of the theoretical issues see G. Kachroo, 'Mapping alimony: from status to contract and beyond' (2007) 5 *Pierce Law Review*, 163.

traditionally refused to do so on the grounds of public policy, although in recent years they have become more sympathetic to them and, if not finding them binding, have at least been willing to attach significance to them.

Many of the arguments in favour of pre-marriage contracts are focussed on autonomy. Stephen Cretney, one of England's finest family lawyers, has argued that the law should 'allow husband and wife the liberty ... to decide for themselves the terms of their own partnership'.[52] Even some feminists have joined in support for such contracts as recognising the private ordering of two equal parties to determine the scope of their relationship and with the freedom to depart from the outdated notion of marriage. Jana Singer argues:

> [H]onoring the decisional autonomy of those individuals and groups who have traditionally been disfavored by the law promises both to enhance personal freedom and promote equality goals. Substituting private for public control over the formation and structure of the family relationship seems to offer a similar double benefit: it expands the opportunities for the exercise of personal choice while affirming the inherent equality of the sexes.[53]

Opponents of pre-marriage contracts tend to emphasise their scope for unfairness: they are open to misuse; can produce results which are unfair; and one party may be taken advantage of. Feminists have expressed concerns that women are most likely to suffer from pre-marriage contracts being enforced. Any assumption of equality ignores the real differences in bargaining power between spouses negotiating a contract.[54] However, my present argument against pre-marriage contracts is not based on such concerns, although I think they have much validity.

Central to an understanding of relationships is their fluid nature. Writers on ethics of care have distinguished an approach based on an ethic of care and one based on an ethic of justice. Virginia Held explains how rights are related to an ethic of justice approach: 'An ethic of justice focuses on questions of fairness, equality, individual rights, abstract principles, and the consistent application of them'.[55] As highlighted by Selma Sevenhuijsen: 'A decision based on the ethic of justice cannot be easily changed or modified. It tends to be made once and for all, even though conditions may change at a later date.'[56] In effect 'rights talk' means that 'real experiences' are

[52] S. Cretney, 'Private ordering and divorce – how far can we go' (2003) 33 *Family Law*, 399, 403.
[53] J. Singer, 'The privatization of family law' (1992) 5 *Wisconsin Law Review*, 1443–1567.
[54] P. Laufer-Ukeles, 'Selective recognition of gender difference in the law'.
[55] V. Held, *The Ethics of Care*, New York: Oxford University Press, 2006, p 15.
[56] S. Sevenhuijsen (1998) *Citizenship and the Ethics of Care: Feminist Considerations about Justice, Morality and Politics*, London: Routledge, p 171.

converted into 'empty abstractions'.[57] As Smart puts it: 'the rights approach takes and translates personal and private matters into legal language. In so doing, it reformulates them into issues relevant to law rather than to the lives of ordinary people'.[58]

These points are particularly relevant to pre-marriage contracts. An attempt to set down in stone the rights and responsibilities of the parties smacks of the ethic of justice, in the sense just described. Relationships are chaotic and messy. The sacrifices called for can be unpredictable and obligations without limit. Ask any partner caring for their demented love one. To seek to tie these down at the start of the relationship in some form of 'once and for all' summation of their claims against each other ignores the realities of intimate relationships.

Any attempt to delineate at the start of the relationship the rights and responsibilities of the relationship are likely to work against the interests of a partner who suffers an unexpected sacrifice or loss. This might include having to take on the care of a disabled partner or other relative or the impact of childcare responsibilities being greater than those imagined. In such cases these are more likely to fall on women. The fixing of responsibilities in advance, therefore, is likely to work to the disadvantage of women particularly.

A further point is that there are important issues of public importance that are determined on the financial orders made on relationship breakdown.[59] A contract which left a woman far worse off after a marriage when she had undertaken the caring work would not just be doing a wrong to her but would be harming society. The lack of respect shown to care work and the lack of respect thereby shown to women in general would be harmful to the wider community.[60] We already live in a society in which care work goes largely unrecognised and unvalued. The making of financial orders on divorce is one of the few areas in which care work is recognised.[61]

Elsewhere[62] I have written of the failure to appreciate the issues of public significance of financial orders on relationship breakdown. Treating them as private disputes ignores these wider issues. One of those is the significance of childcare. If we imagined a world in which there were no financial orders

[57] M. Tushnet, 'A critique of rights' (1984) *Texas Law Review*, 1363, 1364.
[58] C. Smart, 'Children and the transformation of family law', in J. Dewar and S. Parker (eds), *Family Law Processes, Practices, Pressures*, Oxford: Hart, 2003, pp 238–39.
[59] J. Herring, 'Why financial orders on divorce should be unfair' (2005) 19 *International Journal of Law, Policy and the Family*, 218.
[60] K. Silbaugh, 'Turning labor into love: Housework and the law' (1996) 91 *Northwestern University Law Review* 27.
[61] M. Case, 'How high the apple pie? A few troubling questions about where, why, and how the burden of care for children should be shifted' (2001) 78 *Chicago-Kent Law Review*, 1753.
[62] Herring, 'Why financial orders on divorce should be unfair'.

available on divorce, we would thereby be creating a world in which everyone was encouraged to be financially self-sufficient. It would be a foolish parent who gave up employment to care for a child or ailing relative. They would be putting themselves at grave financial risk. If the relationship broke down they would be in an extremely financially disadvantageous position. It would be much more sensible for them to rely on paid care for their children. There are some who would regard that as a good thing.[63] But to many the vision of a world of mass day care, the discouragement of personal care and encouragement for financial independence is a horror. If undertaking personal care is an option that we wish to preserve we must have a system that does not render the undertaking of family care and home-making financially very risky. Hale LJ (as she then was) recognised this clearly in *SRJ* v *DWJ* (*Financial Payments*):

> It is not only in [the child's] interest but in the community's interests that parents, whether mothers or fathers, and spouses, whether husbands or wives, should have a real choice between concentrating on breadwinning and concentrating on home-making and childrearing, and do not feel forced, for fear of what might happen should their marriage break down much later in life, to abandon looking after the home and the family to other people for the sake of maintaining a career.[64]

This issue is, however, more complex than just presented. Lucinda Ferguson, in an illuminating analysis, emphasises how important it is to determine the extent to which compensation for economic loss during a relationship creates an interpersonal obligation (against a partner) or a social obligation (against the state). She sees dangers in expecting a partner to compensate a woman who has lost out, when the obligation is truly owed by the state.[65] As her discussion shows recognition of care work on divorce can only be a tiny part of the work towards properly recognising this work.

If the law were to accept the arguments based on autonomy in favour of enforcing pre-marriage contracts we could easily end up enforcing contracts which devalued childcare. It may be the couple themselves devalue childcare. We have all come across men who claim mothers have it easy just sitting around drinking tea all day; and even mothers who disparage their own role reflect the demeaning view often taken within society of childcare. But that does not mean that the law should accept and enforce their understanding of the value of what they do. Financial orders on divorce can therefore impact on

---

[63] See the discussions in R. Deech, 'The principles of maintenance' (1977) 7 *Family Law*, 229; V. Schultz, 'Life's work' (2000) 100 *Columbia Law Review*, 1881.

[64] [1999] 2 FLR 176.

[65] L. Ferguson, 'Family, social inequalities, and the persuasive force of interpersonal obligation' (2008) 22 *International Journal of Law, Policy and the Family*, 61.

the appreciation and value attached to nurturing work.[66] As Joan Williams has emphasised:

> If we as a society take children's need for parental care seriously, it is time to stop marginalizing the adults who provide it.[67]

Financial orders on divorce will reflect the norms that are said to underlie the marital relationship. The orders made can seek therefore to reinforce certain norms or to downplay others.[68] This might be to privilege independence and autonomy or to recognise the value and vulnerability that care work gives rise to. As Milton Regan explains:

> The ideas of autonomy as independence and obligation as consensual rest upon the valorization of the realm of the market in which men traditionally have been the primary agents, and the marginalization of a realm in which women traditionally have been the primary actors. Relationships marked by personal dependence, vulnerability, care and affection are taken as relevant in conceptualising the fundamental terms of human interaction and in defining autonomy.[69]

Through financial orders on divorce, determined by the values of the law, our community is able to recognise the value and importance of care work. There is much more that our society needs to do to properly value that work, but this is a starting point. Enforcing pre-marriage contracts would deprive the law of this way of acknowledging the importance of care.

Adolescent medical decision making

The debates over the extent to which children should be able to make decisions about their medical treatment are well known and the battle lines firmly drawn.[70] In the one corner there are the welfarists keen to protect

---

[66] J. Williams, *Unbending Gender*, New York: Oxford University Press, 2000, pp 124–27.

[67] J. Williams, 'Towards a reconstructive feminism: reconstructing the relationship of market work and family work' (1998) 19 *Northern Illinois University Law Review*, 119.

[68] C. Smith, 'Philosophical models of marriage and their influence on property division methods at divorce' (2000) *Journal of Contemporary Legal Issues*, 214.

[69] M. Regan, *Alone Together; Law and the Meaning of Marriage* Oxford: Oxford University Press, 1999, p 166.

[70] F. Kelly, 'Conceptualising the child through an ethic of care: lessons for family law' (2005) 1 *International Journal of Law in Context*, 375. For an American perspective see K. Mutcherson, 'Whose body is it anyway? An updated model of healthcare decision-making rights for adolescents' (2005) 14 *Cornell Journal of Law and Public Policy*, 251.

children from harm and ensure that competent children are not denied the medical treatment they need, while also not wanting competent children to be able to veto the treatment that they need. In the other corner are the children's rights supporters, decrying the failure of the law to protect the autonomy rights of competent adolescents. Less prominent, at least in English writing, are yet a third group decrying the law's failure to respect the rights of parents in this area. These positions have been well documented and presented in the literature.[71]

What might a relational autonomy perspective add to this debate? First, it would question the separation of the interests of children and adults that all these approaches take. It is an obvious point, but one which is often overlooked, that the medical treatment which a child may or may not receive can have huge repercussions on the lives of the parents.[72] Medical decisions involving children are rarely issues which affect only the child. Of course it is equally true that medical decisions involving adults will have a huge impact on their children and others close to them.[73] This transcends the merely practical implications of receiving or not receiving a treatment. In one of the best discussions on this issue[74] Joanna Bridgeman writes:

> rather than attempt to articulate justice and provide explanations for forced treatment in terms of the rights of the abstract autonomous individual of liberal legal theory or the paternalistic overriding of those rights, it would be instructive to listen to the parents of sick children, heath care professionals and lawyers acting in partnership in order to secure the well-being of the child. If the 'different voice' can be heard in what they say, decisions relating to the medical treatment of children may be more convincingly explained in terms of the responsibility of caring than presently achieved with expressions of autonomy. What we hear may enable us to develop, out of the vague best interests test, an ethic of care model for health care decision in relation to children which explains why, because we care, sometimes medical treatment may be imposed upon them despite their wishes to the contrary.

Second, as argued above our vision of autonomy presupposes a competent, independent strong adult making choices for themselves. Children, it is commonly argued lack the independence, competence and experience that adults have and so are not entitled to make decisions for themselves. Yet are

---

[71] See e.g. Bridgeman, *Parents, Young Children and Healthcare Law*, Ch. 1.

[72] See, J. Herring, 'Children's abortion rights' (1997) 5 *Medical Law Review*, 257.

[73] J. Herring, 'The place of carers', in M. Freeman, *Law and Bioethics*, Oxford: Oxford University Press, 2008.

[74] J. Bridgeman 'Because we care? The medical treatment of children', in S. Sheldon and M. Thomson, *Feminist Perspectives on Health Care*, London: Cavendish, 1998, pp 97–113.

not adults too vulnerable and open to abuse? Are not adults dependent on others to pursue their vision of a good life and dependent on the co-operation of others to pursue their goals? Are not adults all too often lacking the necessary knowledge and experience to make important decisions? Adults are in many ways as vulnerable, dependent on others and lacking in competence as children. The difficulties that many have in granting adult rights to children in the medical arena have as much to say about our puffed up vision of ourselves as adults as it does about the true vulnerability of children. A vision of autonomy that respected and promoted relationships and saw individuals as interconnected to others would be more appropriate for not only children but adults too.[75]

Hence it is that despite its influence and sophistication there is something troubling about Michael Freeman's vision of children's rights which is based on the suggestion that:

> [t]he question we should ask ourselves is: what sort of action or conduct would we wish, as children to be shielded against on the assumption that we would want to mature to a rationally autonomous adulthood and be capable of deciding on our own system of ends as free and rational beings?[76]

Such an approach promotes rational autonomy as the ideal for our children on the brink of adulthood. While placing children at the age of 18 with the maximum chance of autonomy is a laudable goal, it should not be the only one. Do we also not want children who care, understand their responsibilities, know how to develop relationships; know how not to insist on having their way? This may mean not respecting a child's autonomy interests to the extent Freeman might wish. In relationships of care we do not always get our own way. Sometimes this will mean occasionally that even competent children's wishes in relation to medical treatment will not be followed. Indeed, I suggest that adults' decisions too in respect of their medical treatment should not always be followed. There are times, be we adults or children, where our relational obligations require a limit upon our right to refuse medical treatment.

Tom Cockurn argues:

> If … one looks at the relationship between mother and child, we see human reciprocity based on characteristics of nurturing and dependence, rather than competition and autonomy. In the case of the mother–child

---

75 J. Herring, 'Children's rights for grown-ups', in S. Fredman and S. Spencer (eds), *Age as An Equality Issue*, Oxford: Hart, 2004, pp 145–72.
76 M. Freeman, *The Moral Status of Children*, London: Martinus Nijhoff, 1997, p 38.

relationship, mutual respect and equality of worth are of more importance than any contractarian principles based on equal legal rights. The
moral repertoire also needs to include principles of co-operation, intimacy, trust, connection and compassion to be emphasised as important
sources of moral reasoning.[77]

These values should underpin the legal reasoning in these medical cases too.
As Jo Bridgeman emphasises reaching solutions to these troublesome cases
requires a careful attention to the individual relationships concerned and the
responsibilities that arise from them.[78] This means that it is not possible to
produce a single clear rule to apply in these cases, rather the solution is to be
fashioned from the relationships themselves. Because whatever else happens
in these medical decisions, the child and her carers will need to continue in
their relationships together and those relationships are worth more than any
abstract legal rights.

CONCLUSION

This chapter has examined the concept of autonomy in family law. Against
the growing use of autonomy in arguments concerning family law, it has
argued that individualistic conceptions of autonomy have no place. They are
inconsistent with the realities of family life; are dissonant with how people
understand their intimate lives; and work against the interests of women.
Instead this chapter has promoted the notion of relational autonomy. This
starts with a conception of individuals having been born in and living in
relations with those around them. It argues that most people's vision of how
they wish to live their life is relational and their daily lives are relational.
This means that the traditional image of family members have severable
interests is hard to maintain. The language of 'making my decisions' has no
place in the family context. Instead we need a vision of autonomy which
recognises the interdependency and vulnerability of both children and adults.

---

[77] T. Cockburn, 'Children and the feminist ethic of care', (2005) 12 *Childhood*, 71.
[78] Bridgeman, *Parents, Young Children and Healthcare Law*, Ch. 1.

Chapter 13

Concluding thoughts: The enduring chaos of family law

Helen Rhoades

In his classic 1998 article, 'The normal chaos of family law', John Dewar proposed that family law, insofar as it 'deals in ideas of what families are, how their members should deal with each other, and what the role of law and the state should be with regard to them', was fundamentally incoherent.[1] According to Dewar's assessment, this was not a negative feature, nor an indication of its failure as a legal system. Rather, he argued, this state of affairs was perfectly normal given the subject matter with which the law deals – intimate relationships – and the range of regulatory sites and policy aims involved. The chapters in this collection attest to the resilience of this complexity in English family law, despite the recent imposition of a rights framework. From the perspective of an Australian family law academic, whose national government is presently exploring the possibility of enacting human rights legislation,[2] the analyses contained in this volume are instructive.[3] Not only do they reveal the unsystematic and often limited effects of this development in England, they also offer important insights into the reasons for the apparently enduring chaos of family law.

Variable reception

One explanation for the unpredictability of reform projects in this area of law is what Dewar and Stephen Parker called the 'principle of variable reception'.[4] This concept refers to the scope for different interpretations

[1] John Dewar, 'The normal chaos of family law' (1998) 61 *Modern Law Review*, 467, 468.

[2] Attorney-General for Australia, 'Rudd Government Announces National Human Rights Consultation', Media Release, 10 December 2008, http://www.attorneygeneral. gov.au/www/ministers/robertmc.nsf/Page/MediaReleases_2008_FourthQuarte_10Dec ember2008-RuddGovernmentAnnouncesNationalHumanRightsConsultation

[3] Note that one Australian state, Victoria, has enacted human rights legislation: see Charter of Human Rights and Responsibilities Act 2006 (Vic), which came into operation in January 2007.

[4] John Dewar and Stephen Parker, 'The impact of the new Part VII Family Law Act 1975' (1999) 13 *Australian Journal of Family Law* 96, 112–13.

across the various professional communities that mediate the impact of legislative change on its subjects. First among these interpretive communities
when it comes to human rights legislation is the judiciary. Indeed, the
undemocratic nature of their application, and associated fears of 'judicial
activism', has been the basis of determined opposition to the adoption of
rights charters.[5] Appearing to confirm this fear, a number of the chapters in
this volume suggest that a critical factor affecting the Human Rights Act's
influence on family law has been a differential level of take-up by the courts.
This is not just a matter of divergent compliance rulings. The analyses here
indicate that the impact of rights also involves questions of judicial sympathy
for the values underpinning them, and suggest considerable scope for judges
to shape their meaning for families by under- or over-reading their protective
intentions.[6] For example, Christine Piper's exploration of the child protection
system points to Munby J as an example of a judicial officer who has taken a
strong rights-based stance in the area, using the ECHR principles to impose
positive duties on prison service staff to safeguard young people in detention
from assaults by fellow inmates.[7] In contrast, other judges have adopted
comparatively weak interpretations, limiting protections against decisions by
public authorities to a bare minimum of procedural safeguards,[8] and failing
to advance children's citizenship status beyond a traditional 'welfarist'
approach.[9]

On the other hand, a number of the authors have raised concerns about
judicial rights-advocates. The criticisms here focused on the failure by judges
to incorporate an understanding of the material and social context affecting
an individual's rights into their determinations. These critiques are reminis-
cent of Reg Graycar's gender analysis of family law judgments, which
exhorted us to be alert to 'what judges know about the world' and 'how the
things they know translate into their activity as judges'.[10] Alison Diduck's

---

[5] See in relation to opposition to the proposed Bill of Rights for Australia, Michelle
Grattan, 'Opposition flags bill of rights fight', *The Age*, 11 December 2008; Paul
Kelly, 'Uncharted waters', *The Weekend Australian*, 13–14 December 2008.
[6] See on this point, Jennifer McIntosh and Richard Chisholm, 'Shared care and
children's best interests in conflicted separation: a cautionary tale from current
research' (2007) 20(1) *Australian Family Lawyer* 1, 4, who caution Family Court
judges against 'over-reading' the shared care provisions of Australia's 2006 Shared
Parental Responsibility Act reforms.
[7] *The Queen (On the Application of the Howard League for Penal Reform) v Secretary of State for the Home Department* [2002] EWHC 2497 (Admin), paras 66–68.
[8] See Kaganas Chapter 3 in this volume p 51ff.
[9] See Chapter 1 in this volume p 2ff. It is interesting to note in this respect that s 17
of the Charter of Human Rights and Responsibilities Act 2006 (Vic) provides that
'Every child has the right, without discrimination, to such protection as is in his or
her best interests'.
[10] Reg Graycar, 'The gender of judgments: an introduction', in Margaret Thornton
(ed.), *Public and Private: Feminist Legal Debates* (Oxford University Press, 1995)
pp 262–82, p 267.

examination of matrimonial property cases in this volume illustrates this point. Whilst she notes that Baroness Hale has embraced the rights values of equality and non-discrimination in her decision-making, Diduck is also ambivalent about this development, expressing anxiety about the implications for families of importing moral values designed for 'public, political living' into case law principles governing personal relationships that revolve around notions of commitment, emotional support and reciprocity.[11]

Jo Bridgeman's examination of medical treatment cases is likewise concerned by the failure of judges to engage in a contextual reading of children's welfare, citing a lack of attention to the dependency and care needs of children with disabilities in giving effect to their right to physical integrity. The chapter by Julie Wallbank, too, provides a passionate critique of developments in post-separation contact law and suggests that some judges have been so uncritical in their interpretation of fathers' parenting rights that they have become, in effect, public relations agents for the fathers' lobby. According to Wallbank, what is missing from these judgments is an understanding of the burden on mothers who must facilitate men's contact with their children after separation and adequate regard for the past pattern of caregiving or the (conflicted and sometimes violent) nature of the interparent relationship.[12]

However, while courts may be the ultimate arbiters of rights laws, they are not the only or even the most important, interpretive community when it comes to family law. As Dewar and Parker's 'variable reception' concept suggests, the modern family law system relies on a vast array of regulatory agencies, and the chapters in this volume reveal a diversity of responses to the Human Rights Act among them. Felicity Kaganas' critique of the child protection system suggests that whilst the courts have used rights principles to impose 'fair procedure' requirements, the benefit of this development for families has been limited by the 'court avoidance' tactics of local authorities. Rather than risk rejection of a protective application, local authorities have developed a practice of seeking parents' agreement to 'voluntary

---

[11] See on this, Nareeda Lewers, Helen Rhoades and Shurlee Swain, 'Judicial and couple approaches to contributions and property: the dominance and difficulties of a reciprocity model' (2007) 21 *Australian Journal of Family* 123; Mavis Maclean and John Eekelaar, 'The obligations and expectations of couples within families: three modes of interaction' (2004) 26 *Journal of Social Welfare and Family Law* 117.

[12] See for critiques of the increasing disregard for the past history of the parents' relationship in Australian post-separation parenting law, Zoe Rathus, 'Shifting the gaze: will past violence be silenced by a further shift of the gaze to the future under the new family law system?' (2007) 21 *Australian Journal of Family Law* 87; Helen Rhoades, 'The dangers of shared care legislation: why Australia needs (yet more) family law reform' (2008) 36 *Federal Law Review* 279.

arrangements', such as monitoring or accommodation, under threat of court action. Hence, while the law 'on the books' might suggest a significant advance for families, the reality seems to be a growth in privatised regulation that effectively bypasses the safeguards of the Human Rights Act.

These practices and their avoidance of court-adjudicated responses raise a separate point about the location of the interpreter and their proximity to the formal justice system. Dewar and Parker's 'variable reception' analysis offered a contradiction of Mnookin and Kornhauser's 'shadow of the law' explanation of family law's effects, and suggests that distance from the appellate court level of decision-making may provide some interpretive communities with substantial freedom to resist judicial interpretations of legislative messages.[13] A good example of this phenomenon can be seen in recent research of community-based family mediation services in Australia, which suggests that many mediation practitioners, whose disciplinary grounding is in the social or psychological sciences and who have no formal relationship with the courts, actively challenge the law's autonomy-centred understanding of clients' entitlements in family disputes,[14] and are critical of both (what they consider to be) the narrow legislative construction of children's interests (in terms of equality of time with parents) and the courts' failure to factor the emotional and psychological dimensions of family life into their deliberations.[15]

In addition to the potential diversity of professional practices, a number of authors have highlighted the capacity for different readings of the law among its consumers, and, in particular, the scope for gendered experiences of its implementation. Julie Wallbank and Brid Featherstone each explore the relative implications for women and men of the recent fusion of rights and responsibilities in family law policies, in light of their differential attachments to the paid workforce after children arrive and the persistent gendered nature of unpaid work in the home. Their critiques build on the work of Carol Smart, whose empirical research revealed the gendered nature of the law's intersection with the psychological dynamics of separation: whereas a shared parenting rule may be associated with anxiety for a mother who is concerned about the father's untested parenting abilities, it might involve validation for a father who fears his lack of experience as a hands-on carer will be regarded as an inferior form of parental love.[16] An exploration of

---

[13] Dewar and Parker, 'The impact of the new Part VII Family Law Act 1975', 115–16.

[14] Helen Rhoades, Hilary Astor and Ann Sanson, 'A study of inter-professional relationships in a changing family law system' (2009) 23 *Australian Journal of Family Law* (forthcoming).

[15] See Max Wright, 'Best interests, conflict and harm – a response to Chisholm and Parkinson' (2008) 22 *Australian Journal of Family Law* 72.

[16] Carol Smart, 'Preface', in Sally Sheldon and Richard Collier (eds), *Fathers' Rights Activism and Law Reform in Comparative Perspective* (Hart: 2006), p x.

assisted conception policies would also remind us that the recognition of a right to privacy is likely to have different meanings for the various participants in assisted conception projects – such as a 'donor dad' and the lesbian couple who will raise the child[17] – and may involve different emotional journeys for male and female beneficiaries of donated genetic material.

A further factor contributing to the chaos of family law, as the editors note in the Introduction, involves the clash of rights and other relevant principles, such as welfare, care, justice and autonomy, and how the tensions between these principles, and between competing rights, are resolved in practice. Shazia Choudhry's chapter reminds us that regulatory policies often involve a political decision about the appropriate balance of two or more competing rights. As Choudhry shows, the adoption of a mandatory arrest policy for perpetrators of domestic violence prioritises the woman's right to safety over her autonomy rights. More often, policymakers are called on to strike a balance between the rights of one family member and those of another, as Caroline Jones' analysis of the shifting policy approach to the identity rights of donor conceived children and the privacy rights of donors of genetic material and their families illustrates. Adding to this complexity are political decisions which see governments assigning different weight to the same right in different policy contexts. A good example of this is the lack of any 'consolidated legal position' on the child's right to know her genetic history in English law, where, as Julie Wallbank describes elsewhere, the rights approach sometimes gives way to a utility approach.[18]

Arguably, the most significant variable is the level of financial support for human rights provided by government. As Brid Featherstone argues in her critique of New Labour's minimalist approach to parental leave policies, governments must inevitably make economic decisions about the costs of recognising rights. Yet several authors in this volume imply that an even more influential factor affecting contemporary family law policies is the media. Wallbank's chapter, for example, points to the success of fathers' rights advocates in using the media to popularise the idea that fathers are the victims of a gender biased family law system, triggering law reform inquiries and government-funded research projects. Christine Piper's examination of youth justice policies similarly suggests the influence of the press on recent measures designed to reduce community fears about rising rates of crime and nuisance behaviour among young people and restore public confidence in the justice system.

---

[17] Fiona Kelly, 'In search of a father: sperm donors, lesbian-headed families, and the *Re Patrick* case', in Heather Grace Jones and Maggie Kirkman (eds), *Sperm Wars: The Rights and Wrongs of Reproduction* (Sydney: ABC Books, 2005), p 252.

[18] See Julie Wallbank, 'The role of rights and utility in instituting a child's right to know her genetic history' (2004) 13 *Social and Legal Studies* 245, 246.

The importance of empirical vigilance

Another important theme traversed in this book concerns the increasing privatisation of family law and the implications of this trend for tracking the law's influence on social practices. Allied to the rise in legal policies that encourage autonomy and self-governance by families, has been increasing promotion of alternative dispute resolution processes, such as mediation, as the appropriate way to settle family disputes. In Australia, an element of compulsion has been introduced,[19] such that seeking to enlist the assistance of the legal system is now a strictly limited option.[20] As Jonathan Herring notes, these private ordering developments reflect a concern to reduce government expenditure on the formal justice system, as well as being a response to mounting criticisms of decision making by courts and government departments, and changing community perceptions of divorce that view relationship breakdown as a personal rather than a legal matter.[21]

Accompanying these changes has been a shift in the form of family law legislation. Instead of the traditional focus on providing a framework for judicial determinations, modern policy makers seek to affect family practices and promote social responsibility by lacing the law with aspirational messages about appropriate outcomes and (un)desirable behaviour.[22] To use Dewar's description, the role of modern family law 'is to set the tone' for private ordering and alternative dispute resolution, rather than to confer enforceable entitlements on individual family members.[23] Reflecting the rise of rights-talk, it is not uncommon for these messages to invoke the language of equality – for example, post-separation parenting laws that associate children's well-being with shared (and equal) parenting, and laws governing the division of assets on divorce that construct fairness in terms of

---

[19] E.g. in Australia, parents in conflict over arrangements for their children must attempt to resolve their dispute through mediation before they will be permitted to make an application for court orders, unless there are issues such as family violence or child abuse: Family Law Act 1975 (Cth), s. 60I.

[20] Applications to the Family Court for parenting orders have dropped by around 18 per cent since the compulsory mediation reforms came into effect in July 2007: Family Court of Australia, *Annual Report 2007–2008*, 40–43.

[21] See B. Geldof, 'The real love that dare not speak its name: a sometimes coherent rant', in Andrew Bainham, Bridget Lindley, Martin Richards and Liz Trinder (eds), *Children and Their Families: Contact, Rights and Welfare* (Hart Publishing, 2003), p 171; D. Bagnall, 'Divorce wars: how lawyers hijacked the marriage breakup business', *The Bulletin*, 17 February 2004, 18.

[22] See, e.g. Dewar, above n 1, 483; John Dewar, 'Family law and its discontents' (2000) 14 *International Journal of Law Policy and the Family* 59; Helen Reece, *Divorcing Responsibly* (Hart, 2003); John Eekelaar, 'Family law: keeping us "on message"' (1999) 11 *Child and Family Law Quarterly* 38; Alison Diduck, *Law's Families* (2004, LexisNexis), 103–4; Robert van Krieken, 'The "best interests of the child" and parental separation: on the "civilising of parents"' (2005) 68 *Modern Law Review* 25.

[23] Dewar, 'Normal chaos', p 474.

non-discrimination between husbands and wives. However, as Brid Featherstone demonstrates, governments have also shown a tendency to send mixed messages – such as policy statements that encourage lone mothers to engage in the paid workforce alongside the provision of tax credits to families in with stay at home mothers.

Of particular concern, a number of the chapters here suggest that the paradox of the emphasis on self-governance and family autonomy has been an increasing surveillance of certain families and pressure to conform to the authorised narratives of responsible conduct.[24] Similar reports are coming from Australia, where empirical research has revealed a rise in the number of families being 'channelled' into the authorised outcomes through alternative dispute resolution processes.[25] For example, recent data suggest that the latest 'equal time' shared parenting reforms that mandate mediation for families in dispute have been successful in producing a significant increase in 'substantially shared care arrangements',[26] despite the presence of significant conflict between the parents that would have militated against this outcome in a court setting under the previous regime.[27] Painting an even darker picture, several chapters in this volume hint at the growing surveillance of certain families as a result of recent responsibility messages, with differential impacts according to class, gender and socio-economic status. Felicity Kaganas, for example, notes the 'increasingly coercive flavour' of government 'partnership' schemes, in which local authorities have offered to work with parents on a voluntary co-operative basis to help them raise healthy children. Her analysis of the effects of these policies suggests an effective widening of the definition of 'at risk' families, with particular implications for mothers.

That there should be uneven consequences of such social policy initiatives along gender and class lines is not surprising. However, Richard Collier's analysis warns us against assuming outcome patterns in these terms. Drawing on Carol Smart's latest work, he suggests we need to pay careful attention to people's 'real lives', and avoid analyses in which individuals and their experiences are 'reduced to ciphers for a culturally and historically specific knowledge-building industry'.[28] Collier's empirical study of fathers' groups

---

[24] See also, Shelley Day Sclater and Felicity Kaganas, 'Contact: mothers, welfare and rights', in Andrew Bainham, Bridget Lindley, Martin Richards and Liz Trinder (eds), *Children and Their Families: Contact, Rights and Welfare* (Hart Publishing, 2003), p 155.

[25] See on this point, C. E. Schneider, 'The channelling function in family law' (1992) 20 *Hofstra Law Review* 495, 498; Christine Piper, 'Divorce conciliation in the United Kingdom: how responsible are parents?' (1998) *International Journal of Sociology of Law* 477.

[26] This refers to arrangements in which the child spends at least 5 nights per fortnight in each parent's home.

[27] McIntosh and Chisholm, 'Shared care'.

[28] Carol Smart, *Personal Life* (Polity, 2007), p 190.

members challenges assumptions about men's experiences of fatherhood, and suggests modern policy expectations of 'emotionally engaged, hands-on' parenting by fathers means that many men and women alike may be struggling to balance their work and family commitments.[29] These insights, and the increasing push to privatise regulation, highlight the importance of empirical research in tracking the effects on families of family law policies and understanding the patterns and resistances that would otherwise remain hidden from view.

Relational autonomy: a way forward?

As noted, one of the key problems identified by the authors with the application of rights principles concerns the lack of attention to context by decision makers. What tends to be neglected in the process of implementing the law, whether by design or default, are the relationships of care and dependency within which rights-bearers exist. For this reason, Jonathan Herring has proposed the use of a 'relational autonomy' approach, which combines a concern for the individual's autonomy rights with an understanding of family members as situated and engaged in relationships. As such, a relational autonomy principle may offer a way around some of the drawbacks of the liberal individual rights model raised in this volume.

Adoption of this approach would require decision makers to pay greater attention to the 'real lives' of individuals, rendering our 'fluid, unpredictable and messy' relationships a visible part of the decision-making process. For example, as Herring suggests, its application to interpretation of pre-nuptial agreements would import an understanding of the fluid nature of married relationships, such as the material changes wrought by the birth of children. It would also provide scope for recognition of the emotional dimensions of family relationships, including the perspectives of family members outside the traditionally privileged nuclear circle whose lives may be affected by the decision (such as the families of donors and recipients of genetic material). Moreover, its explicit incorporation of context has the potential to counter the effects of recent policies that seek to minimise the relevance of the past (such as pre-separation care patterns or relationship dynamics). A relational autonomy principle also addresses the issue raised by mediation practitioners who are critical of the legal profession's narrow individual rights-based approach to working with family law clients and its failure to comprehend the psychological dynamics of conflicted relationships and children's needs.[30]

However, as Herring acknowledges, a relational model of autonomy, with its balance of respect for the individual's rights and the value of their

---

[29] See Stephen Lunn, 'The other side of forty', *The Weekend Australian Magazine: The Men's Issue*, 15–16 November 2008.

[30] Rhoades, 'Dangers of shared care legislation', p 285.

relationships, will be difficult to achieve in law and practice. For a start, the project of codifying this approach is likely to be faced with much the same kind of difficulties that recent attempts to legislate for children's post-separation needs have met. Family law scholars like Michael King and Christine Piper argue that the system-like nature of law means that it inevitably oversimplifies and distorts information from other disciplines, such as child psychology.[31] As has occurred in that field, the attempt to legislate a relational autonomy model may well result in the fluidity and nuance of family relationships being reduced to a checklist of relevant considerations, and end up being administered in a way that is effectively a series of binary questions. In other words, it may be that relational autonomy, like children's developmental interests, is 'ultimately unknowable by law'.[32]

There is also no guarantee that a consideration of relationships will increase a decision maker's sensitivity to context, or their understanding of the emotional and psychological meanings of family relationships. Moreover, it may not reduce the production of normative patterns by the courts. One has only to look at the 'sterilisation' jurisprudence of the Australian Family Court, which deals with applications by parents for court orders authorising the surgical sterilisation of a daughter with an intellectual disability, to appreciate this potential. Arguably each of the judges in these cases has engaged in a form of relational autonomy decision making, where the child's right to bodily integrity is considered in the context of her relationship of dependency on her carer mother. Yet in every case the outcome has been the same: the child's rights are ultimately displaced by judicial concern for the mother's care load and an order permitting the surgery has been granted.[33]

A final obstacle to the implementation of a relational autonomy approach is its incompatibility with the current direction of family law policy making. The idea of focusing increased attention on the material context of an individual's family life is contrary to the present trajectory and economic policy desires of government. Whilst it may be useful for judicial decision-makers who can have regard to evidence of relational factors, and it would seem to be well suited to social science professionals such as counsellors and mediators, its inherently nuanced and contingent understanding of family life is unlikely to be attractive to governments that want to send simple messages about socially responsible behaviour. Relational autonomy does not have the same rhetorical attraction as a right to equality or a presumption of shared parenting or an exhortation to raise law-abiding children.

---

[31] Michael King and Christine Piper, *How the Law Thinks about Children* (1995), pp 136–38.
[32] Dewar, 'Normal chaos', p 479.
[33] Linda Steele, 'Making sense of the family court's decisions on the non-therapeutic sterilisation of girls with intellectual disability' (2008) 22 *Australian Journal of Family Law* 1.

Clearly a relational autonomy approach will not reduce the chaos of family law. Yet providing a 'huge space' for 'the diversity of family practices to be played out' is surely the point of the project.[34] In any case, the scholarship in this book suggests that the regulatory chaos of the modern family law system is not easily tamed, no matter what guiding principle is used, and that it may well be the defining feature of family law. And as Dewar has argued, this of itself is no bad thing. On the other hand, the insights and critiques offered in this collection sound a warning about the consequences of the increasingly privatised nature of family law regulation, including the gendered dimensions of these, and challenge us to pay close empirical attention to how the law is being interpreted and experienced by families.

[34] Juliet Behrens, 'The form and substance of Australian legislation on parenting orders: a case for the principles of care and diversity and presumptions based upon them' (2002) 24 *Journal of Social Welfare and Family Law* 401, 407.

Index

Printed in Great Britain
by Amazon